terra australis 39

Terra Australis reports the results of archaeological and related research within the south and east of Asia, though mainly Australia, New Guinea and island Melanesia — lands that remained terra australis incognita to generations of prehistorians. Its subject is the settlement of the diverse environments in this isolated quarter of the globe by peoples who have maintained their discrete and traditional ways of life into the recent recorded or remembered past and at times into the observable present.

List of volumes in Terra Australis

Volume 1: Burrill Lake and Currarong: Coastal Sites in Southern New South Wales. R.J. Lampert (1971)

Volume 2: Ol Tumbuna: Archaeological Excavations in the Eastern Central Highlands, Papua New Guinea. J.P. White (1972)

Volume 3: New Guinea Stone Age Trade: The Geography and Ecology of Traffic in the Interior. I. Hughes (1977)

Volume 4: Recent Prehistory in Southeast Papua. B. Egloff (1979)

Volume 5: The Great Kartan Mystery. R. Lampert (1981)

Volume 6: Early Man in North Queensland: Art and Archaeology in the Laura Area. A. Rosenfeld, D. Horton and J. Winter (1981)

Volume 7: The Alligator Rivers: Prehistory and Ecology in Western Arnhem Land. C. Schrire (1982)

Volume 8: Hunter Hill, Hunter Island: Archaeological Investigations of a Prehistoric Tasmanian Site. S. Bowdler (1984)

Volume 9: Coastal South-West Tasmania: The Prehistory of Louisa Bay and Maatsuyker Island. R. Vanderwal and D. Horton (1984)

Volume 10: The Emergence of Mailu. G. Irwin (1985)

Volume 11: Archaeology in Eastern Timor, 1966–67. I. Glover (1986)

Volume 12: Early Tongan Prehistory: The Lapita Period on Tongatapu and its Relationships. J. Poulsen (1987)

Volume 13: Coobool Creek. P. Brown (1989)

Volume 14: 30,000 Years of Aboriginal Occupation: Kimberley, North-West Australia. S. O'Connor (1999)

Volume 15: Lapita Interaction. G. Summerhayes (2000)

Volume 16: The Prehistory of Buka: A Stepping Stone Island in the Northern Solomons. S. Wickler (2001)

Volume 17: The Archaeology of Lapita Dispersal in Oceania. G.R. Clark, A.J. Anderson and T. Vunidilo (2001)

Volume 18: An Archaeology of West Polynesian Prehistory. A. Smith (2002)

Volume 19: Phytolith and Starch Research in the Australian-Pacific-Asian Regions: The State of the Art. D. Hart and L. Wallis (2003)

Volume 20: The Sea People: Late-Holocene Maritime Specialisation in the Whitsunday Islands, Central Queensland. B. Barker (2004)

Volume 21: What's Changing: Population Size or Land-Use Patterns? The Archaeology of Upper Mangrove Creek, Sydney Basin. V. Attenbrow (2004)

Volume 22: The Archaeology of the Aru Islands, Eastern Indonesia. S. O'Connor, M. Spriggs and P. Veth (2005)

Volume 23: Pieces of the Vanuatu Puzzle: Archaeology of the North, South and Centre. S. Bedford (2006)

Volume 24: Coastal Themes: An Archaeology of the Southern Curtis Coast, Queensland. S. Ulm (2006)

Volume 25: Lithics in the Land of the Lightning Brothers: The Archaeology of Wardaman Country, Northern Territory. C. Clarkson (2007)

Volume 26: Oceanic Explorations: Lapita and Western Pacific Settlement. S. Bedford, C. Sand and S. P. Connaughton (2007)

Volume 27: Dreamtime Superhighway: Sydney Basin Rock Art and Prehistoric Information Exchange. J. McDonald (2008)

Volume 28: New Directions in Archaeological Science. A. Fairbairn, S. O'Connor and B. Marwick (2008)

Volume 29: Islands of Inquiry: Colonisation, Seafaring and the Archaeology of Maritime Landscapes. G. Clark, F. Leach and S. O'Connor (2008)

Volume 30: Archaeological Science Under a Microscope: Studies in Residue and Ancient DNA Analysis in Honour of Thomas H. Loy. M. Haslam, G. Robertson, A. Crowther, S. Nugent and L. Kirkwood (2009)

Volume 31: The Early Prehistory of Fiji. G. Clark and A. Anderson (2009)

Volume 32: Altered Ecologies: Fire, Climate and Human Influence on Terrestrial Landscapes. S. Haberle, J. Stevenson and M. Prebble (2010)

Volume 33: Man Bac: The Excavation of a Neolithic Site in Northern Vietnam: The Biology. M. Oxenham, H. Matsumura and N. Kim Dung (2011)

Volume 34: Peopled Landscapes: Archaeological and Biogeographic Approaches to Landscapes. S. Haberle and B. David.

Volume 35: Pacific Island Heritage: Archaeology, Identity & Community. Jolie Liston, Geoffrey Clark and Dwight Alexander (2011)

Volume 36: Transcending the Culture–Nature Divide in Cultural Heritage: Views from the Asia-Pacific. Sally Brockwell, Sue O'Connor and Denis Byrne (2013)

Volume 37: Taking the High Ground: The archaeology of Rapa, a fortified island in remote East Polynesia. Atholl Anderson and Douglas J. Kennett (2012)

Volume 38: Life on the Margins: An Archaeological Investigation of Late Holocene Economic Variability, Blue Mud Bay, Northern Australia. Patrick Faulkner (2013)

Volume 39: Prehistoric Marine Resource Use in the Indo-Pacific Regions. Rintaro Ono, Alex Morrison, David Addison (eds)(2013)

terra australis 39

Prehistoric Marine Resource Use in the Indo-Pacific Regions

Rintaro Ono, Alex Morrison, David Addison (eds)

Australian
National
University

E PRESS

ANU
E PRESS

© 2013 ANU E Press

Published by ANU E Press
The Australian National University
Canberra ACT 0200 Australia
Email: anuepress@anu.edu.au
Web: http://epress.anu.edu.au

National Library of Australia Cataloguing-in-Publication entry

Title: Prehistoric marine resource use in the Indo-Pacific regions / Rintaro Ono, Alex Morrison, David Addison (eds).

ISBN: 9781925021257 (paperback) 9781925021264 (ebook)

Series: Terra Australis; 39.

Subjects: Fishing, Prehistoric--Indo-Pacific Region.
             Marine resources--Management--Indo-Pacific Region.
             Economic anthropology--Indo-Pacific Region.
             Fish remains (Archaeology)--Indo-Pacific Region.
             Ocean and civilization.
             Indo-Pacific Region--Antiquities.

Other Authors/Contributors:
             Ono, Rintaro, editor.
             Morrison, Alex, editor.
             Addison, David, editor.

Dewey Number: 567.091823

Series Editor: Sue O'Connor

Cover image courtesy of Rintaro Ono.

Back cover map: Hollandia Nova. Thevenot 1663 by courtesy of the National Library of Australia.
Reprinted with permission of the National Library of Australia.

Terra Australis Editorial Board: Sue O'Connor, Jack Golson, Simon Haberle, Sally Brockwell, Geoffrey Clark

Contents

Preface

Rintaro Ono, Alex Morrison, and David Addison

This volume contains a total of eleven papers which constitute a diverse but generally coherent collection on past and present marine resource use in the Indo-Pacific region, within a human-ecological perspective. The geographical focus extends from Eastern Asia, mainly Japan and Insular Southeast Asia (especially the Philippines) to the tropical Pacific (Micronesia, Melanesia, and Polynesia) with geographically outlying papers on sites in coastal Tanzania (Indian Ocean) and coastal California (North Pacific).

Most of these papers were originally presented during the session entitled "Historical Ecology and Marine Resource Use in the Indo-Pacific Region" at the 19th IPPA (Indo-Pacific Prehistory Association) Congress held in Hanoi, Vietnam in 2009, which the editors of this volume organised. Our main purpose in organising this session was to discuss and reconsider the unique position of archaeology in providing a long-term perspective on past marine ecosystems and human ecodynamics in the Indo-Pacific region.

Although historic sources provide information on recent centuries, archaeology can provide longer-term understandings of pre-industrial marine exploitation in the Indo-Pacific region. Archaeological data can provide valuable baseline data for evaluating contemporary ecological trends. With this understanding, we invited papers on current technical, methodological, and theoretical studies on a variety of topics such as fish and shell analyses, prehistoric fishing, ethno-archaeology, or even traditional and modern fishing in the Indo-Pacific region. A total of fourteen papers were presented during the IPPA Congress session. Among these papers, nine papers are contributed and included in this volume, with the addition of three more papers (by Braje et al., Hashimura, and Segi) that were planned for the session, but could not be presented in Hanoi. We are pleased to include these papers in this volume.

The volume divided into four parts based on the paper topics and temporal foci. Part 1 contains five papers that discuss prehistoric-to-historic marine resource use in the Indo-Pacific Region, based on recent excavations and archaeological analyses in Micronesia, Polynesia, the North Pacific coast, and the Indian Ocean.

Richard Olmo argues that archaeological fish bone analyses in the tropical Pacific have rarely provided information below the family level, and this has not only constrained researchers' interpretations of prehistoric behaviour, but has also introduced substantial inaccuracies. To explore and provide a method to allow those interpretations to be enriched, he mainly uses fisheries data compiled by the Guam Division of Aquatics and Wildlife Resources and attempts to reconstruct prehistoric inshore fishing by the Chamorro in Guam, Mariana Islands. His discussion, which focuses on habitation and catch data for major inshore fish families in each species level, provides us with useful information and insight to analyse excavated fish remains and reconstruct past fishing activities in a tropical context.

Judith Amesbury also discusses marine resource use in the Mariana Islands, but she targets the exploitation of pelagic fish species such as *mahimahi* (dolphinfish) and marlin from prehistoric to modern times. In the Marianas, pelagic fishing continued throughout the 3,000-year long Prehistoric Period (ca. 1500 BC to AD 1521) and for nearly 150 years after European Contact in 1521. Based on archaeological data and historical documents, she discusses why the Chamorro people actively engaged in pelagic fishing from initial colonisation, but stopped around AD 1750. Apparently, the availability of boats after World War II brought about a renaissance in pelagic fishing in the Marianas after a hiatus of almost two centuries.

The atoll inhabitants of Tokelau, Polynesia have a more continuous record of offshore fishing and the exploitation of pelagic resources. Rintaro Ono and David Addison discuss ancient to present marine resource use on Atafu Atoll in Tokelau, based on their excavation and ethno-ecological research conducted in 2009 and 2010. Their excavations on Atafu confirm that the atoll has been inhabited at least 600 years, and the early inhabitants depended heavily on marine resources, particularly fish and sea turtle (as well as seabird). Their analysis of the excavated fish remains also reveals that the past islanders actively exploited both inshore and pelagic species, mainly Scarids (parrotfish), Serranids (groupers), Scombrids (tunas), and Carangids (trevally or scads). This pattern is very similar to recent and modern Atafu fishing, which is patterned in part by traditional marine-conservation measures. Integrating the archaeological and ethno-ecological information suggests the possibility that marine conservation measures have played an important part in marine resource exploitation on Atafu since prehistoric times.

In the North Pacific, marine mammals and shellfish have continually been an important protein resource for humans. Todd Braje, Jon Erlandson and Torben C. Rick discuss the case of historic marine resource use in California. Their analysis of a 10,000 year record of shellfish size changes from archaeological sites on California's San Miguel Island documented a millennial-scale pattern of mean size reductions in red abalone (*H. rufescens*) and California mussel (*Mytilus californianus*) shells from archaeological sites, likely from increased human predation pressure. Their archaeological and ecological data also suggest that sea otter hunting, which began at least 9000 years ago in the Santa Barbara Channel waters, reduced otter densities and increased the productivity of near-shore abalone, sea urchin (*Strongylocentrotus* spp.), and other shellfish populations. By comparing the excavated shells from 19th-century midden on San Miguel Island to prehistoric red abalone shell, they suggest that sea otter populations were locally reduced during the Mid-Holocene, allowing abalones to reach unprecedented size and abundance.

The last paper in Part 1 is by Annalisa C. Christie and explores the social context of maritime exploitation along the east African coast in the 12th-18th centuries AD, based on her archaeological research from the Mafia Archipelago, Tanzania. She evaluates the social context of maritime exploitation within the Mafia Archipelago by examining the faunal assemblages recovered during recent excavations at the site of Kua Ruins on Juani Island within a maritime anthropological framework in order to elucidate the influence of social status on resource accessibility, and to evaluate changing patterns of resource exploitation over time. As the site is situated within the Mafia Island Marine Park (MIMP), her study has the potential to inform marine resource management strategies by providing a historical perspective on the influence of the sea on the socio-cultural organisation of maritime interactions including resource exploitation.

Part 2 includes two papers, both of which focus on the use of specific marine species such as baler shell (*Melo* spp.) in the Philippines (Vitales's paper), and *mahimahi* (dolphinfish) in Japan and the Pacific (Hashimura's paper).

Baler shell (*Melo* spp.) has a long history of exploitation in the Indo-Pacific region. This shell species is usually excavated from contexts associated with shell middens along coastal or near-coastal archaeological sites, particularly in Australia and Insular Southeast Asia. In the Philippines, baler shell remains also form a ubiquitous presence in the archaeological record, particularly during the Neolithic and the Metal Age, and Timothy Vitales explores and discusses the significance of their presence in these sites. His analysis of the baler shell assemblage in Ille cave and rockshelter site in northern Palawan, western Philippines reveals that these shells seem to be collected primarily not for subsistence, but rather, for the production of artefacts (shell scoops), which is also observed in other Philippine sites. Such implications are also discussed in an effort to understand the role of baler shells in the bigger picture of marine shell exploitation in Indo-Pacific prehistory.

As discussed by Amesbury's paper in this volume, *mahimahi* (dolphinfish) has been an important pelagic species as a subsistence and cultural resource in the Pacific since prehistoric times. The historical and cultural importance of *mahimahi* is also recognised in Eastern Asia including Japan. Osamu Hashimura's paper reports the regional distribution of the *Tsuke* method (a kind of Fish Aggregative Device) as a major *mahimahi* fishing techniques and highlights the cultural use of the *mahimahi* in contemporary Japan. He also discusses transitions in *mahimahi* fishing from prehistoric through to modern times. After reviewing the distribution of *mahimahi* uses in food and culture in Eastern Asia, Hawai'i and Costa Rica, Hashimura discusses *mahimahi* and human interactions from the past to the present.

Part 3 presents two case studies about the relationship between marine use and material culture in the western Pacific.

Akira Goto reports the historical evidence for adaptation and development of an outrigger canoe fishing gear complex on Hachijo-jima Island in the Bonin (or Ogasawara) Islands, Japan. The Bonin Islands consist of 30 islands to the north of the Mariana Islands. In prehistoric times, the Bonin Islands may have been settled from the Marianas, as indicated by excavated polished stones adze forms. Although the islands were abandoned by the 1st millennium AD, they were re-colonised from Hawai'i in 1830, introducing Hawaiian material culture including the single-outrigger canoe. Soon after this, Japanese people also started to immigrate to the Bonin Islands. Now, the islands are part of Japan and are inhabited by the Japanese, yet the modern fishing boats in the islands still continue to take the form of single outriggers. Some other fishing gear and materials also show Oceanic influences. Goto discusses this hybridised marine exploitation culture in the islands.

Takashi Tsuji discusses the basket trapping of moray eels in the Mactan Islands in the central Visayas Region of the Philippines. Using the individual tracing method and on-board investigations, he clarifies the state of moray trap fishing and the relationship between the technique of using the fish traps and its ecological and environmental impacts, focusing particularly on the bamboo moray trap. He also discusses the structure of the trap, the usage of the trapping grounds, time allocation, and the productivity of the trap. In addition, references are made to contemporary changes in moray trapping techniques and the environment surrounding these five activities. Although the use of fish traps is broadly recognised throughout the world, detailed observational studies on fish traps and moray trap fishing activities in the Philippines or elsewhere in the region are few. Tsuji's ethno-ecological study provides significant data on the trap fishing and exploitation of moray eels in the Indo-Pacific.

The last part of this volume, Part 4 consists of two papers which discuss modern marine resource use and management in the Pacific and Island Southeast Asia.

Marine resources were an important protein source for the initial settlers of the islands of Remote Oceania where indigenous terrestrial animals were scarce. Traditional subsistence of this region consisted of horticulture and the intensive utilisation of marine resources. However, in some parts of the Pacific, subsistence activities have changed in recent times as imported foods such as tinned fish and corned beef have become more important as protein sources. In light of these changes in diet and marine use, Kazuhiro Suda discusses the use of marine resources on Ha'ano Island in Tonga, Polynesia. He reports that subsistence fishing is still the main source of animal protein. The introduction of outboard motorboats and modern fishing gear such as nylon nets and lines are changing Haʻano fishing from a pattern of self-consumption and reciprocal exchange to wage working or commercial fishing. The case of Haʻano Island tentatively shows that, in the face of economic globalisation and modernisation, the role of marine resources has rapidly changed, even on such a remote island as Haʻano.

The paper by Shio Segi examines the informal territoriality over fishing grounds claimed by local small-scale fishers in south-eastern Cebu Island in the Philippines. Models based on self-sustaining site-specific territorial arrangements which are embedded in local cultural and socio-economic contexts have been proposed as one key alternative approach for coastal resource management. Given that there are only very limited studies on such arrangements in the Philippines, he focuses on how informal territoriality over local waters is operated, rationalised, and related to the formal fisheries and coastal resource management framework. Drawing upon the case of territorial claims in bottom-set gillnet fishing in coastal waters and multiple hook-and-line fishing in offshore waters, he demonstrates that longstanding continuity, localness, and social status are key concepts for fishers in justifying their claims. He also argues that the fishers' territoriality emerged out of necessity to protect their livelihoods through avoiding risks and preserving the resources for their own use rather than that of outsiders. Segi contends that in-depth research into local territoriality with multifaceted approaches to the social and political environment is necessary for designing meaningful and realistic forms of co-management.

The eleven papers in this volume indicate the wide range of topics that researchers are exploring in the Indo-Pacific region. These range from prehistoric marine resource use and its temporal changes, to analytical issues for zoo-archaeological and ethno-archaeological studies on shell and fish remains, to past and modern use of specific marine species and their cultural significance, to historical and contemporary relationships between marine resource use and maritime material culture, and to contemporary marine resource use and issues of contemporary resource management.

Lastly, we wish to express our great appreciation to the 2009 Mia J. Tegner Memorial Grants in Marine Historical Ecology, who provided the funding to edit and publish this volume. We give special thanks to the many anonymous referees who reviewed earlier drafts of the papers in this volume and provided invaluable comments and editorial suggestions, and to Sue O'Connor, David Bulbeck and an anonymous reviewer at The Australian National University for their advice and acceptance of the volume for publication in the Terra Australis series.

1

New Flesh for Old Bones: Using Modern Reef Fish to Understand Midden Remains from Guam, Mariana Islands

Richard K. Olmo, Department of Geography, University of Guam

Introduction

In the mid-1990s, I tried to build a strong prehistoric cultural context for the findings from an extensive archaeological survey and testing project sited at the northern end of Guam (Olmo 1996). While I had limited success with this, one area that caused me great consternation was my inadequate treatment of the midden remains, and in particular the fish remains. It is from my discontent with my discussion from that time that I have embarked in the direction outlined below.

I suspect that I am not alone in being frustrated by an inadequate discussion of fish remains after reading what many of my colleagues have written on the subject. I proceed by introducing three of these writings to illustrate why I am, and I think my colleagues are, disquieted. I use as examples only projects that I was involved with, although I could have chosen almost randomly from the wealth of archaeological reports available on Guam. In 1992, at the beginnings of my career on Guam, I had the opportunity to participate in archaeological survey and testing on Orote Peninsula on the west, south-central coast of the island (Figure 1). James Carucci wrote the report for this project, and the late Alan Ziegler analysed the vertebrate remains (Carucci 1993). Ziegler identified the fish remains to the family level, as was/is the common practice. He identified 10 families from 59 skeletal elements (maxillary, quadrate, vertebra, bone fragment and scale). Although only a small amount of midden was excavated for this project, over 1100 skeletal elements were recovered with 1044 not being identified beyond the category "fish" (Figure 2).

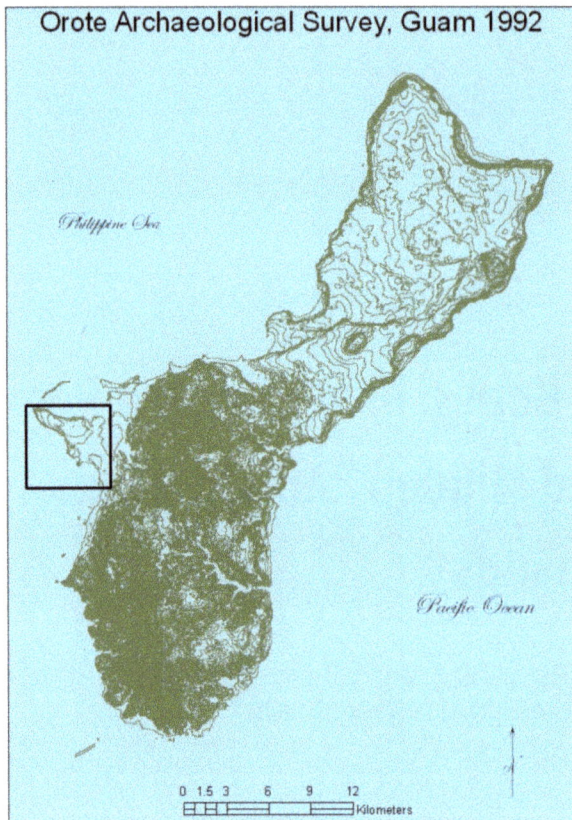

Figure 1. Map of Guam showing Orote Archaeology Project.

Source: Map by Richard K. Olmo.

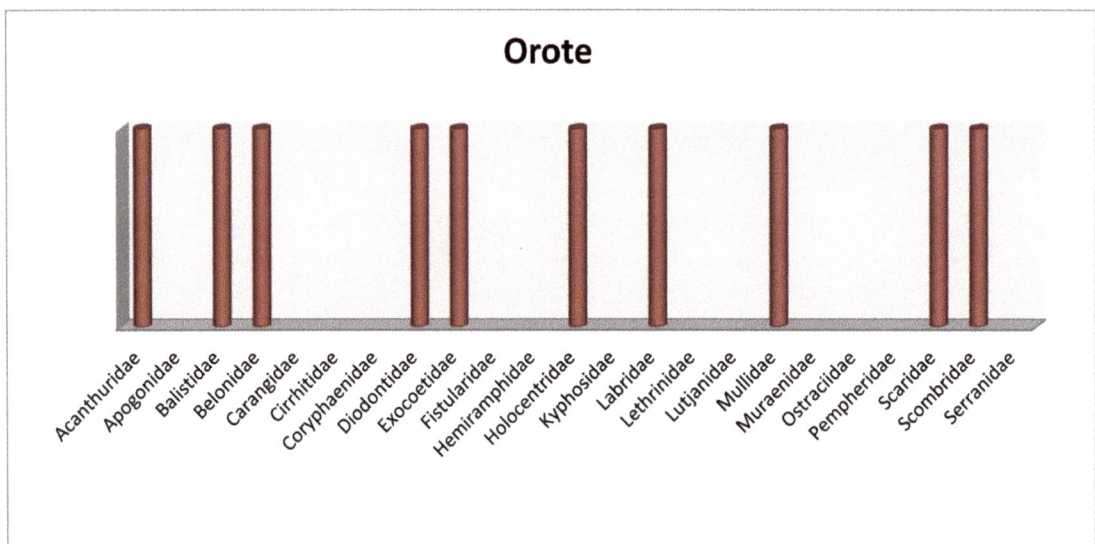

Figure 2. Graph of the fish families identified from the Orote Archaeology Project middens.

Source: Adapted from Amesbury and Hunter-Anderson 2003.

Carucci's discussion of these remains contains a single sentence and reads as follows: "Not only are there several families of inshore fish, but there are also two or three families of fish requiring offshore fishing technology" (Carucci 1993:95).

In 1995, I worked on the project that I introduced in the opening paragraph (Figure 3). Jolie Liston wrote the archaeological volume for this project, and again, Alan Ziegler analysed the vertebrate fauna (Liston 1996). He identified 14 families from 52.67 grams of faunal elements, while 207.33 grams were identified only as "fish" (Figure 4). Liston's discussion of the fish remains reads as an expanded version of Carucci's statement:

> The fish families represented in the collection are all relatively common inshore types, and of only small-to-medium size (usually no greater than about 20 or 25 cm in length). The Lutjanid, Carangid, and Serranid, which occur in small quantities in Sites 7-1605, 7-1614, 8-1588 could have been obtained by fishing from watercraft at least a short distance offshore. They are not, however, represented in enough quantity to indicate an intensive practice of offshore fishing. (Liston 1996:146).

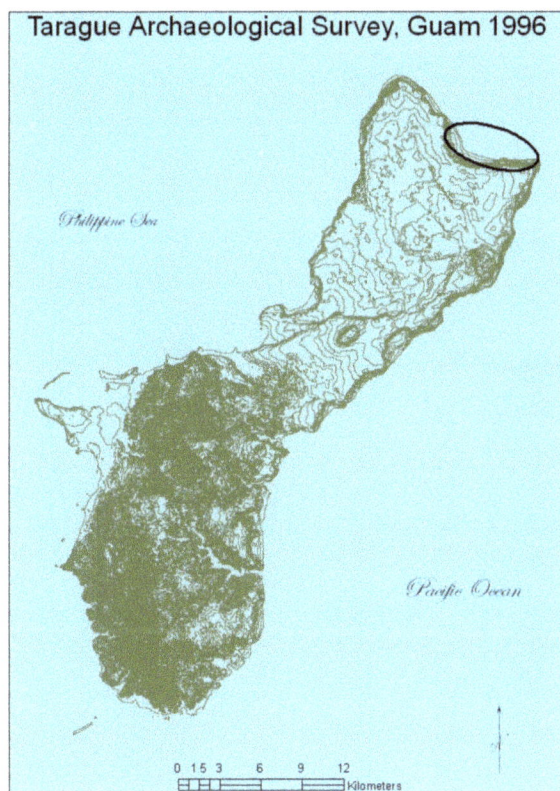

Figure 3. Map of Guam showing the location of the Tarague Embayment Project.

Source: Map by Richard K. Olmo.

Lastly, in 1998 I conducted archaeological survey and testing on several Navy-owned parcels located along the west coast of Guam, between Tanguisson and Urunao (Figure 5). I was first author for the report, along with Tina Mangiere, David Welch and Thomas Dye, and once again Alan Ziegler analysed the vertebrate fauna (Olmo et al. 2000). Fourteen families were identified from 677 skeletal elements (Figure 6).

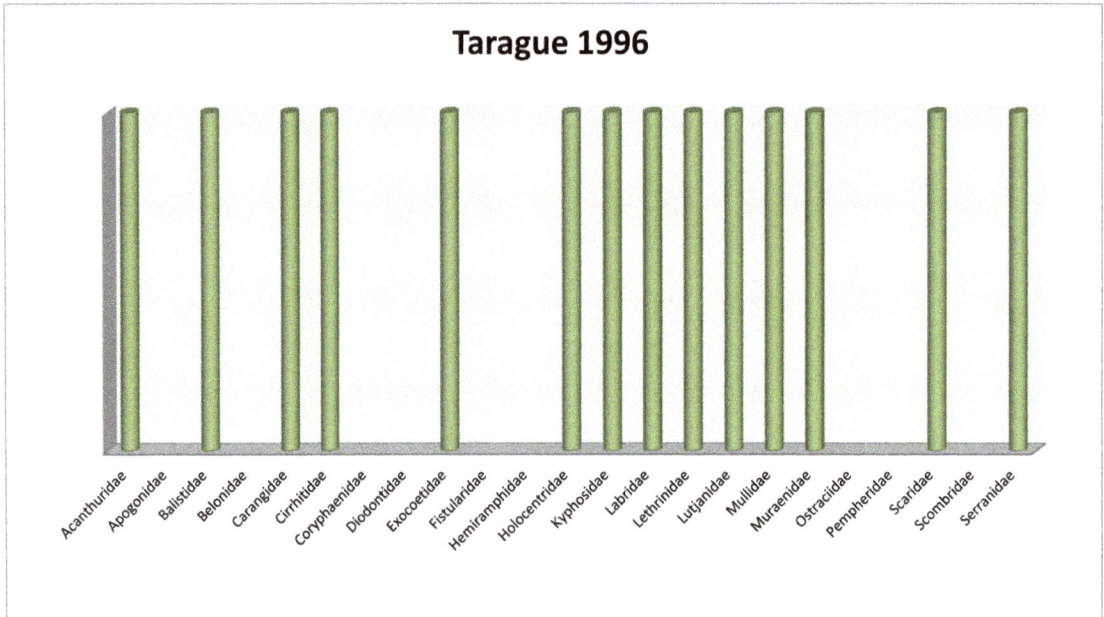

Figure 4. Graph showing the fish families identified for the Tarague Embayment Project.

Source: Adapted from Amesbury and Hunter-Anderson 2003.

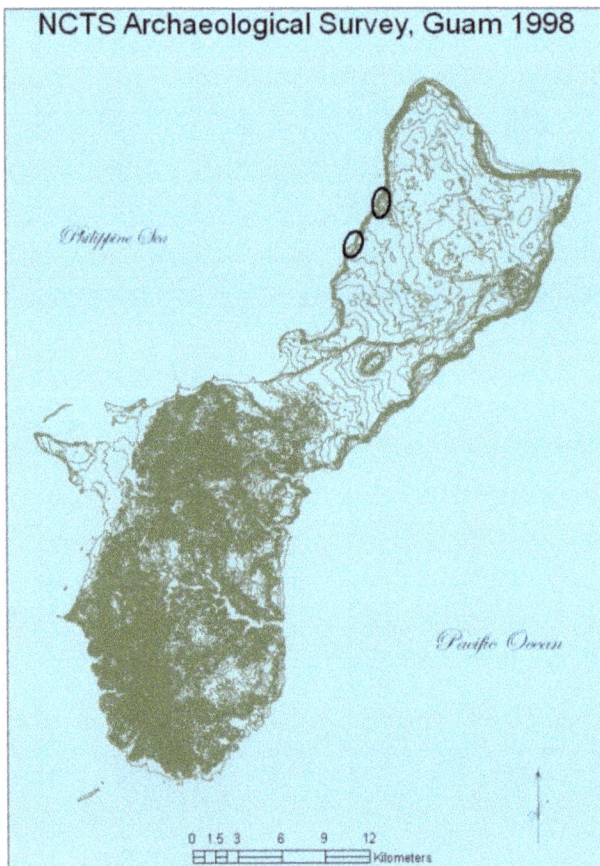

Figure 5. Map of Guam showing the locations of the Naval Computer and Telecommunications Station (NCTS) Archaeology Project.

Source: Map by Richard K. Olmo.

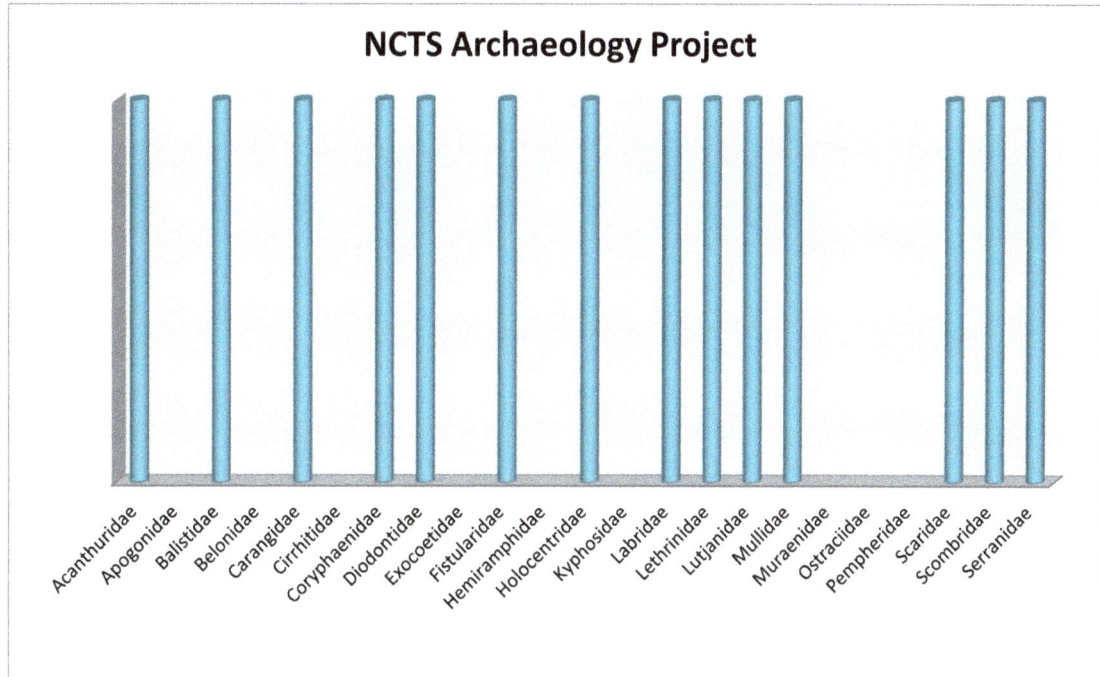

Figure 6. Graph showing the fish families identified for the NCTS Archaeology Project.

Source: Adapted from Amesbury and Hunter-Anderson 2003.

My discussion of the fish remains in the project report is best considered an expansion of Liston's, and reads as follows:

Most of the fish families identified are common inshore groups whose members could have been taken by various traditional and/or modern methods (with or without the use of watercraft) from or near the shore in relatively shallow water. Most individuals of these groups recovered are of no more than small or medium body size (i.e., between about 10 cm or 15 cm and 25 cm or 30 cm in length). Members of the family of Scaridae are noticeably abundant among this material.

There are, however, also a few families represented whose recovered members were very likely taken relatively far from shore – or at least in deeper water – by trolling and bottom fishing. Trolling presumably yielded the large "Coryphaenid" and "Scombrid" individuals, while the "Serranid" and "Lutjanid" individuals could very well have been taken by bottom-fishing, both methods necessitating the use of some type of watercraft. The two or more quite large "Carangid" could have been taken either very close inshore or well out in deeper water. In all, the 14 identified fish taxa provide evidence for at least four fishing strategies. The Acanthurids, Balistids, Mullids, and Scarids were mostly likely caught in nets; Labrids, Lethrinids, Lutjanids, and Serranids, were likely caught with demersal baited hooks; Carangids, Coryphaenids, and Scombrids were caught with pelagic lures; and Diodontids, Fistularids, and Holocentrids were likely captured during general foraging (Davidson and Leach 1988:350). The presence of so many fishes captured with pelagic lures, although relatively common in Mariana Islands faunal assemblages, is unusual in the wider context of Pacific Islands. Coryphaenids or Dolphinfishes in particular, are big fish found rarely in Pacific island archaeological faunal assemblages. The identification of a Coryphaenid bone at Haputo indicates that fishermen here shared the deep-sea fishing skill identified for the people of Rota by Leach and his associates (Leach et al. 1985; Davidson and Leach 1988). (Olmo et al. 2000:208-209).

Even though the above paragraph attempts to more fully link prehistoric activities, e.g., reef gleaning, net fishing, bait fishing, and trolling in open water with the identified fish remains it is far from what is necessary to provide a picture of prehistoric Chamorro life along this stretch of coast as it related to subsistence. When compared with a similar paragraph written by William Lessa, in his short ethnographic monograph on Ulithi, it is easy to see the distance between what we are writing as archaeologists and where we need to be (Lessa 1966:15):

> Spectacular catches come seasonally, when certain kinds of fish come in huge schools to the outer reef and are caught by large numbers of men, working communally, who use long nets to herd the fish together as they wade through the shallow water with the slowly shrinking net. Lagoon fishing is by far the most common of all and has many methods. The most successful involves the cooperation of a large number of men in canoes who assemble in traditional fishing grounds to catch fish with seines. This is the most reliably consistent kind of fishing. Some individuals go out into the lagoon alone or in small groups, using hooks, usually made of tortoise shell or coconut shell, or nowadays steel. Dip nets are often employed in fishing. Some angling is done with gorges made of mussel shell. Composite trolling hooks are used for pelagic fishing, especially to catch bonito, but Ulithians are not fond of leaving the safety of the lagoon, which in any event is the more convenient place to fish. Fishlines are made of sennit or coconut string. Basketry traps and stone weirs are occasionally employed in the lagoon. The traps are usually tied to a drifting log. As much for a sport as anything else, men and boys occasionally indulge in torchlight fishing from the outer reef at low tide, walking along with huge torches whose flames attract the fish, which are then gathered with small nets or clubbed into insensibility.

Lessa's description was chosen for its brevity. Many other ethnographic works contain considerably longer treatments describing indigenous peoples' interactions with marine resources. Although Lessa's account is brief, it remains richer than what I had written from the midden analysis. The ability to personally observe the activities associated with fishing most certainly contributes to the better description. Allowing this, however, I believe that the difficulty others and I have had in writing more descriptively about midden remains comes more from the fact that the lowest taxonomic level we work with is the family and less so from the lack of direct observation. Because there are often many genera and species within each family, a wide range of habitat and behaviour is encompassed and it becomes difficult to be more precise with a discussion of human activities, which are crucially tied to understanding the behaviour of individual species.

Within a family, some members prefer shallow reef environments, some channels, some sandy bottoms, some seagrass beds, some hard substrates, and some lagoons while others prefer reef fronts; some are active at night, while others hide at night, and etc. Acheson, in his survey article on the anthropology of fishing, states that fishermen have not only a good understanding of the ocean, including its currents and bottom topography, but that they have a "detailed knowledge of the species of fish they are seeking – their habits, breeding cycles, enemies, food supply, feeding habits, and especially migration patterns and habitats" (1981:291). Therefore, if we are going to be in the position of discussing the what, when, where and how of a prehistoric peoples' exploitation activities, it is imperative to obtain information on the individual species that are represented by these remains.

Methods

In the effort to expand the possible interpretation from midden analyses an important data source has been explored. These are modern fishery catch data collected and compiled by the Guam Department of Agriculture, Division of Aquatic and Wildlife Resources (DAWR). I am working with two ideas here: (1) that catch data reflect the species that commonly occur in Guam's waters, consequently providing insight to the subset of species most likely associated with the collective midden family results, and, (2) that census data will provide probable species diversity associated with particular midden assemblages. Narrowing down to just a few species the suite of possibilities represented by the broad family designations has the potential of allowing much richer interpretations of prehistoric fishing activities on Guam.

 In 2003, Judith Amesbury and Rosalind Hunter-Anderson published a report on reef fishing in Guam and the Northern Mariana Islands for the Western Pacific Regional Fishery Management Council in Honolulu (Amesbury and Hunter-Anderson 2003). The report was a compilation of prehistoric and historic data and offered the Council a window on long-term trends in species abundance and distributions. After an exhaustive review of the grey literature, Amesbury and Hunter-Anderson were able to identify reports from nine different areas around Guam that contained midden analyses reporting fish remains. Twenty-three families were identified, and their site distributions are displayed in Figure 7. While the goal of these authors was to use midden information to expand the modern data, I am proposing that we go in the opposite direction and use modern data to expand upon our understanding of the past.

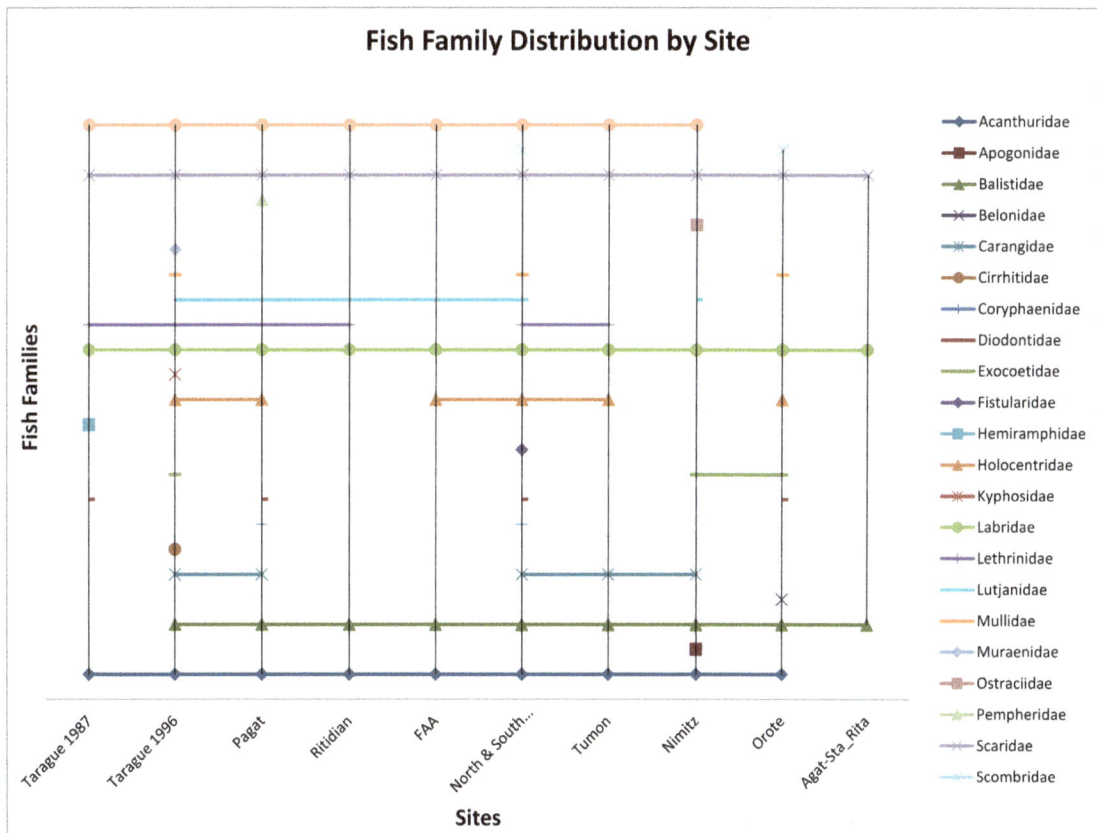

Figure 7. Graph showing the distribution of fish families for nine areas on Guam.

Source: Adapted from Amesbury and Hunter-Anderson 2003.

Analysis and discussion

The data source used in this work was the annual reports from 1986 until 2008 compiled by the Guam Division of Aquatics and Wildlife Resources. I explore several ways of working with the annual reports including the lists of the top-ten families taken, when they were taken, the species that were identified, and the methods that were used. The daytime top-ten were used in this analysis to construct a table showing the families and the species most frequently taken by local fishers. Because data for the kilograms of fish taken was included in the reports, it was possible to provide a sense of the relative contribution of each family over the roughly twenty-year span (Figure 8).

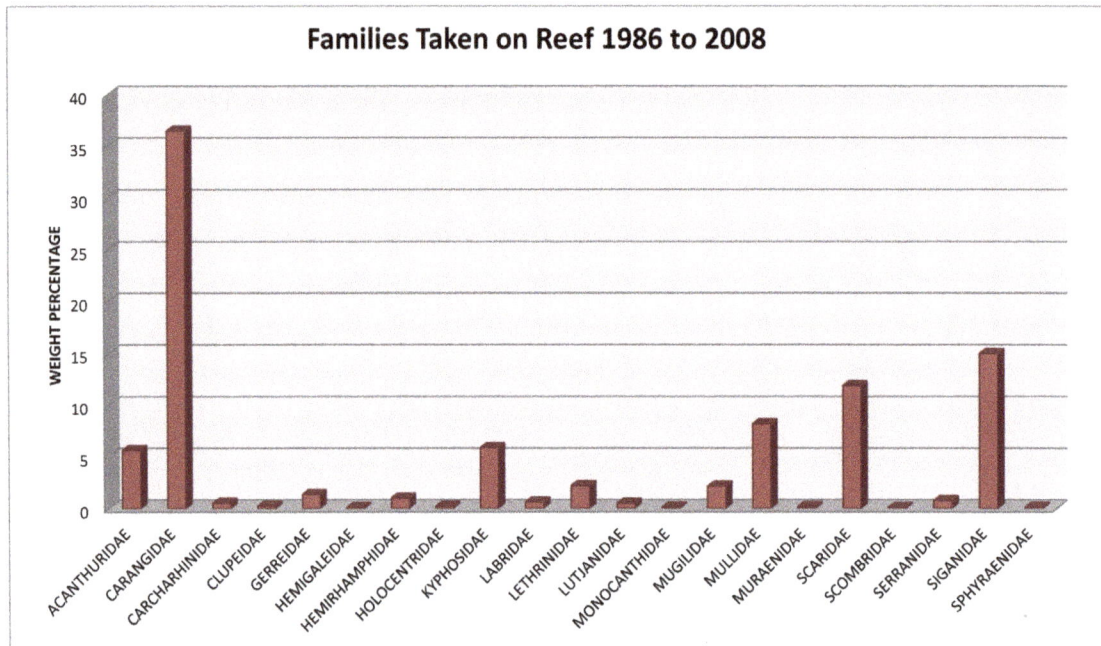

Figure 8. Relative distribution of fish families caught from shore on Guam.

Source: Data from Guam Division of Aquatic and Wildlife Resources (DAWR).

Figure 8 shows that twenty-one fish families comprised t taken over the study period. Acanthurids (surgeonfishes, unicornfishes), carangids (jacks, trevallys), kyphosids (rudderfishes, sea chubs), mullids (goatfishes), scarids (parrotfishes) and siganids (rabbitfishes, spinefoots) are the most frequently represented families. Carangids, mullids and siganids are disproportionately represented due to seasonal runs of juvenile species. When the seasonal component is removed, the resulting graph looks considerably different (Figure 9). Acanthurids, kyphosids, lethrinids and scarids dominate, the presence of carangids is greatly reduced, and the mullids and siganids all but disappear. One reason for removing the juveniles from consideration is that they can be eaten whole or processed in such a way as to contribute little but trace elements to the midden assemblage.

Twenty-one families are represented in the catch data while twenty-three are identified from the combined middens. A comparison of the two data sets shows that thirteen families are common to both. The yearly catch data contain representatives of eight families [carcharinids (requiem sharks), clupeids (herrings, shads, sardines), gerrids (mojarras), hemigaleids (weasel sharks), monocanthids (filefishes, leatherjackets), mugilids (mullets), siganids (rabbitfishes, spinefoots) and sphyraenids (barracudas)], which are not identified from the midden assemblages. Alternatively, the middens contain representatives of seven families [apogonids (cardinalfishes), belonids (needlefishes), cirrhitids (hawkfishes), diodontids (porcupinefishes), fistularids (cornetfishes), ostraciids (trunkfishes, boxfishes) and pempherids (sweepers)] not found among the top-ten families caught (Table 1).

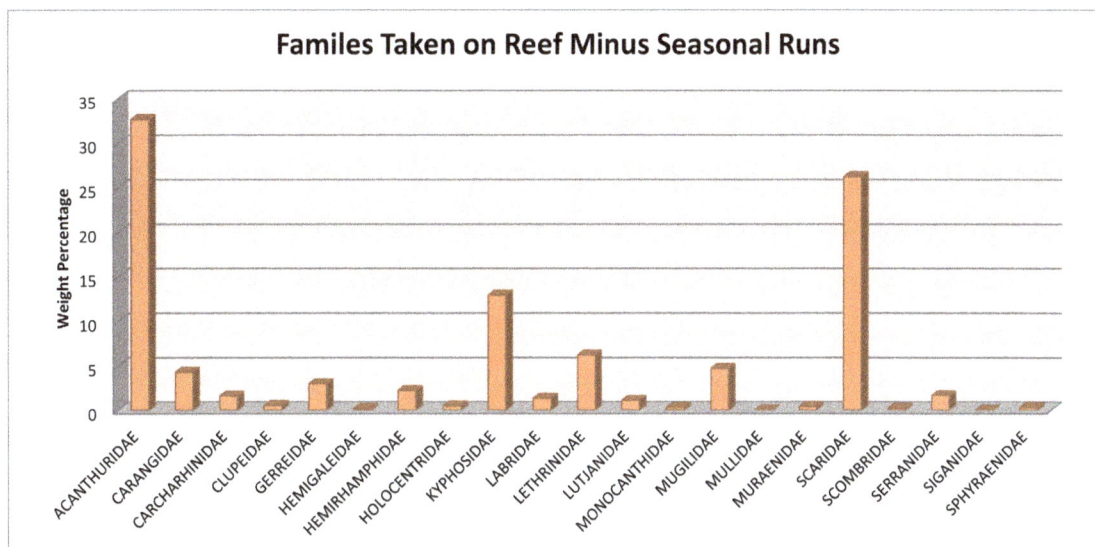

Figure 9. Relative distribution of fish families caught from shore less seasonal component.

Source: Data from Guam DAWR.

A review of the information on these families suggests the possibility that a majority (six out of seven) could have been taken by night fishing. Night fishing with torches is documented in the ethnographic literature for Micronesia. The apogonids and the pempherids are inactive during the day, remaining hidden in caves and crevices, and the cirrhitids, diodontids and ostraciids all spawn in the dark. The belonids are attracted to lights at night and will skip out of the water when disturbed. Although normally diurnal, this behaviour may allow them to be more easily obtained at night. The nocturnal activity of these families might also explain why they are missing from the catch data, which represents only daytime fishing. Because of the prevalence of night-time spear fishing on Guam using a variety of technical advances not available to prehistoric peoples, the night catch was omitted from this analysis. This leaves only the fistularids to be caught during the day. A single species is known from Micronesia, *Fistularia commersonii*. It occurs in all reef habitats, but is often observed in schools in open, sandy areas (Myers 1991).

Table 1. Families identified in middens but not the top-ten catch data.

Family	Habit	Food	Spawn	Caught
Apogonidae	Hide by day, roam reef at night	Zooplankton and small benthic crustaceans		
Belonidae	Surface dwelling, inshore reefs	Small fishes		Casting, trolling, floating nets[b]
Cirrhitidae	Perch on outer branches of coral	Benthic crustaceans and fish	Dusk or early night	
Diodontidae	Adults inshore, young pelagic[a]	Hard-shelled invertebrates[a]	Surface, dawn or dusk	
Fistularidae	Diurnal, all reef areas, open sandy areas	Small fishes and crustaceans		
Ostraciidae	Diurnal, males territorial w/harems	Small invertebrates and algae[a]	Night above outcrops	
Pempheridae	Hide in caves by day, feed at night[a]	Zooplankton1	Pelagic[a]	

Source: All table data are from R.F. Myers (1991), otherwise; (a) data from J.S. Nelson (1994); (b) data from B.B. Collette (2003).

Before continuing with this analysis, one question worth addressing is if the catch data represent a proportional take from the available taxa. The answer seems to be no. Species taken from Marianas waters are not proportional to those available to be taken. A graphical representation of the relationship between species observed versus those obtained is shown in Figure 10. While only the family level data are available for the middens, scarids are identified from all middens and represent the most abundant minimum number of individuals (MNI) when present. Only 25 scarid species are recorded for the Marianas, so the aggregated midden data is also probably not proportional to the available taxa.

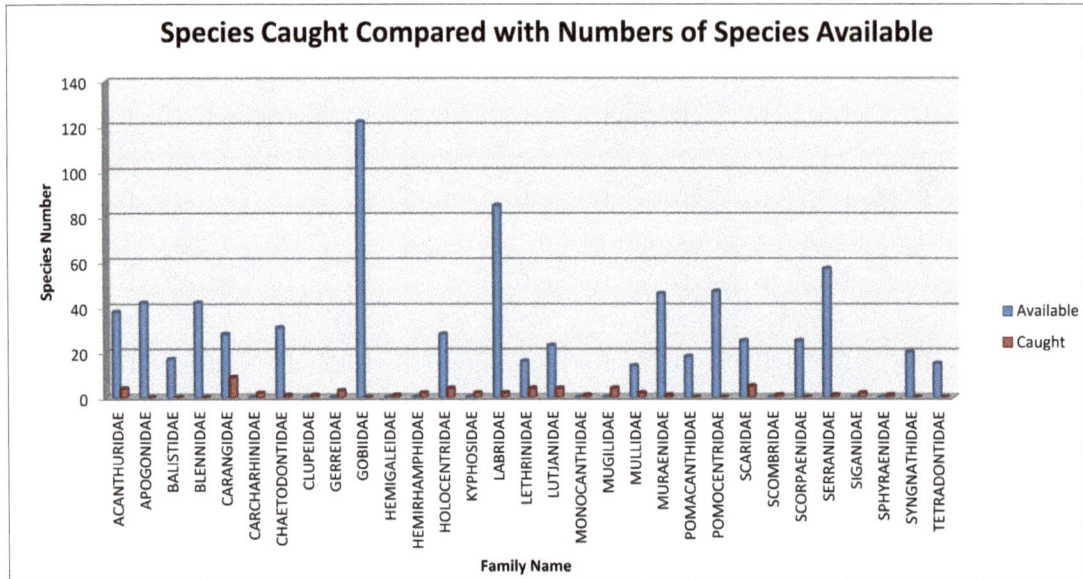

Figure 10. Species available versus numbers caught for each family.

Source: Species data from Myers and Donaldson, 2003; catch data from Guam DAWR1986-2008.

The thirteen families that are common to the middens and the modern catch are acanthurids, carangids, hemirhamphids, holocentrids, kyphosids, labrids, lethrinids, lutjanids, mullids, muraenids, scarids, scombrids, and serranids. The distributions of species identified from the modern catch that represent the common families are shown in Table 2.

Table 2. Species identified in Top-Ten Catch 1986-2008.

Family	Species
Acanthuridae	*Acanthurus lineatus, A. triostegus triostegus, A. xanthopterus, Naso literatus, N. unicornis*
Carangidae	*Carangoides orthogrammus, Caranx ignobilis, C. Melampygus, C. Papuensis, C. Sexfasciatus, Decapterus macrosoma, Scomberoides lysan, Selar crumenophthalmus, Trachinotus blochii*
Hemirhamphidae	*Hyporhampus acutus acutus, Hemiramphus (archipelagicus) lutkei*
Holocentridae	*Myripristis berndti, Neoniphon sammara, Sargocentron spiniferum, S. tiere*
Kyphosidae	*Kyphosus cinerascens, K. vaigiensis*
Labridae	*Cheilinus trilobatus, C. Undulates, Cheilio inermis*
Lethrinidae	*Lethrinus erythracanthus, L. microdon, L. harak, L. obsoletus, L. xanthochilus, Monotaxis grandoculus*
Lutjanidae	*Aprion virescens, Lutjanus bohar, L. fulvus, L. gibbus, L. monostigmus*
Mullidae	*Mulloidichthys flavolineatus, Parupeneus barberinus, P. insularis*
Muraenidae	*Gymnothorax javanicus*
Scaridae	*Bolbometopon muricatum, Cetoscarus bicolor, Chlorurus frontalis, C. microrhinos, C. sordidus, Hipposcarus longiceps, Leptoscarus vaigiensis, Scarus altipinnis, S. psittacus, S. rubroviolaceus, S. schlegeli*
Scombridae	*Gymnosarda unicolor*
Serranidae	*Cephalopholis urodeta, Epinephelus merra, E. polyphekadion, Plectropomus laevis*

Source: All table data are from Guam Division of Aquatic and Wildlife Resources 1986-2008.

In the analysis done by Amesbury and Hunter-Anderson, cited earlier, acanthurids were found at all of the areas except for Agat-Santa Rita. Only three families were identified from that assemblage. There were five species of Acanthuridae identified from the catch data, each exhibiting differences of habit. *Acanthurus lineatus* (lined surgeonfish) commonly occupies the exposed, seaward portions of reefs and prefers the surge zone. It is the most shallow-living of the acanthurids in this list, rarely found below 15 m. Large males are territorial with harems of females (Kuiter and Tonozuka 2001a). Adults are usually found schooling in shallow channels that are from 1 m to 3 m deep (Randall 1986). Data obtained from the DAWR specifically derived from Guam fisheries indicate that about one third of the time *A. lineatus* is caught using hook and line, and about two fifths of the time using a gill net (Figure 11).

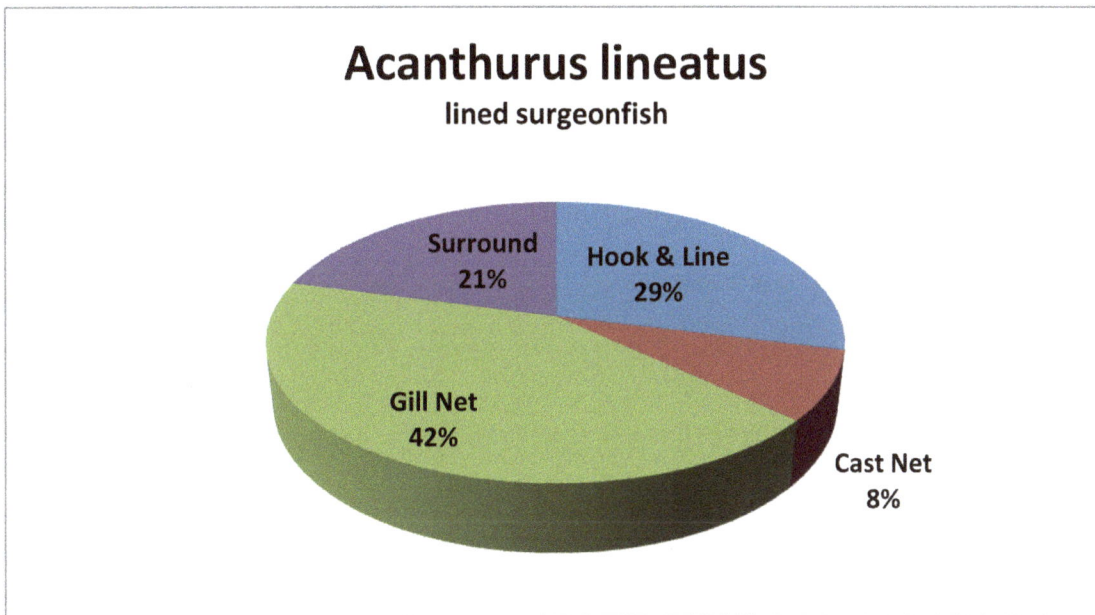

Acanthurus lineatus
lined surgeonfish

Figure 11. Catch methods for the lined surgeonfish.

Source: Guam DAWR 1986-2008.

Acanthurus triostegus triostegus (convict surgeonfish) is found in the wider context of the seaward portions of reefs, the hard-bottomed portions of lagoons, and waters up to 90 m deep (Randall 1956). This species will occasionally school, particularly when feeding on a favourite algae which grows on rocks where there is fresh-water runoff (Kuiter and Tonozuka 2001a). *A. triostegus triostegus* is taken by hook and line 10% of the time, by cast net about half of the time, with gill and surround nets the remainder of the time. This may reflect its wide range and feeding habits (Figure 12).

Acanthurus xanthopterus (yellowfin surgeonfish) inhabits an even wider range of environs including outer and inner reef areas, sand slopes and lagoons (Ibid.). It tends to school and unlike some acanthurids will readily take bait. This is evident in the catch data, as more than 90% of the time it is caught using hook and line (Figure 13).

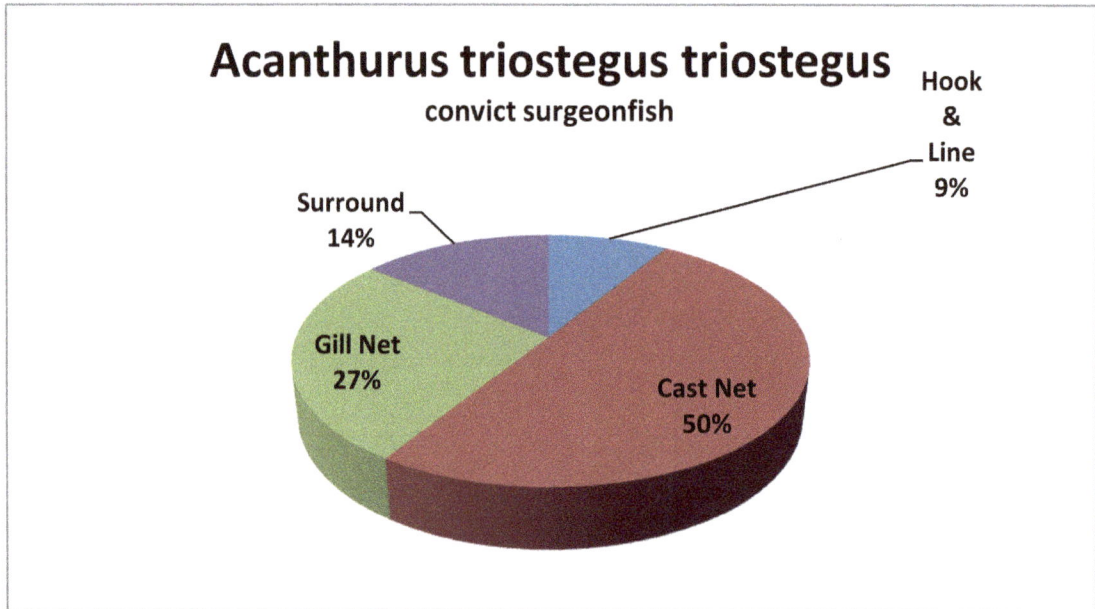

Figure 12. Catch methods for the convict surgeonfish.

Source: Guam DAWR 1986-2008.

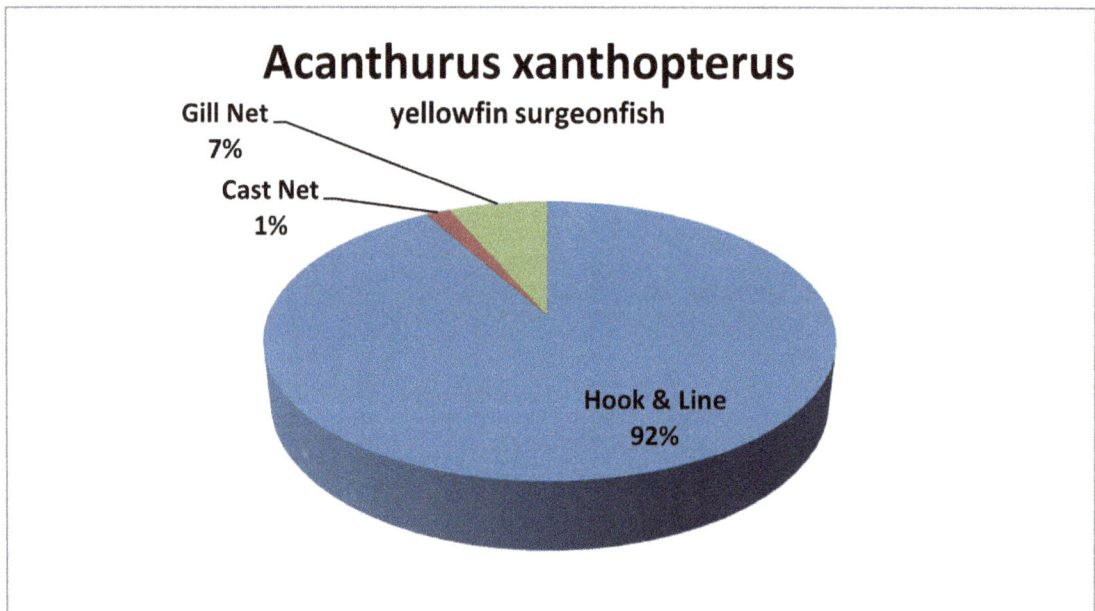

Figure 13. Catch methods for the yellowfin surgeonfish.

Source: Guam DAWR 1986-2008.

Naso literatus (orangespine unicornfish) is found in rock, rubble and coral areas of the lagoon and outer reef (Ibid.). It is usually observed in small groups with other acanthurids but will sometimes form large aggregations (Randall 2001).About 70% of the time *N. literatus* is caught using hook and line, while gill and surround nets account for the remainder of the catch (Figure 14).

Naso literatus
orangespine unicornfish

Surround 13%

Gill Net 13%

Cast Net 5%

Hook & Line 69%

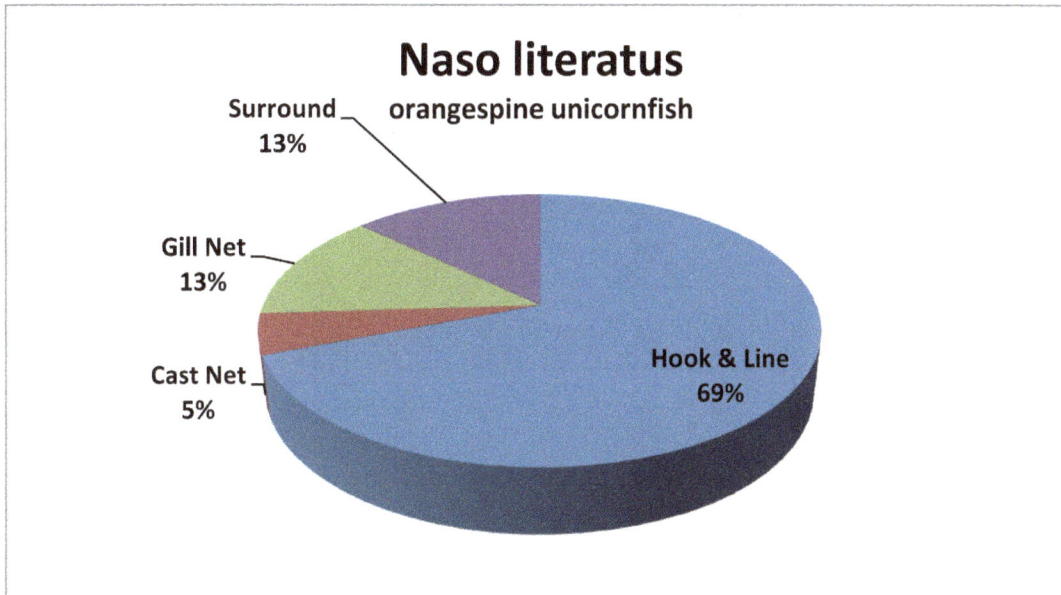

Figure 14. Catch methods for the orangespine unicornfish.

Source: Guam DAWR 1986-2008.

Finally, *Naso unicornis* (bluespine unicornfish) exhibits some behaviour similar to *Acanthurus lineatus*, occupying channels, moats, lagoons and seaward reefs with strong surge. It remains in small groups. Despite the similarity in showing preference for strong moving waters *N. unicornis* is also most often taken using hook and line (Figure 15).

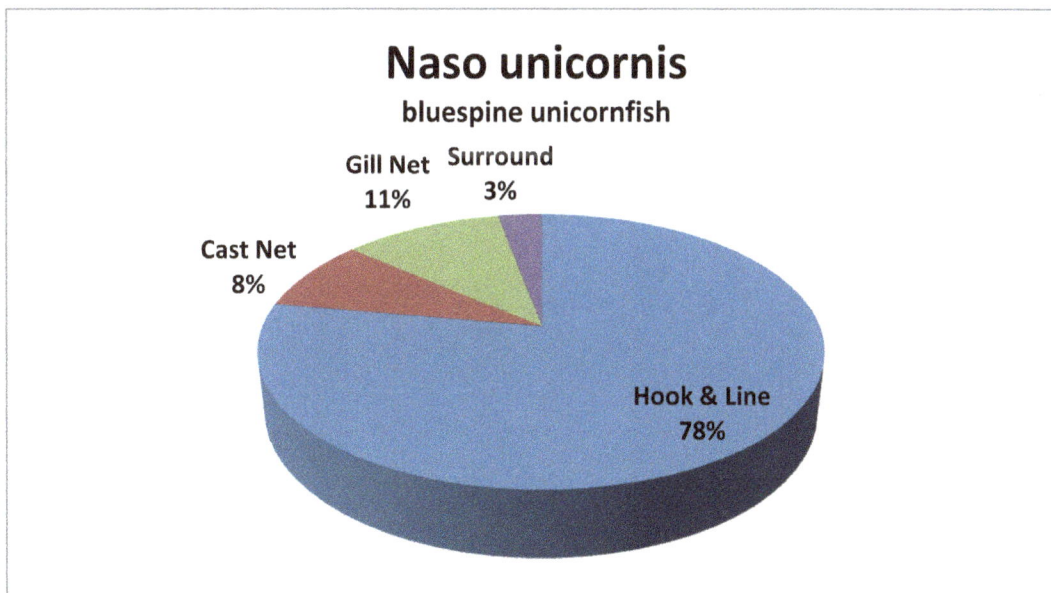

Naso unicornis
bluespine unicornfish

Gill Net 11%   Surround 3%

Cast Net 8%

Hook & Line 78%

Figure 15. Catch methods for the bluespine unicornfish.

Source: Guam DAWR 1986-2008.

By linking prehistoric procurement activities to the fish behaviour for these acanthurids, we can place people at a variety of locations on the reef, including the surge channels building weirs and setting nets, with hand lines and baited hooks in the lagoonal areas and fishing from canoes anchored at or patrolling the reef front, or with a group of lineage mates or fishing partners working a collective surround net in the lagoon. Fishing using weirs and gill nets provides people with different time- and place-engagements than when they are using cast nets, surround nets or angling. Just comparing *Acanthurus lineatus* with *Naso unicornis* reveals some important differences in behaviour. *A. lineatus* provides for people being elsewhere doing other things as they allow their equipment to capture fish in their absence while *N. unicornis* suggests the presence of people at channels and troughs during the changing tides, or when swells are rolling in on the reef. So, the importance of developing a more precise understanding of the midden beyond the family level is not to be underestimated when it comes to illustrating peoples' daily activities.

Carangids were identified in five of the midden locations and nine carangid genera were identified from the catch data. They occupy a wider range of habitats when compared with the acanthurids, in part because they are hunters and eat other fish. Because of their diet they will take bait, and are primarily caught using hook and line. The following table gives a good picture of this relationship. That said, one commonly caught species, *Trachinotus blochii*, departs from this rule, as it is almost exclusively captured using a gill net; and, about one third of the time *C. papuensis* is as well.

Table 3. Carangids and their relative catch methods.

Genera	% Hook and line	% Gill net	% Cast net	% Drag
Carangoides orthogrammus	100	-	-	-
*Caranx i'e'**	73	4	23	-
Caranx ignobilis	71	15	-	14
Caranx melampygus	82	13	1	-
Caranx papuensis	61	31	8	-
Caranx sexfasciatus	78	18	4	-
*Decapterus macrosoma***	100	-	-	-
Selar crumenophthalmus	92	3	5	-
Scomberoides lysan	98	2	-	-
Trachinotus blochii	2	82	15	1

Source: All table data abstracted from Guam Division of Aquatics and Wildlife Resources 1986-2008.

*Commonly taken in large numbers from shore using a cast net.

**Catch data from 1998-2000.

Carangoides orthogrammus (yellow-spotted trevally) is found individually or in pairs or small schools that range from sandy river bottoms to sandy channels of lagoons and the outer reef (Smith-Vaniz 1995). Although they are found over a wide range of depths (3 m to 168 m), larger adults tend to move into the deeper waters (Myers 1991). *Caranx ignobilis* (giant trevally) is the largest of the trevallys. Although it has been observed ranging from 10 m to 188 m, it spawns in the shallow, outer reef zone (Myers 1999). Juveniles are often found in estuarine environments, while adults are found in clear lagoon waters and the outer reef (Lieske and Myers 1994).

Caranx melampygus (bluefin trevally) ranges from river channels to sandy inshore waters to the reef (Ibid.; Marquet 1993). Juveniles are more commonly found in the inshore areas. It will sometimes school. *Caranx papuensis* (brassy trevally) adults range from rivers to lagoons and the outer reef. Juveniles are frequently encountered in estuaries (Kuizer and Tonozuka 2001). *Caranx sexfasciatus* (bigeye trevally) is a reef species that is mainly active at night or twilight. It remains in large fairly slow-moving schools in passes or outside the reef during the day (Bagnis et al. 1984). Juveniles frequent estuaries and may penetrate a good distance up-river (Allen et al. 2002).

Decapterus macrosoma (slender scad) usually schools, and is occasionally observed in small groups feeding on zooplankton along the reef slope near deep water (Kuizer and Tonozuka 2001). The doublespotted queenfish, *Scomberoides lysan,* is found in clear, lagoon and outer reef waters as an adult, and inshore and brackish waters as a juvenile (Lieske and Myers 1994). This carangid is usually solitary, but it is sometimes observed in small, loose aggregates (Kuizer and Tonozuka 2001). *Selar crumenophthalmus* (bigeye scad) prefers clear, ocean waters around islands, but ranges into turbid waters (Cervigón et al. 1992). It is nocturnal, and travels in tight groups numbering in the hundreds of thousands (Smith-Vaniz 1995). The last of the carangids identified from the fishery data is the snubnose pompano, *Trachinotus blochii.* Juveniles inhabit sandy shorelines and shallow sandy or muddy bays near river mouths, while adults school and move into the clearer waters of seaward reefs where they are found in the vicinity of coral and rock (Fischer et al. 1990).

Hemirhamphidae was identified from one midden assemblage and two genera were identified from the catch data, while six species are known in total from the Marianas (Myers and Donaldson 2003). *Hyporhampus acutus acutus* (pacific halfbeak) is found at the surface at the reef front and in lagoons (Lieske and Myers 1994). It is captured about three qurarters of the time on Guam using surround nets and 20% of the time with hook and line. *Hemiramphus lutkei* (jumping halfbeak) is found in immediate coastal waters. Unlike *H. acutus acutus* it is exclusively taken with hook and line.

Myers and Donaldson have recorded twenty-eight genera of holocentrids in the Marianas (2003). Six midden assemblages contained holocentrids and four species were recognised from the catch data. *Myripristis berndti* (big-scale soldierfish) hides in caves and under ledges of the sub-tidal inner reef during the day and becomes active at night (Mundy 2005). It is consequently one of the species captured after dark using gill nets. *Neoniphon sammara* (bloodspot squirrelfish) is found in schools in the reef flats, in seagrass beds and in the lagoon waters over hard substrates such as the coral, *Acropora sp.* (Lieske and Myers 1994).

Catch data for 1995 and 2004 indicate that the majority of *N. sammara* are captured in gill nets, with a small amount caught on hooks. *Sargocentron spiniferum* (long-jawed squirrelfish), like *Myripristis berndti,* is also active at night, hiding under ledges in the lagoon, reef flat and reef front during the day (Lieske and Myers 1994). Unlike *M. berndti,* it is caught using hook and line. The last of the holocentrids that has been identified in the catch is *Sargocentron tiere* (blue-lined squirrelfish). It is reclusive during the day and inhabits deep crevices in surge channels (Myers 1991). *S. tiere* is taken using gill nets. Three of the four commonly taken species of holocentrid are active during the night. While two of the three species can be caught with gill nets set at dusk and then retrieved in the morning, *S. spiniferum* implies active fishing after dark.

Kyphosidae (rudderfishes) were identified from one midden and two species have been identified in the top-ten catch data. Both are caught primarily using gill nets, but about 10% of *Kyphosus cinerascens* are caught with hook and line. *K. cinerascens* (highfin rudderfish) is found grouped in the surf-influenced zone of the outer reef, usually over calcareous algae (Sommer et al. 1996). *Kyphosus vaigiensis* (lowfin rudderfish) occupies the same habitats as its congener and is also found around exposed areas of rock reefs (Masuda et al. 1984). It is most often taken using a gill net.

Labrids (wrasses) were recognised in all ten midden groups and three genera are represented in the top-ten catch data. *Cheilinus trilobatus* (tripletail wrasse) is common in shallow reef margins where good coral cover is available. Consequently, it is found in both lagoon and reef front areas (Lieske and Myers 1994). *C. trilobatus* is almost always taken by net, and in particular, by gill net (Figure 16). *Cheilinus undulatus* (humphead wrasse) is a diurnally active species found over steep areas of the reef front, channel slopes, and the inner reef of the lagoon (Myers 1991). Juveniles are observed in a variety of lagoon habitats including seagrass beds (Ibid.). They rest in caves during the night. Catch method was not available for this species. *Cheilio inermis* (cigar wrasse) is commonly found over algal flats and seagrass beds (Myers 1991). It is recorded as a species taken using spear and snorkel.

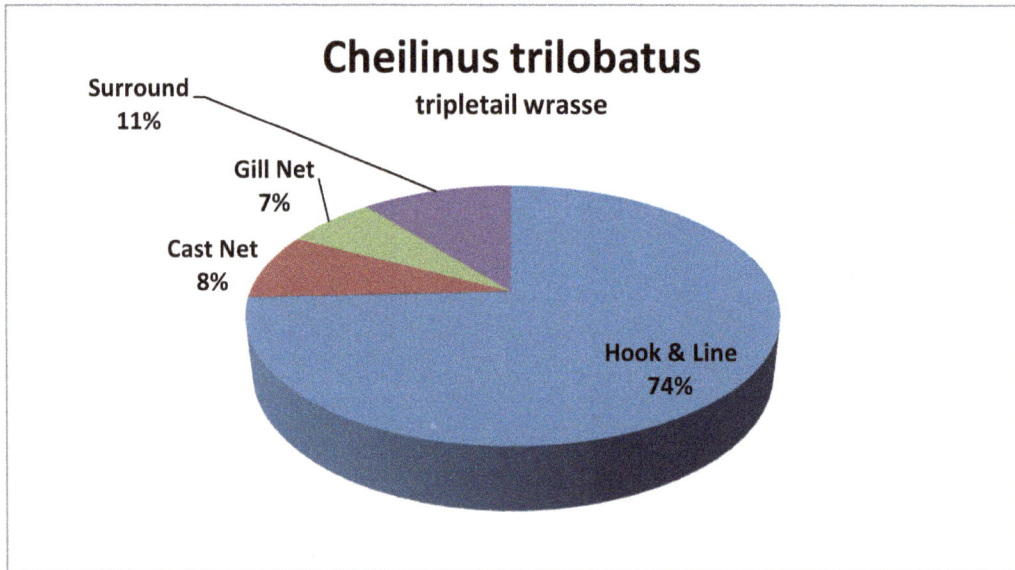

Figure 16. Catch methods for the tripletail wrasse.

Source: Guam DAWR 1986-2008.

Six genera of lethrinids (emperors) appear in the top-ten catch data and the family was identified from six midden assemblages. *Lethrinus erythracanthus* (orangefin emperor) is found in a variety of coral reef habitats: deep lagoons and channels, reef front slopes and sandy-bottomed areas (Sommer et al. 1996). It is taken exclusively by hook and line according to the 1997 data. *Lethrinus harak* (blackspot emperor) is found individually or in small schools within a wide range of coral reef and mangrove habitats. It is usually observed within the upper 20 metres of the water column and is considered the most common emperor in the Marianas (Myers 1991). More than half of the time it is caught using hook and line, otherwise gill nets (31%) and other nets are used (Figure 17).

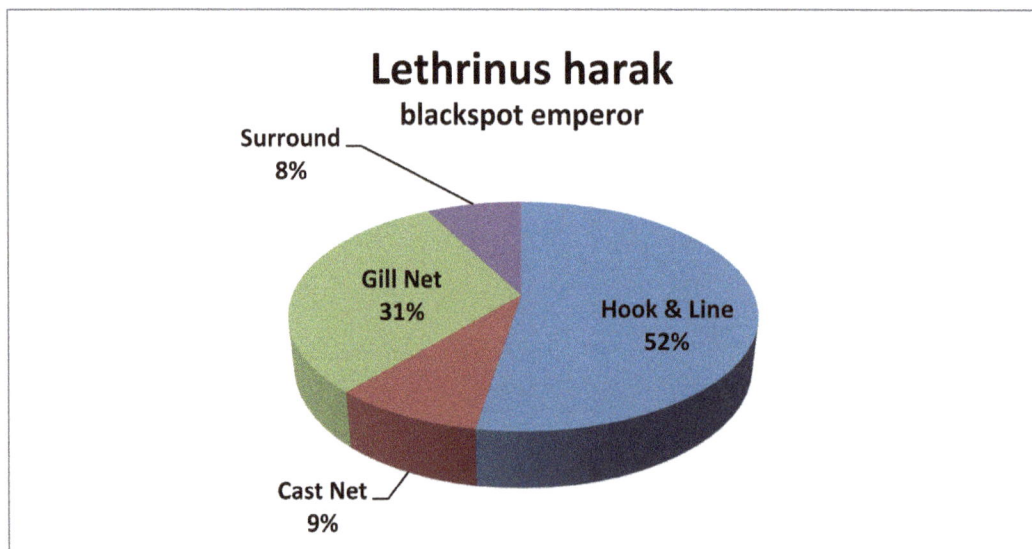

Figure 17. Catch methods for the blackspot emperor.

Source: Guam DAWR 1986-2008.

The small-tooth emperor (*Lethrinus microdon*) is found in small schools and is most frequently observed over sandy areas of the coral reef (Myers 1991). No catch method data were available. *Lethrinus obsoletus* (yellowstripe emperor) occurs individually or in aggregations in sand and rubble areas of the lagoon and in the waters over seagrass beds (Gell and Whittington 2002; Sommer et al. 1996). Approximately three fifths of the time, it is caught with hook and line, otherwise a gill net dominates its capture (Figure 18).

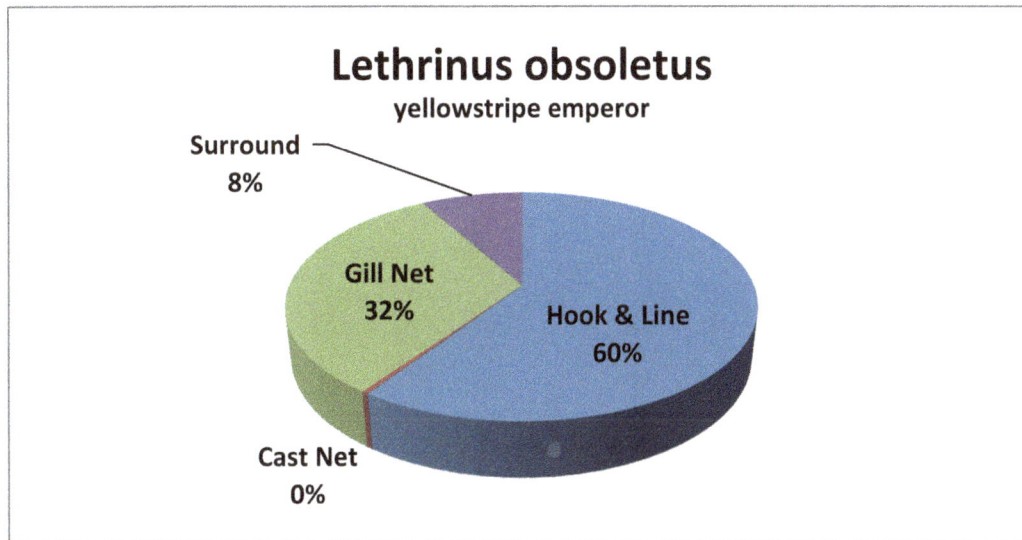

Figure 18. Catch methods for the yellowstripe emperor.

Source: Guam DAWR 1986-2008.

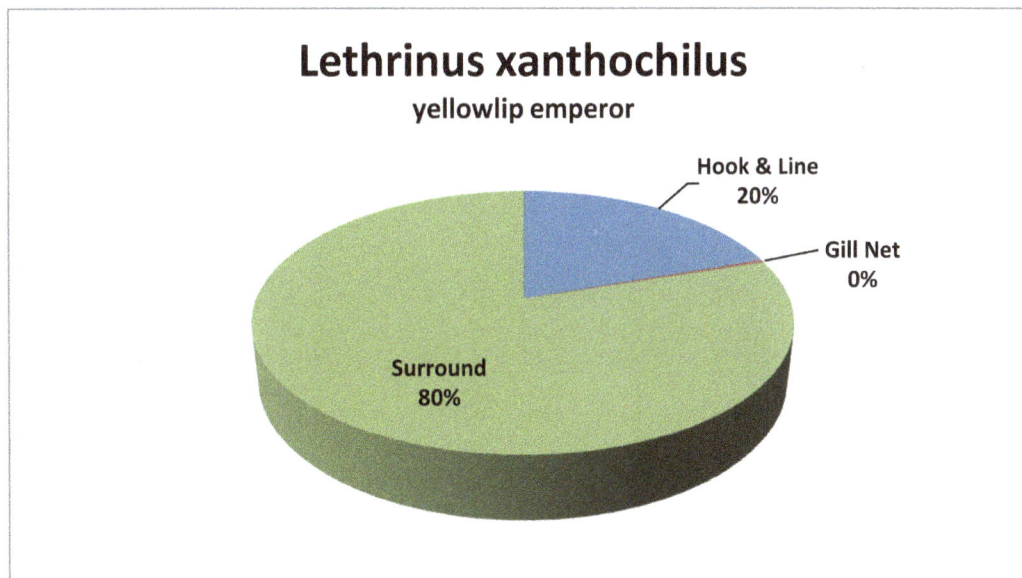

Figure 19. Catch methods for the yellowlip emperor.

Source: Guam DAWR 1986-2008.

Lethrinus xanthochilus (yellowlip emperor) is observed in small schools in the same areas as *Lethrinus obsoletus*, but also in deep channels. Juveniles are most common in seagrass beds (Sommer et al. 1996). Approximately 80% of the time, *L. xanthochilus* is caught with a surround net, and the remainder of the time it is captured using a hook and line (Figure 19). *Monotaxis grandoculus* (bigeye emperor) is the last of the emperors identified in the top-ten catch data. Large adults are most often encountered in groups of approximately fifty individuals (Myers 1991). They are active at night and frequent sand-bottomed and rubble-strewn areas around coral reefs. 65% of the time *M. grandoculus* is caught with hook and line, the remainder of the time using a gill net.

Five genera represent the snappers (lutjanid) in the top-ten catch data and the family is identified from six midden areas. *Aprion virescens* (jobfish) is usually observed in open areas of deep lagoons, in channels and the reef front. It is sometimes found in small groups (Lieske and Myers 1994). It is caught exclusively using hook and line according to 1995 through 2004 data. *Lutjanus bohar* (twinspotted snapper) is usually solitary and can be found on both the reef front and the lagoon side (Sommer et al. 1996). It is most often taken using snorkel and spear. *Lutjanus fulvus* (flametail snapper) is often located in the lagoon or on the reef front where deep holes or large boulders are found (Lieske and Myers 1994). Juveniles are sometimes observed in lower portions of river channels and mangroves (Sommer et al. 1996). About 60% of the time *L. fulvus* is caught with hook and line, and about 40% of the time captured using a gill net (Figure 20).

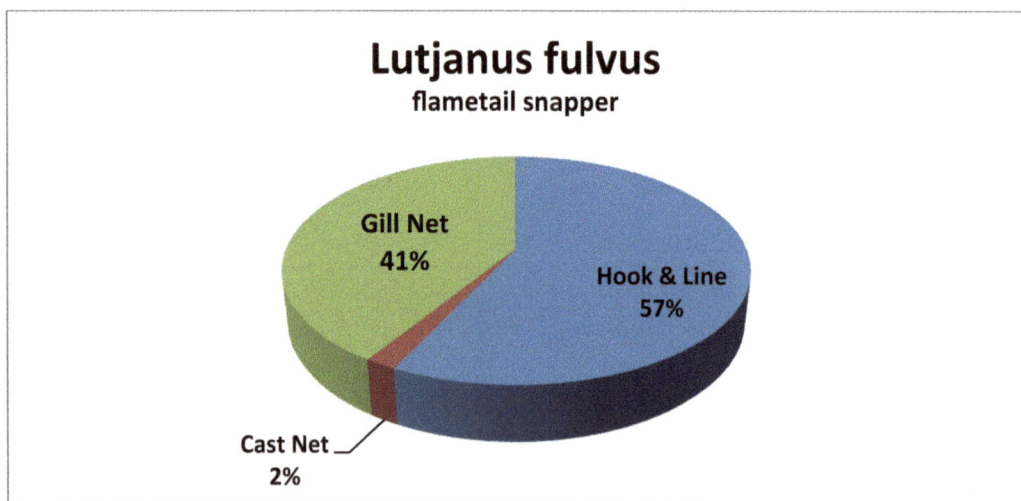

Figure 20. Catch methods for the flametail snapper.

Source: Guam DAWR 1986-2008.

Lutjanus gibbus (humpback snapper) is found in a variety of habitats depending upon its age (Myers 1991). Juveniles are observed in the more sheltered areas of the seagrass beds and in shallow sand and coral environs of the lagoon. Sub-adults cluster in large schools that slowly range or drift over the reef slopes throughout the day. They disperse over the reef at night to feed (Ibid.). According to the 1997 data, *L. gibbus* is exclusively taken by hook and line. *Lutjanus monostigmus* (onespot snapper) is found in the outer lagoon and outer reef during the day and comes into more-shallow reef flat waters at night. It frequents large coral formations, caves and shipwrecks (Sommer et al. 1996). *L. monostigmus* is primarily taken with hook and line; less than 10% of the time it is caught using a cast net, possibly at night.

Three midden assemblages contain mullids (goatfishes) and three genera are identified in the catch data. *Mulloidichthys flavolineatus* (yellowstripe goatfish) is among the more abundant members of the family in shallow, sand-bottomed flats (Myers 1991). It is found in schools in these areas as well as along the outer reef. It is captured using nets, more than 80% of the time using gill nets (Figure 21).

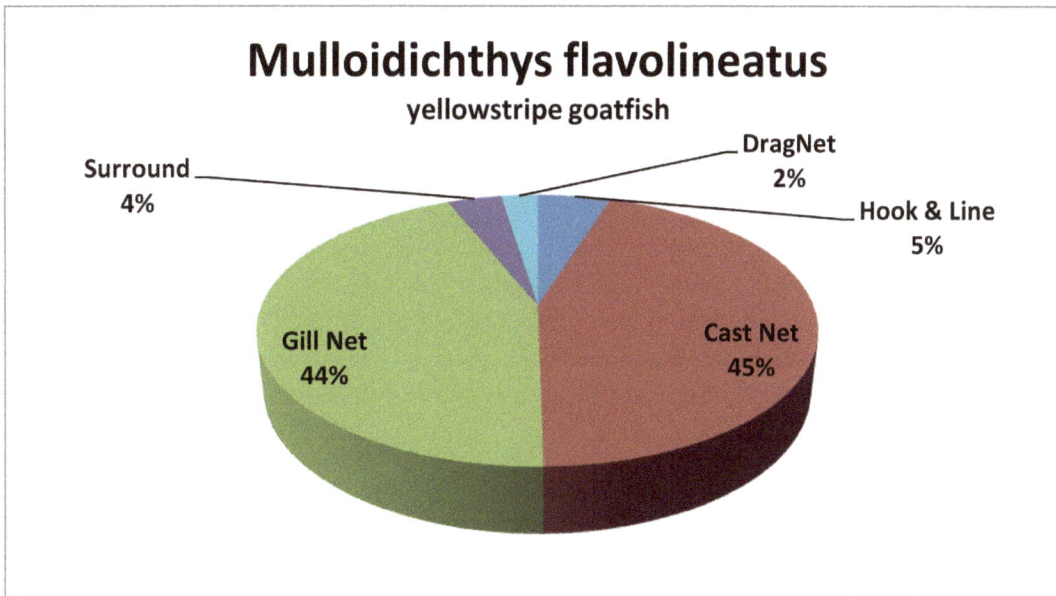

Figure 21. Catch methods for the yellowstripe goatfish.

Source: Guam DAWR 1986-2008.

Mulloidichthys ti'ao is juvenile goatfish that comes in close to shore and is usually taken using a cast net (Amesbury et al. 1986). *Parupeneus barberinus* (dash-and-dot goatfish) is "one of the most abundant species of Parupeneus over large sandy patches as well as sand and rubble areas of reef flats, and lagoon and seaward reef" found in the Marianas (Myers 1991:149). Juveniles are often observed in small, mixed-species groups in areas of seagrass (Kuiter and Tonozuka 2001b). It is captured in gill nets about two thirds of the time, surround nets 15%, and hook and line 12% of the time (Figure 22). *Parupeneus insularis* (two-saddled goatfish) is a relatively newly identified species for Guam whose habitat has not been well defined (Randall and Myers 2002). Catch data indicate that *P. insularis* has been taken using a gill net.

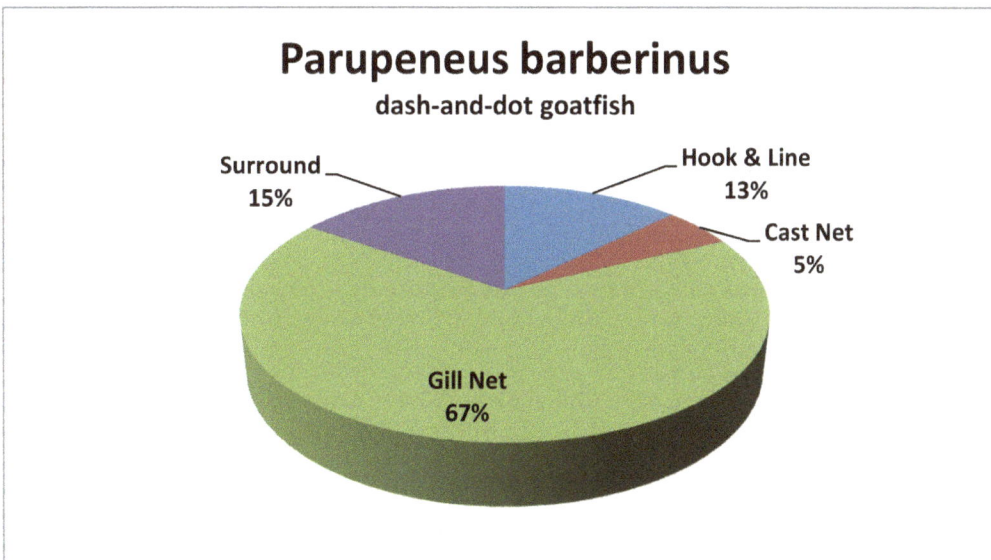

Figure 22. Catch methods for the dash-and-dot goatfish.

Source: Guam DAWR 1986-2008.

One species of muraenid (moray eels) was identified from the catch data for 2007-2008 and the family was identified from only the 1996 Tarague assemblage. *Gymnothorax javanicus* (giant moray) may be the world's largest eel. It is found in the lagoon-side waters of the reef and on the reef front (Myers 1991). Juveniles are frequently observed in fairly shallow water. Catch method data were not available, but considering that this species is usually ciguatoxic, it is perhaps taken only rarely.

Eleven genera of parrotfishes (Scaridae) were identified, making it the family most represented by individual species in the top-ten catch record. Scarids were identified from all of the middens. Parrotfishes are often easily identified in middens because of the differential preservation of their mouthparts. In many of the midden analyses from the late 1980s until the mid-1990s, their relatively easy recognition caused scarids to frequently be the only family identified. Parrotfishes feed on algae and some on live coral.

As a consequence of their food source, they are most often found in clear, outer-lagoon and reef-front areas where corals grow best. Also, as a consequence of their diet, they are frequently speared while snorkelling. The humphead parrotfish (*Bolbometopon muricatum*) is often-times found in schools (Myers 1991). It consumes live coral, and adult males are haremic and territorial (Ibid.). It was taken using scuba gear according to the 1995 catch data.

Cetoscarus bicolor (bicolor parrotfish) is found in the same habitat as *Bolbometopon muricatum*, but adults seem to prefer the upper end of steep coral slopes (Ibid.). Juveniles are frequently observed in areas dense with coral and algae (Kuiter and Tonozuka 2001b). *C. bicolor* is sometimes taken in nets. *Chlorurus frontalis* (tan-faced parrotfish) is observed in small schools on exposed reef flats and in reef front waters (Myers 1991). *C. frontalis* is most often taken using snorkel and spear. *Chlorurus microrhinos* (steephead parrotfish) is found in clear reef waters. While adults congregate, juveniles are usually solitary. No catch method data for this species are included in the records. *Chlorurus sordidus* (daisy parrotfish) range from coral-thick areas to the more open reef flats (Broad 2003). They are observed to behave differently in the different reef habitats (Kuiter and Tonozuka 2001b). *C. sordidus* is caught in gill nets or taken with snorkel and spear according to the 2007-2008 data.

Hipposcarus longiceps (Pacific longnose parrotfish) is often found in groups in turbid waters (Ibid.). Juveniles are observed around patch reefs in lagoons and above coral rubble. Adults and sub-adults frequent sandy areas where their natural colouring provides some protection (Myers 1991:194). The 2008 data show *H. longiceps* as exclusively caught in gill nets. *Leptoscarus vaigiensis* (seagrass parrotfish) lives up to its common name and is found in seagrass areas where it consumes seagrass and algae (Sommer et al. 1996). It is usually found in small groups. No catch method data from 2007-2008 were available.

Scarus altipinnis (filament-finned parrotfish) is known to remain in protected reef habitats while young and to move out into the reef front margins as an adult (Lieske and Myers 1994). The 2008 catch records show *S. altipinnis* as being taken using snorkel and spear. *Scarus psittacus* (common parrotfish) ranges from lagoon to reef flats to the reef front, and is usually found over corals (Fischer et al. 1990). It grazes algae (Bruce and Randall 1984).). *S. psittacus* is sometimes taken in a surround net, but more than 90% of the time by gill net. It cocoons at night and is frequently taken using spear and snorkel when it is thusly immobilised. *Scarus rubroviolaceus* (redlip parrotfish) is found on reef fronts and frequently in the rocky talus and coral substrates below sea cliffs, "where it may occur in large schools" (Kuiter and Tonozuka 2001b). Again, this species is most often taken with spear and snorkel. The last scarid on the list is *Scarus schlegeli* (yellowband parrotfish). The yellowband parrotfish is common to areas rich in coral with high relief (Lieske and Myers 1994). Juveniles and females are found in mixed-species groups; juveniles being more common on slopes rather than flats (Kuiter and Tonozuka 2001b). 50% of the time it is taken using a throw net and about one third of the time using a gill net.

Two midden assemblages contain Scombridae. A single scombrid (tunas and mackerels) is recorded from the top-ten catch record, *Gymnosarda unicolor*, the dogtooth tuna. *G. unicolor* is one of the few tunas that frequent the reef, although it is a pelagic species. Usually solitary, it is sometimes found in small groups along steep slopes and pinnacles (Myers 1991). Tuna are usually taken with hook and line, but according to the 2006 data, *G. unicolor* is taken by gill nets.

The last family common to both top-ten catch and the midden assemblages is Serranidae, which was identified from eight assemblages. Four genera of serranids (groupers) were identified in the top-ten record and all are members of the subfamily Epinephelinae. Serranids are generally large-bodied, voracious bottom dwellers but may be found in a range of habitats (Myers 1991:103). They will take bait and are usually caught using hook and line.

Cephalopholis urodeta (flagtail grouper) is a relatively small grouper and inhabits a variety of reef habitats including front and lagoon side. Although it utilises a greater depth range, it is usually found within the upper 20m of the water column (Lieske and Myers 1994). *C. urodeta* is usually caught on hook and line according to the 1998-1999 data. *Epinephelus merra* (honeycomb grouper) is most often found in protected areas of the reef front and in the shallows of the lagoon. Juveniles are often found in *Acropora sp.* thickets (Myers 1991). According to the catch data more than 80% are caught using hook and line (Figure 23).

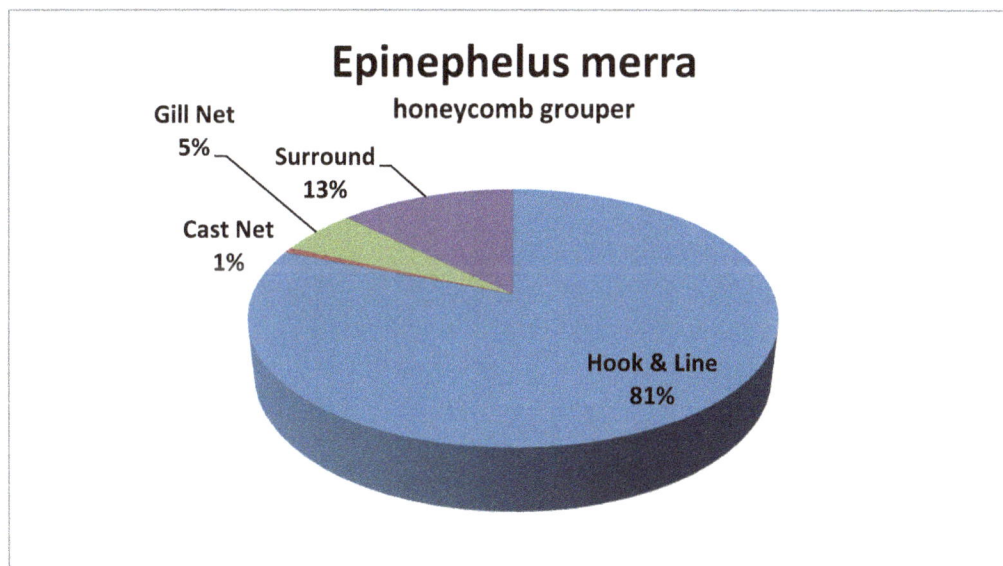

Figure 23. Catch methods for the honeycomb grouper.

Source: Guam DAWR 1986-2008.

Epinephelus polyphekadion (marbled grouper) is usually found in areas of rich coral growth in lagoons and reef fronts (Kuiter and Tonozuka 2001). It is common in un-fished areas, but is rare on Guam as a result of the island's heavy fishing pressure (Myers 1991:108). Data from 2003 suggests that it is taken with spear and snorkel. *Plectropomus laevis* (saddleback grouper) is found most often in channels and outer reef shelves (Kailola et al. 1993). Juveniles inhabit more turbid waters than adults (Myers 1991:110). *P. laevis* is also scarce in the heavily-fished waters of Guam. No catch method data were available for *P.laevis*.

Conclusions

It should be clear from the examples given that family level data obscure important information that is essential to discussions of prehistoric subsistence activities. It also frequently introduces inaccuracies into the interpretive discussion offered by researchers. This is particularly true when entire families are considered to represent either a near-shore, reef flat and/or lagoonal fishery, or an off-shore reef-front or pelagic fishery.

By revisiting two of the more detailed report discussions that were referenced in the introductory pages we can illustrate how the method described in this paper contributes to remedying the problems of interpretation. The Tarague report suggests that carangid, lutjanid, and serranid might indicate fishing offshore from watercraft. While this could be the case, it would depend upon which species are involved. Following the information given in Table 3 for the carangids, we see that the overwhelming majority is caught on hook and line. Significantly, though, *Trachinotus blochii* is caught primarily in gill nets, as is 31% of *Caranx papuensis* and 18% of *C. sexfasciatus*; 29 % of *Caranx ignobilis* are caught in various nets. Cast nets (a tool thought to have been introduced historically) are used to capture an additional 23% of *Caranx* i'e'. Among the lutjanids, ~41% of *Lutjanus fulvus* is obtained using gill nets and a small amount of *Lutjanus monostigmus* is obtained by cast net. Among the Serranids, about 20% of the *Epinephelus merra* is caught in nets. The discussion from Olmo et al. (2000:208,209) highlights additional problems. The first statement from that discussion is that trolling was responsible for the "coryphaenid" and "scombrid" remains. It is the only one that is mostly accurate. Only two species of Coryphaenidae are recorded and one, *Coryphaena hippurus* (common dolphinfish or mahimahi), is common in Guam's waters. As stated, it is almost exclusively taken by trolling. Four species of scombrids are routinely taken by fishing boats in Guam's waters: wahoo, dogtooth tuna, skipjack tuna and yellowfin tuna. Dogtooth tuna also visit the reef and are frequently taken in gill nets, and possibly in weirs. The next statement is that "acanthurids, balistids, mullids, and scarids were most likely caught in nets". There are numerous inaccuracies associated with this statement. Thirteen species of acanthurids were observed in the waters of this project area. Two prehistoric villages that are located in the project area were tested, one located at Haputo and the other at Double Reef. Five of the thirteen species were common to the waters off of each village. Four species were observed at Double Reef and not at Haputo, while four were seen at Haputo and not at Double Reef. The distribution of acanthurids is shown in Table 4.

Table 4. Distribution of acanthurids observed in NCTS waters.

Species	Double reef, outer reef front and submarine terrace	Double reef, patch reef	Haputo
Acanthurus lineatus	X	X	X
Acanthurus nigricans	X	X	X
Acanthurus nigrofuscus	X	X	X
Acanthurus olivaceous			X
Acanthurus pyroferus			X
Acanthurus xanthopterus			X
Ctenochaetus striatus	X	X	X
Naso brevirostris			X
Naso hexacanthus		X	
Naso literatus	X	X	X
Naso unicornus	X	X	
Zebrasoma flavescens	X		
Zebrasoma veliferum	X	X	

Source: All data from Stojkovich 1977.

Pie charts showing catch methods for some of the identified acanthurids are found in the earlier pages. Table 5 provides catch method data available for the species identified in Table 4. As can be seen in Table 5, four of the species of acanthurids identified from NCTS waters were likely not captured in nets, but were probably obtained using hook and line. Of the remainder for which we have catch method data, only three species are mostly taken using nets, and one is exclusively obtained using spear and snorkel. At least for the Acanthuridae known from the project area, the statement that they were most likely obtained using nets is not accurate.

Table 5. Catch method by percentages for acanthurids observed in NCTS waters.

Species	Hook & line	Cast net	Gill net	Surround net	Drag net	Spear
Acanthurus lineatus	29	8	42	21	-	-
Acanthurus nigricans	*	*	*	*	*	*
Acanthurus nigrofuscus	-	-	100	-	-	-
Acanthurus olivaceous	-	-	-	-	-	100
Acanthurus pyroferus	*	*	*	*	*	*
Acanthurus xanthopterus	92	1	7	-	-	-
Ctenochaetus striatus	17	59	24	-	-	-
Naso brevirostris	100	-	-	-	-	-
Naso hexacanthus	*	*	*	*	*	*
Naso literatus	69	5	13	13	-	-
Naso unicornus	78	8	11	3	-	-
Zebrasoma flavescens	*	*	*	*	*	*
Zebrasoma veliferum	*	*	*	*	*	*

Source: Species identifications from Stojkovich, 1977; Catch methods from Guam DAWR, 1986-2008; * no catch method data.

Eight species of Balistidae were recorded from NCTS project waters and these are shown in Table 6. Five species were recorded from Double Reef and four from Haputo. Only the halfmoon triggerfish, *Sufflamen chrysopterus*, was observed at both areas.

Table 6. Distribution of balistids recorded in NCTS waters.

Species	Double reef, outer reef front and submarine terrace	Double reef, patch reef	Haputo
Balistapus undulatus	x	x	
Melichthys niger		x	
Melichthys vidua			x
Pseudobalistes flavimarginatus		x	
Rhinecanthus aculeatus		x	
Rhinecanthus rectangulus			x
Sufflamen bursa			x
Sufflamen chrysopterus	x	x	x

Source: All data from Stojkovich 1977.

Six of the 8 species are usually caught using hook and line (Table 7). One, *Melichthys niger* (black triggerfish) is exclusively captured using a gill net, and *Balistapus undulatus* (orange-lined triggerfish) is obtained with spear and snorkel. Balistids that are found in the project area, like the acanthurids before them, are not accurately depicted as likely caught using nets.

Table 7. Catch method by percentages for balistids observed in NCTS waters.

Species	Hook & line	Cast net	Gill net	Surround net	Drag net	Spear
Balistapus undulatus	-	-	-	-	-	100
Melichthys niger	-	-	100	-	-	-
Melichthys vidua	100	-	-	-	-	-
Pseudobalistes flavimarginatus	100	-	-	-	-	-
Rhinecanthus aculeatus	72	4	24	-	-	-
Rhinecanthus rectangulus	80	18	2	-	-	-
Sufflamen bursa	100	-	-	-	-	-
Sufflamen chrysoptera	100	-	-	-	-	-

Source: Species identifications from Stojkovich 1977; Catch methods from Guam DAWR 1986-2008.

Three (four$^\Delta$) species of Mullidae were recorded for NCTS waters and these are shown in Table 8. Parupeneus barberinus (dash-and-dot goatfish) was only observed at Haputo, while P. cyclostomus (yellowsaddle goatfish) and P. multifasciatus (manybar goatfish) were recorded at both areas.

Table 8. Distribution of mullids recorded in NCTS waters.

Species	Double reef, outer reef front and submarine terrace	Double reef, patch reef	Haputo
Parupeneus barberinus			x
Parupeneus cyclostomus	x	x	x
Parupeneus multifasciatus	x	x	x
Parupeneus trifasciatus	Δ	Δ	Δ

Δ. P. trifasciatus was identified in 1977 as a separate species but is now considered P. multifasciatus.

Source: This table is adapted from WPRFMC (2011) Stojkovich (1977).

While only *Parupeneus barberinus* is most often taken using nets, about half of the time the remaining species are caught using hook and line (Table 9). Including mullids in the list of those families most likely caught using nets is less erroneous than doing so for acanthurids and balistids, but describing them in this way clearly hides significant fishing method diversity.

Table 9. Catch method by percentages for mullids observed in NCTS waters.

Species	Hook & line	Cast net	Gill net	Surround net	Drag net	Spear
Parupeneus barberinus	13	5	67	15	-	-
Parupeneus cyclostomus	56	-	44	-	-	-
Parupeneus multifasciatus	48	30	22	-	-	-

Source: Species identifications from Stojkovich 1977; Catch methods from Guam DAWR 1986-2008; Δ same species as *multifasciatus*.

The last family listed as likely caught using nets is Carangidae. Nine species of carangids were listed in Table 3 and discussed earlier. All, except for *Trachinotus blochii,* which is mostly caught in a gill net, are usually, if not exclusively caught on hook and line. Unfortunately, no carangids were observed in the waters off of NCTS at the time of the marine survey, so it is not possible to more closely match fishing methods with the midden remains for this family.

The remaining fish families referred to in the NCTS report, the labrids, lethrinids, lutjanids and serranids were stated as having been caught with pelagic lures. Again, assigning these families to this catch method is problematic once the habits of individual species are taken into account. While it is true that the serranids and three of the four lutjanid species are mostly caught using hooks, the majority of the labrids and between half and a third of the lethrinids are captured in nets.

More species (23) of Labridae were observed in the waters off of NCTS than were species of any other family. Eight of the 23 species were seen at Double Reef and not Haputo, while 2 species were observed at Haputo and not at Double Reef. The species distributions are shown in Table 10.

Table 10. Distribution of labrids observed in NCTS waters.

Species	Double reef, outer reef front and submarine terrace	Double reef, patch reef	Haputo
Anampses caeruleopunctatus	1	1	
Anampses twisti	1		
Bodianus axillaris			1
Cheilinus trilobatus	1	1	1
Coris aygula	1		1
Coris gaimard	1		1
Epibulus insidiator	1	1	1
Gomphosus varius	1	1	1
Halichoeres hortulanus	1	1	1
Halichoeres margaritaceus	1	1	1
Halichoeres marginatus	1	1	
Halichoeres trimaculatus			1
Hemigymnus fasciatus	1		
Hemigymnus melapterus	1	1	
Labroides bicolor		1	1
Labroides dimidiatus	1	1	1
Macropharyngodon meleagris	1	1	1
Novaculichthys taeniourus	1	1	
Oxycheilinus unifasciatus		1	1
Stethojulis bandanensis	1	1	
Thalassoma hardwicke	1	1	
Thalassoma lutescens	1		1
Thalassoma quinquevittatum	1	1	1

Source: Species identifications from Stojkovich 1977.

Labrids and their catch methods are shown in Table 11. Catch data were available for 18 of the 23 species, and of these only seven could be considered to be preferentially caught using pelagic lures. Ten of the species are most often captured using some combination of gill, cast or surround nets. *Thalassoma trilobatum* is caught in equal amounts by net or hook and line.

Table 11. Catch methods by percentages for labrids recorded from NCTS waters.

Species	Hook & line	Cast net	Gill net	Surround net	Drag net
Anampses caeruleopunctatus	-	25	75	-	-
Anampses twisti	*	*	*	*	*
Bodianus axillaris	*	*	*	*	*
Cheilinus trilobatus	74	8	7	11	-
Coris aygula	-	-	100	-	-
Coris gaimard	86	-	14	-	-
Epibulus insidiator	73	-	27	-	-
Gomphosus varius	65	-	35	-	-
Halichoeres hortulanus	-	-	100	-	-
Halichoeres margaritaceus	-	100	-	-	-
Halichoeres marginatus	*	*	*	*	*
Halichoeres trimaculatus	92	3	5	-	-
Hemigymnus fasciatus	-	-	100	-	-
Hemigymnus melapterus	10	23	67	-	-
Labroides bicolor	*	*	*	*	*
Labroides dimidiatus	*	*	*	*	*
Macropharyngodon meleagris	-	-	100	-	-
Novaculichthys taeniourus	11	6	22	61	-
Oxycheilinus unifasciatus	2	-	35	63	-
Stethojulis bandanensis	-	-	100	-	-
Thalassoma hardwicke	93	-	7	-	-
Thalassoma lutescens	*	*	*	*	*
Thalassoma quinquevittatum	87	-	13	-	-
Thalassoma trilobatum	49	31	20	-	-

Source: Species identifications from Stojkovich 1977; Catch methods from Guam DAWR 1986-2008; * no catch method data.

Two species of Lethrinidae were recorded from the waters off of NCTS (Stojkovich 1977). Both are reef dwellers and are found in less than 30 m of water (Lieske and Myers 1994). *Gnathodentex aureolineatus* (striped large-eye bream) is a night feeder, and the diurnal *Monotaxis grandoculus* (humpnose bigeye bream) is sometimes found in large aggregations (Ibid.). Just over half of the time (55%) *Gnathodentex aureolineatus* is caught with hook and line, see Figure 24. Approximately two-thirds of the time (65%) *Monotaxis grandoculus* is caught with hook and line, and the remainder is captured by using a gill net (DAWR records 1986-2008).

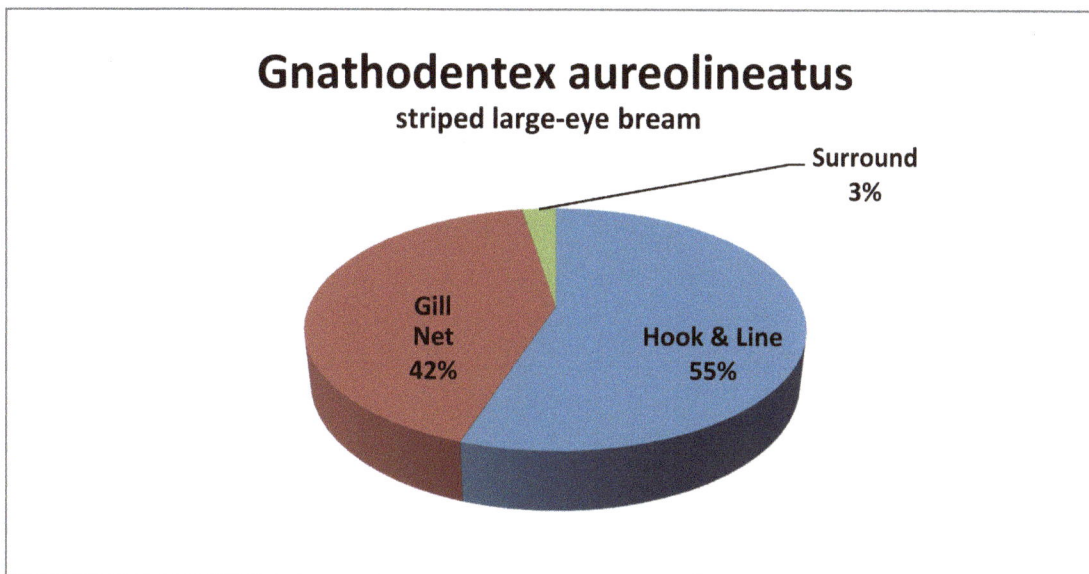

Figure 24. Chart showing catch methods for *Gnathodentex aureolineatus.*

Source: Guam DAWR 1986-2008.

Four species of Lutjanidae (snappers) were identified in the waters of NCTS (Stojkovich 1977). *Aphareus furca* (small toothed jobfish), *Aprion virescens* (green jobfish), and *Lutjanus gibbus* (humpback red snapper) are all most often caught with hook and line (DAWR records 1986-2008). The blacktail snapper, *Lutjanus fulvus,* is taken by both net and hook and line, see Figure 25.

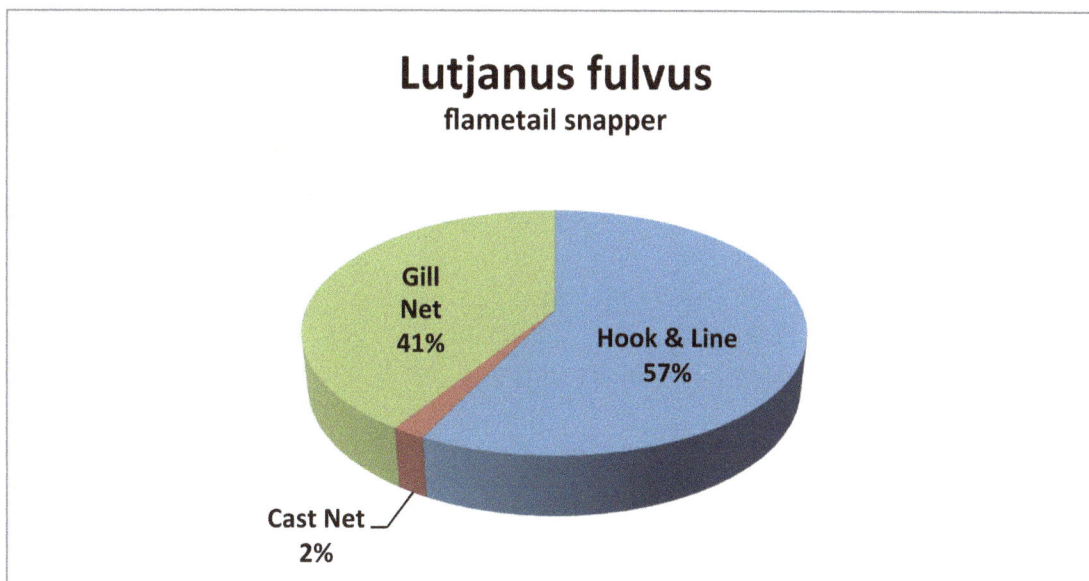

Figure 25. Chart showing catch methods for *Lutjanus fulvus.*

Source: Guam DAWR 1986-2008.

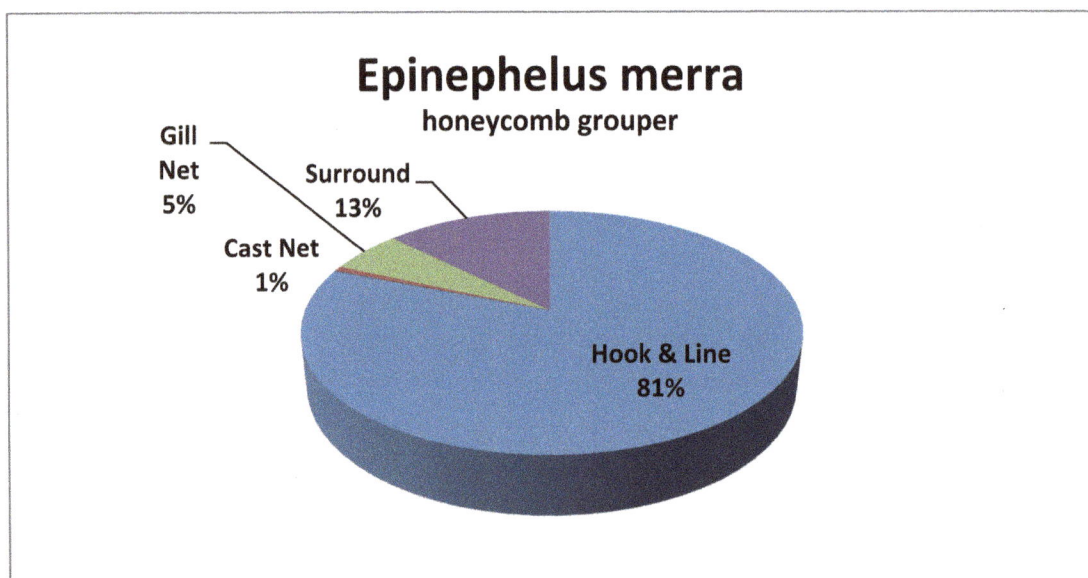

Figure 26. Chart showing catch methods for *Epinephelus mera*.

Source: Guam DAWR 1986-2008.

Lastly, three species of Serranidae were recorded from NCTS waters (Stojkovich 1977). *Cephalopholis urodeta* (darkfin hind) and *Grammistes sexlineatus* (sixline soapfish) are both principally caught on hook and line. These two species were observed at Haputo and not Double Reef. *Epinephelus merra* (honeycomb grouper) was introduced earlier in this paper, and exhibits the greatest variability of catch methods of the serranids from NCTS. About 20% of the time it is captured using nets, otherwise it follows the other serranids in being mostly caught using hook and line. It was only seen at Double Reef.

In addition, two important indigenous fishing methods, trapping (using woven tools or tidal impounds) and stunning (using fish poisons), are not currently in use on Guam, and their species associations and the way these methods might have influenced midden composition remains unknown.

As a consequence of this work, it is strongly recommended that discussions of midden fish remains abandon the general and often misleading interpretations that accompany the use of family data. Instead, family data should be used as a first step that is then fleshed-out with probable representative species from site-local fishery or fish census data. Once that is done, prehistoric fishing strategies can be more accurately assessed, and the associated prehistoric behaviours more meaningfully described.

Acknowledgments

This paper would not have been possible without help from the Guam Department of Agriculture's Division of Aquatic & Wildlife Resources. I would particularly like to thank Thomas Flores of that office for his generous help in first finding, and then providing me with the data used in my analyses. Mitch Warner, also from that office, kindly provided images of fish species common to Guam's waters. I also wish to thank Judith Amesbury for providing me with copies of her reports and for offering the use of her fisheries files.

References

Acheson, J.M. 1981. Anthropology of fishing. *Annual Review of Anthropology* 10:275-316.

Allen, G.R., S.H. Midgley and M. Allen. 2002. *Field guide to the freshwater fishes of Australia*. Perth: Western Australian Museum.

Amesbury, J.R. and R.L. Hunter-Anderson. 2003. *Review of Archaeological and Historical Data Concerning Reef Fishing in the U.S. Flag Islands of Micronesia: Guam and the Northern Mariana Islands*. Honolulu: Western Pacific Regional Fishery Management Council.

Amesbury, S.S., F.A. Cushing and R.K. Sakamoto. 1986. *Fishing on Guam Guide to the Coastal Resources of Guam Vol. 3*. Mangilao: University of Guam Marine Laboratory, Contribution Number 25.

Bagnis, R., P. Mazellier, J. Bennett and E. Christian. 1984. *Poissons de Polynésie, 5th Edition*. France: Société Nouvelle des Editions du Pacifique, Elysées.

Broad, G. 2003. *Fishes of the Philippines*. Pasi City: Anvil Publishing, Inc.

Bruce, R.W. and J.E. Randall. 1984. Scaridae. In W. Fischer and G. Bianchi (eds), *FAO species identification sheets for fishery purposes (Western Indian Ocean Fishing Area 51), Volume 3*. FAO: Rome.

Carucci, J. 1993. *The Archaeology of Orote Peninsula: Phase I and II Archaeological Inventory Survey of Areas Proposed for Projects to Accommodate Relocation of Navy Activities from Philippines to Guam, Mariana Islands*. Honolulu: International Archaeological Research Institute, Inc.

Cervigón, F., R. Cipriani, W. Fischer, L. Garibaldi, M. Hendrickx, A.J. Lemus, R. Márquez, J.M. Poutiers, G. Robaina and B. Rodriguez. 1992. *Fichas FAO de identificación de especies para los fines de la pesca. Guía de campo de las especies comerciales marinas y de aquas salobres de la costa septentrional de Sur América*. Rome: FAO, preparado con el financiamento de la Comisión de Comunidades Europeas y de NORAD.

Collette, B.B. 2003. Family Belonidae Bonaparte 1832 – needlefishes. *California Academy of Sciences Annotated Checklists of Fishes* 16:22.

Division of Aquatics and Wildlife Resources (DAWR) Guam Department of Agriculture 1986-2008. *Shore-based CREEL Survey Species Composition Data*. Mangilao: Division of Aquatics and Wildlife Resources (DAWR) Guam Department of Agriculture.

Fischer, W., I. Sousa, C. Silva, A. de Freitas, J.M. Poutiers, W. Schneider, T.C. Borges, J.P. Feral and A. Massinga. 1990. *Fichas FAO de identificaçao de espécies para actividades de pesca. Guia de campo das espécies comerciais marinhas e de águas salobras de Moçambique*. Roma: FAO, Publicaçao preparada em collaboraçao com o Instituto de Investigaçao Pesquiera de Moçambique, com financiamento do Projecto PNUD/FAO MOZ/86/030 e de NORAD.

Gell, F.R. and M.W. Whittington. 2002. Diversity of fishes in seagrass beds in the Quirimba Archipelago, northern Mozambique. *Marine and Freshwater Research* 53:115-121.

Kailola, P.J., M.J. Williams, P.C. Stewart, R.E. Reichelt, A. McNee and C. Grieve. 1993. *Australian fisheries resources*. Canberra: Bureau of Resource Sciences.

Kuiter, R.H. and T. Tonozuka. 2001a. Pictorial guide to Indonesian reef fishes. Part 1 (Eels – Snappers, Muraenidae – Lutjanidae). *Zoonetics* 2001:1-303.

Kuiter, R.H. and T. Tonozuka. 2001b. Pictorial guide to Indonesian reef fishes. Part 3. (Jawfishes – Sunfishes, Opistognathidae – Molidae) *Zoonetics* 2001:623-893.

Kuiter, R.H. and T. Tonozuka. 2001c. Pictorial guide to Indonesian reef fishes. Part 2. (Fusiliers – Dragonets, Caesionidae – Callionymidae) *Zoonetics* 2001:304-622.

Lessa, W.A. 1966. *Ulithi: A Micronesian design for living*. Prospect Heights: Waveland Press, Inc.

Lieske, E. and R. Myers. 1994. *Collins Pocket Guide, Coral reef fishes, Indo-Pacific and Caribbean including the Red Sea*. London: Harper Collins Publishers.

Liston, J. 1996. *The Legacy of Tarague Embayment and Its Inhabitants, Andersen AFB, Guam, Volume I: Archaeology*. Honolulu: International Archaeological Reasearch Institute, Inc., Prepared for 36 CES/ CEV, Unit 14007, Environmental Flight, Andersen Air Force Base, Guam.

Marquet, G. 1993. Etude biogeographique de la faune d'eau douce de Polynesie Francaise. *Biogeographica* 69(4):157-170.

Masuda, H., K. Amaoka, C. Araga, T. Uyeno, and T. Yoshino. 1984. *The fishes of the Japanese Archipelago. Vol. 1*. Tokyo: Tokai University Press.

Mundy, B.C. 2005. Checklist of the fishes of the Hawaiian Archipelago. *Bishop Museum Bulletins in Zoology* 6:1-704.

Myers, R.F. 1991. *Micronesian Reef Fishes, a Practical Guide to the Coral Reef Fishes of Tropical Central and Western Pacific, 2nd ed.* Barrigada: Coral Graphics.

Myers, R.F. 1999. *Micronesian reef fishes: a comprehensive guide to the coral reef fishes of Micronesia, 3rd revised and expanded edition*. Barrigada: Coral Graphics.

Myers, R.F. and T.J. Donaldson 2003. The fishes of the Mariana Islands in the marine biodiversity of Guam and the Marians. *Micronesica* 5. 35-36:594-648.

Nelson, J.S. 1994. *Fishes of the world, Third edition*. New York: John Wiley & Sons, Inc.

Olmo, R.K. 1996. Theoretical Perspectives: The Human Ecology of the Tarague Embayment. In M.J. Tomonari-Tuggle and R.K. Olmo, *Volume IV: Theoretical Perspectives & the Stewardship of Cultural Resources*, pp. 1-70. Honolulu: International Archaeological Research Institute, Inc.

Olmo, R.K., T. Mangieri, D.J. Welch, and T.S. Dye. 2000. *Phase II Archaeological Survey and Detailed Recording At Commander, U.S. Naval Forces Marianas (COMNAVMARIANAS) Communications Annex (Formerly Naval Computer and Telecommunications Area Master Station, Western Pacific [NCTAMS WESTPAC]), Territory of Guam, Mariana Islands*. Honolulu: International Archaeological Research Institute, Inc.

Parenti, P. and J.E. Randall. 2000. An annotated checklist of the species of the labroid fish families Labridae and Scaridae. *Ichthyological Bulletin (J.L.B. Smith Institute of Ichthyology)* 68:1-97.

Randall, J.E. 1956. A revision of the surgeonfish genus *Acanthurus. Pacific Science* 10(2):159-235.

Randall, J.E. 1986. Acanthuridae. In M.M. Smith and P.C. Heemstra (eds), *Smiths' sea fishes*, pp. 811-823. Berlin: Springer-Verlag.

Randall, J.E. 2001. Surgeonfishes of Hawai'i and the world. Honolulu: Mutual Publishing and Bishop Museum Press.

Randall, J.E. 2004. Revision of the goatfish genus *Parupeneus* (Perciformes: Mullidae), with descriptions of two new species. *Indo-Pacific Fishes* 36:64.

Randall, J.E. and R.F. Myers. 2002. *Parupeneus insularis*, a new central Pacific species of goatfish (Perciformes: Mullidae) of the *P. trifasciatus* complex. *Zoological Studies* 41(4):431-440.

Smith-Vaniz, W.F. 1995. Carangidae, Jureles, pámpanos, cojinúas, zapateros, cocineros, casabes, macarelas, chicharros, jorobados, medregales, pez pilota. In W. Fischer, F. Krupp, W. Schneider, C. Sommer, K.E. Carpenter and V. Niem (eds), *Guia FAO para Identificación de Especies para lo Fines de la Pesca. Pacifico Centro-Oriental*, pp. 940-986. Rome: FAO.

Sommer, C., W. Schneider, and J.M. Poutiers. 1996. *FAO species identification field guide for fishery purposes: the living marine resources of Somalia.* Rome: FAO.

Stojkovich, J.O. 1977. *Survey and Species Inventory of Representative Pristine Marine Communities on Guam. Sea Grant Publication UGSG-77-12*, Mangilao: University of Guam. *University of Guam Marine Laboratory, Technical Report No. 40.*

2

Pelagic Fishing in the Mariana Archipelago: From the Prehistoric Period to the Present

Judith R. Amesbury, Micronesian Archaeological Research Services, Guam

Introduction

The Mariana Islands lie between 13° and 21° north latitude at about 145° east longitude (Figure 1). The geological division of the Mariana Archipelago is not the same as the political division. Politically there are two entities: Guam, which is an unincorporated territory of the United States, and the Commonwealth of the Northern Mariana Islands (CNMI), which comprises the fourteen islands north of Guam. Geologically there are two island arcs. The southern arc includes the six islands from Guam to Farallon de Medinilla, while the northern arc includes the nine islands from Anatahan to Uracas.

The southern arc islands, which began to form about 43 million years ago (Randall 1995), are older and larger than the islands of the northern arc. They are raised limestone islands with volcanic cores and well developed reef flats and coral reefs. The southern arc islands are much more densely inhabited (more than 224,000 people in the 2000 census), and according to one survey they have nearly twice as many species of fishes as the northern arc islands (Donaldson et al. 1994).

The northern arc islands are younger, smaller, high volcanic islands with steep slopes and limited coral development. They are still volcanically active. Pagan erupted in 1981, and Anatahan began to erupt in 2003 (Figure 2). The northern arc islands are sparsely inhabited (6 people in the 2000 census) and have fewer species of fishes than the southern arc islands (Donaldson et al. 1994).

Prehistoric Period

People have lived in the Mariana Islands for at least 3,500 years or about 3,000 years before European contact. The Prehistoric Period lasted from the arrival of the first people by at least 1500 BC until the arrival of Magellan in AD 1521. Spoehr (1957) divided the long Prehistoric Period into the Pre-Latte Phase and Latte Phase (Figure 3). Subsequent authors (Craib 1990; Moore 1983; Moore and Hunter-Anderson 1999) have proposed various subdivisions of the Pre-Latte Phase.

Pre-Latte Phase cultural deposits are found below the surface usually along the coasts. Artefacts that characterise the Pre-Latte Phase include pottery sherds with red-slipped exterior surfaces, some of which are decorated with lime-filled designs, stone and shell tools, and beads and bracelets made from cone shells.

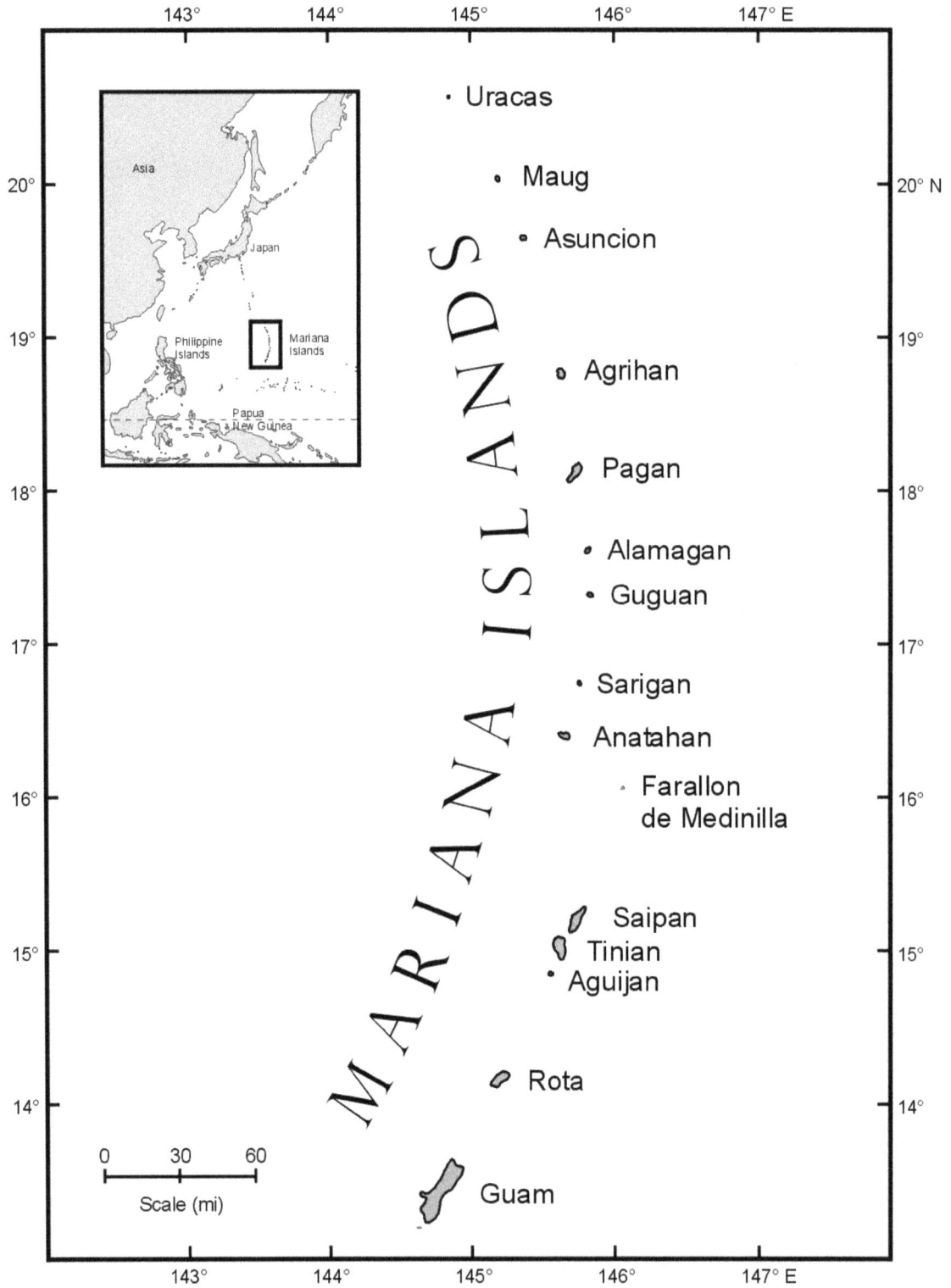

Figure 1. Mariana Islands.

Source: Map courtesy of Barry Smith.

Figure 2. Anatahan erupting on May 11, 2003.

Source: Photo by Allan Sauter.

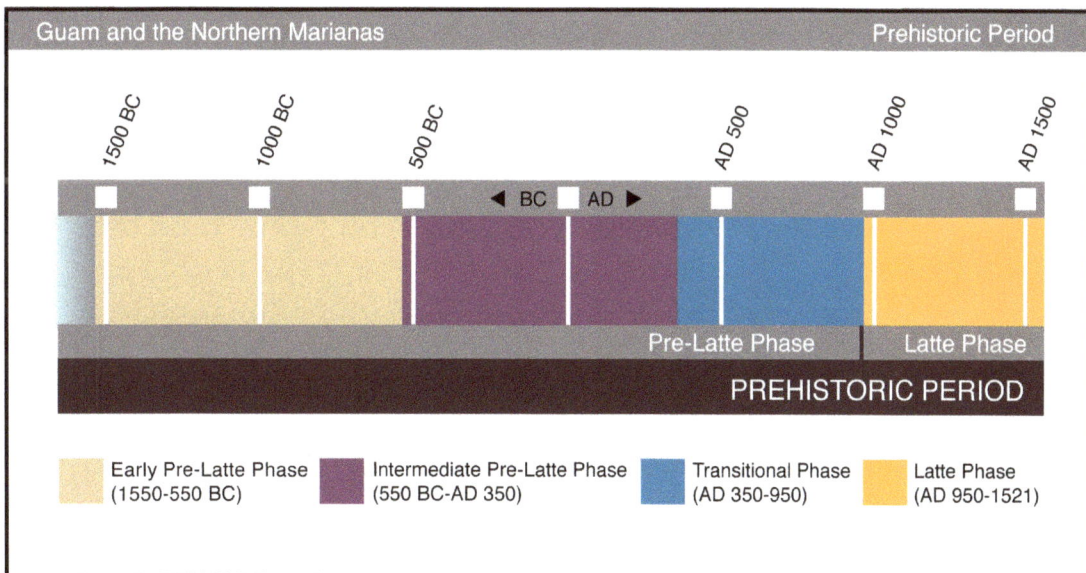

Figure 3. Timeline of the Prehistoric Period in Guam and the CNMI showing Spoehr's (1957) broad phases of Marianas prehistory as subdivided by Moore and Hunter-Anderson (1999).

Source: Figure by Robert Amesbury.

The Latte Phase began by at least AD 1000 and is characterised by the megalithic features called latte sets. A latte set consists of two parallel rows of upright stone shafts (*haligi* in Chamorro) associated with capstones (*tasa*) (Figure 4). The number of shafts in a set varies, but sets with eight, ten, or twelve shafts are common (Graves 1986; Hunter-Anderson and Moore 2002).

Based on the cultural materials and features associated with latte sets, archaeologists believe they functioned as foundations for residential structures. Latte Phase sites are widely distributed along the coastline as well as in the interior of the Mariana Islands. They are found not only on the major islands of the southern arc, but on the smaller islands of the northern arc as well. Characteristic artefacts of the Latte Phase include plain pottery sherds, stone mortars, stone and shell tools, and beads made from *Spondylus* shells.

During the Prehistoric Period the inhabitants of the Mariana Archipelago, who are now known as the Chamorro, were in contact with one another. There is evidence that all the islands shared the same culture and language (Reinman 1977; Spoehr 1957; Thompson 1932). Archaeological assemblages from the various islands are similar. It is possible that the Chamorro were also in contact with their closest Micronesian neighbors, the Refaluwasch people of the Caroline Islands to the south. The ocean-going sailing canoes of both groups would have made that possible.

When the first people arrived in the Marianas between 3,500 and 4,000 years ago, there were no large land mammals to hunt, but the ancient Chamorro had an almost unlimited supply of animal protein from the sea. They fished for both reef and pelagic (open-ocean) species and collected mollusks and other invertebrates, including crustaceans and echinoderms. They also caught sea turtles. Figure 5 shows archaeological sites on Guam with pelagic fish and turtle remains.

Figure 4. The "wall" latte at Mochong, Rota, with upright shafts and fallen capstones along one side and five limestone blocks along the other side.

Source: Photo by Judith Amesbury.

Faunal analysts, such as Foss Leach and Janet Davidson of the Museum of New Zealand Te Papa Tongarewa, calculate the minimum number of individuals (MNI) in archaeological fish bone collections by identifying the unique or paired bones from fishes. They attempt to determine if there were changes through time in the fishes caught. Table 1 is an example of the results of fishbone analysis. From Mangilao Golf Course Site 25, Leach and Davidson (2006a) identified 364 bones. At least 20 families or other groups are present. The minimum number of individuals is 267. Of that number, 237 individuals were assigned to time periods based on the stratigraphy of the site and 41 radiocarbon dates. Most of the fishes date to the Intermediate and Transitional Pre-Latte Phase and the Latte Phase. No changes in the catch through time could be confirmed.

The most abundant family in the catch from all time periods at Mangilao Golf Course is the Scaridae (parrotfishes). The large humphead parrotfish, *Bolbometopon muricatum*, is present throughout the Prehistoric Period. The pelagic families Coryphaenidae (mahimahi or dolphinfishes), Istiophoridae/Xiphiidae (marlins, sailfishes, and swordfishes), and Scombridae (tunas and wahoo) are also found in both Pre-Latte and Latte Phases.

The faunal analysts also suggest what methods were used for catching the fishes based on the technology of the time period, the habits and habitats of the fishes, and ethnographic comparison. Table 2 shows the likely catch methods of fishes from Mochong, Rota, a site occupied from approximately 1000 BC to AD 1700 (Craib 1990). Figure 6 shows archaeological sites on Rota with pelagic fish and turtle remains.

Table 1. Families of fishes (MNI and % MNI) from Mangilao Golf Course Site 25 by time periods.

FAMILY OR OTHER GROUP	EARLY PRE-LATTE PHASE		INTERMEDIATE & TRANSITIONAL PRE-LATTE PHASES		LATTE PHASE		HISTORIC PERIOD	
	MNI	% MNI	MNI	% MNI	MNI	% MNI	MNI	% MNI
Scaridae (Parrotfishes)	6	60.0	33	27.3	43	43.4	2	28.6
Coryphaenidae (Mahimahi)			21	17.4	18	18.2		
Lethrinidae (Emperors)			14	11.6	4	4.0	1	14.3
Coridae/Labridae (Wrasses)			11	9.1	5	5.1		
Istiophoridae/Xiphiidae (Billfishes)			3	2.5	9	9.1	1	14.3
Epinephelidae (Groupers)	1	10.0	8	6.6	2	2.0		
Elasmobranchii (Sharks and rays)	1	10.0	6	5.0	2	2.0	1	14.3
Balistidae (Triggerfishes)	1	10.0	4	3.3	2	2.0		
Diodontidae (Porcupinefishes)					6	6.1	1	14.3
Acanthuridae (Surgeonfishes)			2	1.7	2	2.0	1	14.3
Lutjanidae (Snappers)			3	2.5	2	2.0		
Scombridae, Tribe Scomberomorini (Wahoo)			3	2.5	1	1.0		
Nemipteridae (Monocle breams)			3	2.5	1	1.0		
Teleostomi (includes bony fishes)			4	3.3				
Coridae (Wrasses)	1	10.0	1	0.8				
Scombridae, Tribe Thunnini (Tunas)			2	1.7				
Echeneidae (Remoras)			2	1.7				
Carangidae (Jacks)					1	1.0		
Holocentridae (Squirrelfishes)			1	0.8				
Kyphosidae (Sea chubs or rudderfishes)					1	1.0		
Total	10	100.0	121	100.0	99	100.0	7	100.0

Source: This table is adapted from Leach and Davidson (2006a). For confidence limits of percentages, see Leach and Davidson. Classification of tunas has been updated using Nelson (2006).

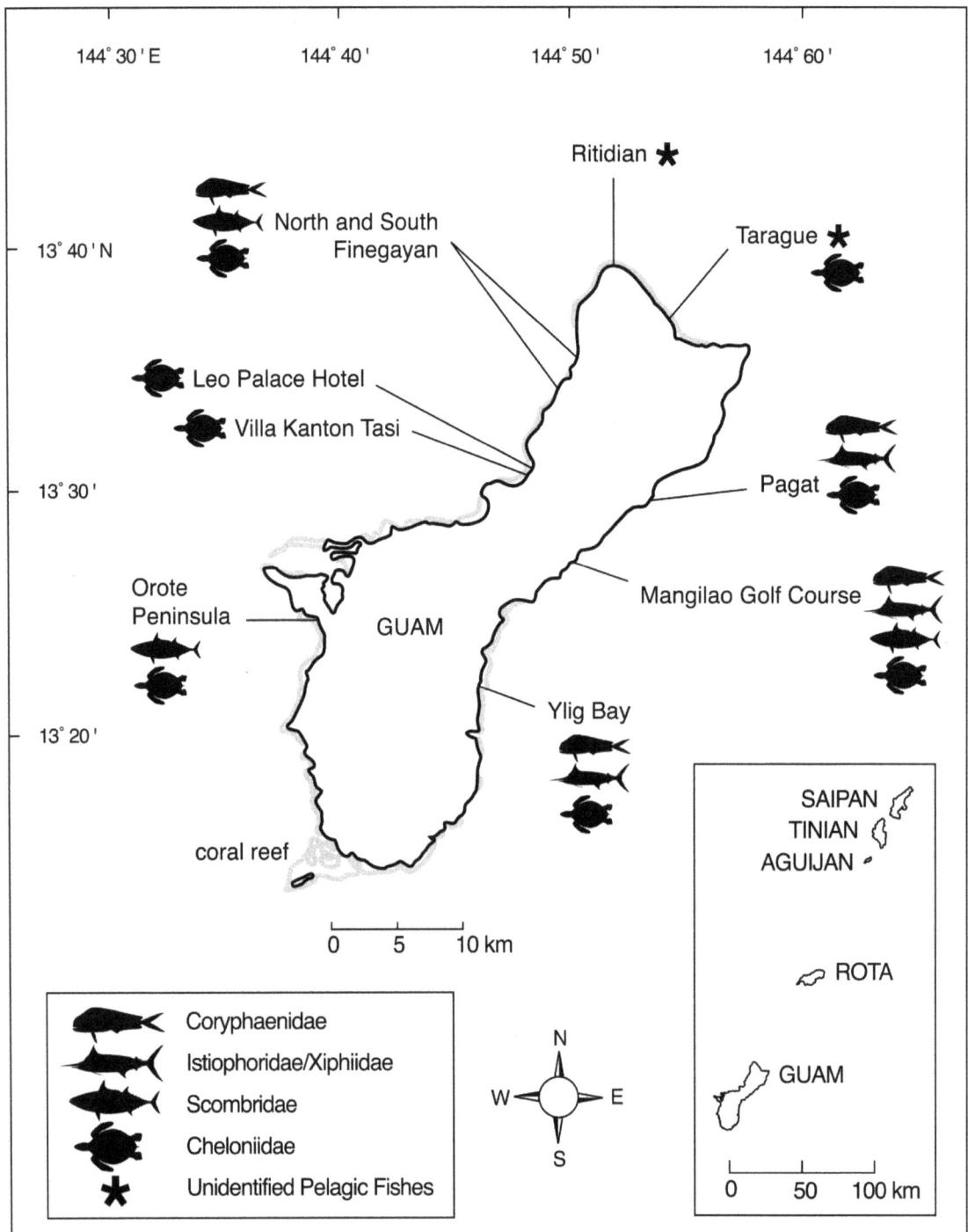

Figure 5. Guam, showing archaeological sites with pelagic fish and turtle remains.

Source: Figure by Robert Amesbury.

Table 2. Likely catch methods of fishes from Mochong, Rota by families (MNI and % MNI).

LIKELY CATCH METHOD	FAMILY OR OTHER GROUP	COMMON NAME	MNI	% MNI
Netting			105	33.5
	Bothidae	Left-eyed flounders		
	Scaridae	Parrotfishes		
	Acanthuridae	Surgeonfishes		
	Balistidae	Triggerfishes		
	Aluteridae	Filefishes		
Demersal Baited Hook			109	34.8
	Epinephelidae	Groupers		
	Lutjanidae	Snappers		
	Nemipteridae	Monocle breams		
	Lethrinidae	Emperors		
	Coridae	Wrasses		
	Coridae/Labridae	Wrasses		
Pelagic Lures			51	16.3
	Scombridae, Tribe Scomberomorini	Wahoo		
	Coryphaenidae	Mahimahi		
	Carangidae	Jacks		
	Scombridae, Tribe Thunnini	Tunas including yellowfin and skipjack		
Harpoons or Bait Trolling			10	3.2
	Istiophoridae	Marlins, sailfishes		
	Istiophoridae/Xiphiidae	Marlins, sailfishes/		
		Swordfishes		
General Foraging			23	7.3
	Holocentridae	Squirrelfishes		
	Aphareidae	Snappers		
	Kyphosidae	Sea chubs or rudderfishes		
	Scorpaenidae	Scorpionfishes		
	Diodontidae	Porcupinefishes		
	Tetraodontidae	Puffers		
Basket Traps			8	2.6
	Muraenidae	Moray eels		
Opportunistic Catch			3	1.0
	Elasmobranchii	Sharks and rays		
Unknown			4	1.3
	Platacidae	Batfishes		
	Teleostomi	Includes bony fishes		
TOTAL			313	100.0

Source: This table is adapted from Leach et al. (1988, 1990). Classification of tunas has been updated using Nelson (2006). This table is designed to reproduce information from its sources and is not a commentary on points raised in Olmo (this volume).

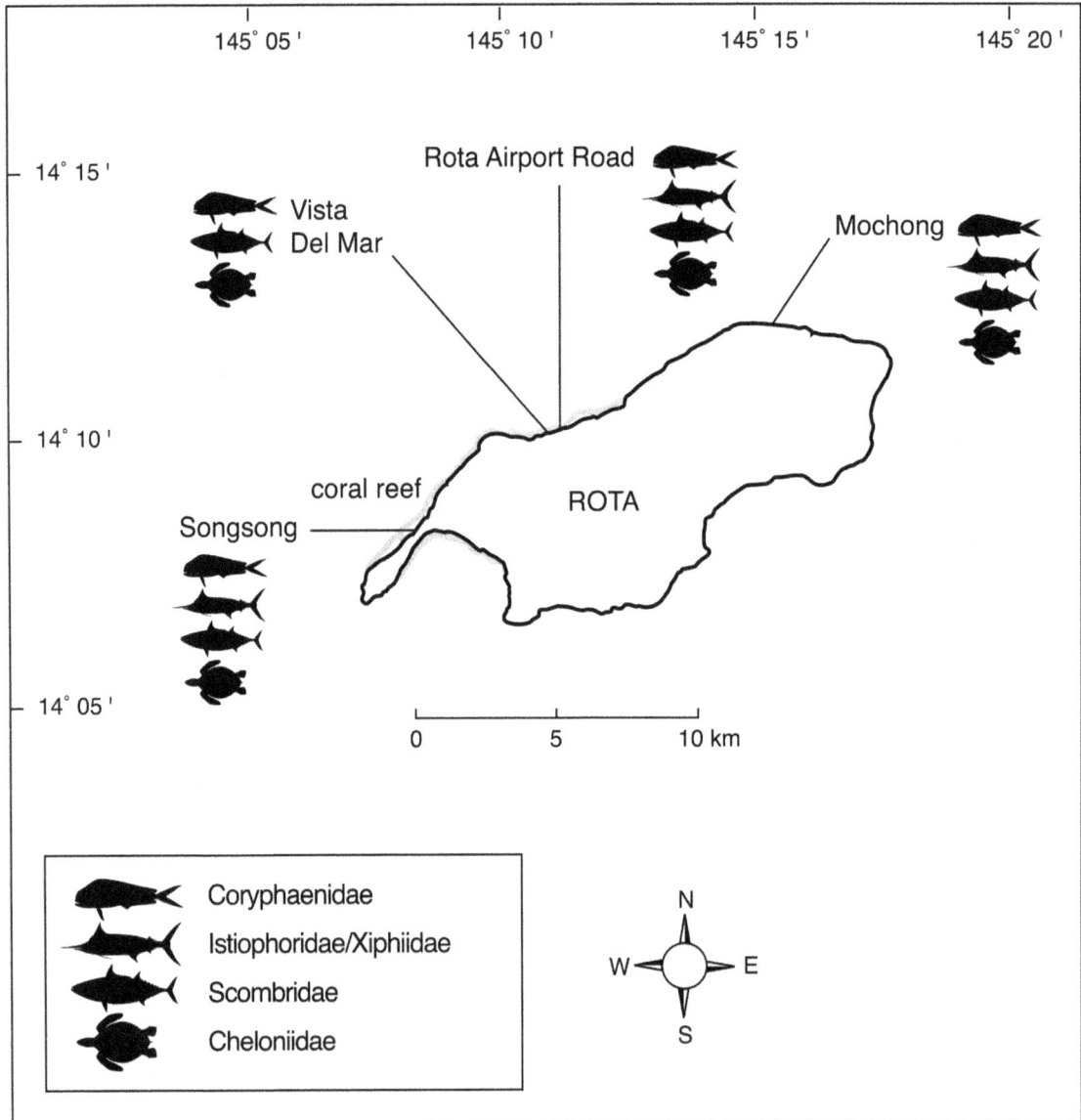

Figure 6. Rota, showing archaeological sites with pelagic fish and turtle remains.

Source: Figure by Robert Amesbury.

Ten sites in the Mariana Archipelago have MNI analysis and pelagic fish remains (Amesbury and Hunter-Anderson 2008). Percentages by MNI of pelagic fishes belonging to the families Coryphaenidae, Istiophoridae/Xiphiidae, and Scombridae are shown in Table 3. The average for the ten sites is nearly sixteen percent pelagics. Since these fishes weigh more than reef fishes, considerably more than sixteen percent of the weight of fish eaten came from pelagic species.

Mahimahi was identified at eight of the ten sites shown in Table 3. Marlin was also identified at eight of the ten sites. This is unusual for Pacific islands. The database of fish remains from archaeological sites at the Museum of New Zealand Te Papa Tongarewa contains information on more than 75 tropical Pacific island sites and more than 125 sites in New Zealand, but none of the sites outside the Marianas have mahimahi remains and only one site outside the Marianas has marlin remains (Leach and Davidson 2006b). Marlin accounted for less than one percent of the MNI at Motupore, Port Moresby, Papua New Guinea.

Table 3. Percent of pelagic fishes in the total MNI of identified fishes from ten sites in the Mariana Islands with pelagic fish remains and MNI analysis.

SITE OR AREA	CORYPHAENIDAE % MNI	ISTIOPHORIDAE/XIPHIIDAE % MNI	SCOMBRIDAE % MNI	ALL PELAGICS % MNI
Pagat, Guam	4.0	1.0		5.0
Mangilao, Guam	15.4	5.2	2.3	22.9
Ylig Bay, Guam	38.9	4.2		43.1
Afetña, Saipan			2.6	2.6
Unai Masalok, Tinian	2.2			2.2
Tachogna, Tinian	0.7	1.3	1.3	3.3
Mochong, Rota	11.8	3.2	1.9	16.9
Airport Road, Rota	16.3	9.2	8.1	33.6
Vista Del Mar, Rota		7.7	11.5	19.2
Songsong, Rota	4.7	3.5	1.2	9.4

Source: This table is adapted from Amesbury and Hunter-Anderson (2008).

However, there is another part of the Pacific with evidence of pre-contact fishing for mahimahi and marlin. This is the area on either side of the Luzon Strait that includes southern Taiwan and the northern Philippines. Coryphaenidae and Istiophoridae are among the most common taxa from archaeological sites at Eluanbi on the southern coast of Taiwan, which date to approximately the same time period as the early Pre-Latte Phase in the Marianas or somewhat earlier (Li 1997, 2002). Across the Luzon Strait from Taiwan in the Batanes Islands of the Philippines, mahimahi bones have been recovered from the Savidug Dune Site dating back to at least 3500 years ago (Campos 2009). The Yami of Botel Tobago, an island off the southeast coast of Taiwan, traditionally fished for mahimahi (Hsu 1982; Kano and Segawa 1956). (Also see Hashimura, this volume, for evidence of pelagic fishing in prehistoric Japan.)

Leach and Davidson (2000, 2006a) noted that people in both southern Taiwan and the Marianas possessed highly specialised fishing skills not seen in other parts of Oceania. Pelagic fishing skills may be one of the pieces of the puzzle that will help to answer the question of where the people of the Marianas came from.

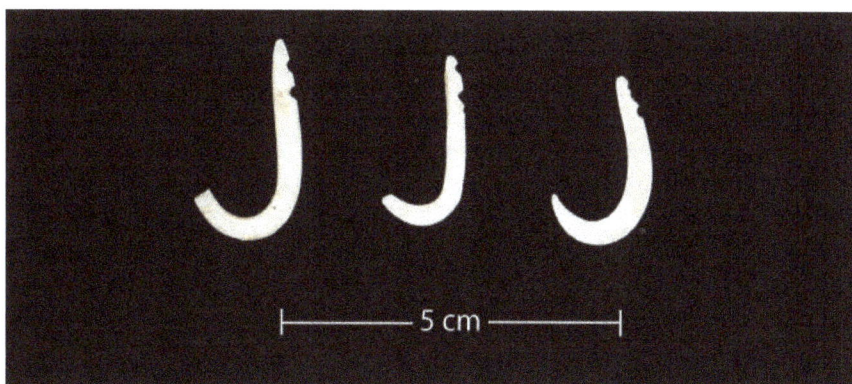

Figure 7. J-shaped fishhooks made from *Isognomon* shell recovered from Villa Kanton Tasi, Tumon Bay, Guam.

Source: Photo by Frank Wells.

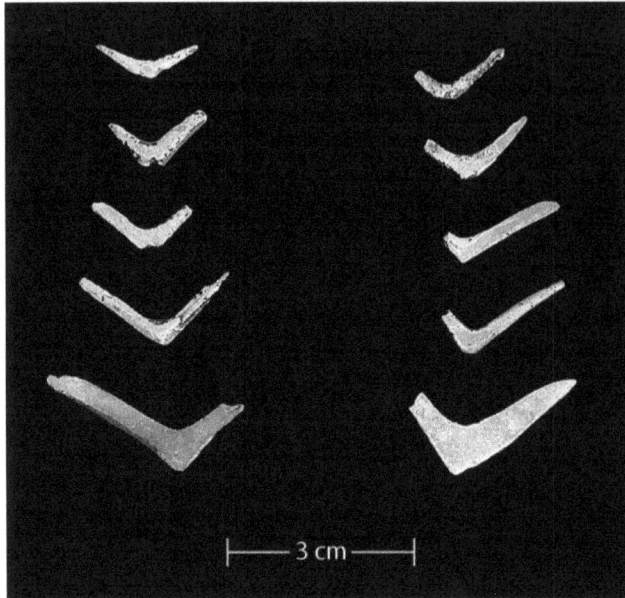

Figure 8. *Isognomon* gorges and gorge fragments from the Mangilao Golf Course site, Guam.

Source: Photo by Frank Wells.

In addition to the actual fish remains, archaeologists find pieces of fishing gear from the Prehistoric Period. Most abundant are one-piece J-shaped fishhooks (Figure 7) and V-shaped gorges (Figure 8) made of *Isognomon* shell. Points (Figures 9, 10) of composite fishhooks are more commonly found than the shanks, which may have been made of more perishable materials. Human bone spear points were used in fighting, but may have been used as harpoons as well (Figure 11).

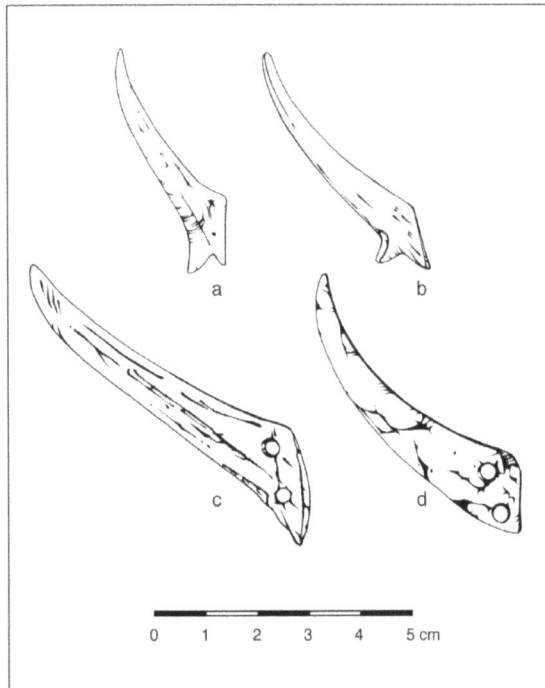

Figure 9. Points of composite fishhooks from archaeological sites in Guam. a = human bone point from Tarague (Ray 1981); b and c = bone points from Pagat (Craib 1986); d = shell point from Pugua Point, North Finegayan.

Source: Olmo et al. 2000.

Figure 10. Human bone point of composite fishhook from Ylig Bay, Guam.

Source: Photo by Rick Schaefer.

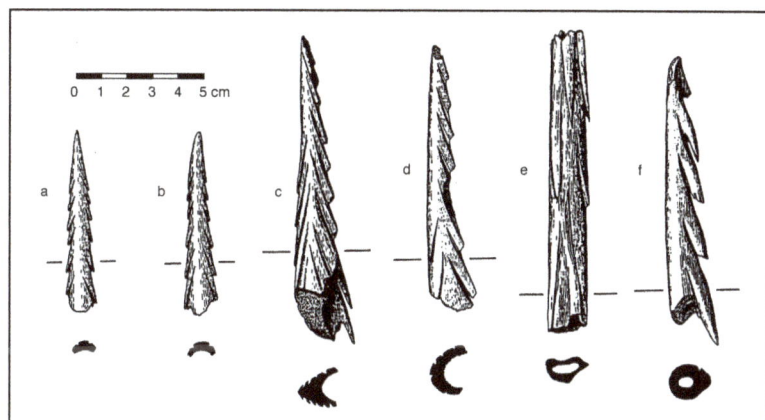

Figure 11. Human bone spear points found in association with Burial 6 at Afetña, Saipan.

Source: from McGovern-Wilson 1989.

Historic Period

In contrast to the long Prehistoric Period, the Historic Period has lasted less than 500 years from European contact until the present (Table 4). Both Guam and the CNMI belonged to Spain for more than 375 years. Twentieth century colonizers include the U.S., Germany and Japan.

Table 4. The Historic Periods in Guam and CNMI.

GUAM	CNMI
Spanish Period (AD 1521 - 1898)	Spanish Period (AD 1521 – 1899)
First American Period (1898 - 1941)	German Period (1899 - 1914)
Japanese Period (1941 - 1944)	Japanese Period (1914 - 1944)
Second American Period (1944 - present)	American Period (1944 - present)

Source: Table by Judith Amesbury.

(1) Spanish Period

Magellan arrived at Guam in 1521, and Legazpi claimed the Mariana Islands for Spain in 1565. In that same year, the Manila galleons began sailing between Acapulco and Manila, stopping in the Marianas on their way west. It was not until 1668 that the Spanish colonised Guam. During the 147-year period between 1521 and 1668, the principal change in fishing technology was due to the introduction of iron used for fishhooks. Much more radical changes in the culture took place in the remaining 230 years of the Spanish Period.

The authors of the earliest written records pertaining to the Marianas all remarked on the exceptional sailing and fishing skills of the Chamorro. Magellan's historian, Antonio Pigafetta, said, "The pastime of the men and women of the said place, and their sport, is to go with their canoes to catch some of these flying fish with some fish-hooks made of fish bones (Lévesque 1992:200-202).

A Spaniard named Sancho, who survived the shipwreck of the *Santa Margarita* in 1601 and became the servant of a Chamorro named Suñama at Pago, Guam, visited another Spaniard, Fray Juan Pobre de Zamora, in Rota in 1602. Fray Juan Pobre recorded what Sancho had to say about how the Chamorro fished for flying fish and used flying fish as bait for mahimahi, billfish, and other large fishes.

> When they fish for these flying-fish, those from one town all come together in a bunch and they go out in their canoes, each one with from ten to twelve gourds; to each gourd is tied with a very slim cord a small two-pointed shell hook [probably an *Isognomon* gorge]. One hook is baited with coconut meat and the other with shrimp or some minnow from the sea. All the fishermen throw these gourds into the sea together, everyone taking care of his own. It is by watching the gourds and seeing them wiggle that they know they have a flying-fish. There are so many fishermen because all those living on the coast of all the islands are fishermen. There are flying-fish for all of them as there are sardines in Spain. The average fish measures about one palm in length, and others about two. The first flying-fish they catch, they then eat it raw. The second one is placed as a bait on a large hook and the cord is thrown over the poop and in this manner they usually catch many dorados [mahimahi], swordfish, and other big fishes. (Lévesque 1993:176, brackets added by Amesbury).

Sancho also told the following fish story about his master Suñama to Fray Juan Pobre. Suñama caught a flying fish and ate the first one raw. With the second flying fish, he baited his hook and hooked a very large billfish (probably a blue marlin) and spent a great deal of time playing the fish to tire it. A large shark came and seized the billfish. When Suñama did not let go of the line, his boat capsized. He tied his line to the capsized boat and followed the line to the shark, diverted the shark, then brought the billfish back to his boat, which he righted and sailed home flying a woven mat from the masthead to indicate a successful catch. Sancho concluded that the Chamorro were "the most skilled fishermen ever to have been discovered" (Driver 1983:15).

The Chamorro culture was drastically impacted by Spanish colonisation in 1668 and the subsequent events. Guam was colonised when the first permanent mission in the Marianas was established. The superior of the mission was Father Diego Luis de Sanvitores, a Jesuit priest who arrived at Guam on June 15, 1668 (Carano and Sanchez 1964). Along with Father Sanvitores were four other Jesuit priests, a scholastic brother and lay assistants. In addition to the missionaries, there was a garrison force consisting of a captain, Don Juan de Santa Cruz, and thirty-two soldiers.

After an initial period of apparent success in converting the islanders to Roman Catholicism, the mission met with hostility. Open rebellion on the part of the Chamorro against the Spaniards broke out in 1670. Father Medina was killed on Saipan in 1670, and Father Sanvitores was killed on Guam in 1672. In his history of the years 1668-1681, García (1985) recorded how Spanish military commanders and governors burned Chamorro villages and canoes, pursued fleeing canoes, and rounded up fugitives who had fled from Guam to Rota. The Spanish-Chamorro Wars continued for 25 years until 1695 when the final battle took place on Aguijan, where the Chamorro people from Tinian had taken refuge but were finally overwhelmed by Governor José de Quiroga and his men. At the end of the Spanish-Chamorro Wars, the Spanish required the people of the Northern Marianas to move to Guam. By the middle of 1699, only Saipan and Rota in the Northern Marianas were still inhabited (Farrell 1991). Rota was never completely depopulated, but all of the islands north of Rota had been depopulated by about 1740.

Pelagic fishing during the Prehistoric Period and the first couple hundred years of the Spanish Period depended on the flying proa, the large ocean-going sailing canoe. In *Canoes of Oceania*, Haddon and Hornell (1975) said, "More than those of any other island group, the sailing craft of the Mariana Islands, by reason of their swiftness and elegance, riveted the attention and aroused the admiration of every navigator who had the good fortune to see them."

The flying proa, which had first been described in the 1500s, was seen and described by William Dampier in 1686 (Dampier 1937), Captain Woodes Rogers in 1710 (Rogers 1928), and George Anson in 1742 (Anson 1748; Barratt 1988). Anson and some of his lieutenants captured a proa on their arrival at Tinian, later dismantled it, and then burned it before they left the island (Barratt 1988:11, 14, 69). Their descriptions and drawings of the proa are among the last in history (Figure 12, below).

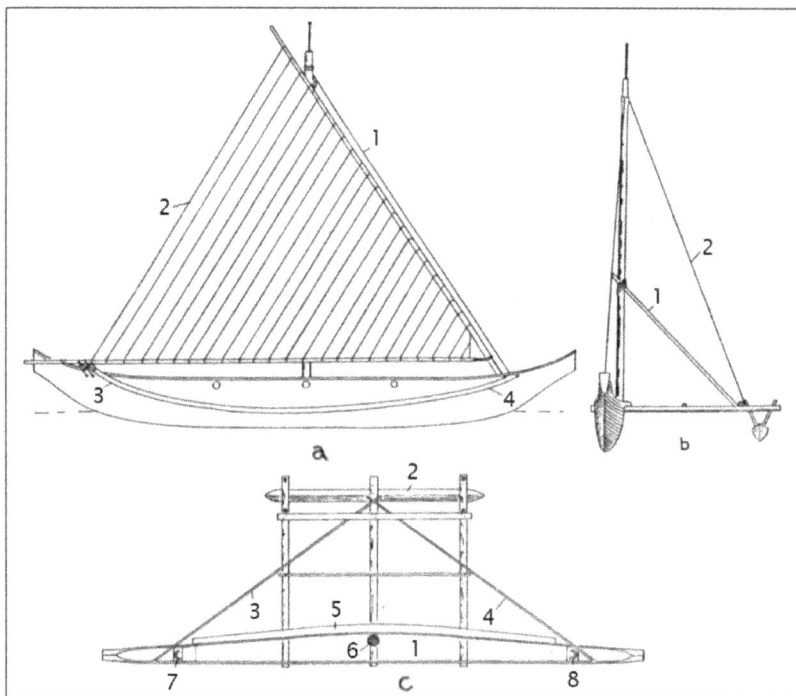

Figure 12. "Flying proa" of the Mariana Islands. a, view from leeward with sail set: 1, one of two stays supporting mast, the other hidden behind sail; 2, matting sail; 3, 4, running stays. b, head view, outrigger to windward: 1, mast shore; 2, shroud. c, plan: 1, proa; 2, "boat" at end of outrigger frame; 3, 4, braces from the ends to steady frame; 5, thin plank placed to windward to prevent shipping of water, to serve as seat for native who bales, and sometimes as rest for goods transported; 6, part of middle outrigger boom on which mast is fixed; 7, 8, horseshoe sockets, in one of which yard is lodged according to tack (after Anson 1748).

Source: Figure and caption from Haddon and Hornell (1975:414).

Anson arrived at Tinian more than 40 years after the Chamorro had been moved to Guam, so he found no permanent population there. Instead he encountered a party of about two dozen men, islanders under the command of a Spanish sergeant, who had come from Guam to kill and cure beef for the garrison in Guam and for the Spanish galleon, which would stop on her way from Acapulco to Manila. The Anson expedition estimated the number of cattle on Tinian at 10,000, and there was an abundance of wild hogs and domestic poultry (Barratt 1988:46).

Haddon and Hornell noted that the last voyager to describe the flying proa of the Chamorro was Captain Crozet (1891), who spent nearly two months on Guam in 1772. However, they questioned his description because it "coincides so closely with that of Dampier that it is impossible to resist the conclusion that Crozet had Dampier's account before him as he wrote and that he based his own almost entirely upon it" (Haddon and Hornell 1975:417). As proof of their conclusion, they cited the fact that Crozet repeated Dampier's error in saying that the outrigger was on the lee side of the boat, rather than the windward side, as correctly reported by other writers.

It appears that Anson was the last European visitor to see the flying proa in use, and even then it was put to the unusual use of transporting meat from Tinian, rather than pelagic fishing. Pelagic fishing by the Chamorro apparently came to an end by about 1750 if not before. When Governor Henrique Olavide took office in 1749, he noted a lack of sea-going vessels. He had three 30-foot vessels built in Guam, and he had eleven *bancas* (sea-going canoes) built for inter-island travel—six in Guam, four in Rota, and one in Tinian (Driver 2005:37). Governor José de Soroa, who took office in 1759, sent *bancas* to Tinian for meat (Driver 2005:38). During Governor José Arlegui's administration (1786-1794), several disasters highlighted the importance of the Refaluwasch or Carolinians and their ocean-going canoes (Driver 2005:54-57). By this time, inter-island travel was dependent on the Refaluwasch. The Refaluwasch *bancas* traveled from Guam to Rota for purposes of the government and church, and they traveled to Tinian to obtain meat and produce.

(2) Early and mid twentieth century

Just prior to the beginning of the 20th century, Spain lost control of the Mariana Islands. Guam was ceded to the U.S. in 1898 as a result of the Spanish-American War, and in 1899 Germany purchased the Mariana Islands north of Guam (Figure 13). The histories of Guam and the Northern Mariana Islands continued to diverge as Japan occupied the Northern Marianas for 30 years, while Guam was occupied by the Japanese for less than three years during World War II. Both Guam and the Northern Marianas have been part of the U.S. since 1944, but their governments have never been reunited.

Georg Fritz, the District Officer of the German (Northern) Mariana Islands from 1899-1907 wrote in *Die Chamorro*, which was published in 1904, that fishing was the main source of food for the islanders, but it took place only inside the reef. He mentioned that the Carolinians sometimes went on the high seas to Aguijan to dive for trepang, which they sold to the Japanese. He also said the Carolinians took turtle, but if they caught pelagic fish, Fritz did not record that.

In 1914, soon after the beginning of World War I, Saipan was seized by Japan. During the 1920s and 30s, the Japanese operated a pole-and-line fishery out of Saipan for bonito (skipjack tuna) and tuna (probably yellowfin tuna), which was the first large-scale commercial fishery in the Marianas. Labour was imported from Japan and Okinawa, and the catch was shipped to Japan. According to statistics obtained from Japan (Higuchi 2007), skipjack catches in Saipan District (Saipan, Tinian, and Rota) peaked at nearly 3700 metric tons or more than 8 million pounds in 1937 (Table 5). Yellowfin catches peaked at 151 metric tons or almost 333,000 pounds in 1936.

Table 5. Bonito and tuna from Saipan District, 1922 through 1941.

YEAR	BONITO* (mt)	BONITO (1000 lbs)	TUNA** (mt)	TUNA (1000 lbs)
1922	2.4	5.2	1.3	2.9
1923	2.8	6.2	1.3	2.8
1924	9.1	20.1	1.5	3.4
1925	14.8	32.6	1.4	3.1
1926	44.8	98.9	2.3	5.1
1927	28.1	62.0	2.9	6.4
1928	26.5	58.4	1.3	2.8
1929	24.7	54.4	0.6	1.2
1930	258.0	568.8	4.5	10.0
1931	564.3	1,244.0	16.7	36.9
1932	1,309.7	2,887.4	48.2	106.4
1933	1,762.3	3,885.2	9.6	21.1
1934	2,516.0	5,546.8	27.3	60.2
1935	1,786.0	3,937.4	42.9	94.6
1936	1,696.0	3,739.1	151.0	332.9
1937	3,697.3	8,151.1	88.9	195.9
1938	2,592.0	5,714.4	33.9	74.8
1939	1,297.4	2,860.2	not available	not available
1940	3,379.0	7,449.5	84.5	186.3
1941	1,297.4	2,860.2	33.7	74.2

* skipjack tuna.

** probably yellowfin tuna.

Source: This table is adapted from Higuchi (2007).

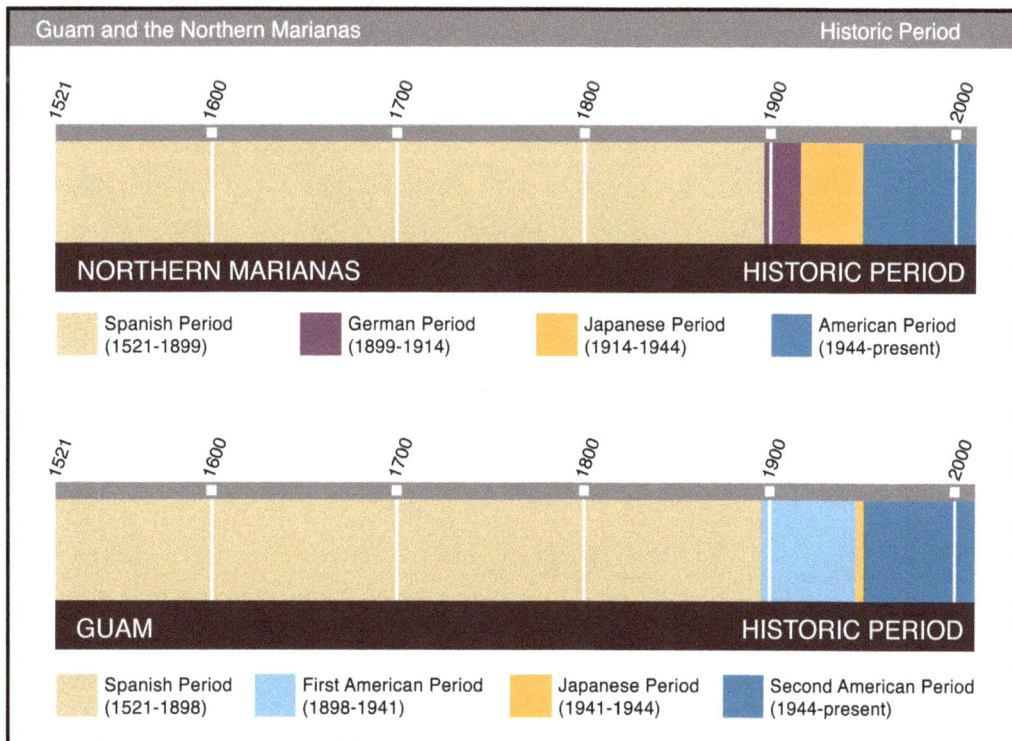

Figure 13. Timelines of the Historic Period in Guam and the CNMI.

Source: Figure by Robert Amesbury.

The American capture of Saipan in July 1944 put an end to the Japanese fishery there. All of the boats were either sunk in the harbour or beached and burned. Soon after the end of hostilities, the sunken hulls were raised from the lagoon and reconstructed by Japanese and Okinawan carpenters prior to the repatriation of Japanese nationals in 1946. Four boats were restored to use in Saipan and Tinian, and the fish caught were used to feed the interned civilians.

From 1946 through 1950, three of the four boats were put to use by a cooperative of Carolinian fishermen, known as the Saipan Fishing Company. Capital for the Saipan Fishing Company came from a small group of Carolinian men who were employed as policemen. One of those policemen was the father of Lino Olopai (Figure 14). The father of Rafael Rangamar (Figure 14) was the captain of one of the boats. Olopai and Rangamar went out on the boats as children and recalled the excitement of pole-and-line fishing in an interview in Saipan in 2005 (Amesbury and Hunter-Anderson 2008).

Post-war production of the commercial fishing industry was greatly reduced from the pre-war Japanese production (Bowers 2001). More than 3500 metric tons (more than 8 million pounds) of bonito were harvested in 1937, compared with fewer than 100 metric tons (fewer than 200,000 pounds) in 1948 (Table 6). Spoehr (2000:129) reported that by 1950 the Saipan Fishing Company was on the verge of bankruptcy. Fewer than 11 metric tons of fish had been caught in the first nine months of 1950, and about two metric tons had been lost to spoilage. When the Saipan Fishing Company ended in 1950 or soon after, the men fished for their own families.

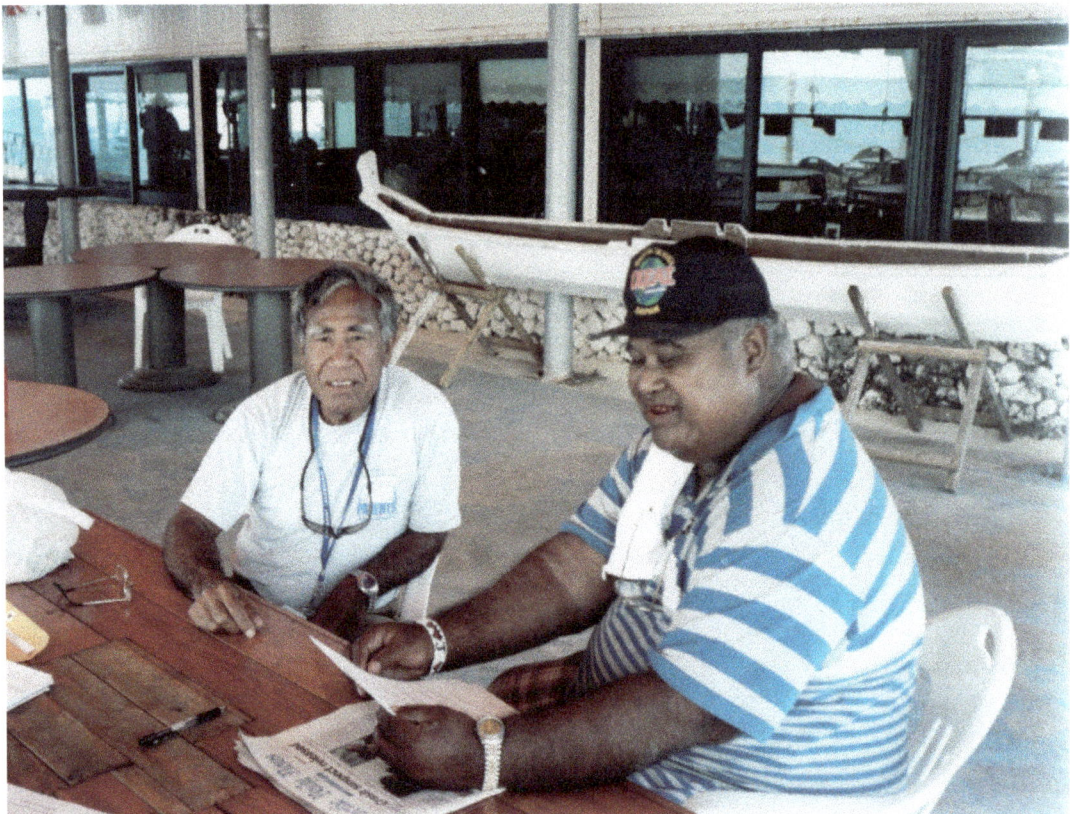

Figure 14. Lino Olopai and Rafael Rangamar at the Seaman's Restaurant, Saipan, February 2005.

Source: Photo by Judith Amesbury.

Table 6. Pre-war and post-war production of the commercial fishing industry, Saipan District.

MARINE PRODUCTS	1937 (mt)	1937 (1000 lbs)	1948 (mt)	1948 (1000 lbs)
Fish				
Bonito	3,697.3	8,151.1		
Tuna	88.9	195.9		
Mackerel	14.5	32.0		
Mullet	0.2	0.4		
Shark	5.8	12.8		
Other fish	153.3	338.0		
Total Fish	**3,960.0**	**8,730.2**	**81.1**	**178.9**
Other Marine Products				
Trepang	22.1	48.7	0.00	0.00
Trochus			0.00	0.00
Turtle			0.03	0.06
Lobster			0.40	0.88
Total Other Marine Products	**22.1**	**48.7**	**0.43**	**0.94**
Grand Total	**3,982.1**	**8,778.9**	**81.53**	**179.84**

Source: This table is adapted from Bowers (2001).

Spoehr (2000:129-130) cited four factors in the demise of the Saipan Fishing Company. The fishermen were more familiar with reef and lagoon fishing than deep-sea fishing for bonito and tuna, and maintenance of the fishing boats was a problem. Management of the commercial venture was lacking, and there were difficulties in transporting the fish to market in Guam and in marketing the fish there.

Meanwhile in pre-war Guam, the U.S. Naval Government decided to teach Chamorro men to fish beyond the reef. From 1933 to 1937, twelve men at a time were trained for a period of three months (U.S. Naval Government of Guam 1934-1937). For safety's sake, the instruction took place within view of a fishing lookout at Orote Point, and each boat carried trained homing pigeons to carry messages in case of emergency. Offshore fishing did not develop at that time due to a lack of boats.

After World War II, cash was scarce, but as the economy improved in the 1950s and 60s, the local people in the Marianas began to buy boats and outboard motors and troll for pelagic species. Most of the boats were imported from the U.S., but some were built locally. The year 1956 is the first year in which tuna or trolling catch is listed separately in the fishery statistics of the post-war governors' annual reports for Guam (Governors of Guam 1951-1970).

In an interview with Amesbury and Hunter-Anderson (2008), Lino Lizama of Tinian told an unusual story about how his father acquired a boat. In the mid-1960s, his father found a large quantity of brass from machine gun shells left by the U.S. military at a place on the northwest coast of Tinian called Dumpcoke, where the military dumped Coke bottles among other things. Lizama's father tied a weapons carrier to a big tree and used the winch on the weapons carrier to raise the drum cans of brass. He sold the brass and used the money to purchase an 18-foot wooden boat built on Saipan by his cousin's husband, Pobio Cabrera. He also bought a 40-horsepower Evinrude engine. The name of the boat was Bithen de Carmen. Lizama said that in the mid-1960s there were only three or four boats on Tinian. The late Antonio Mesngon Sr., a fisherman on Rota, said that in the 1960s there were only about four boats on Rota also, although there were more on Saipan and Guam.

(3) Late twentieth century to the present

Five species make up approximately ninety-five percent of the trolling catch in the Marianas: mahimahi (*Coryphaena hippurus*), skipjack tuna (*Katsuwonus pelamis*), wahoo (*Acanthocybium solandri*), yellowfin tuna (*Thunnus albacares*), and blue marlin (*Makaira nigricans*). An economic boom, which began in the late 1980s and continued through most of the 1990s, led to an increase in number of boats. Now hundreds of thousands of pounds of pelagic fish are landed by small boat fishermen each year.

The Guam Division of Aquatic and Wildlife Resources (DAWR, formerly Division of Fish and Wildlife) began to collect data on fisheries beginning in the 1960s. Surveys done the way they are done now began in 1979 for boat-based fisheries and in 1982 for coastal fisheries. In 1981 the National Marine Fisheries Service's (NMFS) Southwest Fisheries Science Center (SWFSC) started the Western Pacific Fishery Information Network (WPacFIN) to work cooperatively with the U.S. Pacific islands fisheries agencies to collect and disseminate fisheries statistics. These statistics are available through the WPacFIN website and the administrative reports produced by the Honolulu Laboratory, SWFSC.

Beginning in 1987, the Pelagics Plan Team and staff of the Western Pacific Regional Fishery Management Council (WPRFMC) have produced reports to the Council on the pelagic fisheries of the Western Pacific region based on the statistics produced by the island agencies and WPacFIN. The WPRFMC reports use the Guam data from 1982 on. Table 7 shows the estimated total landings in Guam of the five most abundant pelagic species from 1982 through 2009. These include non-charter and charter landings.

The WPRFMC reports provide information on effort, including estimated number of trolling boats, estimated number of trolling trips, estimated number of trolling hours, estimated trip length, and catch per unit effort (CPUE) in terms of pounds per hour. The WPRFMC reports also provide economic data including average price per pound of pelagic species, annual consumer price indexes (CPI) and CPI adjustment factors, inflation-adjusted commercial revenues, annual estimated inflation-adjusted average prices, and annual estimated inflation-adjusted revenue per trolling trip.

Since the early 1980s, the CNMI Division of Fish and Wildlife (DFW) has collected data on fishing. DFW distributes and collects invoice books from participating fish vendors on Saipan. In this way approximately 90 percent of the commercial landings on Saipan are recorded. WPacFIN compiles and expands the data to represent the entire CNMI. The data from 1983 on are considered the most accurate. Table 8 shows commercial landings of pelagic fishes on Saipan from 1983 through 2009.

Table 7. Estimated total landings of pelagic fishes by metric tons & 1000 pounds in Guam.

YEAR	MAHIMAHI		SKIPJACK		WAHOO		YELLOWFIN		BLUE MARLIN	
	mt	1000 lbs	mt	1000 lbs	mt	1000 lbs	mt	1000 lbs	mt	1000 lbs
1982	50.8	112.0	57.5	126.7	25.4	55.9	51.1	112.7	9.9	21.8
1983	70.9	156.3	44.4	97.8	39.2	86.5	29.9	66.0	13.8	30.4
1984	11.9	26.2	99.0	218.3	24.4	53.8	30.8	68.0	22.4	49.4
1985	32.8	72.4	50.0	110.3	56.1	123.7	43.2	95.3	25.4	55.9
1986	45.9	101.1	35.5	78.3	31.9	70.3	25.4	56.0	25.9	57.1
1987	36.1	79.5	28.0	61.8	39.2	86.5	18.8	41.4	22.4	49.4
1988	153.2	337.8	97.2	214.3	44.8	98.7	39.1	86.3	27.9	61.4
1989	43.6	96.0	58.2	128.2	57.8	127.3	18.4	40.5	38.8	85.5
1990	63.8	140.6	67.8	149.5	38.6	85.1	32.8	72.4	43.0	94.8
1991	188.7	415.9	53.8	118.7	25.4	55.9	20.0	44.0	39.9	87.9
1992	39.9	87.9	56.0	123.4	37.4	82.4	60.4	133.2	38.3	84.5
1993	106.6	235.0	49.7	109.6	28.4	62.6	22.8	50.4	26.3	58.0
1994	62.6	138.0	85.6	188.8	22.9	50.5	32.3	71.2	34.8	76.6
1995	148.3	327.0	81.2	179.0	35.1	77.4	42.4	93.5	34.7	76.6
1996	148.9	328.3	108.2	238.6	66.5	146.5	48.6	107.0	29.0	63.9
1997	120.3	265.2	99.4	219.2	29.5	65.0	40.9	90.2	41.2	90.8
1998	120.0	264.5	91.5	201.7	71.8	158.2	62.3	137.4	20.0	44.1
1999	73.5	161.9	56.0	123.5	34.6	76.3	58.1	128.0	36.5	80.5
2000	38.8	85.6	121.4	267.7	31.9	70.4	34.8	76.7	39.2	86.4
2001	83.1	183.3	150.5	331.8	54.3	119.8	26.3	57.9	15.1	33.3
2002	78.5	173.1	80.0	176.4	33.0	72.6	20.5	45.1	24.4	53.8
2003	38.4	84.7	84.2	185.6	29.2	64.3	32.5	71.6	30.9	68.2
2004	88.9	195.9	76.6	168.8	54.6	120.3	47.6	105.0	17.6	38.8
2005	48.0	105.7	45.1	99.4	19.9	43.9	11.3	24.9	4.2	9.3
2006	73.7	162.5	66.5	146.7	48.0	105.9	12.7	28.0	13.3	29.2
2007	117.9	259.8	71.6	157.9	20.2	44.5	21.8	48.1	8.6	19.0
2008	50.7	111.8	133.9	295.3	44.6	98.3	9.0	19.9	4.4	9.7
2009	66.5	146.6	150.2	331.1	59.3	130.7	22.8	50.3	14.8	32.6
28 Year Average	78.6	173.4	78.5	173.2	39.4	86.9	32.7	72.2	25.1	55.3
Percent of Five Species		30.9		30.9		15.5		12.9		9.9

Source: This table is adapted from WPRFMC (2011).

Table 8. Total commercial landings of pelagic fishes by metric tons & 1000 Pounds in the CNMI.

YEAR	SKIPJACK		YELLOWFIN		MAHIMAHI		WAHOO		BLUE MARLIN	
	mt	1000 lbs	mt	1000 lbs	mt	1000 lbs	mt	1000 lbs	mt	1000 lbs
1983	83.2	183.4	9,7	21.3	6.3	13.9	4.0	8.8	1.7	3.8
1984	131.9	290.8	8.9	19.6	3.5	7.6	6.4	14.1	0.7	1.5
1985	80.4	177.3	5.7	12.5	5.9	13.0	8.3	18.3	0.8	1.9
1986	115.4	254.4	7.7	16.9	8.1	17.8	4.1	9.1	1.2	2.7
1987	73.3	161.5	4.7	10.5	4.3	9.5	6.1	13.4	1.1	2.5
1988	120.9	266.5	7.0	15.4	14.0	30.8	5.3	11.7	0.6	1.3
1989	116.9	257.7	4.6	10.1	3.3	7.3	0.7	1.6	2.6	5.7
1990	67.1	148.0	4.7	10.5	4.7	10.4	1.6	3.5	0.9	2.0
1991	52.5	115.8	5.9	13.0	15.3	33.8	0.7	1.5	0.7	1.6
1992	37.3	82.3	11.7	25.7	11.9	26.3	7.8	17.2	3.0	6.6
1993	44.1	97.3	6.8	14.9	17.0	37.5	1.3	2.8	1.7	3.7
1994	41.8	92.2	6.1	13.4	6.8	15.1	1.8	3.9	1.2	2.6
1995	59.6	131.4	9.5	20.9	10.6	23.3	2.6	5.7	3.0	6.6
1996	74.9	165.0	17.3	38.0	16.2	35.7	4.9	10.8	3.9	8.6
1997	60.5	133.4	9.7	21.4	14.2	31.3	3.4	7.6	3.2	7.1
1998	75.8	167.1	6.6	14.6	11.5	25.4	2.9	6.3	1.9	4.2
1999	48.2	106.3	11.1	24.4	5.8	12.9	3.7	8.1	1.6	3.5
2000	63.7	140.4	8.0	17.7	3.3	7.3	1.9	4.1	1.6	3.6
2001	60.7	133.8	6.6	14.5	6.5	14.2	2.1	4.6	0.9	1.9
2002	81.6	180.0	13.6	30.0	8.2	18.0	3.7	8.2	0.6	1.3
2003	77.8	171.6	11.8	26.0	3.3	7.4	3.6	8.0	0.5	1.1
2004	67.3	148.3	12.5	27.5	16.2	35.8	3.1	6.9	0.9	2.0
2005	118.2	260.6	23.6	52.0	12.2	26.9	1.5	3.3	0.7	1.6
2006	120.5	265.8	19.0	42.0	7.8	17.2	1.4	3.1	0.6	1.4
2007	108.4	239.0	15.8	34.9	12.0	26.4	1.1	2.5	0.03	0.1
2008	77.1	170.1	8.5	18.7	6.0	13.2	0.8	1.7	0.9	2.0
2009	58.6	129.2	11.4	25.1	8.9	19.6	1.5	3.4	0.02	0.0
27 Year Average	78.4	172.9	9.9	21.9	9.0	19.9	3.2	7.0	1.4	3.0
Percent of Five Species		76.9		9.7		8.9		3.1		1.3

Source: This table is adapted from WPRFMC (2011).

The composition of the CNMI trolling catch is very different from that of the Guam trolling catch. In the CNMI, the average annual commercial trolling catch of skipjack exceeds 170,000 pounds, but yellowfin, mahimahi, wahoo, and marlin average less than 22,000 pounds each. On Guam, the average annual total trolling catches of both mahimahi and skipjack exceed 170,000 pounds each. The average annual trolling catches of wahoo, yellowfin, and marlin range from 87,000 to 55,000 pounds each.

Figure 15 compares the 27-year average commercial landings in the CNMI (from Table 7) with the 28-year average total landings in Guam (from Table 8). The Saipan catch is more than 75 percent skipjack, while the Guam catch is more evenly divided between the five most abundant species. It is possible that the preference for skipjack in Saipan is a result of Saipan's history with the pre-war Japanese and post-war Carolinian pole-and-line fishery.

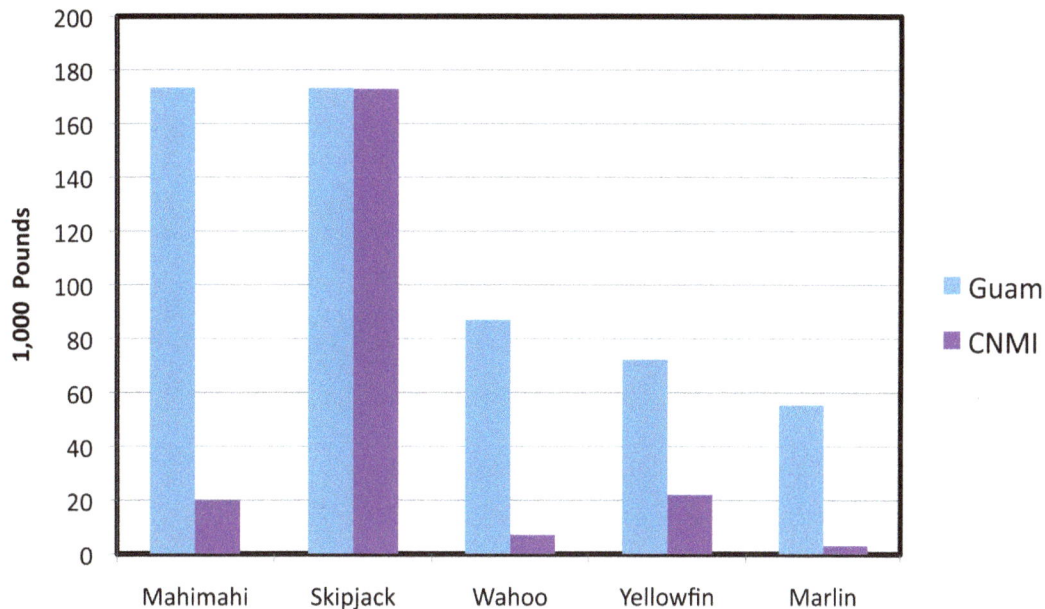

Figure 15. Composition of the trolling catch in Guam and Saipan, based on average annual catches.

Source: Figure by Judith Amesbury.

Summary

The first people to arrive in the Mariana Archipelago at least 3,500 years ago were skilled fishermen. No doubt their ability to reach the Marianas over a long distance of open ocean was accompanied by the ability to fish for open-ocean species. Analysis of fish bones from archaeological sites shows that the Chamorro fished for pelagic species, especially mahimahi and marlin, throughout the long Prehistoric Period (at least 1500 BC to AD 1521). A comparison of ten sites with pelagic species and MNI analysis indicates that approximately sixteen percent of the fishes caught were pelagic species. It is noted that archaeological sites in southern Taiwan and the northern Philippines also have yielded bones of mahimahi and marlin from deposits which date to approximately the same time period as the Pre-Latte Phase in the Marianas.

Pelagic fishing continued into the Spanish Period with the addition of iron for fishhooks. The writers of the early Spanish Period described fishing for flying fish, mahimahi, and billfish. By all accounts the Chamorro were exceptionally skilled sailors and fishermen. However, when hostilities broke out soon after Spanish colonisation in 1668, the Chamorro people and culture were drastically affected. As a result of the 25-year long Spanish-Chamorro Wars and the Spanish policy of requiring nearly everyone in the Marianas to move to Guam, the flying proa was no longer built by about 1750, and the Chamorro people did not participate in pelagic fishing for the next 200 years. Refaluwasch people from the Caroline Islands moved into the Marianas and took over inter-island travel during the second half of the 1700s and the 1800s. Both Chamorro and Carolinian people engaged in reef fishing.

The next major development in pelagic fishing was the pole-and-line fishery operated by the Japanese in Saipan in the 1920s and 30s, which was the first commercial fishery in the Marianas. The labour was mostly Japanese and Okinawan, and the fish were exported to Japan. Extraordinarily large amounts of skipjack were caught. The Japanese fishery ended with the American takeover of Saipan in 1944. For a few years after the war, a cooperative of Carolinian fishermen tried to resume the pole-and-line fishery, but they did so with less success than the Japanese had. Meanwhile in pre-war Guam, the U.S. Navy decided to teach Chamorro men how to fish for pelagic species. A lack of boats prevented that idea from getting off the ground.

Boats became available in the 1950s and 60s as the economy improved after the war. Pelagic fishing had begun by 1956 according to the post-war Guam governors' reports. By the mid-1960s there were only a few boats on Tinian and Rota, but more on Guam and Saipan. Good fishery data from the 1980s on show that the small boat fishermen of the Marianas now land hundreds of thousands of pounds of pelagic fish annually. Five species (mahimahi, skipjack, wahoo, yellowfin, and marlin) make up about ninety-five percent of the catch. The Chamorro fishermen have reclaimed their heritage as great pelagic fishermen.

For additional fishery data from each of the time periods, see Amesbury and Hunter-Anderson (2008). The report is available on the website of the Pelagic Fisheries Research Program at http://www.soest.hawaii.edu/pfrp/ under Other Publications.

Acknowledgments

This project was partly funded by Cooperative Agreement NA17RJ1230 between the Joint Institute for Marine and Atmospheric Research (JIMAR) and the National Oceanic and Atmospheric Administration (NOAA). The views expressed herein are those of the author and do not necessarily reflect the views of NOAA or any of its subdivisions. The author thanks Janet Davidson and Osamu Kataoka for their helpful reviews of this paper.

References

Amesbury, J.R. and R.L. Hunter-Anderson. 2008. *An Analysis of Archaeological and Historical Data on Fisheries for Pelagic Species in Guam and the Northern Mariana Islands*. Report prepared for Pelagic Fisheries Research Program, University of Hawai'i at Mānoa. Guam: Micronesian Archaeological Research Services. Available on the website of the Pelagic Fisheries Research Program at http://www.soest.hawaii.edu/pfrp/ under Other Publications.

Anson, Baron G. 1748. *A Voyage Round the World (1740-1744)*. Compiled by Richard Walter. London: Martin Hopkinson Ltd.

Barratt, G. 1988. *H.M.S. Centurion at Tinian, 1742: The Ethnographic and Historic Records*. Saipan: CNMI Division of Historic Preservation. *Micronesian Archaeological Survey Report* No. 26.

Bowers, N.M. 2001. (First published 1950). *Problems of Resettlement on Saipan, Tinian and Rota, Mariana Islands*. Saipan: CNMI Division of Historic Preservation. *Occasional Historical Papers Series* No. 7.

Campos, F.Z. 2009. *The Ichthyoarchaeology of Batanes Islands, Northern Philippines*. Unpublished master's thesis, Archaeology, University of the Philippines.

Carano, P. and P.C. Sanchez. 1964. *A Complete History of Guam*. Rutland: Charles E. Tuttle Company.

Craib, J.L. 1986. *Casas de los Antiguos: Social Differentiation in Protohistoric Chamorro Society, Mariana Islands*. Unpublished doctoral dissertation, University of Sydney.

Craib, J.L. 1990. *Archaeological Investigations at Mochong, Rota, Mariana Islands*. Report submitted to the Office of Historic Preservation, Commonwealth of the Northern Mariana Islands. Melbourne: Department of Archaeology, La Trobe University.

Crozet, Captain. 1891. *Crozet's Voyage to Tasmania, New Zealand, the Ladrone Islands, and the Philippines in the Years 1771-1772*. Translated by H. Ling Roth. London: Truslove and Shirley.

Dampier, W. 1937. *A New Voyage Round the World*. London: Adam and Charles Black.

Donaldson, T.J., R.F. Myers, J.T. Moyer, and P.J. Schupp. 1994. Zoogeography of fishes of the Mariana, Ogasawara and Izu Islands: A preliminary assessment. In A. Asakura and T. Furuki (eds), *Biological Expedition to the Northern Mariana Islands, Micronesia*, pp. 303-332. Chiba: Natural History Museum and Institute. *Natural History Research Special Issue* No. 1.

Driver, M.G. 1983. Fray Juan Pobre de Zamora and his account of the Mariana Islands. *Journal of Pacific History* 18(3):198-216.

Driver, M.G. 2005. *The Spanish Governors of the Mariana Islands*. Guam: Micronesian Area Research Center, University of Guam. *MARC Educational Series* No. 27.

Farrell, D.A. 1991. *History of the Northern Mariana Islands*. Saipan: CNMI Public School System.

García, F. 1985. *The Life and Martyrdom of the Venerable Father Diego Luis de Sanvitores*. Translated by Margaret Higgens. Guam: Nieves M. Flores Memorial Library.

Governors of Guam 1951-1970. *Annual Reports*. On file at Micronesian Area Research Center, University of Guam.

Graves, M.W. 1986. Organization and differentiation within late prehistoric ranked social units, Mariana Islands, Western Pacific. *Journal of Field Archaeology* 13(2):139-154.

Haddon, A.C. and J. Hornell. 1975. *Canoes of Oceania*. Honolulu: Bishop Museum Press. *Bernice P. Bishop Museum Special Publications* 27, 28, and 29.

Higuchi, W. 2007. Pre-war Japanese fisheries in Micronesia: Focusing on bonito and tuna fishing in the Northern Mariana Islands. *Immigration Studies* 3:49-68. Okinawa: Center for Migration Studies, University of the Ryukyus.

Hsu, Y.C. 1982. *Yami Fishing Practices: Migratory Fish*. Taipei: Southern Materials Centre Inc.

Hunter-Anderson, R.L. and D.R. Moore 2002. *Phase I and Phase II Archaeological Survey at Waterfront Annex and Ordnance Annex, Territory of Guam*. Prepared under Contract No. N26742-97-D-3511, Task Order 12, Task 1 between International Archaeological Research Institute, Inc. and the Department of the Navy, Pacific Division, Naval Facilities Engineering Command, Pearl Harbor. Guam: Micronesian Archaeological Research Services.

Kano, T. and K. Segawa. 1956. *An Illustrated Ethnography of Formosan Aborigines, Volume 1: The Yami*. Tokyo: Maruzen Co. Ltd.

Leach, F. and J. Davidson. 2000. Fishing, a neglected aspect of Oceanic economy. In A. Anderson and T. Murray (eds), *Australian Archaeologist: Collected Papers in Honour of Jim Allen*, pp. 412-426. Canberra: Coombs Academic Publishing and The Australian National University.

Leach, B.F. and J.M. Davidson. 2006a. *Analysis of Faunal Material from an Archaeological Site Complex at Mangilao, Guam*. Technical Report 38. Wellington: Museum of New Zealand Te Papa Tongarewa.

Leach, B.F. and J.M. Davidson. 2006b. *Analysis of Faunal Material from an Archaeological Site at Ylig, Guam*. Technical Report 39. Wellington: Museum of New Zealand Te Papa Tongarewa.

Leach, B.F., M. Fleming, J.M. Davidson, G.K. Ward, and J.L. Craib. 1990. Appendix C, Prehistoric Fishing at Mochong, Rota, Mariana Islands. In J.L. Craib (ed), *Archaeological Investigations at Mochong, Rota, Mariana Islands*, pp. C-1 to C-34. Submitted to the Office of Historic Preservation, Commonwealth of the Northern Mariana Islands. Melbourne: Department of Archaeology, La Trobe University.

Leach, F., M. Fleming, J. Davidson, G. Ward, and J. Craib. 1988. Prehistoric fishing at Mochong, Rota, Mariana Islands. *Man and Culture in Oceania* 4:31-62.

Lévesque, R. (compiler and editor). 1992. *History of Micronesia, A Collection of Source Documents, Volume 1—European Discovery, 1521-1560*. Québec: Lévesque Publications.

Lévesque, R. (compiler and editor). 1993. *History of Micronesia, A Collection of Source Documents, Volume 3—First Real Contact, 1596-1637*. Québec: Lévesque Publications.

Li, K. 1997. *Change and Stability in the Dietary System of a Prehistoric Coastal Population in Southern Taiwan*. Unpublished doctoral dissertation, Arizona State University.

Li, K. 2002. Prehistoric marine fishing adaptation in southern Taiwan. *Journal of East Asian Archaeology* 3(1-2):47-74.

McGovern-Wilson, R. 1989. *Afetña: The Prehistory of South West Saipan*. Prepared for InterPacific Resorts and Historic Preservation Office, Saipan. Dunedin: Anthropology Department, University of Otago.

Moore, D.R. 1983. *Measuring Change in Marianas Pottery: The Sequence of Pottery Production at Tarague, Guam*. Unpublished master's thesis, Behavioral Science, University of Guam.

Moore, D.R. and R.L. Hunter-Anderson. 1999. Pots and pans in the intermediate Pre-Latte (2500-1600 BP), Mariana Islands, Micronesia. In J-C Galipaud and I. Lilley (eds), *The Pacific from 5000 to 2000 BP, Colonisation and Transformations*, pp. 487-503. Paris: IRD Editions.

Nelson, J.S. 2006. *Fishes of the World*. Fourth Edition. Hoboken: John Wiley and Sons, Inc.

Olmo, R.K., T. Mangieri, D.J. Welch, and T.S. Dye. 2000. *Phase II Archaeological Survey and Detailed Recording at Commander, U.S. Naval Forces Marianas (COMNAVMARIANAS) Communications Annex (formerly Naval Computer and Telecommunications Area Master Station, Western Pacific [NCTAMS WESTPAC]), Territory of Guam, Mariana Islands*. Prepared for Department of the Navy, Pacific Division, Naval Facilities Engineering Command, Pearl Harbor, Hawai'i. Honolulu: International Archaeological Research Institute, Inc.

Randall, R.H. 1995. Biogeography of reef-building corals in the Mariana and Palau Islands in relation to back-arc rifting and the formation of the Eastern Philippine Sea. *Natural History Research* 3(2):193-210.

Ray, E.R. 1981. *The Material Culture of Prehistoric Tarague Beach, Guam*. Unpublished master's thesis, Arizona State University.

Reinman, F.R. 1977. *An Archaeological Survey and Preliminary Test Excavations on the Island of Guam, Mariana Islands, 1965-1966*. Guam: Micronesian Area Research Center, University of Guam. *Miscellaneous Publication* No. 1.

Rogers, Captain W. 1928. *A Cruising Voyage Round the World*. New York: Longmans, Green and Co.

Spoehr, A. 1957. *Marianas Prehistory*. Chicago: Chicago Natural History Museum Press; Fieldiana: *Anthropology* Vol. 48.

Spoehr, A. 2000 (Second Edition). *Saipan: The Ethnology of a War-Devastated Island*. Saipan: N.M.I. Division of Historic Preservation.

Thompson, L.M. 1932. *Archaeology of the Marianas Islands.* Honolulu: Bishop Museum Press. *Bernice P. Bishop Museum Bulletin* 100.

U.S. Naval Government of Guam 1901-1941. *Annual Reports on Guam.* On file at the Micronesian Area Research Center, University of Guam.

WPRFMC 2011. *Pelagic Fisheries of the Western Pacific Region: 2009 Annual Report.* Honolulu: Western Pacific Regional Fishery Management Council.

3

Historical Ecology and 600 Years of Fish Use on Atafu Atoll, Tokelau

Rintaro Ono, School of Marine Science and Technology, Department of Maritime Civilization, Tokai University, Japan

David J. Addison, Samoan Studies Institute, American Samoa Community College

Introduction

A NZ dependency, Tokelau is a group of three atolls as including Fakaofo, Nukunonu and Atafu, which located around 500-600km north of Samoa at a latitude of S8-10° and longitude of W171-173° (Figure 1). Marine exploitation, especially fishing, is the most important subsistence activity in Tokelau and has multifarious cultural implications (e.g., Hooper 1985, 1991, 2008, 2010; Huntsman and Hooper 1996; Mafutaga a Toeaina o Atafu i Matauala Porirua 2008; Matagi Tokelau 1991; Ono and Addison 2009). For instance, the Mafutaga a Toeaina o Atafu i Matauala Porirua (2008) report Atafu's rich traditions of fishing lore and a total of 108 fishing methods on Atafu Atoll, one of the atolls in Tokelau. Our recent ethno-ecological study on Atafu also confirms active marine use by the islanders and collected over 160 fish names and 12 mollusc names (see Ono and Addison 2009: Appendix 1).The classification and diversity of fish and mollusc names on Atafu clearly show the overwhelming importance of fish resources, as opposed to molluscs.

An analysis of fish name classification also enables us to consider people's preferences regarding fish and other marine resources. Also, the variety and character of fishing methods and fish name classification on Atafu reveal that there are more variations in names and fishing methods for larger pelagic fish species, such as those in the families Carangidae and Scombridae, and show a high dependence on outer-reef and offshore resources. Such tendencies possibly indicate that outer-reef and offshore resources were significant both economically and culturally in the past on Atafu as well.

In terms of prehistoric fishing, however, a previous archaeological study on Atafu and Fakaofo by Best (1988) and zoo-archaeological analysis of fish remains from Fakaofo by McAlister (2002) report absent or a very limited number of tunas (Scombridae) among the assemblage. A possible reason for the near absence of tunas in their studies might be because of their limited scope of analysis; for their identifications they did not analyse vertebra, which are one of the most diagnostic and solid parts of tuna skeletons (e.g., Davidson et al. 1999; Leach et al. 1997; Ono 2003, 2004, 2010; Ono and Intoh 2011). Alternatively, it is also possible that tunas and other pelagic fish were not the major marine resource exploited in prehistoric times on Fakaofo. In any case, since McAlister's study has been the only analysis of archaeological fish remains from Tokelau, it is impossible to say whether the much higher dependence on reef and lagoon fish resources prehistorically on Fakaofo is replicated at other location in Tokelau for the prehistoric period.

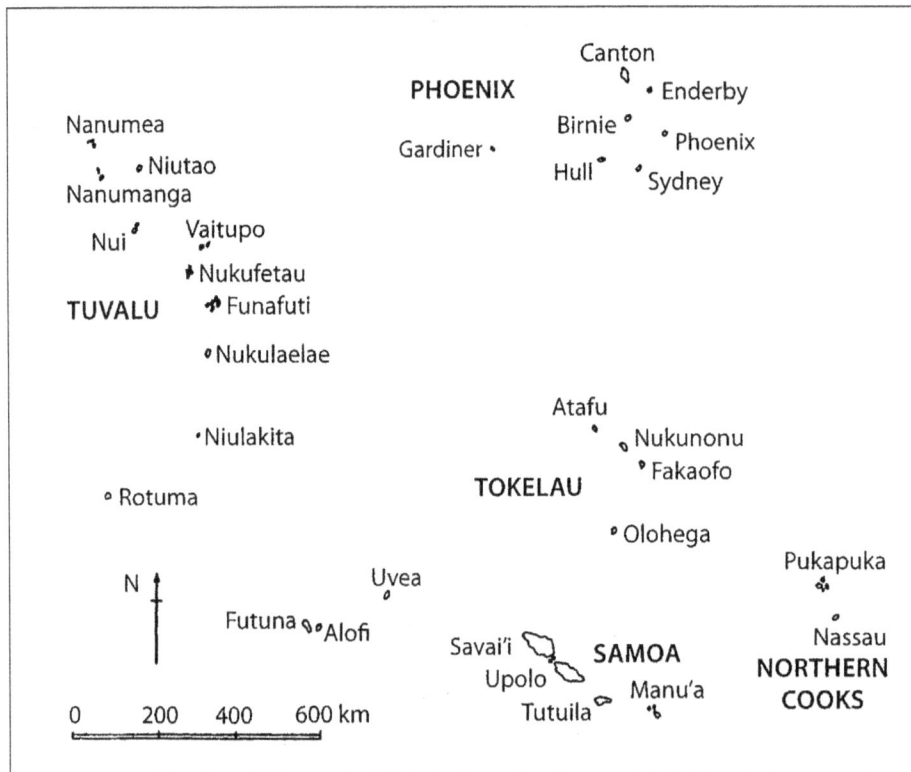

Figure 1. Tokelau and its location.

Source: Matagi Tokelau. 1991. *Matagi Tokelau: History and traditions of Tokelau*. Apia (Samoa) and Suva (Fiji): Office of Tokelau Affairs and the Institute of Pacific Studies, University of the South Pacific.

To improve such archaeological limits of prehistoric fishing data in Tokelau, we conducted excavations on Atafu in 2008 and 2009. We have included vertebra for identification of fish species in analysing our excavated fish remains. In this paper, we first discuss Tokelau fishing lore, focusing on fishing practices and technologies as well as materials and the conservational aspect of fishing on Atafu. Secondly, we examine prehistoric fish use and fishing strategies on Atafu based on our recent excavations. At the final stage of this paper, we try to combine both ethno-ecological and archaeological data to discuss 600+ years of fish use on Atafu from a historical ecology perspective.

Geo-Ecological Background of Tokelau

Among the three atolls in Tokelau, Atafu is located at the north-west end of the archipelago, with Nukunonu in the middle and Fakaofo to the south-east. Besides these three atolls, another atoll named Olohega is located at the south end of the archipelago. Olohega (or Swains Island) is politically a part of the U.S. Territory of American Samoa and is situated ~160km to the south of the other three atolls at S11° and W171°.

The total land area of Tokelau is tiny; the combined dry land area of all three atolls (excluding Olohega) comprises only 12.2km² of dry land (Huntsman and Hooper 1996). Tokelau's exclusive economic zone is considerably larger, covering some 290,000km² of ocean (Passfield 1998:2). The average mean annual temperature in Tokelau is 28°C, and the annual rainfall is 2900mm (Toloa et al. 1994). Geoculturally, Tokelau is located at a crossroads between East and West Polynesia (Burrows 1939), about 400km east of Tuvalu and 400km west of the Northern Cook Islands.

As is the case with most low and exposed atolls, Tokelau is particularly susceptible to wave surge during tropical storms. Between November and March, the weather is often unsettled, and the atolls are exposed to high winds and rough seas. During these months, sea travel is frequently restricted to the sheltered waters inside the reef (Matagi Tokelau 1991:6). Occasionally, the atolls are struck by cyclones during this stormy season.

Geologically, Atafu, Nukunonu, and Fakaofo are typical atolls with a large central lagoon surrounded by an intermittent chain of sandy islets known as motu; Olohega has a landlocked brackish water lake in the centre instead of a central lagoon. The largest of the atolls is Nukunonu, with a land area of about 5.5km², the second largest is Fakaofo with 3km², and Atafu is the smallest with 2.5km², while the land area of Olohega is about 1.5km². Lagoon size is even more variable between atolls: Atafu's lagoon is considerably smaller than the other two, covering only 19km², compared to 109km² for Nukunonu and 59km² for Fakaofo (Huntsman and Hooper 1996).

Most of the motus of Tokelau's atolls are covered with dense groves of coconut palms except some areas where littoral forest dominates. The most common terrestrial plant species are Cordia subcordata, Guettarda speciosa, Hernandia nymphaeifolia, and Pisonia grandis, while Pandanus tectorius and Tournefortia argentea prevail on the margins of the littoral forest (Whistler 1988). The main food plants are mostly root crops (pulaka or Cyrtosperma chamissonis and taamu or Alocasia macrorrhizos.) and fruit trees (screwpine - Pandanus tectorius, breadfruit – Artocarpus altilis, bananas – Musa spp., coconut – Cocos nucifera, and papaya *Carica papaya*). *Pulaka* is cultivated in swampy pits excavated in the centre of some sandy motus where the Ghyben-Herzberg fresh-water lens is close to the surface, while fruits trees are planted both around houses in the village and on motus.

Every island except Olohega has a large inner lagoon with a variety of fish and mollusc species. The major fish habitats in the lagoons support species of Holocentridae, Chaetodontidae, Pomacentridae, Muridae, Siganidae, and small-sized species of Serranidae, Lethrinidae, Balistidae, and Labridae. Some species of *Tridacna* are widely distributed and are targeted by islanders when grown large enough to harvest and eat, while the harvest of small-sized individuals is prohibited. Pearlshell (perhaps *Pinctada marginifera*) formerly inhabited Tokelau's lagoons, and once were utilised to produce lure shanks, though this species was very limited in Atafu (Macgregor 1937). It may have been locally extirpated from Tokelau by the 1950s, when it was reported that 10 years had passed since any pearlshell was found on Fakaofo (Van Pel 1958). Other important invertebrate species include about ten species of crab, such as *tupa* (a land crab, *Cardisoma* sp.), *ugauga* (coconut crab or *Birgus latro*), and *kamakama* (rock crab or *Grapsus* sp.) are also common around the lagoon coasts, and are usually exploited as food or fishing bait.

The ocean-side coasts are surrounded by narrow coral reefs that have a greater variety of fish and mollusc species than the lagoons. The major fish inhabiting the outer reefs are various species of Scaridae, Labridae, Balistidae, Acanthuridae, and small species of Carangidae, Serranidae, Lethrinidae and Lutjanidae which mainly swim around reef edges. For molluscs, some species of Turbinidae and Trochidae inhabit mainly the reef edges, but in recent times only *Turbo* shells are taken to eat. According to Passfield (1988), *Trochus* is not native to Tokelau but was introduced to the atolls in 1986 from Fiji as part of a development project. Some larger fishes inhabit the outer reef waters, particularly between the reef edges and the pelagic ocean. They are species of Carangidae, Scombridae, Lutjanidae, Serranidae, Sphyraenidae, and shark species. Flying fish (*Cypselurus* sp.) and sea turtles are also mainly captured in this biotope.

Wild bird species inhabit the islands, and Tokelauans still occasionally capture wild birds for food (Huntsman and Hooper 1996; Matagi Tokelau 1991). Seabirds, such as terns and noddies (*lakia*), are generally caught with nets and nooses (Matagi Tokelau 1991: 201). There are no terrestrial mammals native to Tokelau; all are introductions either by the early Polynesian settlers or later European visitors. Archaeological finds (Addison and Kalolo 2009; Best 1988) suggest that the first people to arrive at Tokelau brought with them the dog (*Canis canis*) and the Polynesian rat (*Rattus exulans*). Dogs were no longer present in Tokelau at European contact. Tokelauans have no tradition of dogs, either as a source of food or of companionship and they are not kept today. *R. exulans* are still found in Tokelau along with recently introduced rat species; rats are now considered a pest. Pig (*Sus scrofa*) was introduced to Tokelau after European contact. The timing of the introduction of chicken is ambiguous.

The People and Language

In terms of population in Tokelau, Atafu is the most populous with ~600 people, followed by Fakaofo with ~500, and Nukunonu with ~400 (Statistics New Zealand 2001); Olohega currently has fewer than 20 people. Tokelau has been an incorporated territory of New Zealand since 1948. Over 1,500 Tokelauans now live on the main islands of New Zealand (Statistics New Zealand 2001), with several thousand more Tokelauans living in Samoa, Hawai'i, and Australia. Although Olohega is currently part of the American Samoa, many Tokelauans consider it a historical and cultural part of Tokelau (Matagi Tokelau 1991:41-43).

The people of Tokelau are Polynesian, with strong affinities to the atoll peoples of Tuvalu to the west, and the Northern Cook Islands to the east. Interaction to the south with Samoa has been an important process for at least the last century and possibly much longer. However, oral tradition is silent on the earliest origins of the Tokelau peoples (Huntsman pers. comm.; Huntsman and Hooper 1996; Matagi Tokelau 1991). Archaeologically, the Lapita cultural complex is the first indication of people in West Polynesia at ~3000-2800 cal BP (e.g., research summarised in Kirch 1997). In the "Hawaiki" model (Kirch and Green 2001), an "Ancestral Polynesian Society" (APS) with unique cultural and linguistic traits developed in the Fiji, Tonga, Samoa, Uvea, and Futuna area over the following millennium of regular interarchipelagic contact. A dialect chain developed over this area and eventually split into a northern and southern branch. At ~1300-1100 cal BP and subsequent to this breakup, East Polynesia and the Polynesian Outliers were settled, mostly from islands speaking the northern branch of the dialect chain – Proto Nuclear Polynesian (Green 1966, 1988; Marck 2000; Pawley 1966, 1967).

Tokelau was probably first settled during this period of expansion. The previous archaeological excavations in Tokelau (Best 1988:104) dated unidentified charcoal from basal cultural deposits on Atafu to 1150-690 cal BP.[1] On Fakaofo, turtle bone from the lowest cultural deposits dates to 790-530 cal BP (Best 1988: 115). The apparent discrepancy between these two dates could be resolved by arguing that the area of overlap represents the actual initial settlement period for Tokelau. Coconut endocarp excavated by our research in 2008 from a basal cultural layer about 100m from Best's 1986 sample location dates to 660-550 cal BP (Addison et al. 2009; Addison and Kalolo 2009; Petchey et al. under review), further reinforcing the idea that the overlap in Best's basal dates is the actual period of initial colonisation. Many more dating samples from a variety of stratigraphically secure contexts on all three atolls will be required to resolve this question.

---

1   Reported at 2σ, calibrated using OxCal v3.10 with InterCAL04. For justification for Northern-Hemisphere curve (see Petchey and Addison 2008 and also Addison and Asaua 2006).

The Tokelauan language is typically Polynesian. It contains five vowel sounds (written as a, e, i, o and u), and ten consonants (written as f, g, h, k, l, m, n, p, t, and v). The f is pronounced like wh, and the h is a glottal fricative, while it sounds the same as English h before the vowels i and e. On the other hand, before the back vowels a, o, and u, is pronounced more like hy (e.g., Tokelauan Dictionary 1986). The last century has seen an increase in cultural and linguistic influence on the Tokelauans by Samoa, and this has affected some of the names of plants (Whistler 1988). Some Tokelauan fish names have also been affected or introduced from adjacent islands, mainly the Northern Cook Islands, Tuvalu, Samoa, and Tonga (see Hooper 1994; Rensch 1994).

In a comparative linguistic analysis of Proto Polynesian (PPN) and Proto Nuclear Polynesian (PNP) fish names, Robin Hooper (1994) checked for shared retentions and innovations, or borrowings between Polynesian islands. Her analysis indicates that out of 112 PPN reconstructions for fish names, Tokelauan retains reflexes of 94 (84%), which is an extraordinarily high figure (Hooper 1994:187). As Hooper mentions, the high figure for Tokelauan could indicate either a more nearly complete inventory of local fish names than other islands, or the more conservative nature of the Tokelauan lexicon (Hooper 1994:187). In any case, it is clear that Tokelauan fishing terms and fish names are good candidates for inclusion in core vocabulary lists for the region.

A Brief Sketch of Atafu

Here, we briefly describe Atafu, its people and social structure. Atafu is located at the northwest end of Tokelau, which is the part of Tokelau most distant from Western Samoa (600km). There is ship transport roughly every two weeks between Western Samoa and Tokelau, and it usually takes about 48 hours from Samoa to Atafu via Fakaofo and Nukunonu. As noted earlier, Atafu is the smallest atoll in Tokelau both in lagoon size and land area. The only village is on an islet at the northwest corner of Atafu. The current human population is ~600. Atafu's other 41 islets have no permanent human habitations (Figure 2).

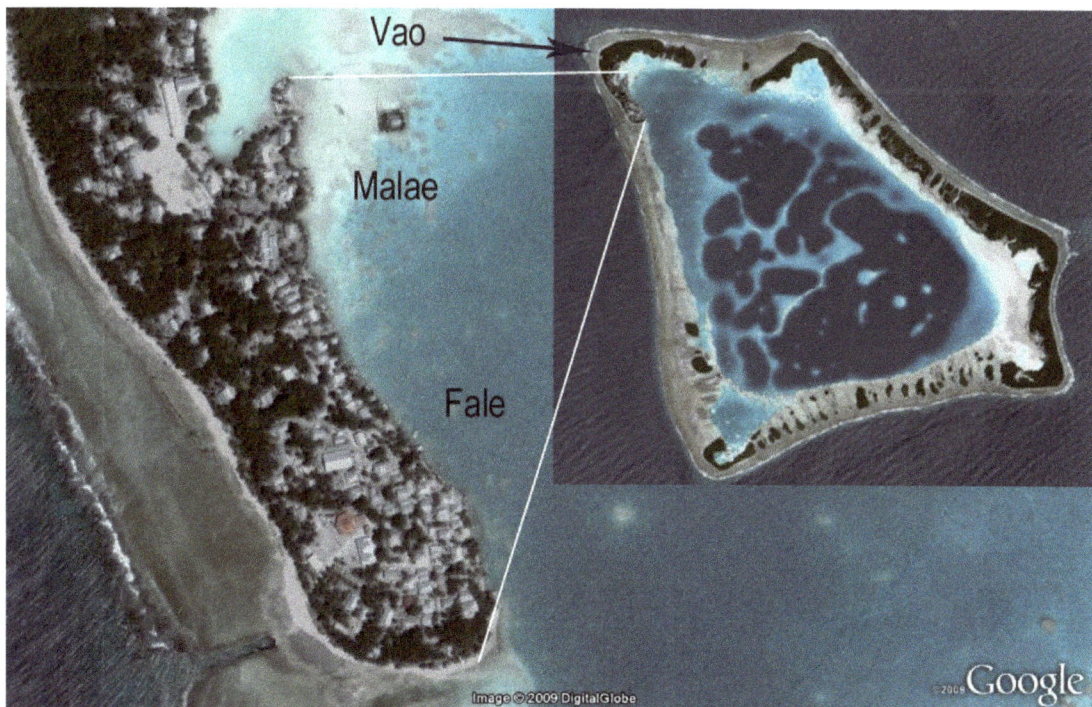

Figure 2. Atafu Atoll and the village location on Vao Island.

Source: Map by authors, based on Google Map. Retrieved from http://maps.google.com

The subsistence activity of the Atafu people falls into three major spheres: fishing, root-crop cultivation, and fruit-tree harvesting. Coconut gardens are used for human and pig food. Traditionally, only men were allowed to fish on the outer reefs, while fishing and gathering in the lagoon and on the reef were also practised by women and children. Large repertoires of fishing techniques and strategies (~120) were formerly employed throughout the lagoon, inner reef, and outer-reef-to-offshore zones of Atafu (Mafutaga a Toeaina o Atafu i Matauala Porirua 2008). A variety of coral-reef fish, sharks, sea turtles, pelagic fish, and some invertebrates were caught by use of seines, hand nets, stone weirs, lines, spears, ropes, and lures. Gathering of molluscs, crabs, and other marine resources were also occasionally practised. The range of techniques and strategies has considerably narrowed in recent decades (Mafutaga a Toeaina o Atafu i Matauala Porirua 2008).

The major root crop cultivated on Atafu is giant swamp taro (*pulaka* or *Cyrtosperma chamissonis*), which is mainly cultivated on some of the large islets on Atafu's west and south west sides where the Ghyben-Herzberg freshwater lens is easily accessible from the surface. Villagers must travel to the islets where their gardens are located to maintain and cultivate their land and crops. Besides root crops, some fruit trees such as coconut, breadfruit, banana and pandanus are also cultivated both in the village and on other islets. Among them, coconut has also been planted for copra production. Copra was the major commercialised economic crop of Atafu for some decades, but is no longer exported.

Some pandanus-leaf crafts such as hats and bags made by women and wooden carvings produced by men are exported. An annual grant provided by the New Zealand government is used for building and running public services including roads, the hospital, the power plant, and the school. The main shop on Atafu is a cooperative run by the community, and it imports various foods and other products. These public services are administered by a council of male elders known as the *Taupulega o Atafu*. A council of women, the *Fatupaepae*, and a men's society, the *Aumaga*, are each responsible for coordinating other important economic, social, and cultural activities.

Tokelauan Fishing Lore and Fishing at Atafu

The people of Tokelau use the term faiva[2] to refer to the capture of all edible animals (Matagi Tokelau 1991). The most important of these activities is fishing (Gillett 1985). Traditionally, a great range of fishing techniques was employed in Tokelau, including various methods of angling, netting, trapping and spearing. Gillett (1985) reports that some traditional fishing methods such as casting for skipjack with pearl shell lures has been seldom practised in Tokelau since the 1980s, while some new and modern fishing methods and gear are widely employed.

Most of such fishing activities on Atafu and other Tokelau atolls are also closely related to the phases of the moon as well as the seasonal cycle (see Ono and Addison 2009). For instance, Tokelauan atolls are occasionally struck by cyclones during the November-to-March period, while rather mild south-east trade winds blow during the May-to-November period. Because outer-reef-to-offshore fishing of the inhabited side of islands is periodically difficult or impossible during the cyclone season, fishing activities are more actively pursued during May to November, and the season is regarded as the best fishing season on Atafu and other atolls in Tokelau (see also Gillett 1985; Hooper 1985; Matagi Tokelau 1991). The detailed classification and terms of the lunar cycle on Atafu and other atolls in Tokelau indicates that the lunar and tidal cycle is also important for fishing activities, and some inshore and offshore fish species are well known and recognised to have seasonality by the people in Tokelau (see Ono and Addison 2009:Table 1).

---

2   However, "Faiva" does not just refer to fishing/hunting (Tokelau Dictionary 1986).

In Tokelau, traditional fishing lore and knowledge was closely related to the "tautai" title system. This title was a status which could be achieved only by men. It can be glossed as "master fisherman" – someone who has a considerable amount of expertise in the entire spectrum of fish-catching methods and also the leadership skills and experience necessary for directing and managing fishing expeditions (e.g., Gillett 1985; Hooper 1985, 2010; Matagi Tokelau 1991). Traditionally, until achieving tautai status, a young man was not supposed to take the stern seat in a canoe, the position from which all operations were directed (Hooper 1985). After years or decades of instruction, he would be eligible for a kau kumate ceremony in which the title of tautai was conferred.[3] However, there have been no kau kumate held since the late 1970s in Tokelau (Hooper 1985).

On contemporary Atafu and other Tokelau atolls, basically three types of fishing zones are identified: offshore (*tuakau*), reef (*uluulu*) and lagoon (*namo*). Although each of these three zones is characterised by a set of distinctive fishing methods, there is considerable overlap in the types of fish that are commonly caught across the three zones. Beside these three zones, land and beach zones are also recognised as part of fishing areas on Atafu (Mafutaga a Toeaina o Atafu i Matauala Porirua 2008), particularly in relation to bait for fishing, as some important bait species such as coconut crab (*ugauga*) are caught ashore. Here, we first briefly introduce the major fishing in each fishing zone and secondly discuss the material culture of fishing and aspects of marine conservation in Tokelauan fishing.

Outer-reef-to-off-shore fishing

According to Atafu informants, offshore fishing is more important than reef or lagoon fishing, because of the relatively small size of their lagoon. In fact, the book written and published by the Atafu-born elders living in New Zealand (Mafutaga a Toeaina o Atafu i Matauala Porirua 2008) reported 47 methods of offshore fishing against 29 methods for lagoon fishing and 45 methods for reef fishing on Atafu. The number and variety in methods are largest for the offshore fishing zone. Most of the fishing activities observed during our stay on Atafu in August 2008 and on July 2009 were on the outer reef or offshore.

Casting a hook or lure for *atu* (skipjack or *Katsuwonus pelamis*) and *kakahi* (yellowfin tuna or *Thunnus albacares*) has probably been the most important single type of fishing practised traditionally on Atafu, both economically and socially (e.g., Gillett 1985; Hooper 1985; Hooper and Huntsman 1991; Huntsman 1990; Macgregor 1973; Matagi Tokelau 1991). This pattern continues today. Skipjack fishing is called *alo atu* or just *alo*. Decades ago, this involved paddling through a group of shoaling fish while casting a hook and lure. Today, aluminium boats with outboard engines are commonly used for outer-reef to offshore fishing including *alo atu,* although some Atafu fishermen maintain the tradition of using wooden outrigger canoes (albeit with outboard engines).

Skipjack and yellowfin tuna fishing is traditionally a communal, family, or fishing crew based activity involving a number of boats (see also Hooper 2008 and Hooper 2010 for the Fakaofo case in the 1970s).[4] Skipjack went to inati and yellowfin to inati or kaiga depending on what kind of fishing the Taupulega decreed, then catch from the kaiga canoe was taken to the fatupaepae who shared it to the family and to members of the crew who were not of the kaiga.

Hahave (flying fish or *Cypselurus* sp.) are usually caught at night in waters close to the shore using scoop-nets called *heu* and torch light. This fishing is called *lama hahave* (*lama* = torch) on Atafu,

---

3   The detail of the *kau kumate* ceremony are described by Hooper (1985:18-26) and other documents (e.g., Matagi Tokelau 1991:177-179).

4   Among them, skipjack was communal, highly controlled fishing, while yellowfin was usually by family fishermen and far more common in Atafu, where the bait-fish (*uli*) were used.

and traditionally coconut leaf torches were used (see also Mafutaga a Toeaina o Atafu i Matauala Porirua 2008). Catches of up to three hundred fish per night are not uncommon (Passfield 1998). *Hahave* are available throughout the year, but are most abundant July through October. During this time of year, they are consumed in greater numbers than tuna (Passfield 1998), although they are a much smaller fish, growing to a length of around 25cm, and with a weight of about 300g (Froese and Pauly 2002). Similar fishing methods with scoop-nets are also employed to catch *talagogo* (a seabird species, possibly *Sterna fuscata*) on the outer reefs during the day time.

Noosing *pala* (wahoo or *Acanthocybium solandri*) is also a well-regarded traditional fishing method in Tokelau (Matagi Tokelau 1991) and it is called *takiulu*. A small baitfish, such as a flying fish is towed behind a canoe to lure the *pala* into a prepared noose, which catches the fish by the tail. Groups of *hakula* (marlin or *Xyphias gladius*), *kakahi* (yellowfin tuna or *Thunnus albacares*), and *mago* (sharks) were also occasionally caught using this method. Among these, *hakula* is traditionally regarded as one of the sacred fish (*ika ha*) by the Atafu people and its meats are equally distributed to each household with the *inati* system. Both inshore and deep-sea (80-100 fathoms) shark fishing with large hooks and lines is another popular fishing method, particularly for elders who relish shark meat, especially the liver. Deep-sea shark fishing called *fakatu* (Mafutaga a Toeaina O Atafu I Matauala Porirua 2008: 106), is a rather new method developed in the early 20th century (Matagi Tokelau 1991:191). *Pala* and *ono* (barracuda or *Sphyraena barracuda*) are also caught using this method.

Sea turtle (*fonu*) is one of the important catches in traditional fishing among all the atolls of Tokelau (Matagi Tokelau 1991:188). Although there are different methods to catch sea turtle, the most popular method is to catch a pair of mating turtles, usually as two men swim to the turtles, each seizing a turtle (see also Macgregor 1937:99-100). There were also many traditional restrictions (*lafu*) for turtle fishing, such as a man whose wife was pregnant, who was not allowed to join a fishing party since his presence with the team would make the turtles timid and shy (Matagi Tokelau 1991:189). Turtle was regarded as one of the sacred marine resources (*ha*) by Atafu people, and meat was equally distributed to each household by the *inati* system similar to other sacred species such as skipjack tuna and marlin. The season of turtle fishing is closely related to the turtle's mating period, usually September to November on Atafu. As in most Pacific countries, today turtle fishing is officially prohibited throughout Tokelau.

Reef fishing

For reef fishing, fishing with nets (*kupega, heu, kalele*) is the most common technique practised today in Tokelau (see also Passfield 1998), while angling (*hi*) is also actively employed on Atafu (Mafutaga a Toeaina o Atafu i Matauala Porirua 2008). In the recent past, nets were made locally, using 30kg breaking-strain monofilament. Passfield (1998:10) reported that mesh size ranged from ½in. (12.7mm) to 4in. (100mm), with 2in. (50mm) being the most common size. Although most of the nets used today on Atafu are commercial products made of nylon filament, the techniques of netting are quite similar to those of the recent or traditional past; nets are usually set on the reef flat to catch fish moving in and out of the lagoon. Fishing with a net attached to a circular wooden frame which can be closed by pulling a line is called *tata*, and is commonly employed in the reef zone.

Smaller and long-handled scoop nets (*heu*) are used by groups of two or three people to catch groupers (e.g., *Epinephelus melanostigma*, *Epinephelus merra*, *Epinephelus hexagonatus*) and squirrelfish (*Myripristis* sp.) on Atafu (see also Mafutaga a Toeaina o Atafu i Matauala Porirua 2008:86-88). Large scoop nets (*kalele*) were frequently used for fishing in outer reef channels (e.g., Macgregor 1937:95), and this method is called *tatago* on Atafu. On Atafu today, large netting drives with seines (*talitali*) are also occasionally employed for communal fishing involving over 100 people (men and children but not adult women). Fish captured by such netting include high numbers of *ulahi* (*Scarus harid*), *umeihu* (*Naso unicornis*), *umelei* (*Naso lituratus*), *kanae* (*Mugil cephalus*), and *nanue* (*Kyphosus cinerascens*).[5]

Fishing with a hook (*matau/kafilo*) and line (*uka*) is occasionally practised, mainly around reef channels on Atafu today. Among 45 traditional fishing methods mainly employed in reef zones, 13 are recognised as hook-and-line fishing (Mafutaga a Toeaina o Atafu i Matauala Porirua 2008). Interestingly, most of these hook-and-line fishing methods are named and identified with targeted fish names such as *hi gatala* (*gatala* = *Epinephelus quoyanus*), *hi patuki* (*patuki* = *Cirrhitus pinnulatus* or hawkfish in general), *hi api* (*api* = *Acanthurus guttatus*), *hi mutu* (*mutu* = *Abudefduf* sp.), and *hi ulafi* (*ulafi* = *Hipposcarus longiceps* or *Scarus harid*). In recent times, lures are also used where the sea bottom is sandy (so that hooks do not get snagged).

Stone weir fish traps (*fota*) were also used as one of the traditional fishing methods on Atafu. However, the use of such stone weirs ended by the late 1970s. On Atafu, basically two types of *fota* were built and employed; the former one is called *fota tali ihe* and mainly aims at school of *Caranx* sp. The trap is a *fota* about 60 feet long with the mouth facing the land and lagoon side. The other is called *tali ihe i na fota* and is mainly aimed at schools of garfish with a trap about 60 feet long, with the mouth also facing toward land (Mafutaga a Toeaina o Atafu i Matauala Porirua 2008: 55-58). Our interviews with elder men confirm that there were at least two of each *fota* on Atafu in the late 1970s. Huntsman and Hooper (1996:24) report that traps were constructed beside the shallow passes in the reef to catch fish on their spawning runs from the lagoon to the sea. While most traps were operated communally, some were owned and operated by individual families (Matagi Tokelau 1991).

Fishing methods aimed at octopus (*feke*) and crayfish (*ula*) was also mainly employed in the reef zone. The capture method of octopus, called *fagota feke*, mainly consist of three different methods: (1) *fagota feke*, capture using a wooden stick made from specific tree called *gagie* (*Pamphis acidula*) and fishing string called *kalava* made from the outer skin of a coconut frond petiole (which attracts the octopus so it can be caught); (2) *taki feke*, fishing with an octopus lure (*pule takifeke*) made from a large cowrie shell (*pule*) and pandanus leaf (*laufala*); and (3) *toko feke*, capture using a metal rod at low tide. A canoe was occasionally used for moving around the reef to seek octopus. The capture method of crayfish called *holi ula*, in which feet and hands are used to catch crayfish during a rising tide on a moonlit night when the crayfish come out to feed (Mafutaga a Toeaina o Atafu i Matauala Porirua 2008:46). Among these, *toko feke* is the main capture method used today.

Lagoon fishing

On Atafu, lagoon fishing is not considered as productive as open-sea fishing, and is often only done when the weather prohibits going out to sea, especially during the hurricane season between November and April. A number of different species are caught with hook and line. Among 29 fishing methods mainly employed in the lagoon, 16 are recognised as hook-and-line fishing (Mafutaga a Toeaina o Atafu i Matauala Porirua 2008:23). Similar to reef fishing, most of these line fishing methods are named and identified with targeted fish names such as *hi kulapo* (*kulapo*

---

5   We had a chance to observe the large netting drive during our stay on 11 July 2009. The netting was practised as the community fishing during the *Aumaga* festival with over 100 men involved. The fishing was started around noon for about an hour to catch ~480-600kg (25 baskets each of which was ~20-25kg) of inshore fish. All the fish captured were distributed equally to each household with *inati* system, and our count of each fish species confirm that *ulahi* (305 specimens), *umelei* (240 specimens), and *umeihu* (81 specimen) are major captures and far exceed other species in number and weight.

= small-sized *Scarus harid* or *Hipposcarus longiceps*), *hi mu* (*mu* = *Monotaxis grandoculis*), *hi umu* (*umu* = *Balistoides viridescens*), *hi mutu* (*mutu* = *Abudefduf* sp.), *hi papo* (*papo* = *Cheilinus fasciatus*), and *hi kafa* (*kafa* = *Liza vaigiensis* or *Liza subviridis*).

Flying fish moving into the lagoon are also targeted by line fishing during the daytime and this method is termed as *hi havane ite ao* (*ite ao* = during daytime). Line fishing is also employed at night to catch *gatala* (*Epinephelus quoyanus*) and *talatala* (*Myripristis violaceus*). The one to catch *gatala* is termed *hi gatala i te tete*, and another one to catch *talatala* is termed *hi talatala*. Swimming fishing with goggles and line is called *fakatakoto*. Octopus meat is mainly used for the bait for this kind of fishing (Matagi Tokelau 1991:201). Sometimes a sack full of coral gravel is tipped into the lagoon to attract fish before the line is cast. This is known as *tuki akau* (Matagi Tokelau 1991:200) or *tuki toka* (Mafutaga a Toeaina o Atafu i Matauala Porirua 2008:35).

Smaller hand and scoop nets (*heu*) have been also used by groups of two or three people in lagoon fishing. The major fishing with *heu* is called *lama ihe*, which aims to catch garfish or half-beak (*ihe* = Hemiramphidae and Belonidae) inside the lagoon at night. Baskets (*faga*) made from the *gagie* tree are also used in lagoon fishing. Some net fishing such as *tata* (see the description in reef fishing) and *tali tafega*, which targets some fish species moving between reef and lagoon during low tide, are employed as lagoon fishing methods (Mafutaga a Toeaina o Atafu i Matauala Porirua 2008:41). Basket traps were also employed mainly in the lagoon on Atafu and other atolls in Tokelau. Macgregor (1937:94) reported that he did not see basket traps at Atafu during his visit in 1932, although he saw a few of one type at Fakaofo and Nukunonu. Our interviews confirm that there were some at Atafu in the recent past, though none were seen at Atafu during our stay. Such basket traps might not be commonly used in Tokelau, particularly at Atafu with the smallest sized lagoon in Tokelau.

Gathering molluscs is also part of lagoon fishing. Giant clams (*fahua* or *Tridacna maxima* and *Tridacna squamosa*) are regularly harvested from shallow parts of the lagoon, and they are levered from below the water with a knife-like instrument called a *nao*; this fishing technique is called *naonao fahua* (Mafutaga a Toeaina o Atafu i Matauala Porirua 2008:37). At present, there is some concern over the diminishing abundance of clams (e.g., Toloa et al. 1994). The introduction of underwater goggles and the recent development of commercial harvesting for the export market have both contributed to the decline in clam numbers (e.g., Gillett 1985; Passfield 1998). The *Taupulega* on Atafu has now imposed strict limits on *Tridacna* harvest.

Material culture of fishing

Gear and equipment associated with fishing have changed since prehistoric times, particularly subsequent to contact with the Western world. Historical evidence indicates that Tokelauans used lines, hooks, lures, rods, nets of various kinds, as well as traps and stone weirs before European contact (e.g., Hooper 1985; Macgregor 1937). Archaeological research on Fakaofo and Atafu by Best (1988) unearthed four one-piece pearl-shell or bone hook fragments and recovered a complete pearl-shell lure shank.

Traditionally, the hook portion of the lure was made from the shell of *fonu una* (hawksbill turtle or *Eretmochelys imbricate*), while in modern times cow horn, coconut shell, whale teeth, marlin spikes, aluminium and plastic are also occasionally used (Gillett 1985). Typologically, historic-period Tokelau lures styles, with attachment of the leader line to both the head of the pearl-shell shank and to the base of the turtle shell hook, conform to the typically West Polynesian types such as those from Samoa, Pukapuka, Tuvalu, Wallis and Polynesian outliers in Melanesia (e.g., Anell 1955; Gillett 1985; Hiroa 1932; Macgregor 1937).

The records of the United States Exploring Expedition (Hale 1846; Wilkes 1845), which visited Atafu and Fakaofo in 1841, mention the people's extreme eagerness to trade for metal fish hooks and pieces of iron for making hooks. Gillett (1985) reported that pearl-shell was also brought to Tokelau from Papua New Guinea by Tokelauan missionaries during the early 1940s. The shells were also imported from other localities including Pukapuka and Nassau in the Northern Cook Islands and finished lure shanks from Samoa (Gillett 1985). This evidence indicates the eagerness of Tokelauans for exogenous material for making fishing gear, especially pearl shell. This may suggest a motivation for extensive voyaging in prehistoric times, supporting archaeological evidence for Tokelau long-distance exchange in basalt and ceramics (Addison and Kalolo 2009; Addison et al. 2009; Best 1988; Best et al. 1992).

By the late 1960s, imported fishing equipment had almost entirely replaced items of local manufacture, except canoes. Cotton lines, which had supplanted lines made of coconut sennit or other braided fibres such as *Hibiscus tiliaceus* since the early 20th century, are now completely replaced by monofilament nylon lines (e.g., Hooper 1985). Nets used to be locally made with braided sennit or other fibers but now are also replaced by nylon. Spears are not so actively used in Tokelau, while spear-guns and goggles have been more in use since their introduction during the 1940s.[6] The use of pearl-shell lures stopped or dramatically decreased by the early 1970s (Gillett 1985; Hooper 1985, 2010), and most of the hooks have been made from metal. The traditional pole for skipjack fishing was made from the wood of *puka* (*Hernandia nymphaeifolia*), while imported bamboo has been used in recent times (Gillett 1985) as well as fibreglass fishing poles.

A variety of plant woods were used in the manufacture of fishing gear until a few decades ago. For example, to build a traditional canoe, *kanava* (*Cordia subcordata*) was used for the hull and outrigger spars, *gagie* (*Pemphis acidula*) for the attachment of spars to outrigger, and *puka* (*Pisonia grandis* or *Hernandia nymphaeifolia*) for the outrigger (Gillett 1985; Whistler 1988). Breadfruit wood has also been used for the hull on occasion (Huntsman pers. comm. 2009). All terrestrial resources are owned and controlled by *kaiga* (extended family unit in the sense that they jointly own resources and co-operate in exploiting them), which is one of the traditional social structures in Tokelau. Canoes also were unequivocally *kaiga* property in the past. Until the 1970s, each extended family had at least one canoe, and could hardly have existed as an independent unit without it (Hooper 1985). However, the number of traditional canoes has been decreasing since the 1970s, after the widespread introduction of aluminium skiffs and outboard engines.[7]

Today on Atafu, traditional canoes are a common site beside houses and around the village, though most are in disrepair and currently seldom or never used. People mainly use aluminium skiffs, although several traditional canoes are regularly maintained and used. Both skiffs and canoes are propelled by outboard engines and are regarded as the property of individuals or of married couples now, and no longer of *kaiga* (see also Hooper 1985 for the Fakaofo case). This may be an example of the rapid replacement of traditional gear and materials for fishing by the introduced modern ones since the middle-to-late 20th century, weakening the tight connections that formerly existed between material culture, the social system, and the island ecosystem.

---

6   Gillett (1985) suspects the introduction of diving goggles to Fakaofo in the 1940s was a major factor contributing to the virtual absence of pearl-shell in the lagoon by the 1950s.

7   For example, Hooper reported that about 60 canoes were in serviceable condition at Fakaofo in 1971, while their number had decreased to only 8 in 1981 (Hooper 1982:31).

Marine conservation measures

A number of measures are in place in contemporary Tokelau societies that act to limit the exploitation of certain taxa (McAlister 2002:34). One of the most important conservation measures is the periodic imposing of a *lafu*, or use-restrictions, on specific areas of the reef by the *Taupulega* (Toloa et al. 1994). In addition to protecting fisheries that are periodically depressed because of human exploitation and seasonal changes, a *lafu* is sometimes declared to ensure that fish stocks are built up in anticipation of future needs for specific events, such as important festivals (Toloa et al. 1994). On contemporary Atafu, for example, most of the reef fronting the islet where the village is located is restricted from private fishing, and only communal fishing (*faiva fakamua*) is allowed at certain times of the year as described by Toloa and colleagues (Toloa et al. 1984).

The distinctive *inati* system of distribution practised in the atolls is another aspect of Tokelau fishing strongly related to marine conservation. All resident members of the village are assigned to an *inati* group, often on the basis of kin relationships, but sometimes for a variety of other reasons (Passfield 1998). In this system, certain types of fish are considered as *ha* (sacred), meaning that they must be shared among the village when they are caught. As described above, these sacred fish (*ika ha*) were traditionally *fonu* (sea turtle), *hakula* (billfish/marlin), and *atu* (skipjack tuna), and they were divided among the whole population through the *inati* system on Atafu and the rest of Tokelau (see Hooper 1985). Even today, *fonu* and *hakula* are still regarded as *ika ha*, while *atu* is usually not, except in cases when there is an especially large catch. In effect, the *inati* system deters the exploitation of these taxa by reducing individual incentives for capturing certain animals. Other species mainly of reef fish are also distributed through the *inati*, particularly at the time of communal fishing.

Reconstructed Prehistoric Fish Use on Atafu

Archaeological background

On Atafu, prehistoric remains are concentrated on a single motu where the village is currently located. The atoll was archaeologically excavated by Simon Best (1988) in 1986. He excavated 14 test units (nine 2 x 2m² and five 2 x 1m²) on the village islet. Eleven of them ran the length of the contemporary village and were situated about 50 metres apart and about 40 metres from the lagoon shore (Best 1988:106). His excavations confirmed that each test unit had different character and stratigraphy, with some units possibly part of a burial area (e.g., Unit 5), whereas some units were possibly part of habitation areas with significant amounts of faunal remains, mainly fish and bird bones (e.g., Unit 9). The deepest deposits, with several stratigraphic layers down to over 2 metres, were only found around the middle part of the islet (Units 10 and 11) in his excavation. Some ¹⁴C dates were also acquired; the oldest date from the charcoal at the lower layer of his Unit 5 is 1000 +/- 100 BP (Best 1988: 115; see Petchey et al. 2010 for a review of Tokelau's radiocarbon chronology). Although the number and variety of excavated artefacts were not larger than those from Fakaofo, Best excavated some pieces of potsherds, stone and shell adzes, shell-made fish hooks, and faunal remains on Atafu. For the faunal remains, pig, dog, rat, turtle, bird, fish and shell remains were excavated, while pig remains were found only from upper layers possibly dated back after the European contacts (Best 1988:116).

Based on his previous excavations in the 1980s, we opened eight 1 x 1 metre test units (TU 1, 2, 3, 4, 6, 7, and 8) on Atafu during 2008 and 2009. All the ¹⁴C dates obtained by the previous study (Best 1988) and our recent excavations are shown in Figure 3.

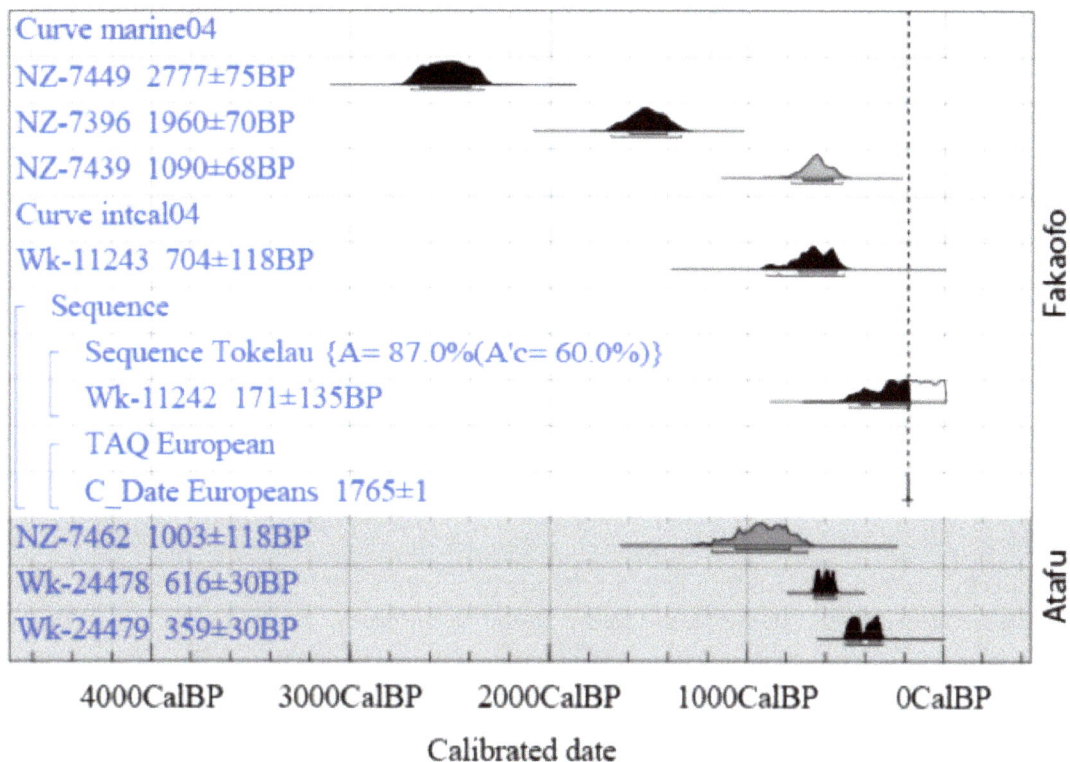

Figure 3. All the ¹⁴C dates obtained on Atafu.

* 2009 calibrated radiocarbon ages for Tokelau. Black probability distributions = identified charcoal and shell/coral determinations. Dark grey = unidentified charcoal and turtle bone determinations.

Source: After Petchey et al. 2010.

Methodology of fish bone analysis

The water sieving with 3, 5 and 7mm mesh was employed at all units to compare the different recovery method of sieving by different mesh size. After the excavation, all the fish remains together with other faunal remains and artefacts were borrowed under the permit by Tokelauan government, and brought to The Australian National University for further analysis. In this stage, however, we only selected the fish remains sieved by 1/2 and 1/4 inch screen for the identification as there were too many small and tiny bones recovered by 1/8 inch screen.

The methods of fishbone analysis here closely followed the technique developed by Ono and others for the treatment of tropical fish remains from Island Southeast Asia (e.g., Campos 2009; Ono 2003, 2004), Oceania (e.g., Intoh and Ono 2006; Leach 1986; Leach and Davidson 1977; Ono and Intoh 2011; Vogel 2005) and Okinawa (e.g., Toizumi 2007). Cranial elements, special elements, vertebrae and teeth were used for identification. The cranial elements used here include maxilla, premaxilla, dentary, articulate, quadrate, pharyngeal clusters,[8] opercular,[9] preopercular, hyomandibular, palatine,[10] cleithrum,[11] supra-cleithrum, post-temporal, scapula,[12] ephiyal, and ceratohyal; special elements included the erectile spines of Balistidae (triggerfish) and Acanthuridae

---

8 Pharyngeal clusters were used for identification of Scaridae, Labridae, and Lutjanidae for this study.

9 Opercular can be used for identification of Mugillidae.

10 Palatine was used of identification of Serranidae and *Lethrinus* sp. for this study.

11 Cleithrum was used for identification of Siganidae for this study.

12 Scapula can be used for identification of Scaridae and Scombridae, though we could not find any of these on Atafu so far.

(unicornfish), scale of Ostrachiidae (boxfish), spines of Diodontidae (porcupinefish), scute of Carangidae (trevelley) and Acanthuridae (unicornfish), and caudal peduncle of Scombridae (tuna). Teeth were also used only for identification of sharks, triggerfish, and one species in Lethrinidae (*Monotaxis granoculis* or sea breams).

Vertebra were also used for the identification for Elasmobranchii, mainly sharks and some bony fish families such as Scombridae, Carangidae, Belonidae, Muraenidae, Siganidae, Balistidae, and Scaridae as the vertebra belonging to these families are diagnostic in their shapes and relatively easy to identify. Thoracic and caudal vertebrae (caudal peduncle) were mainly used. It is also the fact that many of pelagic fishes such as Scombridae are usually much easier to identify by use of vertebrae rather than cranial elements which are much more fragile than those of other bony fishes (see Davidson et al. 1999; Leach et al. 1997; Ono and Intoh 2011).

For the purpose of the analysis, an assemblage was divided as the contents of any single excavation unit. Thus, all bones from one excavation unit and one excavation level were designated as an assemblage. Following the method of Leach (1986), each assemblage was sorted into identifiable and not identifiable piles, and all materials were re-bagged, then identifiable fragments were sorted anatomically and re-bagged again. Taking each part of the anatomy in turn, bones were sorted into species, genera, and families, and identified with reference to the comparative collections. The Minimum Number of Individuals (MNI) and Number of Identified Specimens (NISP) were calculated with the technique of Chaplin (1971), although size mismatches were also taken into account (e.g., Intoh and Ono 2006; Ono 2002, 2004, 2005; Ono and Intoh 2011). The exception is shark vertebrae which have a wide size range in a specimen, thus, the MNI of each shark group is always counted as "1" even if there are more numbers and size varieties in the excavated assemblage.

Results

A total of 8,160 fish bones were counted from the seven of 1 x 1 m² units (TU 1, 2, 3, 4, 6, 7 and 8) in 2008 and 2009. The total number of bones should be increased when other much smaller bones sieved by 1/8 inch screen are added by further study. The distribution of identified anatomical elements (29 components) in all the excavated sites was indicated in Table 1. Among these elements, vertebrae exhibited the largest numbers. Beside vertebrae, the major anatomical elements of cranial part are (1) premaxilla, (2) dentary (3) maxilla (4) pharyngeal (upper cluster), (5) pharyngeal (lower cluster), (6) articular, and (7) quadrate. The total number of identified fish remains in family levels counted up to 608 (MNI) and 1,655 (NISP) in total.

Table 1. Number of Identified Elements from Atafu Excavation in 2008 and 2009.

ANATOMY	LEFT	RIGHT	TOTAL		TOTAL
Dentary	85	92	177	Vomor	22
Premaxilla	81	75	156	Tooth(c)	19
Quadrate	60	65	125	Posttemporal	17
Articulaer	59	58	117	Ceratohyal	14
Maxilla	44	52	96	Tooth(b)	12
Cleithrum	39	35	74	Postopercle	11
Preopercle	30	37	67	Palatine	9
Erectile Spines(A)			95	Scapula	9
Scute (Carangids)			75	Spine(Diodontidae)	4
Erectile Spines(B)			67	Scute(A)	2
Caudal Peduncle			67	Ulophyal	2
Pharyngeal (U)			62	Epihyal	9
Hyomandibular			57	Pharyngeal	9
Pharyngeal (L)			57	skull?	48
Supracleithrum			39	Others	163
Opercle			34	Fragments	3001
Vertebrae (b)	1752			Total	8,160
Vertebrae (c)	106				
Scale	1132				
Spines	541				

Source: Table by the authors.

Twenty-six taxa were identified including 22 families and 1 species (*Monotaxis granoculis*). As shown in Table 2, the MNIs of Scarids (parrotfish) is the highest as they occupied around 15 to 20% in total MNI in each unit. In some units, the MNI of Scombrids (tunas) exceed that of Scarids and can be recognised as the second major fish species on Atafu. Acanthurids, Serranids and Balistids are also major fish taxa in most units. The relatively high abundance of Holocentirds is another trend in the prehistoric fish use on Atafu. In general, relative abundance of inshore or reef species and outer-reef to pelagic species are equally exploited in most of units. In terms of outer-reef to pelagic species, the shark bones were classified into four taxa including at least 2 families as Carcharhinids and Lamnids based on morphology of its vertebrae. For other fish species, Scombrids, Carangids (trevally or scads) and Sphyraenids (barracudas) are identified. In some units, such as TU 1 and TU 2, the MNI numbers of Scombrids exceed that of Scarids, and occupy the first rank fish exploited in these units.

Similarly, in terms of NISP count, the numbers of Scombrids and Carangids dramatically increase (see Table 3). This may be caused by the larger number of excavated vertebra indentified into these species, and we should stress again that tunas were mainly identified by use of vertebrae and caudal peduncles since the number of these elements was very large, while the number of cranial bones for this family was very limited and far smaller than that of other bony fish species (e.g., Serranidae, Lutjanidae, and Lethrinidae). On the other hand, the total number of vertebrae identified to other bony fish taxa was very small, except Scarids as shown in Table 4, and these taxa were mainly identified by their cranial bones (e.g. premaxilla, maxilla, quadrate, and dentary).

Table 2. Identified fish remains from each unit* (MNI).

TU	1		2		3		4		6		7		8		Total	
Bony fish	MNI	%	MNI	%	MNI	%	MNI	%	MNI	%	MNI	%	MNI	%	MNI	%
Scaridae	16	18.6	7	20.5	7	19.4	9	19.4	16	21	19	15.9	32	15.3	106	17.4
Scombridae	20	23.2	12	35.2	3	8.3	7	14.8	12	15	9	7.5	11	5.2	74	12.1
Serranidae	9	10.4	2	5.8	4	11.1	4	8.5	9	12	13	10.9	26	12.5	67	11
Carangidae	3	3.4	0		0		3	6.3	2	2.5	11	9.2	8	3.8	27	4.4
Acanthuridae	9	10.4	2	5.8	5	13.8	1	2.1	6	7.6	16	13.4	58	27.8	97	15.9
Balistidae	6	6.9	1	2.9	1	2.7	10	21.2	15	19	20	16.8	16	7.6	69	11.3
Holocentridae	4	4.6	0		2	5.5	3	6.3	4	5.1	11	9.2	19	9.1	43	7
Myipeistis sp.			0								6		12			
Sargocentron sp.			0								5		7			
Labridae	1	1.1	0		1	2.7	1	2.1	6	7.6	5	4.2	12	5.7	26	4.2
Siganidae	1	1.1	1	2.9	0		0		1	1.2	0		3	1.4	6	0.9
Lutjanidae	1	1.1	0		1	2.7	1	2.1	1	1.2	1	0.8	5	2.4	10	1.6
Sphyraenidae	1	1.1	0		0		2	4.2	0		0		1	0.4	4	0.6
Belonidae	2	2.2	2	5.8	1	2.7	0		0		0		0		5	0.8
Lethrinidae	1	1.1	0		1	2.7	2	4.2	0		6	5	2	0.8	12	1.9
Monotaxis sp.	1		0		1		2		0		2		0		6	
Lethrinus sp.	0		0		0		0		0		4		2		6	
Diodontidae	0		2	5.8	0		0		0		0		1	0.4	3	0.4
Muraenidae	0		0		1	2.7	1	2.1	0		0		1	0.4	3	0.4
Mullidae	0		0		0		0		0		0		2	0.8	2	0.3
Osteridae	0		0		0		0		0		0		1	0.4	1	0.16
Coryphaenidae	0		0		0		0		0		1	0.8	0		1	0.16
Mugilidae	0		0		1	2.7	0		0		0		0		1	0.16
Tetradontiae	0		0		1	2.7	0		0		0		0		1	0.16
sub-total	75		29		30		46		72		129		219		600	92.2
Erasmobranchii	MNI	%	MNI	%	MNI	%	MNI	%	MNI	%	MNI	%	MNI	%	MNI	%
TypeA	4	4.6	2	5.8	4	11.1	1	2.1	4	5.1	3	2.5	5	2.4	23	4.7
TypeB	5	5.8	1	2.9	1	2.7	1	2.1	1	1.2	3	2.5	5	2.4	17	2.7
TypeC	1	1.1	2	5.8	2	5.5	1	2.1	1	1.2	0		0		7	1.1
TypeD	0		0		0		0		0		1	0.8	0		1	0.16
sub-total	10	11.6	5	14.7	7	19.4	3	6.3	6	7.6	7	5.8	10	4.8	48	7.8
Total	86		34		36		47		78		119		208		608	

Source: Table by the authors.

Table 3. Identified fish remains from each unit* (NISP).

TU	1		2		3		4		6		7		8		Total	
Bony fish	NISP	%	NISP	%	NISP	%	NISP	%	NISP	%	NISP	%	NISP	%	NISP	%
Scaridae	32	20.1	19	18.8	7	19.4	25	30.8	30	27	127	38.1	277	33.2	704	42.5
Scombridae	53	33.3	64	63.3	3	8.3	16	19.7	21	18.9	51	15.3	120	14.3	501	30.2
Serranidae	12	7.5	3	2.9	4	11.1	5	6.1	15	13.5	36	10.8	110	13.1	185	11.1
Carangidae	3	1.8	0		0		5	6.1	3	2.7	26	7.8	66	7.9	103	6.2
Acanthuridae	9	5.6	2	1.9	5	13.8	1	1.2	6	5.4	16	4.8	59	7	98	5.9
Balistidae	6	3.6	1	0.9	1	2.7	10	12.3	15	13.5	22	6.6	28	3.3	83	5
Holocentridae (M)	6	3.6	0		2	5.5	4	4.9	4	3.6	11	3.3	36	4.3	63	3.8
Holocentridae (S)	0		0						0		9	2.7	27	3.2	36	2.1
Labridae	1	0.6	0		1	2.7	2	2.4	9	8.1	13	3.9	29	3.4	55	3.3
Siganidae	1		1		0		0		1		0		23	2.7	26	1.5
Lutjanidae	1		0		1		1		1		2		12	1.4	18	1
Sphyraenidae	5	3.1	0		0		3	3.7	0		0		5	0.5	13	0.7
Belonidae	8	5	2		1		0		0		0		0		11	0.6
Monotaxis	1		0		1		2		0		2		2		8	0.48
Lethrinus	0		0		0		0		0		4		2		6	0.36
Diodontidae	0		2		0		0		0		0		1		3	0.18
Muraenidae	0		0		1		1		0		0		1		3	0.18
Mullidae	0		0		0		0		0		0		2		2	0.12
Osteridae	0		0		0		0		0		0		1		1	0.06
Coryphaenidae	0		0		0		0		0		1		0		1	0.06
Mugilidae	0		0		1		0		0		0		0		1	0.06
Tetradontiae	0		0		1		0		0		0		0		1	0.06
sub-total	138		94		29		75		105		320		801		1562	94.4
Erasmobranchii	NISP	%	NISP	%	NISP	%	NISP	%	NISP	%	NISP	%	NISP	%	NISP	%
TypeA	9	5.6	4	3.9	4	11.1	3	3.7	4	3.6	3	0.9	20	2.3	47	2.8
TypeB	10	6.2	1	0.9	1	2.7	1	1.2	1	0.9	9	2.7	13	1.5	36	2.1
TypeC	2	1.2	2	1.8	2	5.5	2	2.4	1	0.9	0		0		9	0.5
TypeD	0		0		0		0		0		1	0.3	0		1	0.06
sub-total	21	13.2	7	6.9	7	19.4	6	7.4	6	5.4	13	3.9	33	3.9	93	5.6
Total	159		101		36		81		111		333		834		1655	

Source: Table by the authors.

Table 4. Number of vertebra identified into taxa.

TAXA/UNIT	TU8	TU7	TU6	TU4	TU3	TU2	TU1	TOTAL
Scombridae	113	46	20	16	3	60	45	303
Scaridae	113	36	7	6	1	4	4	171
Sharks	38	21	9	5	4	7	22	106
Siganidae	17	0	0	0	0	1	3	21
Carangidae	5	1	0	6	0	0	5	17
Belonidae	0	0	0	0	1	0	9	10
Sphyraenidae	1	0	0	2	0	0	0	3
Muraenidae	1	0	0	0	1	0	0	2
Serranidae	0	1	0	0	0	0	0	1
Balistidae	1	0	0	0	0	0	0	1

Source: Table by the authors.

Concerning the spatial distribution of fish remains on the islet, TU 1 to 6 were located in the northern part of the village and produced about 100 NISP of the total identified fish bones in each unit, while TU 7 and 8 were located in the southern part of the village and produced 300 to 800 NISP of the total identified fish bones (see Table 3). The result tentatively indicates that the intensive use and discard of fish (bones) was done around TU 7 and 8. As described above, TU

4 and 6 produced some human remains including skulls and they were possibly part of a mainly burial area on the islet, while no human remains except teeth were found in TU 1, 2, 3, 7 and 8 and thus these units might be part of a mainly habitation area.

In relation to each fish taxa and excavation unit, a high abundance of Scombrids (about 14-35% of the total MNI) is confirmed in TU 1, 2, 4, and 6, while the relative abundance of Scombrids is lower in TU 3, 7, and 8. Similarly, the relative abundance of Balistids and Acanthurids also show differences between each unit. The relative abundance of Balistids is higher in TU 4, 6, and 7 (16-21%), while lower in TU 1, 2, and 8 (2.9-7.9%). On the other hand, the relative abundance of Acanthurids is higher in TU 1, 3, 7 (10-13%), and particularly in TU 8 (27.8%). It is yet uncertain why so many Acanthurid bones (n=58) were concentrated at TU 8 while TU 7, which is located next to TU 8, did not produce as many (n=16). Other major fish taxa such as Scarids and Serranids are generally high in all units, except Serranids in TU 2 whose relative abundance is a bit lower (5.8%).

In terms of temporal change in fish use, we only have ^{14}C dates from TU 1 and 7 (see 3.3). These ^{14}C dates indicate the lower layer of TU 1 dated to ~600 cal BP, while TU 7 and possibly TU 8 might have been formed at ~200 cal BP. As shown in Table 5, a higher abundance of inshore fish species is the trend in TU 7 and 8 while TU 1, which currently has the oldest date from a reliable context on Atafu, contains a higher abundance of pelagic species such as Scombrids (Table 5). If this result is not an effect of differential spatial patterns in site use, there is a possibility that more intensive inshore use was practised during the later times on Atafu. On the other hand, the relative abundance of Scombrids and Scarids are both high in the lower layers at TU 1, and their abundances are continually high in the middle-to-upper layers (see Table 5). Although no ^{14}C dates were processed from the middle-to-upper layers and hence we do not know the exact dates of these layers, the results of the fish assemblage in TU 1 tentatively indicates that Scombrids and Scarids were the most important fish family in Atafu's prehistory, dating back ~600 cal BP.

Table 5. Identified fish taxa in spit level at TU1.

TAXA/SPIT	1	2	3	4	5	6	7	8	9	10	11	12	13	TOTAL
Scombridae	3	0	1	2	1	1	0	4	1	0	3	2	2	20
Scaridae	1	2	0	1	1	1	0	2	1	2	2	1	2	16
Serranidae	0	1	2	0	0	1	0	1	0	1	2	0	1	9
Acanthuridae	4	0	0	0	0	2	0	1	1	0	0	0	1	9
Balistidae	1	1	0	0	0	0	0	0	0	2	1	0	1	6
Holocentridae	1	2	0	0	0	0	0	0	0	0	0	0	1	4
Carangidae	0	2	0	0	0	0	0	1	0	0	0	0	0	3
Lethrinidae	0	0	0	0	0	0	0	1	0	0	0	1	0	2
Belonidae			1	0		0		0		1	0	0	0	2
Lutjanidae	0	0	0	1	0	0	0	0	0	0	0	0	0	1
Labridae	0	0	0	0	0	0	0	0	0	1	0	0	0	1
Spyraenidae			1		0		0		0	0	0	0	1
Monotaxis sp.	0	0	0	0	0	0	0	0	0	0	0	0	1	1
Siganidae	0	1	0	0	0	0	0	0	0	0	0	0	0	1
sub-total	10	9	4	5	2	5	0	10	3	7	8	4	9	76
SharkA	0	1	0	0	0	0	0	1	1	0	0	0	1	4
SharkB	1	1	0	0	0	1	0	0	0	1	0	0	1	5
SharkC	0	0	0	1	0	0	0	0	0	0	0	0	0	1
sub-total	1	2	0	1	0	1	0	1	1	1	0	0	2	10
Total	11	11	4	6	2	6	0	11	4	8	8	4	11	86

Source: Table by the authors.

Discussion and Conclusion

The amount of fish remains excavated from Atafu clearly indicate that marine fish, both inside and outside of the lagoon, was one of the most important subsistence activities since the early settlement period, which may date to ~600 cal BP. Since no archaeological data of prehistoric fishing or fish use on Atafu were provided by previous studies, these data are the only light currently shed on prehistoric fish use on Atafu.

Our current analysis of Atafu fish remains clearly indicates that various marine fish taxa, both inshore and offshore species, were exploited in the past on Atafu. Particularly, the number and relative abundance (MNI) of Scombrids and Scarids were highest among these taxa. The abundance of Scombrid bones in our recent excavations on Atafu shows a clear contrast with the results of the past studies on Fakaofo by Best (1988) and McAlister (2002), which could identify only a few Scombrid bones. Neglect of vertebra for the identification seems to be the possible major factor for such difference between our result and those of past studies, and thus we strongly recommend using more elements, including vertebra for fish identification in future studies. For instance, vertebra are also useful to identify Elasmobranchii, Carangids, Muraenids, Belonids, Siganids, and Scarids (see also Ono and Intoh 2011), while palatine is useful to identify Serranids and *Lethnrinus* sp. Thus, using more elements for fish bone identification may increase the variety of fish taxa and relative abundance of each taxon at each site.

On the other hand, the high number and relative abundance of Scombrids among some units, particularly TU 1 which dated back to ~600 cal BP, tentatively indicates that offshore fish species were important marine resources since the earliest currently known human presence on Atafu. The high number and relative abundance of Carangids, Serranids, Holocentrids, and sharks also indicate such a possibility. Although these fish taxa are also captured within inshore and lagoon zones, our ethno-ecological study of contemporary fishing by Atafu people (Ono and Addison 2009) and other research on Tokelau fishing (Gillett 1985; Hooper 1985, 2008, 2010; Mafutaga-a-Toeania-o-Atafu-i-Matauala-Porirua 2008) show that these taxa are usually captured in the outer-reef to pelagic zones by angling or lure fishing.

Our ethno-ecological study also reveals that there are more variations in names and fishing methods for larger pelagic fish species such as Scombrids and Caranginds (Ono and Addison 2009), and thus we suggest that a high dependence on offshore marine resources has been one of the prominent characteristics of Atafu fishing from the early human colonisation to the present.

The limited amount of molluscan remains in our excavations and the limited number of mollusc names on contemporary Atafu (Ono and Addison 2009:16) indicate the relative scarcity of shellfish resources on Atafu with its small-sized lagoon and limited reef area around the atoll. These biogeographical constraints of Atafu might be a major factor in the apparent long-term high dependence of its human population on offshore resources. Although the detailed analysis of the molluscsan remains excavated by our research is still in progress, initial examination suggests that most of them are occupied by species of the genera *Tridacna* and *Turbo*.

As for inshore fish exploitation, however, our archaeological analysis of fish remains reveals that a variety of inshore fish species have also been exploited since the ancient past. Particularly, MNI and relative abundance of Scarids, Acanthurids, and Balistids were the highest among the inshore fish identified. Our ethno-ecological study of fish names on Atafu also confirms the relative higher variety of individual names in these fish family. For instance, Scarids (*ufu*) have 20 different individual fish names, while Acanthurids (*ume*) have 14 names and Balistids (*humu*) have 7 names (Ono and Addison 2009:21-22).

Other ethno-archaeological or ethno-ecological studies on contemporary fishing in the Pacific and Southeast Asia (e.g., Kirch and Dye 1979; Masse 1989; Ono 2007, 2009, 2010; Ono and Addison 2009; Rolett 1989; Wright and Richard 1985) as well as Butler's (1994) zoo-archaeological study focusing on fish feeding behaviour and fish capture, clearly indicate that the most suitable method to capture slow swimming herbivorous fish with a small mouth such as Scarids, Acanthurids and Balstids is netting and spearing, while the method to capture fast swimming or bottom dwelling carnivorous fish with a large mouth such as those belonging to Serranids, Lutjanids, Labrids, Scombrids, Holocentrids and sharks is angling. Trolling-lure fishing is another major method to capture fast-swimming pelagic fish such as Scombrids and Sphyraenids. Some fish families such as Lethrinids and Carangids are mainly captured by both netting and angling, while some certain species such as *Monotaxis* sp. (sea bream) or larger species are more frequently caught by angling.

When we apply such ethno-ecological or ethno-archaeological fishing data for archaeological reconstruction based on the excavated fish species, the reconstructed possible major fishing methods during the early colonisation time on Atafu were both netting and angling, with the possible use of spearing and other methods. The high relative abundance (%MNI) of Scombrids also indicates the possible use of trolling in the pelagic zone from this early period. Although the associated dates are unclear, the previous excavations by Best found numbers of fish hooks and lures including a complete pearl-shell lure (Best 1988:110; McAlister 2002:48). Such archaeological evidence also indicates intensive use of angling and trolling in prehistoric Tokelau, including Atafu. On the other hand, the relatively large number of Holocentrids among the excavation units on Atafu indicates the possible use of small-sized fish hooks and lures to capture these smaller-sized fish species. In fact, the previous excavations by Best found five pieces of worked shell that resembled the small lures used today in Tokelau for catching Holocentrids (McAlister 2002:48).

All the evidence we have discussed here tentatively indicates that the prehistoric populations on Atafu, unsurprisingly, arrived with developed fishing techniques, particularly for outer-reef to pelagic zone fishing such as angling and trolling. The existence of a number of shark and sea turtle bones from the lower excavation layers also indicates that the people have continually captured these larger-sized offshore marine species as well. It should be noted, however, that the people also targeted inshore species inhabiting the lagoon to fringing reef zones and such trends of fish use in the past seem very similar to what Atafu's fishers practice today.

Based on current information, the only exceptions we note are the exploitation of flying fish and marlins, whose bones are not yet identified from the fish bone assemblages we analysed, although both taxa are highly important in traditional and contemporary fishing in Tokelau, including Atafu (e.g., Mafutaga-a-Toeania-o-Atafu-i-Matauala-Porirua 2008; Matagi Tokelau 1991). Regarding flying fish exploitation, however, there is a possibility to find and identify them when we analyse all the small fish bones sieved by 1/8 inch screen, as most flying fish bones are relatively smaller and hard to find when sieving by 1/2 or 1/4 inch screens. On the other hand, marlin bones are usually much larger, though this fish species might be rarely captured; we did not observe Atafu fishers capture this species during our stays. Also, marlins are regarded as one of the sacred fish and its meat should be equally distributed to all the households on the island, even today. If marlin species were rarely captured in the past as well, it will be harder to find their bones in small-sized test units and larger areal excavations will be required to find them in future research.

In terms of tradiational marine-conservation measures on Atafu, we should mention again the *inati* system of distribution, which is currently practised on all atolls in Tokelau. As described above, all resident members of the village are assigned to an *inati* group and certain types of marine food, including sea turtles, schools of skipjack tunas and marlins are considered as *ika ha* (sacred fish) to be shared among the village when they are caught. Although we do not know when such a system of distribution was started in Tokelau, it might be a long-time tradition (at least over a few hundred years) since all the atolls maintain the same system and it is well-known ethnographically.

It should also be noted that the *ika ha* that are always shared by the whole community are all offshore species. A possible reason for this might be because these species could be captured only rarely or seasonally, such as sea turtles which can only be captured during October to March. The recent drop of skipjack tunas from the *ika ha* category also supports this possibility, because modern fishing gear and boats have made skipjack tunas relatively easier to capture. However, it is also quite obvious that skipjack tunas were culturally and socially a very significant fish species (see Hooper 1985, 1991, 2008, 2010; Hooper and Huntsman 1991). Our analysis of the excavated fish bones also confirms that Scombrids, including skipjack tunas, were one of the major and important protein sources in prehistoric times. Such cultural and social significance can be another major reason why these species have been regarded as *ika ha*.

On the other hand, it is also true that the *inati* system does not directly work on marine conservation since there is no control of the amount and number of capture. It is possibly because all the fish or animals regarded as *ika ha* are offshore species, and thus it is not necessary to control their capture since their capture is naturally controlled by luck or seasonal effects, etc. In considering marine conservation measures in small island ecosystem such as on atolls, measures to control inshore fish capture become more important.

In this regard, Atafu and other atolls in Tokelau have the *lafu* system, which is the periodic imposing of use-restrictions on specific areas of the reef by the *taupulega*, or the island ruling council (Toloa et al. 1994). As described above, most of the reef fronting the village on Atafu is restricted from private fishing, and only communal fishing (*faiva fakamua*) is allowed at certain times of the year. It is also important that all the catch (mainly inshore fish species) by such communal fishing is shared and distributed by the *inati* system. In this way, the *inati* and *lafu* system are connected together as the major marine conservation measure in Tokelau, especially in regard to limited resources, such as inshore fish on Tokelau. Although, as in the case of the *inati* system, we do not know when the *lafu* system was started in Tokelau, our preliminary reconstruction of a well-balanced exploitation of both inshore and offshore fish species in Atafu's past tentatively indicates that marine conservation measures have played an important part in marine resource exploitation since prehistoric times.

Lastly, concerning mesh-size effects on the recovery of fish bones, Butler (1994:85) noted relative fish family abundance was similar across screen mesh fractions (3mm, 5mm, and 7mm in her case) based on material excavated from Manus in the Bismarck Archipelago, and indicates that mesh size did not skew the recovery of remains of fish taxa of particular sizes in the assemblages were considered. However, it is generally accepted that mesh size does affect results of faunal analysis (Thomas 1969), particularly for fish bone analysis (e.g., Casteel 1972; Nagaoka 2005; Wheeler and Jones 1989). An initial examination of our Atafu material collected by 1/8 inch size mesh suggests that the total number of fish bones, particularly of smaller-bodied species, will be dramatically increased when we finish their analysis.

Although our analysis of fish remains sieved by 1/8 inch size mesh is under progress, we would like to stress the importance of employing fine mesh (with 1/8 inch at minimum) screening (see also Ono 2010; Ono and Clark 2010; Reitz et al. 2009:17) as well as increasing the variety of elements analysed in order to recover and identify as many faunal remains (particularly fish bones) as possible. Once this type of analysis is conducted on fish bone assemblages, we should be able to reconstruct the past changes of fish exploitation and fishing strategies in greater detail.

Our study in Tokelau has just started, and it is now required to extend our ethno-ecological and archaeological investigations not only on Atafu but also on the other atolls of Tokelau including Nukunonu and Fakaofo so that we can compare characteristics and trends in past and present marine resource use, fishing lore, material culture and the social aspects related to marine use. Once this is done, we can begin to infer how each different atoll environment affected fish and marine use on each atoll and also to consider future use and conservation measures on marine resources in Tokelau and also other islands in Indo-Pacific region.

Acknowledgements

We wish to express our appreciation to the people of Atafu, particularly for their warm friendship and support of our research and hospitality during our stays on their atoll. Although it is impossible to name each individually here, we wish to thank all of our friends in Atafu. This work would not have been possible without the active support the Atafu Taupulega, the Fatupaepae, and the Aumaga, which were each helpful, engaged, and profoundly interested in helping to understand their atoll's past. All the government offices on Atafu extended the hospitality and assistance to us, especially. The crew of the MV Tokelau has always been generous, kind, and accommodating. Staff at the Tokelau Office in Apia have also been of great help and assistance on many occasions. We also have special thanks to David & Gail Funk, and Ann & Barry Lange for their kind help and volunteering to take us to Atafu with their sail boats. Without their help and kindness, we could not have conducted our 2008 season research in Atafu. The 2008 research was carried out as a part of the "Tokelau Science Project" funded in part by the University of South Pacific and Tokelau government. The Tokelau Science project is truly a collaboration between Tokelau communities and outside people. We offer this paper as a small and humble contribution to this collaboration. All mistakes and faults in fact and interpretation remain ours.

References

Addison D.J. and T.S. Asaua. 2006. 100 new dates from Tutuila and Manu'a: Additional data addressing chronological issues in Samoan prehistory. *Journal of Samoan Studies* 2:95–117.

Addison D.J. and J. Kalolo. 2009. *Tokelau Science Education and Research Program: Atafu fieldwork August 2008*. Pago Pago and Atafu: Samoan Studies Institute and Tokelau Department of Education.

Addison D.J., B. Bass, C.C. Christensen, J. Kalolo, S.P. Lundblad, P.R. Mills, F. Petchey, and A. Thompson. 2009. Archaeology of Atafu, Tokelau: Some initial results from 2008. *Rapa Nui Journal* 23(1):5–9.

Best, S.B. 1988. Tokelau archaeology: A preliminary report of an initial survey and excavations. *Bulletin of the Indo-Pacific Prehistory Association* 8:104–18.

Best, S.B., P.J. Sheppard, R.C. Green, and R.J. Parker. 1992. Necromancing the stone: Archaeologists and adzes in Samoa. *Journal of the Polynesian Society* 101(1):45–85.

Buck, P. (Te Rangi Hiroa). 1930. *Samoan material culture*. Honolulu: Bishop Museum Press. *Bernice P. Bishop MuseumBulletin* 75.

Burrows, E.G. 1939. *Western Polynesia: A study in cultural differentiation*. Gothenburg: Ethnological Studies 7.

Burrows, E.G. 1940. Culture-areas in Polynesia. *Journal of the Polynesian Society* 49(195):349–66.

Butler, V.L. 1994. Fish feeding behaviour and fish capture: The case for variation in Lapita fishing strategies. *Archaeology in Oceania* 29:81–89.

Campos, F.Z. 2009. The *Ichthyoarchaeology of Batanes Islands, Northern Philippines*. Unpublished master's thesis, Department of Archaeology, University of Philippines.

Casteel, R.W. 1972. Some biases in the recovery of archaeological faunal remains. *Proceedings of the Prehistoric Society* 36:382-388.

Chaplin, R.E. 1971. *The Study of Animal Bones from Archaeological Sites*. London: Seminer Press.

Davidson, J.M., K. Fraser, B.F. Leach, and Y.H. Sinoto. 1999. Prehistoric fishing at Hane, Ua Huka, Marquesas Islands, French Polynesia. *New Zealand Journal of Archaeology* 21:5-28.

Froese, R. and Pauly D. (eds). 2009. Fish-Base. World Wide Web electronic publication, available at http://www.fishbase.org/

Gillett, R.D. 1985. *Traditional tuna fishing in Tokelau*. Noumea: South Pacific Commission. *South Pacific Regional Environmental Programme Topic Review* 27.

Green, R.C. 1966. Linguistic subgrouping within Polynesia: The implication for prehistoric settlement. *Journal of the Polynesian Society* 75:6–38.

Green, R.C. 1988. Subgrouping of the Rapanui language of Easter Island in Polynesia and its implications for east Polynesian prehistory. In C.F. Cristino, P.C. Vargas, R.S. Izaurieta, and R.P. Budd (eds), *First International Congress, Easter Island and East Polynesia 1*, pp. 37–58. Santiago: University of Chile.

Hale, H. 1846. *United States Exploring Expedition*. Ethnography and philology. Philadelphia: Lee and Blanchard.

Hooper, A. 1985. Tokelau fishing in traditional and modern contexts. In R.E. Johannes and K. Ruddle (eds), *Traditional knowledge and management of coastal systems in Asia and the Pacific*, pp. 7–38. Jakarta: UNESCO.

Hooper, A. 1991. Aspects of skipjack fishing: Some Tokelau words of the sea. In A.K. Pawley (ed), *Man and a half: Essays in Pacific anthropology and ethnobiology in honour of Ralph Bulmer*, pp. 249–256. Auckland: The Polynesian Society.

Hooper, A. 2008. Old men and the sea. In C. Sather and T. Kaartinen (eds), *Beyond the horizon: Essays on myth, history, travel and society*, pp. 91–100. Helsinki: The Finnish Literature Society.

Hooper, A. 2010. Two Tokelau fishing texts. *Journal of the Polynesian Society* 119 (3):227-268.

Hooper, A. and J. Huntsman (eds). 1991. *Matagi Tokelau. History and traditions of Tokelau*. Apia and Suva: Office for Tokelau Affairs and University of the South Pacific.

Hooper. R. 1994. Reconstructing proto Polynesian fish names. In A.K. Pawley and M. Ross (eds), *Austronesian terminologies: Continuity and change*, pp. 185–229. Canberra: Department of Linguistics, The Australian National University. *Pacific Linguistics Series* C-127.

Huntsman, J. and A. Hooper. 1996. *Tokelau: A historical ethnography*. Auckland: Auckland University Press.

Johannes, R.E. 1981. *Words of the Lagoon: Fishing and marine lore in the Palau district of Micronesia*. Berkeley: University of California Press.

Kirch P.V. 1997. *The Lapita peoples: Ancestors of the oceanic world*. Oxford: Blackwell Publishers.

Kirch P.V. and T.S. Dye. 1979. Ethno-archaeology and the development of Polynesian fishing strategies. *Journal of the Polynesian Society* 88:53–76.

Kirch, P.V. and R.C. Green. 2001. Hawaiki: Ancestral Polynesia. Cambridge: Cambridge University Press.

Leach, B.F. 1986. A method for analysis of Pacific island fishbone assemblages and an associated data base management system. *Journal of Archaeological Science* 13(2):147-159.

Leach, B.F., J.M. Davidson, M. Horwood, and P. Ottino. 1997. The fishermen of Anapua Rock Shelter, Ua Pou, Marquesas Islands. *Asian Perspectives* 36(1):51-66.

Leach, B.F. and J.M. Davidson. 1977. Fishing methods and seasonality at Paremata (N160/50). *New Zealand Archaeological Association Newsletter* 20(3):166-175.

Macgregor, G. 1937. *Ethnology of Tokelau Islands*. Honolulu: Bishop Museum Press. *Bernice P. Bishop Museum Bulletin* 146.

Mafutaga a Toeaina o Atafu i Matauala Porirua. 2008. *Hikuleo: I te Papa o Tautai*. Wellington: Steele Roberts Ltd.

Marck, J. 2000. *Topics in Polynesian language and culture history*. Canberra: Pacific Linguistics, Research School of Pacific and Asian Studies, The Australian National University.

Masse, W.B. 1986. A millenium of fishing in the Palau Islands, Micronesia. In A. Anderson (ed), *Traditional fishing in the Pacific: Ethnographic and archaeological papers from the 15th Pacific Science Congress*, pp. 85–117. Honolulu: Bishop Museum Press.

Masse, W.B. 1989. *The archaeology and ecology of fishing in the Belau Islands, Micronesia*. Unpublished doctoral dissertation. Department of Anthropology, Southern Illinois University.

Matagi Tokelau. 1991. *Matagi Tokelau: History and traditions of Tokelau*. Apia and Suva: Office of Tokelau Affairs and the Institute of Pacific Studies, University of the South Pacific.

McAlister, A.J. 2002. *Prehistoric fishing at Fakaofo, Tokelau: A case for resource depression on a small atoll*. Unpublished master's thesis. Department of Anthropology, University of Auckland.

Nagaoka, L. 2005. Differential recovery of Pacific Island fish remains. *Journal of Archaeological Science* 32:941-955.

Statistics New Zealand. 2001. *New Zealand Census 2001*.

Ono, R. 2003. Prehistoric Austronesian fishing strategies: A tentative comparison between Island Southeast Asia and Lapita Cultural Complex. In C. Sand (ed), *Pacific Archaeology: assessments and prospects*, pp. 191-201. Noumea: New Caledonia Museum.

Ono, R. 2004. Prehistoric fishing at Bukit Tengkorak rock shelter, east coast of Borneo Island. *New Zealand Journal of Archaeology* 24:77-106.

Ono, R. 2006. *Marine Exploitation and Subsistent Strategies in Celebes Sea: An Ethnoarchaeological Studies to Area Studies*. Unpublished doctoral thesis, University of Sophia, Tokyo. (in Japanese).

Ono, R. 2007. Tradition and modernity in fishing among the Sama, eastern coast of Borneo, Malaysia. *Bulletin of the National Museum of Ethnology* 31(4):497–579 (in Japanese).

Ono, R. 2009. Ethnoarchaeology in coral seas. *Quarterly of Archaeological Studies* 55(4):75–94 (in Japanese).

Ono, R. 2010. Ethnoarchaeology and the early Austronesian fishing strategies in near-shore environments. *Journal of the Polynesian Society* 119(3):269-314.

Ono, R. and D. Addison. 2009. Ethnoecology and Tokelauan fishing lore from Atafu atoll, Tokelau. *SPC Traditional Marine Resource Management and Knowledge Information Bulletin* 26:3-22.

Ono, R. and M. Intoh. 2011. Island of pelagic fishermen: Temporal change in prehistoric fishing on Fais, Micronesia. *Journal of Island and Coastal Archaeology* 6:255-286.

Passfield, K. 1998. *A report of a survey of the marine resources of Fakaofo Atoll, Tokelau.* Fisheries and Environmental Resource Consultants Ltd., available at http://www.spc.int/coastfish/ Countries/ Tokelau/Fakaofofishery.pdf

Pawley, A. 1966. Polynesian languages: A subgrouping on shared innovations in morphology. *Journal of the Polynesian Society* 75:39–64.

Pawley, A. 1967. The relationships of the Polynesian outliers languages. *Journal of the Polynesian Society* 76:259–296.

Petchey, F., D.J. Addison, and A.J. McAlister. 2010. Re-interpreting old dates: Radiocarbon determinations from the Tokelau Islands (South Pacific). *Journal of Pacific Archaeology* 1(2):161-167.

Rensch, K. 1994. *Fish names of Western Polynesia.* Canberra: Archipelago Press.

Reitz, E.J., I.R. Quitmyer, and R.A. Marrinan. 2009. What are we measuring in the zooarchaeological record of prehispanic fishing strategies in the Georgia Bight, USA? *Journal of Island and Coastal Archaeology* 4(1):2-36.

Rolett, B.V. 1998. *Hanamiai: Prehistoric colonization and cultural change in the Marquesas Islands, East Polynesia.* New Haven: Department of Anthropology and The Peabody Museum Yale University. *Yale University Publications in Anthropology* No. 81.

Tokelau Dictionary. 1986. *Tokelau Dictionary.* Apia: Office of Tokelau Affairs.

Toloa F., M. Pelasio, and R.D. Gillett. 1994. Adapting traditional marine conservation in Tokelau. In R.J. Morrison, P.A. Geraghty, and L. Crowl (eds), *Science of Pacific Island peoples Vol. 1*, pp. 121–127. Suva: Institute of Pacific Studies, University of the South Pacific.

Thomas, D.H. 1969. Great Basin hunting patterns: a quantitative method for treating faunal remains. *American Antiquity* 34:393-401.

Toizumi, T. 2007. Analytical problems with identification of fish remains in prehistoric Ryukyu: influences from differences in screening methods and identified elements used in analysis. In M. Marui (ed), *Archaeological Studies on the Cultural Diversity in Southeast Asia and Its Neighbors*, pp. 307-20. Tokyo: Yuzankaku Press. (in Japanese).

Vogel, Y. 2005. *Ika.* Unpublished master's thesis, Department of Anthropology, University of Otago.

Whistler, W.A. 1988. Ethnobotany of Tokelau: The plants, their Tokelau names, and their uses. *Economic Botany* 42(2):155–176.

4

Red Abalone, Sea Otters, and Kelp Forest Ecosystems on Historic Period San Miguel Island, California

Todd J. Braje, San Diego State University

Jon M. Erlandson, Museum of Natural and Cultural History, University of Oregon

Torben C. Rick, National Museum of Natural History, Smithsonian Institution

Introduction

With prominent marine scientists calling for deeper historical perspectives to overcome the "shifting baselines" syndrome and help restore fisheries and ecosystems degraded by human overexploitation (e.g., Dayton et al. 1998; Jackson et al. 2001; Lotze et al. 2006; Pauly et al. 1998; Worm et al. 2006), archaeological data play an increasingly significant role in documenting the structure of past fisheries and foodwebs (see Rick and Erlandson 2008). Recent archaeological and historical ecological research on California's Northern Channel Islands (Figure 1) has focused on building trans-Holocene sequences of human-environmental dynamics to better understand the long histories of local marine ecosystems and the effects of human exploitation on them (Braje 2010; Braje et al. 2009; Erlandson et al. 2008, 2011a; Rick et al. 2008). One line of research has investigated possible links between prehistoric human hunting of sea otters, shellfish harvesting, and human induced trophic cascades beginning about 7500 years ago (Braje et al. 2009; Erlandson et al. 2005).

Sea otters play an important role in structuring North Pacific kelp forest ecosystems (Dayton 1985; Dayton and Tegner 1984; Simenstad et al. 1978). When feeding in kelp forests, sea otters focus on abalones (*Haliotis* spp.), sea urchins (*Strongylocentrotus* spp.), and crabs, shifting to California mussels (*Mytilus californianus*), other shellfish, and fish when their preferred prey is unavailable (Estes et al. 1981). In Alaska and British Columbia, the historical removal or reduction of sea otters has resulted in local kelp deforestation by sea urchin blooms, trophic cascades, and reduced marine biodiversity and productivity in nearshore ecosystems (Estes and Duggins 1995; Simenstad et al. 1978). In Southern California and the Channel Islands, kelp forest foodwebs are more complex, stable, and resilient (Graham et al. 2008; Steneck et al. 2002). Despite the historic decimation of sea otter populations in the mid-1800s, there has been no wholesale collapse of kelp forests since California sheephead (*Semicossyphus pulcher*), sunflower stars (*Picnopodia helianthoides*), spiny lobsters (*Panulirus interruptus*), and humans also prey on urchins and help control their populations when sea otters are reduced.

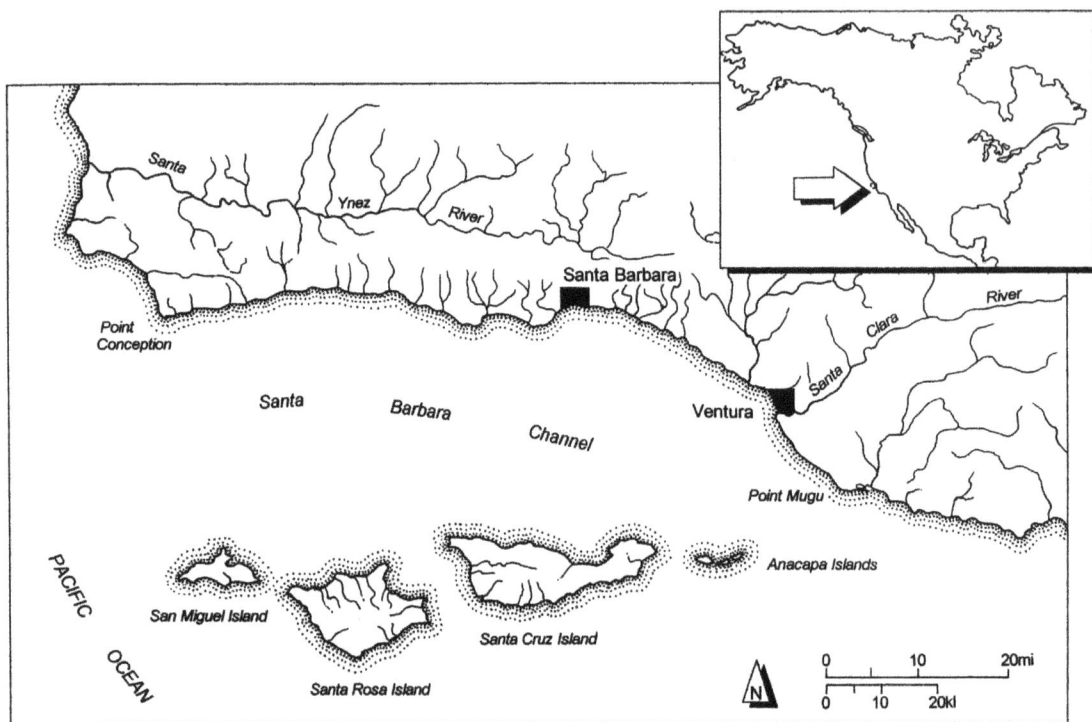

Figure 1. The location of the Northern Channel Islands and the Santa Barbara Channel off the coast of California.

Source: Adapted from Kennett (2005).

Dayton (1985:234) and Dayton and Tegner (1984:471) argued that Native American hunters may have controlled sea otter populations along the California Coast, releasing shellfish populations from predation and increasing their size and abundance. Using archaeological data to test this hypothesis, Erlandson et al. (2005, 2008) suggested that the Island Chumash and their ancestors hunted otters on San Miguel from at least 9000 years ago until the Historic Period, increasing the productivity of nearshore shellfish communities. They argued that the exceptional size and abundance of red abalone (*Haliotis rufescens*) shells and the presence of sea urchin lenses (dense concentrations of sea urchin tests) from numerous Northern Channel Island shell middens dated between ~8000 and 3000 years ago (also see Braje et al. 2009; Sharp 2000) provided evidence for prehistoric sea otter exploitation and anthropogenic changes in local shellfisheries. Whether such changes were an inadvertent by-product of otter hunting or part of an intentional environmental management strategy is difficult to determine using archaeological data.

Sea otter remains have been found in numerous San Miguel Island sites dating between about 9000 and 200 years ago, but the sample sizes for most sites and time periods are relatively low (Erlandson et al. 2005). In particular, there is relatively little faunal evidence for otter hunting prior to 7500 years ago, when large red abalone middens first appear widely in the archaeological record. Technological evidence, in the form of numerous finely-made stemmed and barbed projectile points, has emerged recently to suggest that marine hunting was an important activity on San Miguel and the other Northern Channel Islands between ~12,000 and 8000 years ago (Braje 2010; Erlandson et al. 2009, 2011b; Glassow et al. 2008). There is also evidence of increasing demographic expansion through the Early, Middle, and Late Holocene. Likely, the islands were being used more intensively, by larger groups of hunter-foragers through the Early to

Middle Holocene, with clear evidence for the first permanent island villages at the beginning of the Late Holocene (~3500 years ago). This would have resulted in increasing predation pressure on both shellfish and sea otters. A deeper understanding of the long history of interaction between humans, otters, and abalones might prove useful in designing conservation programs aimed at restoring healthy otter populations and re-establishing a productive abalone fishery in Southern California (Braje et al. 2009).

In this chapter, we provide a new dataset to help test the intensity of ancient sea otter hunting on the Northern Channel Islands. We report on the largest assemblage of historic red abalone shell measurements from California's Northern Channel Islands, data gathered from a 19th century Chinese abalone processing camp at CA-SMI-614H, occupied after the local extinction of sea otters from San Miguel Island. Historically, black abalone (*Haliotis cracherodii*) were once common in Southern California's intertidal ecosystems and highly susceptible to human predation, while red abalone are largely subtidal and more susceptible to sea otter predation. When sea otters are common, red abalone are largely confined to cracks and fissures, limiting their sizes and densities (Wendell 1994). In the absence of sea otters, abalone populations can become very large and abundant, a phenomenon recorded historically in coastal California (Dayton et al. 1998:317). Using historical shell sizes as a proxy for the structure of a red abalone population released from the effects of otter predation, we compare these measurements to Middle (~7500-3500 years ago) and Late Holocene (~3500 years ago to AD 1820) red abalone shell measurements from San Miguel Island reported by Erlandson et al. (2008).

Because late 19th century commercial fisheries focused largely on intertidal black abalone, we begin with a discussion of a Chinese-dominated black abalone fishery that began in the mid-1800s, after the local extirpation of sea otters. This early historical fishery provides a baseline for our analysis of prehistoric red abalone exploitation by the Chumash and their ancestors.

Nineteenth Century Sea Otter Hunting and Abalone Predation

Beginning in the early 1800s, commercial hunting organised by Russian and Euro-American merchants resulted in the local extirpation of sea otters from Southern California waters (Ogden 1941). After the decimation of coastal Native American populations by Old World diseases and the relocation of the Island Chumash to Spanish towns and missions on the mainland by about AD 1822, abalone populations flourished in the absence of human and sea otter predation. Chinese immigrants were among the first to commercially exploit the rich abalone stocks along the California Coast on a large scale. In the mid-1850s and 1860s, numerous abalone fishing camps were established in the San Francisco, Monterey, Channel Island, San Diego, and Baja California areas (Berryman 1995; Braje and Erlandson 2007; Braje et al. 2007). While subtidal abalone species were also released from predation and their numbers and sizes likely exploded, Chinese fishermen on the Channel Islands largely focused their collecting efforts on easy-to-access intertidal black abalone along rocky shores, processing and drying the meat on the islands, then shipping their product to overseas markets in China and Japan.

Historic abalone camps have been documented on San Clemente (Axford 1984, 1987; Berryman 1995; McKusick and Warren 1959), San Nicolas (Berryman 1995), Santa Rosa (Bentz 1996; Morris 1994), and San Miguel (Braje et al. 2007) islands. Most of these sites are dominated by large black abalone shells, with some containing hearth features, wood planks, Asian pottery, opium paraphernalia, bullet cartridge casings, and/or metal and glass fragments. Since the commercial sale of abalone shell for ornamental and construction (lime) uses began in the mid-1860s (Berryman 1995), most historic abalone middens probably represent the remains of early sites. After the mid-1860s, sites are probably under-represented as fishermen shipped both the processed meat and the shell to overseas markets. This is further supported by the lack of red, pink (*H. corrugata*), green (*H. fulgens*), and white abalone (*H. sorenseni*) in historic sites, species that were not systematically harvested until the late 18th century when Japanese and Euro-American hardhat divers expanded the industry to include subtidal taxa.

Historic black abalone middens offer an important dataset against which to test prehistoric impacts on sea otter populations and anthropogenic alteration of nearshore ecosystems. These historical sites shed light on an anthropogenic intertidal ecosystem free of sea otters, which were locally extirpated by the 1850s (Scammon 1968:169). As part of a San Miguel Island-wide study of shellfish size changes through the Holocene, Erlandson et al. (2008) compared mean black abalone sizes from six historic sites (using a total of 416 individual shell measurements) to numerous Native American sites spanning the Holocene. They found little evidence for a decline in the size of black abalone shells across the Holocene, but several Middle Holocene assemblages dating between about 6000 and 4000 years ago produced relatively large mean sizes of black abalone shells only slightly smaller than the 19th century sample (Erlandson et al. 2008:Figures 3 and 4).

The present study expands this research and focuses on size comparisons between historic period and archaeological red abalone shells. Red abalone shell sizes should be more closely correlated with both human predation pressure and local sea otter populations than were black abalone shell sizes. As a subtidal species, red abalones are a preferred and accessible resource for sea otters. Erlandson et al. (2008:Table 3) demonstrated that red abalone shell samples from the past 9000 years showed a steep and statistically significant decline in the mean size of shells through the Holocene. Although several prehistoric sites between 7500 and 6000 years old yielded mean red abalone shell sizes nearly comparable to those from historic sites, only two historic sites yielded whole red abalone shells, producing just 11 shell measurements and limiting inferences about historic versus prehistoric size changes. Since the discovery of a new historic age site on western San Miguel Island, we have been able to generate a robust sample of post-AD 1850 red abalone shell size measurements and fill an important gap in the dataset.

Site Setting and Results

In 2005, Dr. Robert DeLong of the National Marine Fisheries Service brought us to a remarkable historic site (CA-SMI-614H) located just behind the beach at Adams Cove near Point Bennett that yielded a large sample of whole, well-preserved red and black abalone shells (Figure 2). According to DeLong, a marine biologist who has worked in the Point Bennett area for over 30 years, Adams Cove is unique on San Miguel Island in having large numbers of red abalone in the intertidal zone. The shoreline adjacent to CA-SMI-614H drops off sharply, is characterised by intensive upwelling of cool waters, and may have been a place where red abalone were available to Chinese fishermen harvesting abalones from the intertidal or shallow subtidal zones. Little archaeological work has been conducted in this area due to its proximity to a large pinniped breeding colony and blowing sands that have reduced visibility and obscured archaeological remains. Due to concerns over disturbing pinnipeds hauled out near the site, we were limited in the amount of time we could spend at CA-SMI-614H. Our investigations, therefore, have been limited to survey, surface collection, site mapping, and small subsurface probes. This work has provided the first sizable assemblage of red abalone shells dating to a 19th century Chinese abalone camp on San Miguel Island.

CA-SMI-614H is a historic site with multiple components scattered across an area of approximately 750 m². Recent pinniped activity, wave action, and coastal erosion have heavily disturbed the site, mixing modern flotsam with historic debris and older artefacts diagnostic of Early and Late

Holocene Native American occupations (Braje and Erlandson 2008; Braje et al. 2007). We have conducted several reconnaissance trips to the site to surface collect diagnostic artefacts, record historic features, and map the area. Continued monitoring of the site has been productive as shifting beach and dune sands reveal and obscure cultural materials and features every season. Thus far, we have documented a circular hearth feature, two roughly rectangular rock features, a large assemblage of Asian and Euro-American artefacts including ceramic sherds of Asian origin, sawn Steller sea lion teeth, bullet cartridge casings, and various metal and glass objects.

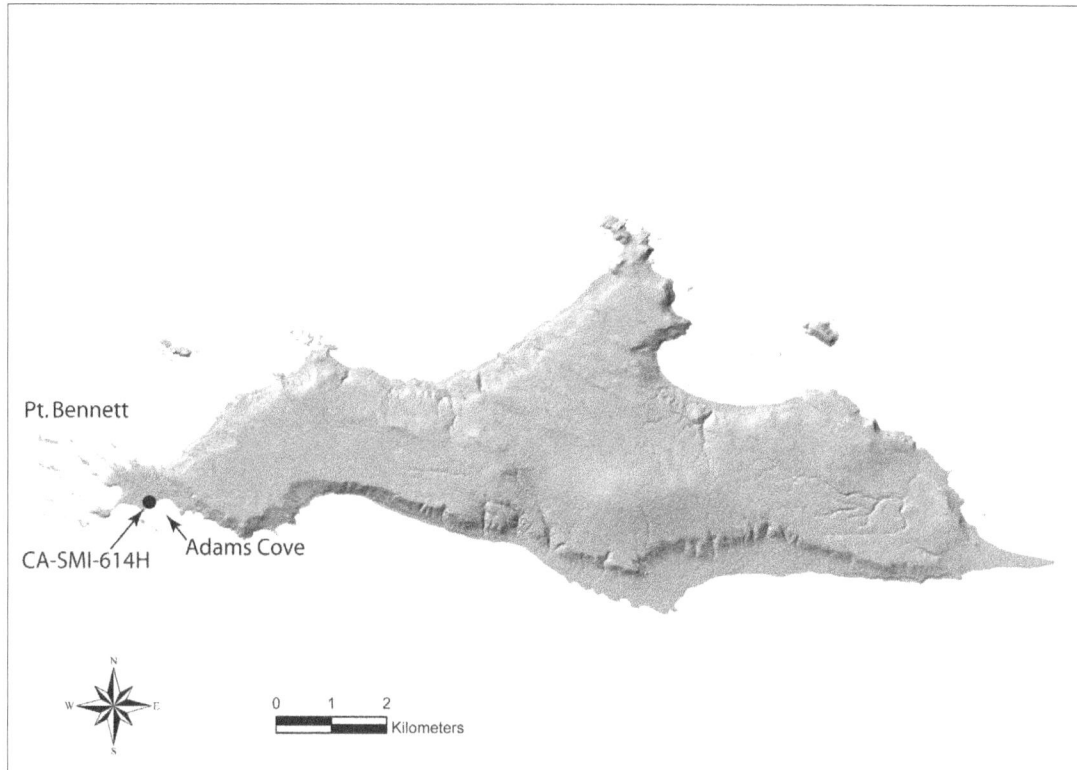

Figure 2. The location of Adams Cove and CA-SMI-614H.

Source: Map by T. Braje.

During a visit in December 2007, shifting sands had exposed a pavement (at least 12 m east-west by 9 m north-south) of whole red and black abalone shells associated with two rectangular rock features (Figure 3). Similar rectangular rock hearths have been recorded elsewhere on San Miguel (Braje et al. 2007) and San Clemente islands (Berryman 2005). Based on the association of the abalone pavement at SMI-614H with these historic hearth features, the presence of historic artefacts embedded within the shells, and the large shell sizes, we are confident that the abalone shells are of 19th century origin. Similar abalone scatters are common at many historic fishing camps on the Channel Islands and probably represent the remnants of shell piles created by some of the first Chinese fishermen to exploit the local intertidal for abalone meat in the mid-1800s.

The CA-SMI-614H abalone feature is unique because of the relatively large number of red abalone shells. In a single, randomly selected 1.0 x 1.0 m test unit, 9 of 34 (26.5%) abalone shells were reds. A sample of whole red abalone shells was measured from CA-SMI-614H following methods described by Erlandson et al. (2008). The 65 whole red abalone shells from CA-SMI-614H had an average length of 189.2 mm (standard deviation = 15.4 mm), a maximum length of 214.0 mm, and a minimum of 132.0 mm. In much smaller numbers, red abalone shells have been documented in just two of the other 21 San Miguel Island historic abalone processing sites [CA-

SMI-553 (n=10) and CA-SMI-654H (n=1)]. To our knowledge, CA-SMI-614H has yielded the largest assemblage of red abalone size measurements from later 19th century Southern California, when abalone populations were largely free of predation by otters and Native American foragers.

Figure 3. Photograph of one of the two rectangular rock features at CA-SMI-614H.

Source: Photographs and graphic by T. Braje.

Adams Cove may offer a unique set of environmental conditions that allow for abundant red abalone populations in the intertidal, but our data should be comparable to subtidal populations in other locations. Measurements of modern red abalone from marine protected areas without sea otters are nearly equivalent to our Adams Cove sample and environmental reconstructions suggest that marine productivity and sea-surface temperature (SST) were comparable during the Middle Holocene and 19th century (see below).

Red abalone shells are rare in Channel Island sites older than ~8000 years, but Erlandson et al. (2008:2147) reported a mean shell length of 166.3 mm (n=548 shell measurements) from ten Middle Holocene sites on San Miguel Island (Erlandson et al. 2008: Table 1). Average sizes at each site ranged from 188.5 to 124.0 mm. Six sites dated between about 7500 and 4500 years ago produced mean shell sizes approaching the mean for CA-SMI-614H, including CA-SMI-603 at 188.5 mm (n=34) and CA-SMI-172 (n=131) at 186.9 mm. Only three of ten Middle Holocene sites [CA-SMI-161 at 137.8 (n=116), CA-SMI-261 at 126.0 (n=4), and CA-SMI-628 at 124.0 (n=10)] produced means less than 152 mm (Figure 4). A reduction in average red abalone size occurs from the Middle (166.3 mm) to Late (94.4 mm) Holocene, a pattern Erlandson et al. (2008:2147) attributed to human predation and the increased use of large red abalone shells to make dishes, ornaments, beads, and fishhooks after ca. 3500 cal BP (see also Braje et al. 2007; Kennett 2005:193).

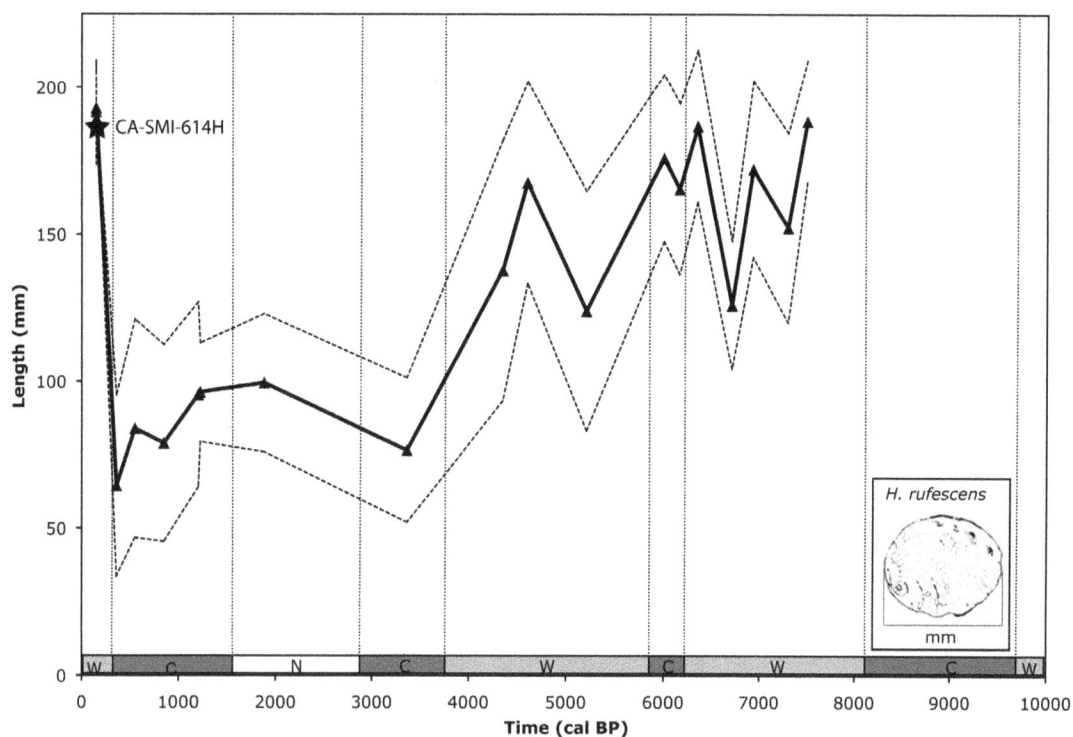

Figure 4. Mean red abalone size changes in San Miguel Island archaeological sites (adapted from Erlandson et al. 2008:2150) and mean red abalone size at CA-SMI-614. Data points are from Table 1 and the dashed lines represent the standard deviation around the mean. The shaded bar along the x-axis shows sea-surface temperatures from Kennett (2005): w = warm, c = cold, n = variable.

Source: Figure by T. Braje.

The similarity of the red abalone shell measurements from CA-SMI-614H—occupied ~20-30 years after sea otters were extirpated from San Miguel Island waters—and the Middle Holocene sites reported by Erlandson et al. (2008) support the notion that Native American hunters suppressed otter populations around the Northern Channel Islands during the Middle Holocene. The maximum size of red abalone shells from several of the Middle Holocene components (~220-230 mm) exceeds the largest specimens from our mid-19th century sites, however, a fact that may be related to the great age (~20-30 years) of such individuals and the limited period of growth available between the local extinction of sea otters and the inception of the Chinese abalone fishery.

Palaeoecological reconstructions of SST and marine productivity suggest that marine conditions during the occupation of CA-SMI-614H and the majority of the Middle Holocene were both characterised by periods of predominantly warm SST (Kennett 2005:64-69), so upwelling and marine productivity do not appear to be primarily responsible for larger red abalone size profiles during these times. Even in the Middle Holocene, however, we should not expect mean red abalone sizes to equal historic ones, as otters and humans both appear to have been present as predators in nearshore Channel Island waters.

Discussion and Conclusions

Since the collapse of California abalone fisheries in the 1980s and 1990s, marine conservationists and resource managers have worked to develop a sustainable abalone fishery. Except for one highly regulated recreational fishery for red abalone north of San Francisco, there has been a moratorium on all abalone fisheries in California (Jones 2008:66). At best, abalone management and restoration plans have had mixed success and they often put fisheries managers and fishermen at odds with one another. In February 2009, after sixteen years of closure of commercial and recreational harvests, the National Oceanic and Atmospheric Administration (NOAA) granted black abalone endangered species status (Center for Biological Diversity 2006). Today, the commercial abalone market in California is fed exclusively by thirteen abalone farms, where adult abalone (primarily reds ranging in size from ~85-115 mm) are grown in tanks (Jones 2008:66). Between 7300 and 4300 years ago, every red abalone shell assemblage measured on San Miguel has mean sizes larger (>120 mm) than these modern farm-raised red abalone.

Fanshawe et al. (2003) reported demographic data for modern red abalones at nine sites along the California Coast, including six in marine protected areas, four of which had local sea otter populations. They found that sea otter predation restricted abalones to a limited number of microhabitats and to densities and sizes inadequate to sustain a healthy fishery, concluding that "…marine protected areas with sea otters restored as top-level carnivores cannot serve the dual purposes of biodiversity enhancement and abalone fishery conservation off California" (Fanshawe et al. 2003:281). They reported a mean red abalone size of 183 mm for marine protected areas without sea otters, 142 mm for unprotected areas without sea otters, and 94 mm for marine protected areas with sea otters (Fanshawe et al. 2003:Table 3). Mean red abalone sizes from most of the Middle Holocene red abalone middens (~166 mm) on San Miguel are roughly equivalent to or greater than Fanshawe et al.'s (2003) data from unprotected areas without sea otters and much larger than the marine protected areas with sea otters. All three of the historical assemblages and two of our Middle Holocene assemblages had mean sizes that exceed Fanshawe et al.'s (2003) populations from marine protected areas without sea otters, suggesting that humans harvesting abalones at these sites were collecting "pristine" populations where adult abalones had been largely released from predation pressures.

Archaeological data from CA-SMI-614H provide a rare example of the size of a 19th century red abalone population on San Miguel Island, providing a baseline for a period when sea otters were known to be absent from Channel Island waters. Combined with work by Erlandson et al. (2005) and Braje et al. (2009), these historical data support Fanshawe et al.'s (2003) modern findings, and suggest that a productive red abalone fishery may not have developed on the Channel Islands until ~8000 cal BP when Native American hunters began suppressing local sea otter populations. The recent discovery of large red abalone shells in terminal Pleistocene shell middens at CA-SMI-678 on San Miguel Island—where they are associated with numerous sophisticated projectile points (Erlandson et al. 2011b)—might extend the evidence for localised sea otter depletion back to ~11,600 cal BP, although no sea otter bones have been identified at this or other sites prior to 9000 cal BP. The presence of sea otter bones in San Miguel Island archaeological assemblages for much of the Holocene suggests that a subsistence red abalone fishery persisted and co-existed with sea otters—the latter probably in low densities—on the Northern Channel Islands for at least 8000 years. Average red abalone sizes collected by the Chumash in the Late Holocene were relatively small, but there is no evidence for a wholesale collapse in the fishery until modern, commercial exploitation.

The precise mechanism behind this balance between productive red abalone fisheries and at least low densities of sea otters remains difficult to establish with existing archaeological data. Comparison of Middle Holocene, 19th century, and modern ecological datasets suggests that the abundance and large sizes of prehistoric red abalones may only have been reached through the human suppression of sea otter populations. As it did historically, substantial reduction in prehistoric sea otter populations would have caused an ecological re-organisation in the nearshore environment where humans replaced otters as the keystone abalone predator. This resulted in a highly productive red abalone fishery on the Channel Islands during the Middle Holocene.

Historical, archaeological, and ecological data suggest that a limited but sustainable red abalone fishery and the recovery of sea otters may be able to co-exist in California. This would require, however, a healthy (fully recovered) red abalone population and a carefully controlled sea otter population. Future debates between ecologists and environmental advocates who call for sea otter recovery in Southern California waters and fisherfolk who yearn to restore economically productive abalone harvests may be mediated by a better understanding of the archaeological and historical relationships between humans, otters, and abalone over the last 8000 years.

Continued archaeological, historical, and ecological research on the Channel Islands may provide historical baselines and ecological linkages to guide effective recovery and management plans and help further investigate the relationships between ancient peoples, sea otters, and kelp forest ecosystems. For now, archaeological data lend some support to the notion that healthy red abalone populations and sustainable human fishing practices can co-exist with sea otter populations, but only where both human harvests and the density of sea otter populations are carefully monitored and controlled. Sustaining such a fishery in modern times may only succeed if various parties compromise by limiting commercial and recreational harvests of red abalones to sustainable levels, as well as limiting the density or distribution of sea otter populations within a broader geographic range. Ultimately, it will be critical to determine how to best mediate the conflicting requirements of restoring and protecting endangered populations of sea otters and abalones, especially when one endangered species feeds on the other.

Acknowledgments

Our research was supported by the National Science Foundation (BCS-0613982 to Braje and Erlandson), Channel Islands National Park (CINP), the Western National Parks Association, and our home institutions. We are indebted to Bob DeLong (U.S. National Marine Fisheries Service) for facilitating our work at CA-SMI-614H. At CINP, we thank Ann Huston, Kelly Minas, and Ian Williams for their support. We are grateful to David Addison, Rintaro Ono, Ian Smith, and an anonymous reviewer for their constructive comments and assistance in the revision and final production of this paper.

References

Axford, M. 1984. *Four years of archaeological investigations on San Clemente Island, California.* Manuscript on file. San Diego: Natural Resource Office, North Island Naval Reservation.

Axford, M. 1987. *Late historic Chinese abalone collectors on San Clemente Island.* Manuscript on file, San Diego: Natural Resource Office, North Island Naval Reservation.

Bentz, L. 1996. *Chinese abalone collectors of Santa Rosa Island.* presented for contract fulfillment to National Park Service, Channel Islands National Park.

Berryman, J.A. 1995. *Archival information, abalone shell, broken pots, hearths, and windbreaks: Clues to identifying nineteenth century California abalone collection and processing sites, San Clemente Island: A case study.* Unpublished doctoral dissertation, Department of Anthropology, University of California, Riverside.

Braje, T.J. 2010. *Modern oceans, ancient sites: Archaeology and marine conservation on San Miguel Island, California.* Salt Lake City: University of Utah Press.

Braje, T.J. and J.M. Erlandson. 2007. Measuring subsistence specialization: Comparing historic and prehistoric abalone middens on San Miguel Island, California. *Journal of Anthropological Archaeology* 26:474-485.

Braje, T.J. and J.M. Erlandson. 2008. Early maritime technology from western San Miguel Island, California. *Current Research in the Pleistocene* 25:31-32.

Braje, T.J., J.M. Erlandson, and T.C. Rick. 2007. A historic abalone fishery on California's Northern Channel Islands. *Historical Archaeology* 41(4):117-128.

Braje, T.J., J.M. Erlandson, T.C. Rick, P.K. Dayton, and M.B.A. Hatch. 2009. Fishing from past to present: Long-term continuity and resilience of red abalone fisheries on California's Northern Channel Islands. *Ecological Applications* 19(4):906-919.

Center for Biological Diversity. 2006. *Petition to list the black abalone (*Haliotis cracherodii*) as threatened or endangered under the endangered species act.* Submitted to the United States Secretary of Commerce, 21 December 2006.

Dayton, P. 1985. Ecology of kelp communities. *Annual Review of Ecology and Systematics* 16:215-245.

Dayton, P.K., and M.J. Tegner. 1984. The importance of scale in community ecology: A kelp forest example with terrestrial analogs. In P.W. Price, C.N. Slobodchikoff, and W.S. Gaud (eds), *A New Ecology: Novel Approaches to Interactive Systems*, pp. 457-481. New York: John Wiley and Sons.

Dayton, P.K., M.J. Tegner, P.B. Edwards, and K.L. Riser. 1998. Sliding baselines, ghosts, and reduced expectations in kelp forest communities. *Ecological Applications* 8:309-322.

Erlandson, J.M. and T.J. Braje. 2008. Five crescents from Cardwell: The context of eccentric crescents from CA-SMII-679, San Miguel Island, California. *Pacific Coast Archaeological Society Quarterly* 40(1):35-45.

Erlandson, J.M., T.C. Rick, and T.J. Braje. 2009. Fishing up the food web?: 12,000 years of maritime subsistence and adaptive adjustments on California's Channel Islands. *Pacific Science* 63(4):711-724.

Erlandson, J.M., T.J. Braje, T.C. Rick, N.P. Jew, D.J. Kennett, N. Dwyer, A.F. Ainis, R.L. Vellanoweth, and J. Watts. 2011a. 10,000 years of human predation and size changes in the owl limpet (*Lottia gigantea*) on San Miguel Island, California. *Journal of Archaeological Science* 38:1127-1134.

Erlandson, J.M., T.C. Rick, T.J. Braje, M. Casperson, B. Culleton, B. Fulfrost, T. Garcia, D.A. Guthrie, N. Jew, D.J. Kennett, M.L. Moss, L. Reeder, C. Skinner, J. Watts, and L. Willis. 2011b. Paleoindian seafaring, maritime technologies, and coastal foraging on California's Channel Islands. *Science* 331:1181-1185.

Erlandson, J.M., T.C. Rick, T.J. Braje, A. Steinberg, and R.L. Vellanoweth. 2008. Human impacts on ancient shellfish: A 10,000 year record from San Miguel Island, California. *Journal of Archaeological Science* 35:2144-2152.

Erlandson, J.M., T.C. Rick, J.A. Estes, M.H. Graham, T.J. Braje, and R.L. Vellanoweth. 2005. Sea otters, shellfish, and humans: A 10,000 year record from San Miguel Island, California. In D. Garcelon and C.A. Schwemm (eds), *Proceedings of the Sixth California Islands Conference*, pp. 9-21. Arcata: Institute for Wildlife Studies.

Estes, J.A. and D.O. Duggins. 1995. Sea otters and kelp forests in Alaska: Generality and variation in a community ecological paradigm. *Ecological Monographs* 65:75-100.

Estes, J.A., R.J. Jameson, and A.M. Johnson. 1981. Food selection and some foraging tactics of sea otters. In J.A. Chapman and D. Pursley (eds), *Worldwide Furbearer Conference Proceedings*, pp. 606-641. Frostburg: Worldwide Furbearer Conference, Inc.

Fanshawe, S., G.R. VanBlaricom, and A.A. Shelly. 2003. Restored top carnivores as detriments to the performance of marine protected areas intended for fishery sustainability: A case study with red abalones and sea otters. *Conservation Biology* 17:273-283.

Glassow, M.A., P. Paige, and J. Perry. 2008. *The Punta Arena site: Early and Middle Holocene cultural development on Santa Cruz Island, California.* Santa Barbara: Santa Barbara Museum of Natural History. *Santa Barbara Museum of Natural History Contributions in Anthropology* No. 3.

Graham. M. H., B. Halpern, and M. Carr. 2008. Diversity and dynamics of Californian subtidal kelp forests. In T.R. McClanahan and G.M. Branch (eds), *Food webs and the dynamics of marine reefs*, pp. 103-134. New York: Oxford University Press.

Jackson, J.B.C., M.X. Kirby, W.H. Berger, K.A. Bjorndal, L.W. Botsford, B.J. Bourque, R.H. Bradbury, R. Cooke, J. Erlandson, J.A. Estes, T.P. Hughes, S. Kidwell, C.B. Lange, H.S. Lenihan, J.M. Pandolfi, C.H. Peterson, R.S. Steneck, M.J. Tegner, and R.R. Warner. 2001. Historical overfishing and the recent collapse of coastal ecosystems. *Science* 293:629-637.

Jones, G.A. 2008. 'Quite the choicest protein dish': The costs of consuming seafood in American restaurants, 1850-2006. In D.J. Starkey, P. Holm, and M. Barnard (eds), *Ocean's past: Management insights from the history of marine animal populations*, pp. 47-76, 606-641. London: Earthscan.

Kennett, D.J. 2005. *The Island Chumash: Behavioral ecology of a maritime society.* Berkeley: University of California Press.

Lotze, H.K., H.S. Lenihan, B.J. Bourque, R.H. Bradbury, R.G. Cooke, M.C. Kay, S.M. Kidwell, M.X. Kirby, C.H. Peterson, and J.B.C. Jackson. 2006. Depletion, degradation, and recovery potential of estuaries and coastal seas. *Science* 312:1806-1809.

McKusick, M.B. and C.N. Warren. 1959. *Introduction to San Clemente Island archaeology.* Los Angeles: University of California. *University of California Los Angeles Archaeological Survey Annual Report* 1:106-183.

Morris, D.P. 1994. Santa Rosa Island survey. Paper presented at the *Fourth California Islands Symposium.* Santa Barbara: Santa Barbara Museum of Natural History.

Ogden, A. 1941. *The California sea otter trade 1784-1848.* Berkeley: University of California Press.

Pauly, D., V. Christensen, J. Dalsgaard, R. Froese, and F. Torres Jr. 1998. Fishing down marine food webs. *Science* 279:860-863.

Rick, T.C. and J.M. Erlandson (eds). 2008. *Human impacts on ancient marine ecosystems: A global perspective.* Berkeley: University of California Press.

Rick, T.C., J.M. Erlandson, T.J. Braje, J.E. Estes, M.H. Graham, and R.L. Vellanoweth. 2008. Historical ecology and human impacts on coastal ecosystems of the Santa Barbara Channel region, California. In T.C. Rick and J.M. Erlandson (eds), *Human impacts on ancient marine ecosystems: A global perspective*, pp. 77-101. Berkeley: University of California Press.

Scammon, C.M. 1968. *The marine mammals of the northwestern coast of North America.* New York: Dover.

Sharp, J.T. 2000. *Shellfish analysis from the Punta Arena site, a Middle Holocene red abalone midden on Santa Cruz Island, California.* Unpublished master's thesis, Department of Anthropology, Sonoma State University.

Simenstad, C.A., J.A. Estes, and K.W. Kenyon. 1978. Aleuts, sea otters, and alternate stable-state communities. *Science* 200:403-411.

Steneck, R.S., M.H. Graham, B.J. Bourque, D. Corbett, J.M. Erlandson, J.A. Estes, and M.J. Tegner. 2002. Kelp forest ecosystems: Biodiversity, stability, resilience, and future. *Environmental Conservation* 29(4):436-459.

Wendell, F. 1994. Relationship between sea otter range expansion and red abalone abundance and size distribution in central California. *California Fish and Game* 80:45-56.

Worm, B., E.B. Barbier, N. Beaumont, J.E. Duffy, C. Folke, B.S. Halpern, J.B.C. Jackson, H.K. Lotze, F. Micheli, S.R. Palumbi, E. Sala, K.A. Selkoe, J.J. Stachowicz, and R. Watson. 2006. Impacts of biodiversity loss on ocean ecosystem services. *Science* 314:787-790.

5

Exploring the Social Context of Maritime Exploitation in Tanzania between the 14th-18th c. AD: Recent Research from the Mafia Archipelago

Annalisa C. Christie, University of York

Introduction

This paper presents some of the results of recent research in the Mafia Archipelago, Tanzania. The archipelago is situated approximately 21 kilometres off the coast of mainland Tanzania, opposite the Rufiji Delta. It comprises four main islands – Mafia, Chole, Juani and Jibondo – as well as several smaller islands and uninhabited coral atolls formed by the emergences of the fringing reef, which extends along the East African coast (Baumann 1895:5) (Figure 1).

Part of the archipelago was designated as a marine park in 1995 (Walley 2004:3). This has resulted in a number of studies that have examined the nature of the coastal ecology within the park as well as the biodiversity of the surrounding reefs (Dulvy et al. 1995; Garpe and Ohman 2003; Gaudian and Richmond 1990; Horrill 1991; Jidawii and Ohman 2002; Kamukuru et al. 2005).

This paper focuses on the preliminary analysis of the faunal assemblages collected during excavations at the site of Kua Ruins on Juani Island (Figure 1(a)). These excavations aimed to elucidate the socio-cultural context of maritime exploitation (specifically fishing and shellfish collections), looking in particular as to whether, in line with data from other anthropological studies (Conte 2006; D'Arcy 2006; Hviding 1996), there was any evidence to suggest that higher status individuals controlled access to marine resources.

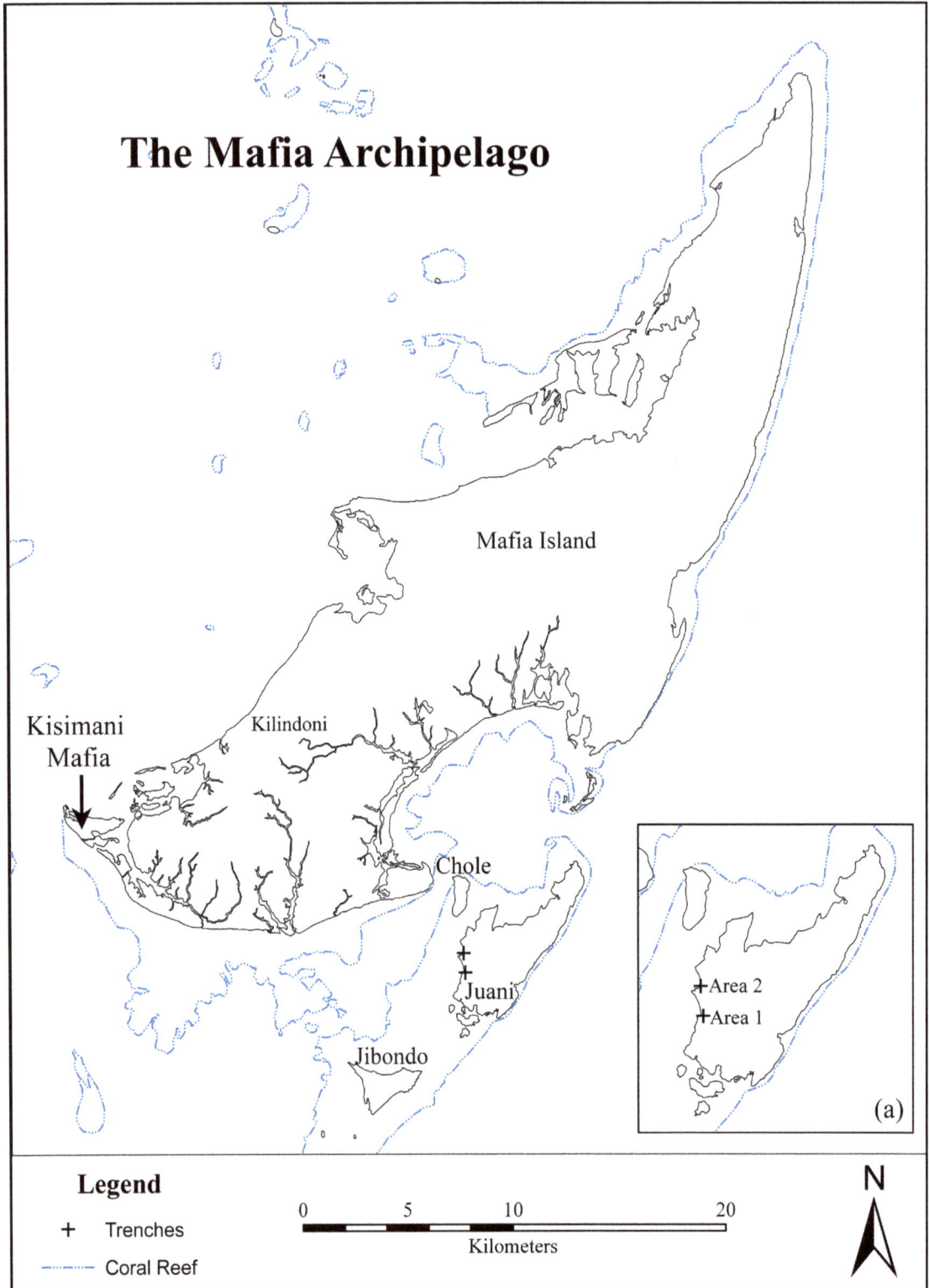

Figure 1. Map of the Mafia Archipelago. Inset (a) Showing the location of the excavation areas at Kua.

Source: Map by author.

In recent years, research into the nature of the subsistence economy of the Swahili communities living along the East African coast between the 8th – 15th centuries AD has become more prominent. Studies such as Horton and Mudida's analysis of some of the faunal assemblages from the site of Shanga in the Lamu Archipelago, Kenya (Horton 1996; Horton and Mudida 1993), van Neer's examination of the assemblages from Kizimkazi Dimbani on Zanzibar (van Neer 2001), and Fleisher's analysis of remains recovered from several sites around Pemba Island (Fleisher 2003), have highlighted the importance of marine resources within Swahili subsistence strategies. While these are useful developments, much of this recent work has aimed to elucidate the nature of Swahili diet, or changing patterns of resource exploitation, rather than on the socio-cultural context of maritime interactions. The work at Kua was part of a larger research project, one aim of which was to develop a theoretical and methodological framework within which to explore the diverse meanings and manifestations of 'maritime-ness' and 'maritime identities'.

Research Context

Maritime archaeology has developed considerably over the last fifty years, incorporating a wide range of remains both on land and underwater, and tackling a variety of socio-cultural questions. However, with the greater integration of terrestrial remains into the remit of maritime archaeology over the last twenty years, more emphasis has been placed on understanding the nature of the societies responsible for the creation, manipulation and destruction of the submerged heritage that had once been the focus of maritime archaeological studies. Consequently, archaeologists have started to question 'what makes a society maritime?' or 'what is a maritime culture?'. In answer to this, Westerdahl (1992:5) proposed that we situate these societies within the context of their surrounding landscape and research a set of five components (shipwrecks, land-based remains, tradition of usage, natural topography and place names), which collectively comprised what might be termed a 'maritime cultural landscape'. Defined as the archaeological examination of "the human utilisation (economy) of maritime space by boat: settlement, fishing, hunting, shipping and its attendant sub-cultures" (Westerdahl 1992:5), the concept has since been expanded to address some of the socio-cultural aspects of these communities through the examination of 'ritual landscapes' (Westerdahl 2005, 2007). Despite this, most maritime cultural landscape studies have continued to focus on examining the technology and economy of coastal communities – and this has led to the underlying implication that a maritime society is one that lives by the sea and exploits marine resources.

The lack of an explicit statement outlining what maritime societies are is problematic, if maritime archaeology is to be considered a worthwhile area of study. After all, the archaeologies of 'coastal' communities have been comparatively well-examined by archaeologists more generally—what, if anything, differentiates these communities from specifically maritime communities? Until these differences are clarified and any unique features indicative of maritime communities identified, calls for archaeologists to engage more fully with maritime archaeological approaches and provide a "more holistic understanding of the development of maritime traditions" (Breen and Lane 2003:470) can never be fully realised.

In postulating some of these questions, it became apparent during this research that perhaps it was the presence of the sea itself (as opposed to the resources it provides and the communication and trade networks it facilitates), that shapes explicitly 'maritime' identities —creating a maritime-ethos—and which has the potential to influence the broader socio-cultural and ideological organisation of such societies. Similar perspectives, that 'maritime-ness' is as much a social construct as it is a technological or environmental one, are often presented by literature pertaining to anthropological studies within maritime societies (Chapman 1987; Conte, 2006; Cooney 2003; D'Arcy 2006; Hau'ofa 1994; Hviding 1996). Although the social context of the maritime interactions observed and recorded in these ethnographies were both culturally specific and representative of living traditions, it should be noted that in some cases, these social complexities can be manifested in the archaeological record. When examined within an anthropologically informed framework and in conjunction with locally derived ethnographic and ethnoarchaeological datasets, archaeological data could therefore be used to examine this maritime ethos using a multi-faceted research strategy.

Existing archaeological and historical evidence suggest that the Swahili communities living on the East African coast were clearly maritime societies (Middleton 1992; Nurse and Spear 1985; Prins 1965, 1971). Much of the archaeological work in the region has focused on the role of the Swahili as cultural brokers between the African interior and the broader Indian Ocean trading networks (Horton and Middleton 2000:89), examining, in particular, the role of this trade on architectural styles, religion, linguistics, social and settlement organisation (Abungu 1998; Kusimba 1999). However, more recently, projects such as Breen and Lane's research around Mombasa Harbour (Breen and Lane 2003) or Pollard's (2007, 2008a, 2008b, 2008c) work around Kilwa have started to examine these coastal communities within the context of their broader maritime cultural landscapes. While this recent work has broadly followed the implicit archaeological perspectives of the features that make a society maritime, these studies and the extensive body of previous research conducted along the coast provide a strong foundation from which to develop anthropologically informed frameworks and explore the socio-cultural context of maritime interactions. To this end, I decided to focus my research in the heretofore comparatively under-investigated Mafia Archipelago.

Kua - Historical and Archaeological Context

Described as the "Pompeii of East Africa" (Wheeler 1955:46), Kua is an extensive complex of coral-stone architecture that may have been surrounded by a network of smaller villages similar to other stone town sites along the Swahili coast (Wynne-Jones 2006:7). Extending over 30-40 acres, recent surveys of the site indicate that the settlement once comprised seven mosques, four cemetery areas, a large double-storied 'palace', at least 10 'complex structures' (likely houses, containing several distinct spaces/rooms), approximately 30 "walled courts" (Garlake 1966:109), which may have been associated with houses constructed from non-stone materials (Freeman-Grenville 1962:193), and numerous internal and external latrines. The site is extensively overgrown, a problem documented in several of the historical sources (e.g., Chittick 1957:3; Kirkman 1964:191; Piggott 1941a:5; Wheeler 1955:46) and this seems to have influenced how much of the site has been observed and recorded in the past. The history of Kua recorded by Freeman-Grenville in 1955 (Freeman-Grenville 1962:211-215; referred to as the 'Kua Chronicle') states that the site was initially founded by Shirazi settlers "who had come long ago from Persia" (Freeman-Grenville 1962:211). The original settlement was concentrated in an area south of the main ruin complex, known as *Mkokotoni* (Freeman-Grenville 1962:211) and although the precise date for the foundation of Kua is unknown, it is shown on the maps of Arab geographer Al-Idrisi in 1154 as Kahua (Chittick and Rotberg 1975:141). Numismatic evidence from the site suggests that it was occupied by at least the 13th century AD, and Freeman-Grenville (1962) notes the presence of possible 14th century AD celadon ware. Piggott (1941a) and Chittick (1957) were both less convinced of the antiquity and elegance of the settlement. Chittick (1957) argues that "most of the buildings at Kua are uninspiring and... of no great antiquity" (Chittick 1957:3). The Kua Chronicle (Freeman-Grenville 1962) indicates that the main settlement area was founded at a later date by Arabs who approached the Shirazi settlers asking for a place to build. "The Arabs were given the north part of... [*Mkoktoni*]... After they had finished building their town, they called their hosts, that is, the Shirazi and said to them: The name of our town will now be called Kua" (Freeman-Grenville 1962:211). On this basis, discrepancies between Chittick's (1957) and Freeman-Grenville's (1962) dating of the site could be explained by the fact that Chittick only visited the later phase of settlement. The fact that Freeman-Grenville (1962:172) records the presence of seven mosques whereas Chittick (1957:3) only records five suggests that Freeman-Grenville had also visited the mosque in the *Mkokotoni* Area to the south of the site. While he does not note the large burial ground surrounding this mosque, as shown by his observation that there were only two cemeteries at Kua and his suggestion that "earlier burials ... [may have taken place]... elsewhere in cemetery not yet found" (Freeman-Grenville 1962:172), it is possible that the graves were obscured by the dense vegetation. Many of the burials in this area are marked by stones at the head and foot of the grave and even today, they are not easily visible.

Although dates for the foundation of Kua still need to be firmly established though further archaeological reconnaissance, an account of the collapse and subsequent abandonment of the site derived from local traditions is referred to by many historians (Freeman-Grenville 1962; Kirkman 1964; Piggott 1941a, 1941b; Revington 1936). A popular narrative suggests that Kua was raided in the early 19th century AD by the Sakalava from Madagascar who "arrived in their small canoes call '*laka*' and captured many people" (Piggott 1941b:25). It is possible that this attack was orchestrated by an artisan from Kua, who was upset with the poor way slaves and others were treated by their rulers, escaped and returned with reinforcements (Freeman-Grenville 1962:213). The dates of the attack can be further refined to sometime between "1810 and 1835" (Piggott 1941b:7) as news of the attack was sent to the Sultan of Zanzibar, whose control of Mafia was well-established by 1812. As a result of this, "an expedition was made up and sent to chase the invaders ...[who] ... were found on a small island and defeated, the prisoners brought triumphantly back to Mafia" (Piggott 1941a:7). In light of the reported response to the raid, it is also probable that it occurred prior to 1838, when the Sultan is said to have "made a treaty with Queen Seneekoo of the Sakalava" (Piggott 1941b:7). Despite this victory, the tradition holds that Kua never recovered from the attack and the site was subsequently abandoned when the Sultan's seat of power was moved to nearby Chole Island. During this subsequent period, Chole had considerable involvement in long-distance trading networks, playing an important role in the supply of cowrie shells to other parts of Africa (Hongerdon and Johnson 1986; Piggott 1941a:7). Although Kua was involved in long-distance trading networks—as evidenced by the presence of considerable quantities of imported material including pottery and beads, the nature of the harbour led Piggott to suggest that the "population [could not] have depended on sea trade" (Piggott 1941a:5). Whether this comment refers exclusively to long-distance trade, or whether it includes their involvement in local networks and maritime exploitation is unclear; however, it is likely that fishing was an important part of the subsistence economy of the site's inhabitants.

Excavation Context

While a similar study could have been conducted at the other stone town settlement site in the archipelago—Kisimani Mafia (Figure 1), Kua was selected for excavation as the standing ruins and their associated archaeology were more extensive. This was beneficial from two perspectives: first, the surviving standing remains lent themselves to mapping using a handheld Global Positioning System (GPS), which could then be used to evaluate the influence of the sea on settlement organisation. Second, and more relevant from the perspective of this paper, local ethnographies collected during the course of the broader project had suggested that rubbish was disposed of on a house-by-house basis. It was therefore hypothesised that the examination of the midden deposits associated with two households of different social status (determined based on the ethnographic and architectural data and the associated cultural material within the midden deposits that could be used as social markers), could be used to evaluate whether access to marine resources was influence by social or economic status in the past.

Site selection

Two 2 x 3 m trenches (Trenches 1 and 2) and one additional 1 x 1 m trench extension (Trench 1A) were excavated during the field season (Figure 1(a)), selected based on local knowledge of the site, ethnographic data, surveys and small-scale Shovel Test Pit (STP) excavations. The assemblages recovered from Trenches 1 and 1A were combined during the spatial analysis and these Trenches are referred to collectively as 'Area 1', as their deposits are thought to have been associated with the same household. To maintain consistency, Trench 2 is therefore referred to as 'Area 2'. All deposits were dry-screened using a 3mm mesh, with a 0.5mm mesh used in a secondary screen for the initial deposits of Trench 1. This smaller mesh size was subsequently abandoned after heavy rains left the deposits waterlogged. Although wet screening would have been preferable, maximising the recovery of smaller bones, this was not logistically feasible as the water supplies on the island were limited.

Area 1

Situated approximately 1 km south of the main ruins complex, Area 1 is probably situated within the area of the original settlement of *Mkokotoni*, mentioned by Freeman-Grenville (1962:211). Located over 80 m from the shore, Trenches 1 and 1A were associated with a low circular mound of large coral rocks (Figure 2), which ethnographic surveys had suggested were the remains of a collapsed house.

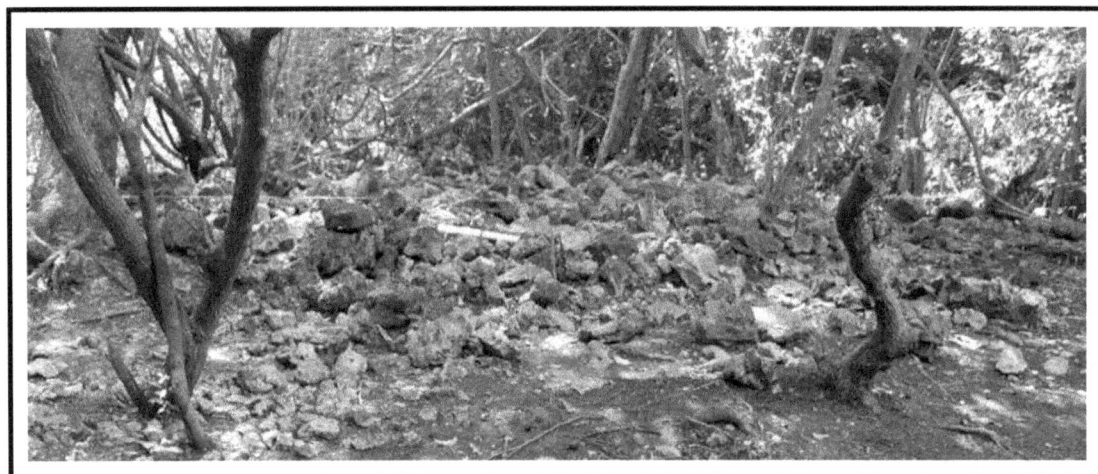

Figure 2. Low circular stone mound in Area 1.

Source: Photo copyright author.

Trench 1 was opened in this area as a sizeable scatter of marine shells, land-snail shells, local and imported pottery, and bone had been identified. It was believed to be the remains of part of a rubbish dump deposit created by the occupants of the associated house. A number of similar mounds were identified during a small-scale survey of the surrounding area and marked with GPS coordinates using the Garmin eTrex Vista. One of these 'house' mounds was considered to have the potential for further excavation, however, despite the excavation of four 0.5 m x 0.5 m test pits, the location of its associated rubbish dump remained uncertain. To identify a second area for excavation, additional surveys were conducted within the main ruins complex.

The coastline west of Area 1 is covered with a thin humic layer and considerable leaf litter. As the name of the area ('*Mkokotoni*' literally 'at the mangroves') suggests, direct access to the sea is limited by a dense band of mangrove at least 150 m thick, and unlike Area 2 (discussed below), there are no distinct breaks in the mangroves along the immediate coastline. The nearest coastal access point is approximately half a kilometre north of the area, towards the main ruin complex. The dense mangrove forest in this area is an ideal environment for mangrove mollusc species, such as *Terebralia palustris* and surface scatters of the shells from these molluscs around the excavation area suggest they have been quite extensively exploited, at least in recent years. Trench 1A was opened towards the end of the field season as an extension to the southeast corner of Trench 1. A large proportion of the faunal remains recovered from Trench 1 had been concentrated in this area and there was a lot of material still in the section. The excavation of Trench 1A had two aims: first, it aimed to determine the maximum extent of the deposits identified in Trench 1. Second, as a wall feature running along the west of Trench 1 had been uncovered, I hoped the excavation of Trench 1A would help clarify whether the deposits excavated were internal or external.

Area 2

To identify the second excavation area, archaeological scatters – particularly those associated with shell and bone debris – were identified during the surveys of the ruins. Test pits were excavated at four of these scatters to gauge the extent of the subsurface remains. These test pits were productive and Trench 2 was opened next to Test Pit 5 (TP5), which had the richest deposits (Figure 3).

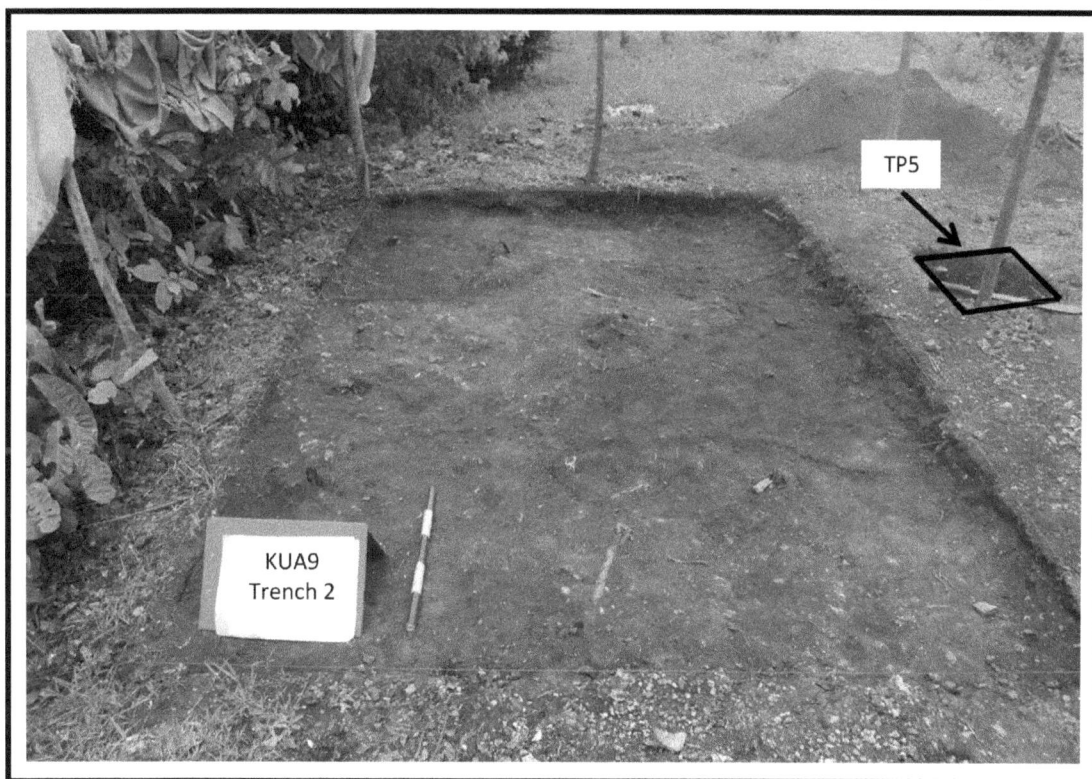

Figure 3. View of Excavation Area 2 looking North (Scale with 10cm divisions).

Source: Photo copyright author.

Bisecting a low mound close to the coastal edge on the top of a small but steep cliff which is exposed to water during the high tides of the *Ba Mvua* (times of the month when there is a high tidal range), Trench 2 is located slightly to the north of the main ruins complex. The beach immediately below the trench is quite rocky and the mangroves open out slightly to provide access to the bay. The beach in this area is strewn with a comparatively dense concentration of local and imported pottery, bone, beads, shell and iron slag; all of which extend seawards approximately 10-15 m.

Beyond the mangroves, the inter-tidal zone becomes increasingly silted with occasional concentrations of seagrass, and though difficult, it is possible to walk between Juani and Jibondo on foot during the *Ba Mvua* at which times shellfish and seagrass are intensively exploited. The seagrass species frequently used as bait in the *Madema* fish traps is also collected in this area.

The terrestrial environment around Trench 2 was relatively open compared to other parts of the site, and while the trench was not directly associated with visible standing remains, there are a number of plastered remains and toilets in the immediate vicinity. The coastal edge to the west of the trench (extending north and south of the unit) was lined with trees and shrubs including a large baobab tree—which is often considered indicative of past human settlement (Wynne-Jones 2006:10) was growing approximately 10 m to the south. Human skeletal remains were observed eroding out of a path providing access to the beach; however, these were not examined out of respect for local customs and because of the issues associated with obtaining permission to excavated human remains in Tanzania. The presence of a grave this close to the high water mark (HWM), and the dense concentration of slag and other cultural deposits on the immediate inter-tidal zone, does suggest that this area of coast may have been exposed to a certain degree of coastal erosion in the past in which cultural material may have been washed out of the cliff section.

Site chronology

To evaluate the influence of social or economic status on patterns of resource exploitation, it is important to consider each of the excavation areas within their chronological context. To this end, twelve charcoal samples were collected at various stages of the excavation from sealed layers or undisturbed contexts; three of which were sent to Rafter GNS science labs in New Zealand for dating.

While radiocarbon dating tends to provide more refined chronological data than other indicators such as pottery sequences, it can produce quite a wide date range as the calibration curve can oscillate. Thus, the peak of the radiocarbon age signal can bisect the calibration curve at several date ranges.

KU1 (NZA33897)

Taken from a layer near the bottom to Trench 1A in Area 1, this sample yielded a date of 531 ± 25 years BP. Calibrated, this gave two possible date ranges at a 95% confidence interval of either AD 1325 to 1346 or AD 1393 to 1437 (Figure 4).

The calibrated date range suggested above is difficult to refine further. Other chronological indicators recovered from this area were limited to one piece of Chinese celadon ware, which could be associated with either of the dates suggested (14th-15th century AD).

KU2 (NZA 33898)

The second sample, taken from an undisturbed context near the top of the midden deposition in Trench 1A in Area 1, yielded a date of 470 ± 25 BP, which gave a calibrated date range of AD 1415 to 1451 at a 95% confidence interval (Figure 5).

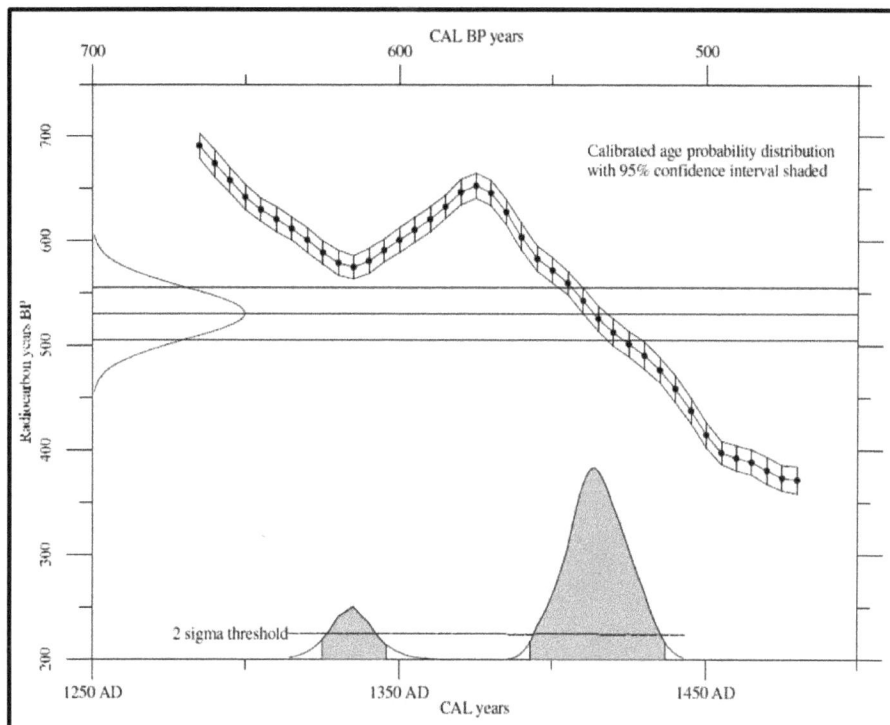

Figure 4. GNS radiocarbon calibration curve for sample KU1 (NZA33897).

Source: Rafter Radiocarbon Laboratory report for KU1 (NZA338978).

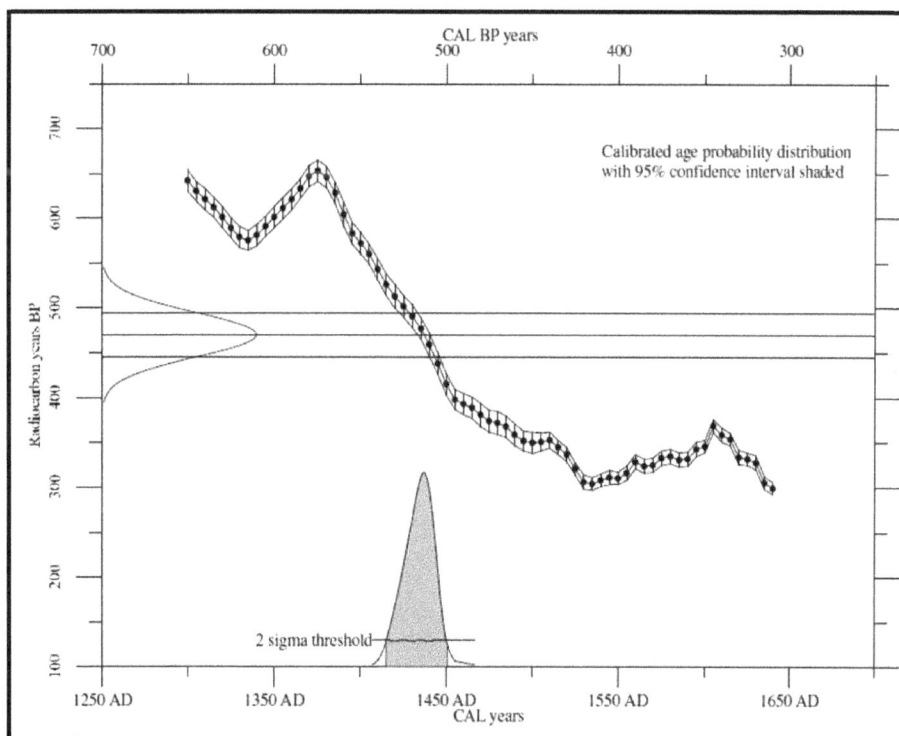

Figure 5. GNS radiocarbon calibration curve for sample KU2 (NZA33898).

Source: Rafter Radiocarbon Laboratory report for KU2 (NZA33898).

As the date ranges from KU1 could not be refined further, it is difficult to assess the period of deposition. The midden could have accumulated over a period of approximately 100 years, although it is also possible that this period could have been rather shorter, around 10-20 years. Whether this period reflects the entire occupation of the associated household or whether an as yet unidentified site was selected for additional deposition at the end of this sequence remains unclear, and remains to be determined through further excavation.

KU3 (NZA 33899)

Taken from a deposit considered to represent an initial phase of midden deposition in Trench 2 (Area 2), this sample yielded a date of 263 ± 30 BP. Unlike the previous two samples, there were more oscillations on the calibration curve resulting in four possible ranges suggested at a 95% confidence interval. The ranges were as follows: AD 1520 to 1593, AD 1619 to 1669, AD 1781 to 1798, and AD 1945 to 1950 (Figure 6).

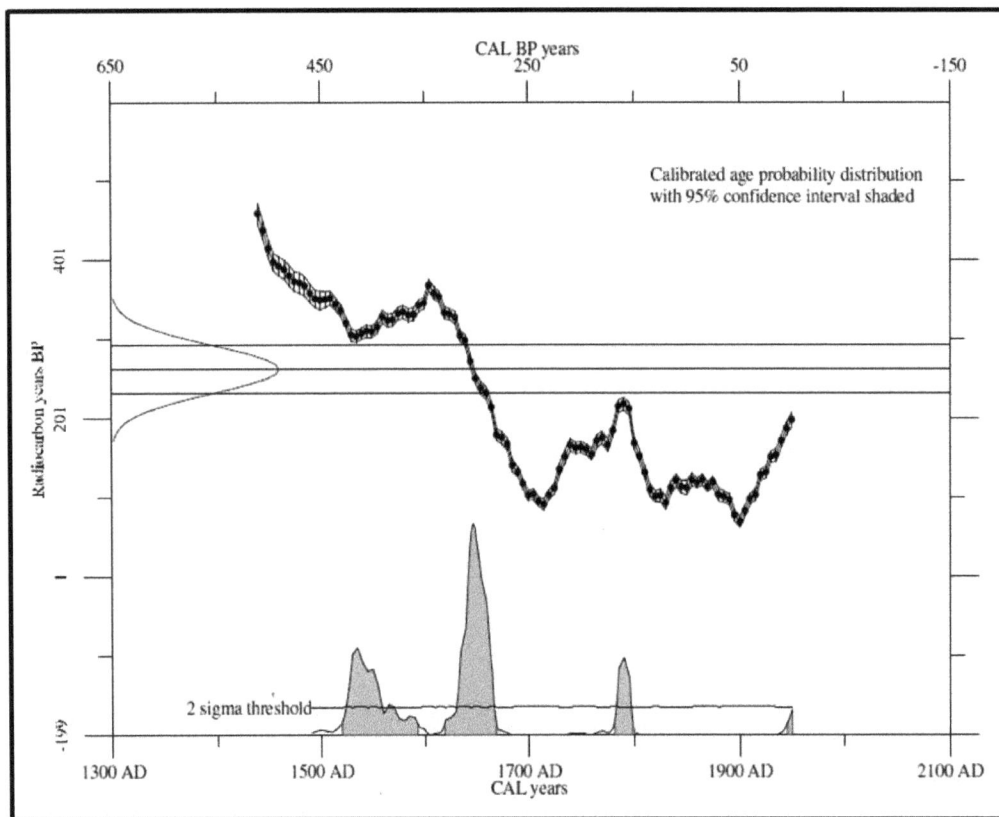

Figure 6. GNS radiocarbon calibration curve for sample KU3 (NZA33899).

Source: Rafter Radiocarbon Laboratory report for KU3 (NZA33899).

These dates can be refined when examined in conjunction with other chronological indicators including historical sources, architectural features, pottery sequences and beads, (see Christie 2011 Vol. 1:262-264 for more details). Based on the historical data, it is possible to eliminate the date range of AD 1945 to 1950, while the architectural, inscriptional and historical sources would all seem to suggest that the date ranges AD 1619 to 1669 and AD 1781 to 1798 could both be applicable. Based on these ranges, there seems to have been a gap of at least two centuries between the final deposits in Area 1 and the founding deposits in Area 2. Although the historical sources point to a possible status differentiation between the two areas, arguing that the Arabs who built Kua, "resolved after they had settled down to make themselves the rulers and subdue the inhabitants" (Freeman-Grenville 1962:212), in light of the radiocarbon dates, it is possible that any differences in the patterns of consumption observed between the two excavation areas could also have resulted from chronological changes.

Status differentiation: Archaeological and historical indicators

One factor considered in the selection of the excavation areas was the likely status of the associated households. While this was initially determined based on ethno-historical data and small-scale surveys, analysis of the associated cultural materials within the midden deposits has been used to test whether the preliminary status differences noted were justifiable archaeologically. The primary indicators for status differentiation were the imported pottery assemblages and the beads, amongst others, as these items are often associated with prestige and higher status (c.f Donley-Reid 1990).

The assemblages from Area 2 have a much higher proportion of each of these materials, with the recovery of beads limited to the deposits from this area. From the perspective of the imported pottery and the beads, the difference in the quantities between the two excavation areas could support the interpretation that they represent households of differing social status, with the household in Area 2 having increased access to commodities available through long-distance trade and exchange. Additionally, Donley-Reid (1990:122) proposes that imported pottery, particularly Chinese porcelain (particularly Chinese blue-on-white), is frequently considered to be a marker of social status. It should be noted that the lack of beads recovered from the lower status household is not likely to have resulted from differential recovery procedures, as the deposits from Area 1 were screened through a finer sieve.

In addition to the archaeological assemblages, the architectural and historical data also suggest that, at least to some extent, there was some status differentiation between the two areas. From the perspective of architectural data, a buildings survey was conducted as part of the broader project, during which status markers within the standing remains were identified and recorded. Given the likely importance of Islam within the community, the mosques were considered to have been representative of higher status buildings. Pollard (2007:110) suggests that "the position of stone mosques probably indicates wealthier areas; status symbols showing the piety of the inhabitants, as well as places for Muslim sailors to head towards for navigation and worship." On this basis, several of the features observed within the mosques were used as status indicators at other buildings around the site. Status markers included evidence of plastering, particularly red plastering, the number of rooms, the number and the degree of elaboration of niches within the structure, the presence of other decorative features including "plaster decorations on the walls, with beautiful geometrical designs around doors and entrances" (Sheriff 2001:66), the use of marine coral or non-coral building materials, and evidence for a second floor.

During the surveys, it was noted that the majority of the houses recorded within the main ruins complex can be interpreted as being of high social status based on the criteria discussed above. While there are some slight variations within this, in terms of the fact that some of the buildings have more status indicators than others, this interpretation seems to fit with the traditional history of the site. Specifically, the history of Kua suggests that the "Arabs [who built Kua] gain a considerable footing and strength and became rulers of both parts of the town" (Freeman-Grenville 1962:212). The poor survival of the mounds interpreted as structures in the Mkokotoni area of the site when compared to the levels of preservation of the higher status buildings like K012 or K037, when examined in conjunction with the predominance of 'lower status' burials recorded in that area could suggest that individuals living in Mkokotoni had a different status to those living in Kua.

Results

Description of the assemblage

Over 3000 bones were recovered from the two excavation areas, of which 2700 specimens were identifiable to element, taxa, or both. Once the assemblages had been sorted by element, and the remains from 'marine' and 'terrestrial' taxa separated, the terrestrial remains were further subdivided into the following categories (Table 1).

Table 1. Size classes for terrestrial taxa.

CATEGORY	CLASSIFICATION METHOD	LIKELY TAXA	LATIN NAME
Large Ungulate	Bones from taxa weighing 76-500 kg	Cow	*Bos spp.*
Medium Ungulate	Bones from taxa weighing 26-75kg	Goat, Sheep	*Capra spp.; Ovis spp.*
Small Ungulate	Bones from taxa weighing 0-25kg	Blue Duiker	*Philantomba monticola*
Bird		Chicken	*Gallus gallus*
Other		Rat, Dog	*Rattus spp.; Canis familiaris*

Source: Primary data from author's analysis of the excavated materials.

The ungulate size divisions were arbitrarily created to reduce potential errors arising from the misidentification of remains to species level. For example, although most 'large ungulate' remains are likely to have been representative of cattle bones, there are a number of other cattle-sized antelope which could have been exploited. The NISP for each of the taxa recorded is shown in Table 2.

Table 2. Representation (NISP) of taxa from each excavation area.

TAXA	AREA 1	AREA 2
Fish	1391	455
Large Ungulate	144	331
Medium Ungulate	59	158
Small Ungulate	3	2
Bird	43	93
Marine Mammals	4	4
Other	10	1
TOTAL	1654	1044

Source: Primary data from author's analysis of the excavated materials.

Over fifteen mollusc species were also recorded. Of these, the food species *Volema pyrum (Nalwale)* and *Terebralia palustris (Tondo)* were most frequently recovered, with non-subsistence molluscs such as cowrie shells *(Cypraea tigris)* and *Cypraea annulus (Kikete)* also well-represented, particularly in Area 2. Molluscs were recorded in the field using their local names and, where possible, these have been identified to species level following further examination. The MNI for the most frequently represented species within the assemblages is shown in Table 3. For gastropod species, MNI was calculated based on the counts of the numbers of complete specimens. For bivalve species, these counts are based on the number of intact right side valves to avoid the same animal being counted twice.

Table 3. MNI mollusc species identified in the excavated material (identified after Richmond 1997).

LOCAL NAME	LATIN NAME	AREA 1	AREA 2
Nalwale	*Volema pyrum*	833	272
Tondo	*Terebralia palustris*	604	19
Kiboko	*Nerita textilus*	109	51
Makome	*Chicoreus ramosus/ Pleuroploca trapezium*	36	20
Cowrie	*Cypraea tigris*	30	24
Combe	*Anadara antiquata*	23	42
Kikete	*Cypraea annulus*	8	156
Other		9	8
TOTAL		1900	647

Source: Primary data from author's analysis of the excavated materials.

Spatial analysis

Several levels of spatial analysis were conducted, three of which are presented below.

1. the proportions of marine and terrestrial fauna recovered from each excavation area were examined to evaluate patterns of resource use on an intra-settlement scale.

2. the proportions of the different ungulate size classes were evaluated, particularly from the perspective of element representation in each of the excavation areas to determine whether the different households had access to different parts of the carcass.

3. the molluscs assemblages from each of the excavation areas were studies from the perspective of the spatial distributions of subsistence and non-subsistence molluscs and the proportions of shell exploited.

1. Proportions of marine and terrestrial resources

Analysis of the Kua assemblages has indicated that there were differences in patterns of resource use between the two excavation areas. Material from Area 1 was comprised primarily of fish bones from much larger fish. In contrast, the assemblage from Area 2 comprised a more diverse assemblage with only a few smaller fish bones (Figure 7).

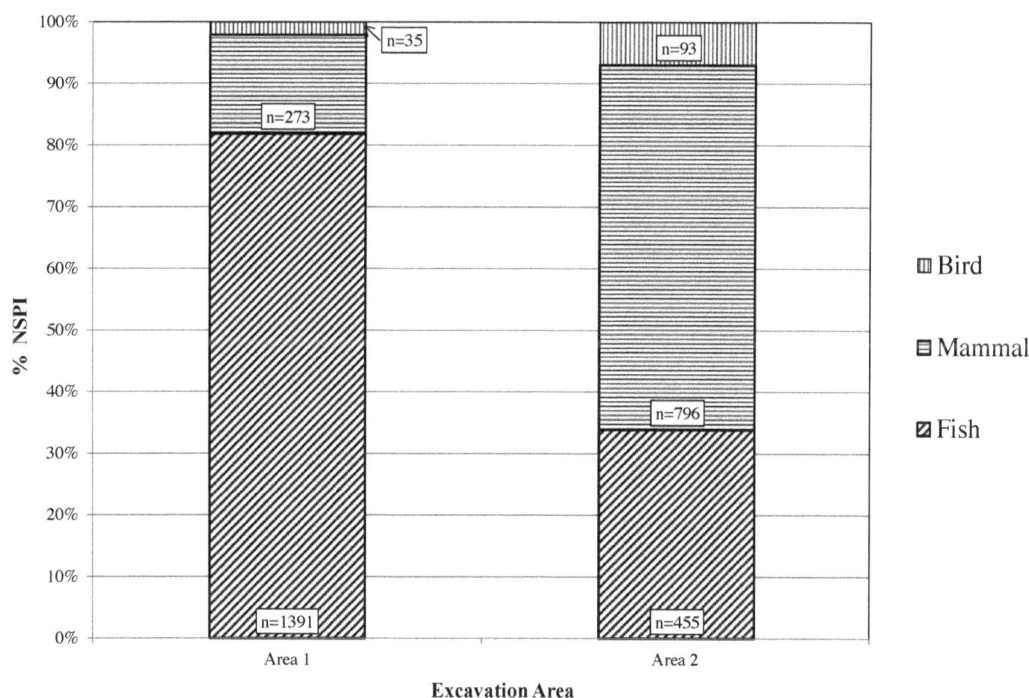

Figure 7. % NISP of different taxa recovered from each of the excavation areas.

Source: Created by author from primary data.

I had expected that the assemblages of both households would comprise equal proportions of marine resources, but also that the assemblages from Area 2 would have been made up of a higher proportion of larger marine taxa. This was based on the observation that higher status individuals would have had access to improved fishing technologies, or could afford bigger boats that would have given them access to fishing grounds further offshore (or more simply, as wealthier households, they could afford to purchase better quality/more expensive fish). Instead, in this deposit, most of terrestrial taxa and many of the fish remains were representative of smaller specimens. The higher proportion of terrestrial remains in Area 2 suggests that status was actually manifested through the control of access to terrestrial taxa, rather than through the direct control of marine resources. The higher proportion of marine remains (in terms of fish and edible shellfish) in Area 1 could then be seen to have been a means by which this household was able to make up the shortfall in their subsistence requirements.

2. Ungulate remains

Although a higher number of terrestrial resource were consumed at Area 2 (Table 2), when examined in terms of specific ungulate size classes, the contributions of each taxa within the total assemblage was fairly consistent. It should be noted that these figures are based on identifiable elements. Bone chips and unidentifiable fragments have been excluded.

While there are not any considerable differences in the proportions of large or medium sized ungulates being considered by each household, there is a difference in the elements represented at each area, particularly in the large ungulate category. Specifically, at Area 1, the identifiable large ungulate elements recovered are either from the cranium (zygomaticus/mandible), or from the forelimbs (humerus, radius, ulna and metacarpals). In contrast, the large ungulate elements recovered from Area 2 are more varied, with the majority coming from the skull, or the hind limbs (femur, tibia) and pelvis (Figure 8).

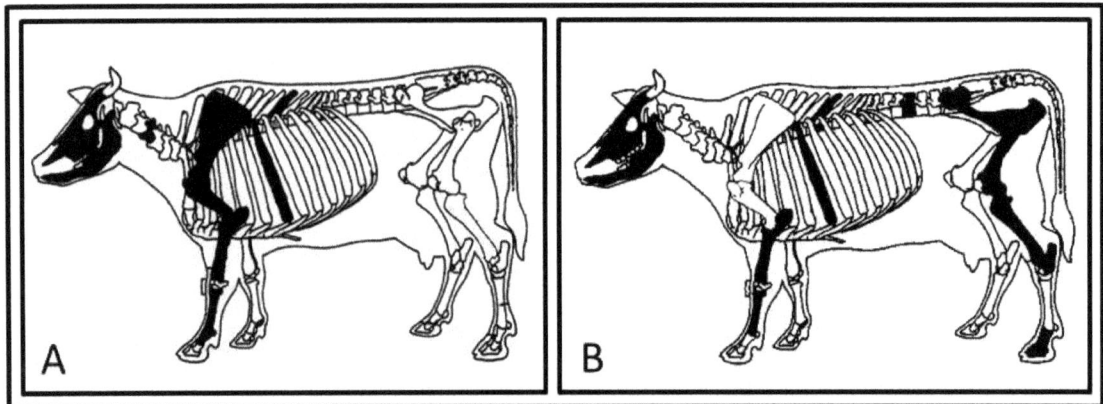

Figure 8. Large ungulate element representation in A) Area 1 and B) Area 2.

Source: Adapted from http://www.tumblr.com/tagged/animal%20science

This is interesting from the perspective of butchery practices as the leanest steaks such as the fillet, the rump or the sirloin are normally removed from the rear of the cow, whereas cuts from the front of the animal tend to be tougher, more suitable for stewing or for use as mince meat (c.f. Shultz and Gust 1983:48). The distribution of different meat cuts has implications for understanding socio-economic status. As Crabtree (1990:171) notes, "the most commonly examined indicator of status [when assessing faunal remains] include: differences in the quality of the meat cuts consumed… generally measured by examining differences in body part frequencies." While element distribution has in this case been used as a marker of socio-economic status, as Enloe (2003:4) highlights, "the ethnographic literature makes it clear that food sharing is neither universal nor uniform." The ways in which animal carcasses are divided is likely to depend on the size of the animal, its value within society and, most importantly, the cultural context of food sharing. This is particularly well-demonstrated by Mooketsi's (1991) examination of the distribution of meat cuts within different Tswana clans. Although part of the same cultural unit, different parts of the carcass are assigned a different value depending on relationships within specific clans (Mooketsi 1991:119-120). Further work would need to be conducted to assess the cultural value of specific meat cuts amongst the Swahili, however, ethnoarchaeological observation of the butchery of a goat carcass during the field season suggests a preference for cuts from the haunches of the animal over the lower limbs (e.g., metacarpals, metatarsals, phalanges) and cranium, which were quickly discarded. When queried as to why these elements were not retained, my informants suggested that they were not considered a worthwhile source of meat. Archaeologically, lower limb elements accounted for only 5% of the total ungulate assemblage, and over half of these were recovered from Area 2. Lower limb/feet bones were also the third most common elements showing evidence of butchery.

When considered in the context of the ethnographic data, it is possible that the low representation of lower limb bones within the total assemblage is the result of differential discard practices. In the case of the goat butchery, the carcass was butchered on the shore, and the lower limbs were thrown into the mangroves. Of the lower limb bones recovered from the archaeological deposits, over half of them would have been removed from a large ungulate (likely cow). In her report on *Food and food security on Mafia,* Caplan (2002) stipulates that cattle tend to be utilised in rituals and ceremonies rather than as a general food source (Caplan 2002:25). Given this association, it is possible that cows were butchered in a different way to goats. The lower limbs of a cow are also meatier, so may have been considered a more valuable food source. This does seems to be supported archaeologically as the observed patterns of medium ungulate element distribution are different to that noted for large ungulates. Specifically, there is a larger variation in the elements represented in Area 1. Medium ungulate elements recovered from Area 2 tend to come from the skull and upper forelimbs (scapula, radii and ulna) (Figure 9).

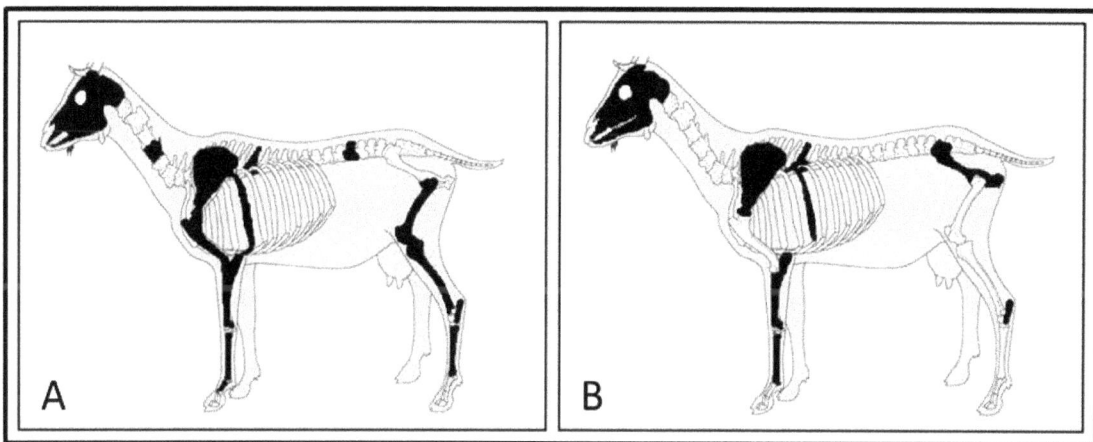

Figure 9. Medium ungulate element representation in A) Area 1 and B) Area 2.

Source: Adapted from http://thekebun.wordpress.com/2008/10/02/goat-skeleton/

Given that the representation of large ungulate elements in Area 2 is quite varied, the reduced variety of medium ungulate remains could suggest that medium sized taxa were less favoured by this household, possibly because they had access to a wider variety of large ungulate meat cuts.

Birds

Comparative analysis in conjunction with a modern reference collection would seem to indicate that most of the archaeological bird remains are chicken (*Gallus gallus*). There is a slight difference in terms of the proportions of bird remains recovered from each of the excavation areas, with a higher proportion of the bird assemblage recovered from Area 2; however, unlike the ungulates, there is very little difference in the elements represented at the two areas. The only difference between the two areas was the presence of two additional wing bones (the humerus and carpometacarpus), and a chicken cranium recovered from the deposits in Area 1. The similarity between the two units in terms of the spatial distribution of elements is not unexpected given the average size of the chicken, as the entire carcass can be eaten by one family. As Wilson (1996:67) states, "large carcasses are extensively butchered, small ones scarcely."

Although there is little difference in the spatial distribution of elements, the higher proportion of chicken remains in Area 2 could suggest that access to chickens may have been restricted.

Marine Resources

To assess the fish remains within the assemblages, a small reference collection of Indian Ocean reef fish (now stored at the University of York) was made. Fish were purchased from local fishermen and the fishing technique used was recorded. The catch was measured and identified, then subsequently cooked to remove the majority of the meat and skin. The bones were collected and allowed to soak overnight in a separate bowl of warm water to soften any excess flesh. These were then sorted and the cleaned bones were submerged and left in a second bowl of warm water, this time mixed with biological washing powder, for up to two days to break down any fatty residues. The bones were subsequently removed and allowed to dry before being soaked in white spirits to preserve them and mitigate against mould and rot. The dried bones were bagged and labelled with the following information: Common Name, Latin Name, Swahili Name, Size of Fish, Date of Collection and Fishing Method.

The collection comprised 57 specimens from over 22 different families and was used to identify the archaeological fish bone assemblages. As my expertise in fish identification was limited, ten cranial elements with clear differences were selected as the basis for the analysis to reduce any errors. Any uncertainties in identification were marked as such. The cranial elements selected included: the upper and lower jaw bones (dentary, articular, maxilla, premaxilla), the pharyngeal bone, the vomer, the palatine, the hyomandibular, the cleithrum, the quadrate and the post temporal.

Given the small selection of elements from which to identify the specimens, the sample size of elements identified to family level is necessarily small, representing just over 14% (n=271) of the entire fish bone assemblage from all three trenches. Of this, 32% (n=87) of the cranial elements available remained unidentified. The proportion of identifiable elements in each of the excavation areas generally reflects the contribution of the fish bones in the assemblages from each of the excavation areas (Figure 10).

The analysis of the identifiable elements suggests that at least nine families are represented in the archaeological assemblages, with emperors (*Lethrinidae*) and groupers (*Serranidae*) being the most abundant (Table 4).

Table 4. Frequency of elements from specific families.

COMMON NAME	LATIN NAME	FREQUENCY	
		AREA 1	AREA 2
Emperor	Lethrinidae spp.	58	6
Grouper	Serranidae spp.	55	5
Snapper	Lutjanidae spp.	29	4
Parrotfish	Scaridae spp.	17	3
Sweetlips	Haemulidae spp.	3	0
Rabbitfish	Siganidae spp.	1	0
Triggerfish	Balistidae spp.	0	2
Goatfish	Mullidae spp.	0	1

Source: Primary data from author's analysis of the excavated materials.

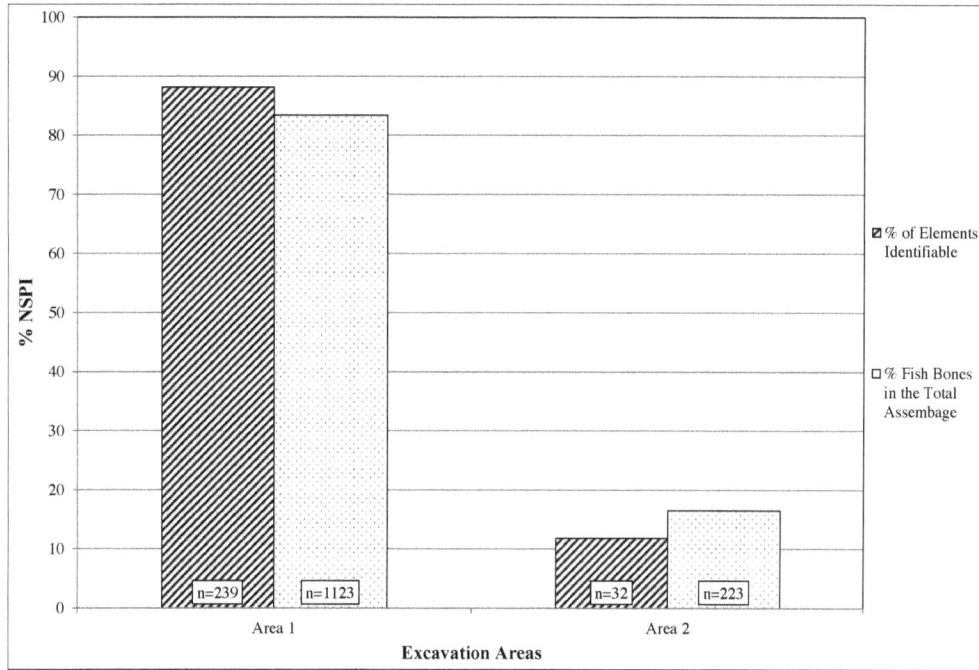

Figure 10. % Fish bones in the total assemblage compared to the % of the assemblage representing identifiable elements.

Source: Created by author from primary data.

As shown in Figure 11, the proportion of the families represented in each of the excavation areas is similar. While Area 1 has a slightly higher proportion of elements identified as groupers (*Serranidae*) and emperors (*Lethrinidae*), it is possible that this is the result of the differential sample size from each of the excavation areas. The higher proportion of goatfish (*Mullidae*), triggerfish (*Balistidae*) and parrotfish (*Scaridae*) in Area 2 is interesting, as data collected during the fish catch surveys suggested that these families are caught more frequently in the *Madema* fish traps. That said, there is still considerable overlap in the composition of fish catch between *Madema* and *Mshipi* techniques. McClanaghan and Mangi (2004) conducted a detailed examination of fish catch off the Kenyan coast near Mombasa, correlating fish catch composition with fishing technologies. Their observations indicated that catch from hand lines *(Mshipi)* had a high dominance of emperor (*Lethrinus*) families, while big traps (*Madema*) had a high dominance of parrotfish (*Scaridae*) (McClanghan and Mangi 2004:57).

Examination of the families identified, in the context of marine zones/habitats, suggests a likely explanation for this overlap, as the habitat preferred by each of these families is quite similar (Table 5). These types of habitat are common around Kua and Juani in general.

Table 5. Habitats of the represented families (after Richmond 1997: 338-364).

COMMON NAME	LATIN NAME	ECOLOGY/HABITAT
Emperor	*Lethrinidae spp.*	Coral and sea grass beds
Grouper	*Serranidae spp.*	Shallow coral reefs and lagoons
Snapper	*Lutjanidae spp.*	Coral and rocky reefs, mangrove forests
Parrotfish	*Scaridae spp.*	Reefs, lagoons and sea grass beds
Sweetlips	*Haemulidae spp.*	Coral reefs
Rabbitfish	*Siganidae spp.*	Inshore areas, especially sea grass beds
Triggerfish	*Balistidae spp.*	Reefs, lagoons and sea grass beds
Goatfish	*Mullidae spp.*	Sandy Bottoms especially around reefs

Source: After Richmond (1997: 338-364).

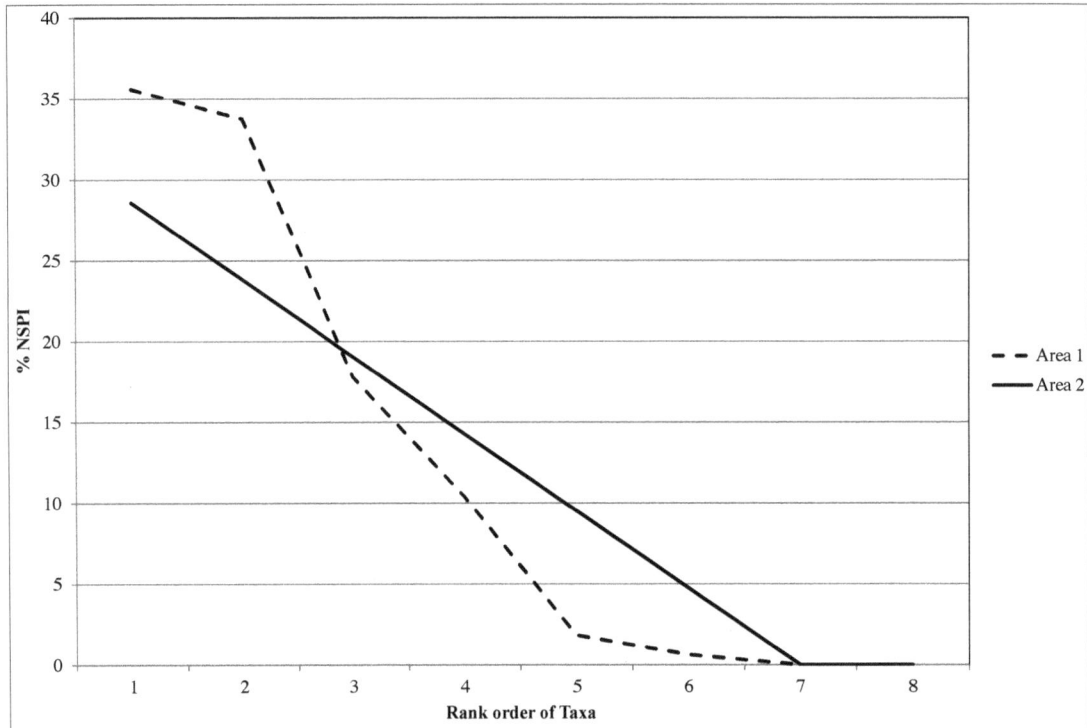

Figure 11. Rank order of taxa between the two excavation areas.

Source: Created by author from primary data.

Interestingly, several of the families that were proportionately more abundant in the assemblage from Area 2 tend to prefer nearshore lagoon and sea grass areas, whereas the families that were proportionately more abundant in Area 1 tend to prefer coral and rocky reefs, which are often slightly further offshore, and while additional data would be needed to make a more conclusive interpretation, it could be indicative of some differences in fishing practices between the two areas either in terms of selection of fishing technique or in terms of access to different vessel types.

Bones from larger pelagic species, often caught outside the reef by large gill nets, are notably absent from the assemblages of both excavation areas. This could suggest that these communities were not exploiting marine zones farther offshore, or did not have access to net technologies. Walley (2004) suggests that net fishing was only introduced as a viable fishing practice after the independence of Tanzania, proposing that nylon seine nets and shark nets were considered as "modern... fishing gear" (Walley 2004:149). It is also possible, however, that their absence is either the result of sampling biases and taphonomy. While preparing the reference collection, it was noted that the remains of both sharks and rays had very poor survival rates, and that the cranial elements in particular were very soft and friable. It is possible, therefore, that the cranial elements of these taxa have since been lost through poor preservation, and thus have not been identified. The slightly more robust vertebral elements were not included in the range of elements selected for analysis.

It is also possible that the remains of many of the more robust pelagic families such as trevally (*Carangidae*), barracuda (*Sphyraenidae*) and tuna (*Scombridae*) were not identified archaeologically, as these families were not included in the reference collection. These families were not collected as their size and weight made them expensive and too large to be shared amongst only three people. Additionally, fish from these larger pelagic families tend to be sold directly to local fishmongers where it is butchered and sold by the kilogram.

3. Mollusc Assemblages

Several of the patterns observed in the analysis of the osteological remains were also noted in the mollusc assemblages. Specifically, it was noted that a higher proportion of mollusc remains were recovered from the lower status units in Area 1 (c.f. Table 3). Within this, a much higher proportion of these remains were from species likely to have been exploited for consumption (such as *Tondo* and *Nalwale*) (c.f. Horton 1996:389-390) (Figure 12):

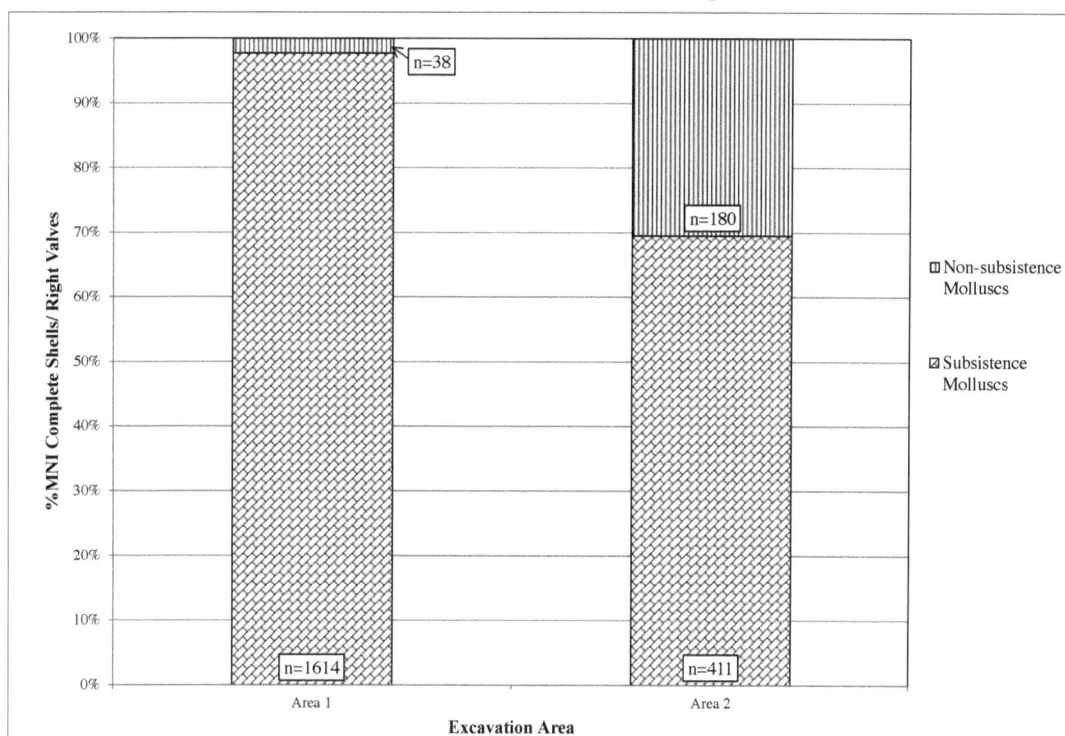

Figure 12 % MNI of molluscs used for subsistence and non-subsistence practices between the two excavation areas. This is based on complete specimens or the right valve of bivalve species.

Source: Created by author from primary data.

The higher proportion of molluscs (and indeed subsistence molluscs) in the assemblages from Area 1 is particularly interesting in light of several ethnoarchaeological studies that have proposed that shellfish consumption is generally associated with lower social status (Chittick 1974; Fleisher 2003; Lyall 2007; Moss 1993; Szasbo 2002; amongst others). These assertions have equally been referred to in a local context, as several informants interviewed as part of the project suggested that the consumption of shellfish was only preferable when access to other marine or terrestrial resources is restricted. Although these restrictions could have been imposed as a result of status differentiation, it is also possible that restrictions to other fish and terrestrial resources could have been the result of environmental stresses. While examination of longer-term environmental or climatic conditions was not possible in the scope of the project, it would be an interesting avenue for further research.

More generally, comparative examination of the species represented in each of the assemblages also has the potential to inform our understanding of the marine environment, and zones of resource exploitation, as different mollusc species are exploited from different parts of the intertidal zone (Table 6). Similar to the interpretations made about the shovel-test-pit assemblages, the high proportion of the mud whelk *Tondo* in the assemblage from Area 1 could suggest that individuals from this household were more actively exploiting mangrove resources. This seems likely given the coastal environment around the *Mkokotoni* area.

Table 6. Habitats of the mollusc species identified (after Richmond 1997:247-261, 274-277).

SWAHILI NAME	LATIN NAME	HABITAT	USE
Nalwale	*Volema pyrum*	Eulittoral sand and sea grass flats	Food
Tondo	*Terebralia palustris*	Upper eulittoral mud or in mangrove swamps	Food, bait
Kiboko	*Nerita textilis*	On rocks in the littoral fringes	Food
	Chicoreus ramosus	Around shallow, sheltered reefs	Food
Makome			
	Pleuroploca trapezium	Sea grass Beds	Food
Kikete	*Cypraea annulus*	In shallow water, tide pools under stones or amongst sea grasses	Decoration
Cowrie	*Cypraea tigris*	Under coral and boulders in shallow or deep water	Decoration
Combe	*Anadara antiquata*	Eulittoral buried in muddy sand	Food
Panga	*Pinna muricata*	Semi buried in eulittoral and shallow sea grass beds	Food

Source: After Richmond (1997:247-261, 274-277).

Discussion

Status differentiation

One of the main aims of the excavation was to evaluate whether there was any evidence to suggest that resource exploitation was influenced by social or economic status, and from this perspective, the results of the spatial analysis are of most interest.

Analysis of the architectural data, and the ceramic and bead assemblages would seem on one hand to support the hypothesis that the two excavation areas represent the midden deposits associated with two households of different social or economic status. The higher proportion of imported pottery – particularly Chinese blue-on-white porcelain associated with the display of social status (Donley-Reid 1990:122) – and the presence of both imported and likely locally manufactured beads both suggest that the midden deposits excavated from Area 2 would seem to be associated with individuals of higher social status.

If we accept that the two areas are representative of households of different social status, the faunal analysis suggests that marine exploitation (most evident in Area 1) was conducted primarily by individuals of lower social status. Furthermore, while these individuals also had access to some livestock, the presence of hind-limb bones in the assemblage from Area 2, and the lack of the same in the assemblages from Area 1 implies that the higher status household would have had access to leaner cuts of meat. While this could be interpreted as suggesting that the lower status household had preferential access to marine resources, this is very unlikely. What seems more reasonable is that the lower status individuals, unable to access the more expensive subsistence base provided by the exploitation of terrestrial remains, demonstrated an increased dependence on marine resources to supplement their diet.

The high proportion of terrestrial exploitation in the higher status household (Area 2) could be interpreted as a way of signifying their status. If the sea was commonplace within society – as one would expect in a maritime society that derives its livelihood from the sea in terms of its role in the subsistence economy and as a facilitator of local and international exchange networks and involvement in local and international exchange networks – then consumption of terrestrial resources may have been a form of distanciation (Garnham and Williams 1996:57-58), by which the 'elite' differentiated themselves from the ordinary. The association between high status and the exploitation of terrestrial remains is also interesting when considered in light of anthropological observations concerning the role of cows as status symbols, used more in ritual activities and feasting than for everyday consumption (Caplan 2002:25).

Parallels could be drawn with Moss's (1993) ethnographic study of shellfish consumption among the Tlingit society on the northwest coast of the United States of America. Her research suggested that although shellfish were likely to have been a primary protein source amongst the community, the consumption of shellfish was considered to be associated with poverty and low social status. Consequently, members of the elite were "encouraged to avoid eating shellfish as part of a larger strategy to achieve wealth and status" (Moss 1993:646).

So where does this leave us in terms of exploring differential access to marine resources? When evaluated wholly from the perspective of the faunal assemblages, it could be argued that access to marine resources is not restricted by status. However, this is not the full story. Although details of the buildings' surveys conducted at the settlement have not been discussed in detail in this paper, the differential patterns of consumption observed could be evaluated differently when examined in light of the buildings' survey data (see Christie 2011 for more details). These data suggest that higher status individuals lived closer to the sea than those of lower social status. If we accept the interpretation that the two areas represent households of different social status, the proximity of the higher status houses to the sea could be regarded as a further iteration of this status as, although they are not actively exploiting marine resources (as evidenced by the higher proportion of terrestrial remains in the associated midden deposits), they are still controlling access to the sea. To a certain extent, this is supported by the ethnographic data on Juani. During one interview, the informant suggested that access to the landing site closest to the 'palace' was restricted, as the people of Kua were not allowed to walk past the palace to gain access to the shore. He also suggested that access to the fishing grounds immediately adjacent to Kua was also limited, as only the king or people carrying out his requests could fish there.

Alternative interpretations

While status differentiation between the two units is a reasonable argument for the interpretation of differences in the patterns of resource exploitation discussed above, in light of the historical data that suggests that the main complex of ruins at Kua (surrounding Area 2) were built sometime after the settlement in *Mkokotoni* (near Area 1) was founded, it is possible that the two units are not directly contemporary. This is further complicated by the fact that these historical sources also suggest that the majority of the ruins around Area 2 were built by a group of foreign Arabs who approached the existing community in *Mkokotoni* and asked for land on which to build.

On this basis, three alternative interpretations to explain the different patterns of resource exploitation between the two excavation areas could be proposed. First, it could be argued that the differences between the two areas were the result of a changing preference from marine resources to terrestrial resources over time. One possible explanation for this change could be that the marine resources were overexploited to the point that they were no longer viable. This seems unlikely, however, as modern observations of marine consumption suggest that communities are currently exploiting a similar range of marine resources to those identified in the archaeological assemblages. This could be tested through further research through the collection and analysis of larger faunal assemblages in a secure chronological sequence – specifically, fish bones identified to family level could be measured to determine whether there is any evidence to suggest over-fishing (possibly indicated by a decline in the average size of the catch, or the elimination of specific families from the sequence). Such levels of over-fishing are possible – for example, analysis of the faunal remains from Shanga suggested that one family (*Siganidae*) that was exploited in the past is now "hardly ever caught…[hypothesising]… perhaps it was over-exploited in the thirteenth century and populations have never recovered" (Horton 1996:384).

A second explanation for the differential patterns of resource exploitation observed during the faunal analysis is that the incoming Arab population that was said to have built Kua (Freeman-Grenville 1962:211) had a preference for terrestrial resources such as cows or goats. This would also need to be evaluated through further research to determine whether similar patterns of resource use are present in other midden deposits within the main ruins complex. This could possibly be examined by comparing the midden deposits associated with houses close to the shore with a midden associated with houses slightly inland. Interestingly, Caplan (2002:25) suggests that there may be a division between individuals involved in animal husbandry and those involved in fishing, which is attributed to the preferences of different population groups (the Arabs and Shirazi compared to the *Wambwera*). One reason suggested for the abandonment of Shanga in the 14th century AD is that it might have run out of water (Horton 1996:427). Reduction in the water supply – a resource that is comparatively scarce on Juani today - might have encouraged a decline in the exploitation of domestic terrestrial taxa, with less livestock kept at the site in order to preserve the water available, thus resulting in a higher dependency on the exploitation of marine resources.

Finally, given Caplan's (2002:25) assertion that "cattle are sold to be slaughtered at big rituals such as funerals and weddings, and also at spirit healing rituals," one final interpretation for the high proportion of terrestrial remains in the assemblage from Area 2 is that the deposits from this midden were primarily associated with 'ritual' activities. This could explain the higher quality of locally produced ceramics and the higher quantity of imported remains – also often associated with protection and ritual, however, it seems unlikely given the high proportion of other terrestrial and marine remains (that are likely to have been less ritually important) within the same contexts. This would need to be examined through further research – possibly through a close study of the butchery and discard practices involved in these ritual activities. Do they result in different butchery marks? Is the entire carcass utilised in these activities, or are only select elements likely to be deposited?

Conclusion

The data from Kua have highlighted the multi-faceted nature of archaeological interpretation. While these alternative interpretations need to be examined in more detail, I would argue that status differentiation between the two excavated areas is likely to have at least *contributed* to the observed differential patterns of resource exploitation. On this basis, the Kua excavations have highlighted that, to some extent, maritime interactions including exploitation were socially complex. From the perspective of developing anthropologically-informed maritime frameworks to elucidate the maritime nature of the communities living along the East African coast, these excavations have highlighted the importance of examining the social context of maritime exploitation, rather than just the technological and economic aspects of the Swahili subsistence economy. The targeted analysis of faunal remains within a spatial framework has the potential to develop our understanding of the maritime nature of the Swahili, and the influence of the sea in the construction of the Swahili maritime identity.

References

Abungu, G.H.O. 1998. City States of the East African Coast and their Maritime Contacts. In G. Connah (ed), *Transformations in Africa: Essays on Africa's later past*, pp. 204-218. London and Washington: Leicester University Press.

Baumann, D. 1957 [1895]. Mafia Island. *Tanganyika Notes and Records* 45:1-24

Breen, C. and P.J. Lane. 2003. Archaeological approaches to East Africa's changing seascapes. *World Archaeology* 35(3):469-489.

Caplan, P. 2002. *Local Understandings of Modernity: Food and Food Security of Mafia Island, Tanzania.* Unpublished report to COSTECH, Tanzania. Available from Goldsmith's website. http://www.gold.ac.uk/media/COSTECH%20REPORT%20final%20060803.doc

Chami, F.A. 2000. Further Archaeological Research on Mafia Island. *Azania* XXXV:208-214

Chami, F.A. 2004. The Archaeology of Mafia archipelago, Tanzania: New evidence for Neolithic Trade Links. In F. Chami, G. Pwiti, and C. Radimilahy (eds), *The African Archaeology Network Reports and a Review*, pp. 73-101. Dar es Salaam: University of Dar es Salaam Press. *Studies in African Archaeology* 4.

Chapman, M.D. 1987. Women's fishing in Oceania. *Human Ecology* 15(3):267-288.

Chittick, N. 1957. Mafia Group. *Mafia Island District Book – History.* Dar es Salaam: Tanzania National Archives.

Chittick, N. 1974. *Kilwa: An Islamic trading city on the East African coast.* Nairobi: British Institute in Eastern Africa.

Christie, A.C. 2011. *Exploring the Social Context of Maritime Exploitation in the Mafia Archipelago, Tanzania: An Archaeological Perspective.* Unpublished doctoral dissertation, University of York.

Chittick, N. and R.I. Rotberg. 1975. *East Africa and the Orient: Cultural Syntheses in pre-colonial times.* London and New York: Holmes and Meier Publishers Ltd.

Conte, E. 2006. Ethnoarchaeology in Polynesia. In I. Lilley (ed), *Archaeology in Oceania*, pp. 240-259. Malden, Oxford and Victoria: Blackwell Publishing.

Cooney, G. 2003. Introduction: Seeing Land from the Sea. *World Archaeology* 35(3):323-328.

Crabtree, P.J. 1990. Zooarchaeology and complex societies: some uses of faunal analysis for the study of trade, social status and ethnicity. *Archaeological Method and Theory* 2:155-205.

D'Arcy, P. 2006. *The People of the Sea: Environment, Identity and History in Oceania.* Honolulu: University of Hawaii Press.

Donley-Reid, L. 1990. The power of Swahili porcelain, beads and pottery. *Archaeological Papers of the American Anthropological Association* 2:47-59.

Dulvy, N.K., D. Stanwell-Smith, W.R.T. Darwall, and C.J. Horrill. 1995. Coral mining at Mafia Island, Tanzania: A management dilemma. *Ambio* 24:358-365.

Enloe, J.G. 2003. Food Sharing Past and Present: Archaeological Evidence for Economic and Social Interactions. *Before Farming* 1(1):1-23.

Fleisher, J. 2003. *Viewing stone towns from the countryside: An archaeological approach to Swahili regional systems: AD 800 – 1500.* Unpublished doctoral dissertation, University of Virginia.

Freeman-Grenville, G.S.P. 1962. *The Medieval History of the Coast of Tanganyika.* London: Oxford University Press.

Garlake, P.S. 1966. *The Early Islamic architecture of the East African Coast.* Nairobi and London: Oxford University Press.

Garnham, N. and R. Williams. 1996. Pierre Bourdieu and the sociology of culture: an introduction. In J. Palmer and M. Dodson (eds), *Design and Aesthetics: A reader*, pp. 49-62. New York: Routledge.

Garpe, K.C. and M.C. Ohman. 2003. Coral and Fish distribution patterns in Mafia Island Marine Park, Tanzania: Fish and habitat interactions. *Hydrobiologia* 498(1-3):191-211.

Gaudian, G. and M.D. Richmond. 1990. *Frontier Tanzania Mafia Island Marine Park Survey: Interim Report No. 1.* London: The Society for Environmental Exploration.

Hau'ofa, E. 1994. Our Sea of Islands. *The Contemporary Pacific: A Journal of Island Affairs* 6(1):148-161.

Fleisher, J. 2003. *Viewing stone towns from the countryside: An archaeological approach to Swahili regional systems: AD 800 – 1500.* Unpublished doctoral dissertation, University of Virginia.

Horrill, J.C. 1991. *Mafia Island Project Report No. 2: Results of physical, biological and resource use surveys: rationale for the development of a management strategy.* London: The Society for Environmental Exploration. *Frontier Tanzania Technical Report* No. 8.

Horton, M. 1996. *Shanga: the archaeology of a Muslim trading community on the coast of East Africa.* London: British Institute in Eastern Africa.

Horton, M. and J. Middleton. 2000. *The Swahili: The social landscape of a mercantile society.* Oxford and Boston: Blackwell Publishers.

Horton, M. and N. Mudida. 1993. Exploitation of maritime resources: evidence for the origin of Swahili communities of East Africa. In T. Shaw (ed), *Archaeology of Africa: Foods, Metals and Towns*, pp. 673-693. London and New York: Routledge.

Hviding, E. 1996. *Guardians of Marovo Lagoon: Practice, place and politics in maritime Melanesia.* Honolulu: University of Hawaii Press.

Jidawii, N.S. and M.C. Ohman. 2002. Marine fisheries in Tanzania. *Ambio* 31(7-8):518-527.

Juma, A.M. 1996. The Swahili and the Mediterranean worlds: Pottery of the late Roman Period from Zanzibar. *Antiquity* 70:148-154.

Kamukuru, A.T., T. Hecht, and Y.D. Mgaya. 2005. Effects of exploitation on age, growth and mortality of the blackspot snapper, *Lutjanus fulviflamma,* at Mafia Island, Tanzania. *Fisheries Management and Ecology* 12:45-55.

Kirkman, J. 1964. *Men and Monuments on the East African Coast.* London: Lutterworth Press.

Kusimba, C.M. 1999. *The Rise and Fall of Swahili States.* Walnut Creek, London and New Delhi: Altimira Press.

Lyall, C. 2007. *Marine Ecology and Shellfish Exploitation in the Rio Parita, Panama.* Unpublished doctoral dissertation, St Francis Xaviar University

McClanahan, T.R. and S.C. Mangi. 2004. Gear-based management of a tropical artisanal fishery based on species selectivity and capture size. *Fisheries Management and Ecology* 11:51-60.

Middleton, J. 1992. *The World of the Swahili: An African Mercantile Civilisation.* New Haven: Yale University Press.

Mooketsi, C. 1991. Butchery and the processing of cattle carcasses in Botswana. *Botswana Journal of African Studies* 15(1):108-124.

Moss, M. 1993. Shellfish, gender and status on the Northwest coast: reconciling archaeological, ethnographic and ethnohistorical records of the Tlingit. *American Anthropology* 95(3):631-652.

Nurse, D. and T. Spear. 1985. *The Swahili: reconstructing the history and language of an African society 800-1500.* Philadelphia: University of Pennsylvania Press.

Piggott, D.W.I. 1941a. History and Archaeology. *Mafia Island District Book.* Dar es Salaam: Tanzania National Archives.

Piggott, D.W.I. 1941b. Mafia – History and Traditions (collected by Kadhi Amur Omar Saadi). *Tanganyika Notes and Records* 11:35-40.

Pollard, E.J.D. 2007. *An Archaeology of Tanzanian Coastal Landscapes in the Middle Iron Age (6th – 15th centuries AD).* Unpublished doctoral dissertation, University of Ulster.

Pollard, E.J.D. 2008a. The maritime landscape of Kilwa Kisiwani and its region, Tanzania, 11th to 15th century AD. *Journal of Anthropological Archaeology* 27:265-280.

Pollard, E.J.D. 2008b. Inter-tidal causeways and platforms of the 13th-16th century city-state of Kilwa Kisiwani, Tanzania. *International Journal of Nautical Archaeology* 37(1):98-114.

Pollard, E.J.D. 2008c. *The Archaeology of Tanzanian Coastal Landscape in the 6th to 15th Centuries AD: BAR International Series 1873.* Oxford: Archaeopress.

Prins, A.H.J. 1965. *Sailing from Lamu: A Study of Maritime Culture in Islamic East Africa.* Assen: van Gorcum & Comp.

Prins, A.H.J. 1971. *Didemic Lamu: Social stratification and spatial structure in a Muslim maritime town.* Groningen: Institut voor culturele antropologie der rijksuniversiteit.

Revington, T.M. 1936. Some notes on the Mafia Island Group. *Tanganyika Notes and Records* 12:23-27.

Richmond, M.D. 1997. *A guide to the seashores of Eastern Africa and the Western Indian Islands.* Stockholm: Sida's Department for Research Co-operation, SAREC.

Sheriff, A. 2001. The spatial dichotomy of Swahili towns: The case of Zanzibar in the nineteenth century. *Azania* XXXVI(1):63-81.

Shultz, P.D. and S.M. Gust. 1983. Faunal Remains and Social Status in 19th Century Sacramento. *Historical Archaeology* 17(1):44-53.

Szabo, K. 2002. *Prehistoric shellfish gathering.* Available at: http://www.manandmollusc.net/history_food.htm

van Neer, W. 2001. Animal remains from the medieval site of Kizimkazi Dimbani, Zanzibar. In B.S. Amoretti (ed), *Islam in East Africa: New Sources (Archives, Manuscripts and Written Historical Sources. Oral History. Archaeology)*, pp. 385-410. Rome: Herder.

Walley, C.J. 2004. *Rough Waters: Nature and Development in an African Marine Park.* Princeton: Princeton University Press.

Westerdahl, C. 1992. The Maritime Cultural Landscape. *The International Journal of Nautical Archaeology* 21(1):5-14.

Westerdahl, C. 2005. Seal on Land, Elk on Sea: Notes on the Applications of the Ritual Landscape at the Seaboard. *International Journal of Nautical Archaeology* 34(1):2-23.

Westerdahl, C. 2010. Horses are Strong at Sea': The liminal aspects of the Maritime Cultural Landscape. In A. Anderson, J.H. Barrett and K.V. Boyle (eds), *Global origins and development of seafaring,* pp. 275-288. Cambridge: McDonald Institute for Archaeological Research.

Wheeler, M. 1955. Archaeology in East Africa. *Tanganyika Notes and Records* 40:43-47.

Wilson, B. 1996. *Spatial patterning among animal bones in settlement archaeology: An English regional exploration. BAR 251.* Oxford: Archaeopress.

Wynne-Jones, S. 2006. *Reconstructing the Long-Term History of the Mafia archipelago.* Unpublished report submitted to COSTECH and the Antiquities Department, Ministry of Natural Resources and Tourism, Tanzania.

6

Beyond Subsistence: Cultural Usages and Significance of Baler Shells in Philippine Prehistory

Timothy Vitales, National Museum of the Philippines

Introduction

For apparent reasons, Molluscan remains constitute a very large portion of materials recovered from archaeological sites in the Indo-Pacific. The tropical Indo-Pacific biogeographic region has the largest diversity of marine molluscs in the world (Vermeij 1993); however, despite the variety of molluscan species, only certain taxa were significantly collected for food consumption and for shellworking and utilisation. Some of the taxa collected for the manufacture of artefacts include species in the Tridacnidae (giant clams), Trochidae (top shells), Turbinidae (turban shells), Conidae (cone shells), Pteriidae (*Pinctada* spp. pearl oysters), and Volutidae (volute and baler shells) families (Szabó 2005, 2008).

Baler shells (genus *Melo*) represent the largest members of family Volutidae, with sizes ranging from 175 to almost 470mm in length (Weaver and DuPont 1970). These marine gastropods are characterised by their inflated ovate shell, elongated but wide aperture, large dome-shaped protoconch (hidden or exposed), and thick folds in the columella. There are seven known species patchily distributed from the eastern Indian Ocean to the western Pacific Ocean, generally living on mud-sand substrates in littoral and sublittoral zones (Springsteen and Leobrera 1986; Weaver and DuPont 1970). These molluscs are edible and are used extensively as raw materials, as seen from ethnographic accounts in Australia, Papua New Guinea, and some regions in Southeast Asia, being fashioned into different objects, such as containers (Chen 1969; McCarthy 1967; McCarthy and Seltzer 1960; Schall 1985 in Smith and Veth 2004; Thomson 1934), valuable adornments (Akerman 1973; Hughes 1977; Mulvaney and Kamminga 1999; Przywolnik 2003), and tools (Akerman 1975; Schall 1985 in Smith and Veth 2004; Tindale 1977).

The widespread presence of baler shell remains in the archaeological record attests to a long history of exploitation in the Indo-Pacific (Figure 1). The earliest evidence to date comes from northwest Australia, as early as 32,000 years ago in Mandu Mandu Creek Rockshelter, Northwest

Cape (Morse 1993; O'Connor and Veth 2000). Other sites include Sumatra (van Heekeren 1972), Sarawak (Szabó *et al.* 2008), Vietnam (Szabó unpublished data), and the Philippines (Fox 1970; Vitales 2009a), ranging from 10,000 years to as recently as 500 years ago.

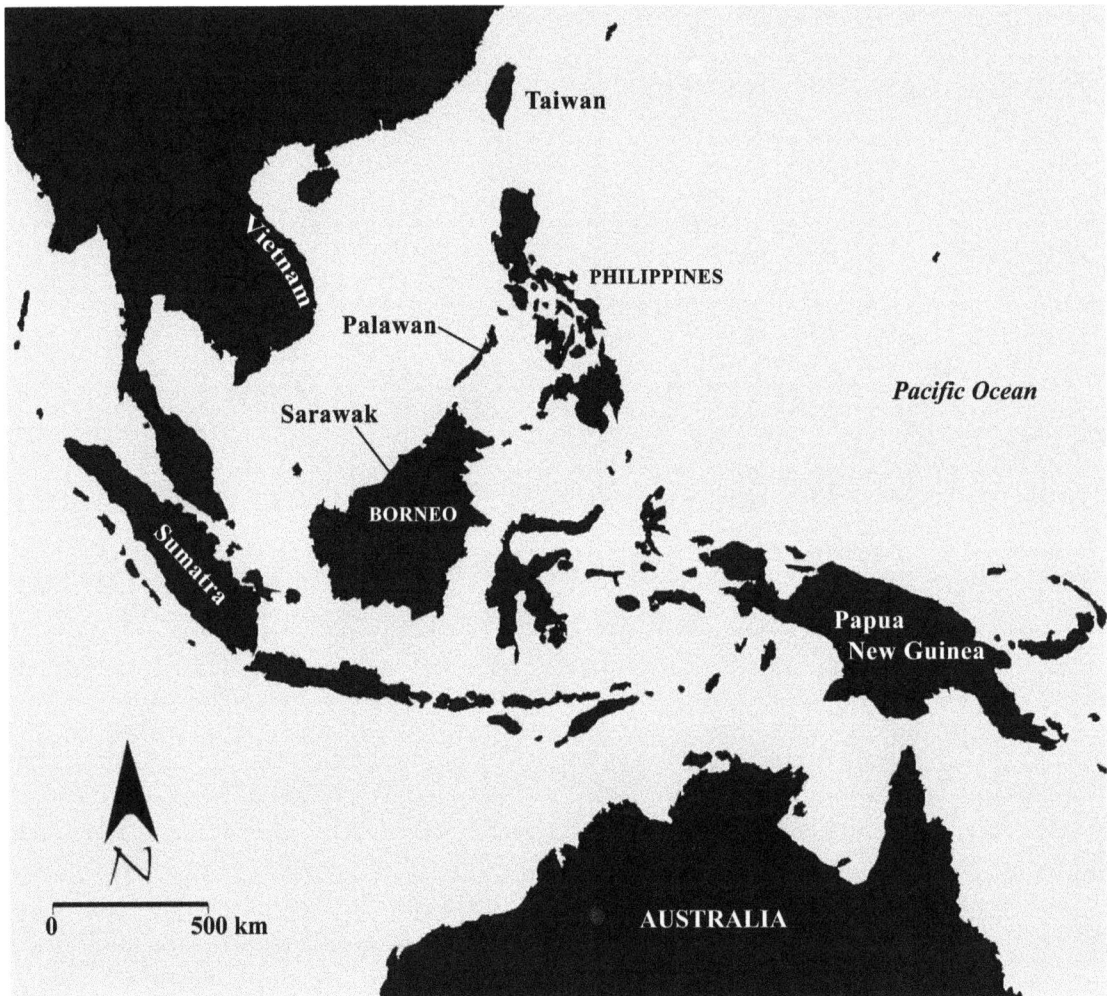

Figure 1. The Indo-Pacific and the Philippines.

Source: Modified from http://commons.wikimedia.org/wiki/File:Se_asia_malaysia.png

This paper will focus on the long history of baler shell exploitation and their significance in Philippine prehistory. The primary data used in this study comes from the baler shell assemblage recovered from the excavations in Ille Cave and Rockshelter site in northern Palawan, western Philippines. Ille Cave and Rockshelter, located in the eastern part of El Nido, Palawan (Figure 2), is a multi-phase site, with evidence of cave utilisation ranging from periods as early as the terminal Pleistocene to as late as the 18th century (Lewis *et al.* 2006; Lewis *et al.* 2008; Paz *et al.* 2008; UP-ASP 2005-2006). A majority of the materials investigated in this paper come from a shell midden deposit, with associated artefacts from the Neolithic and Metal Ages, such as decorated and undecorated pottery, polished stone adzes, and various worked shells. Human remains were also found at these levels, indicating the cave was also used for burial purposes during these periods. However, evidence of continuous reworking of most parts of the site has blurred the distinction between the Neolithic and Post-Neolithic (Metal Age to 18th century), subsistence-related deposits (e.g., shell midden (see Faylona 2003, 2008)), and burial deposits.

Nevertheless, they will still constitute the samples to be studied in this paper; since the author will be investigating the nature of the baler shell remains found in Ille, whether they mainly represent evidence of marine resource-based subsistence or evidence of artefact production and utilisation.

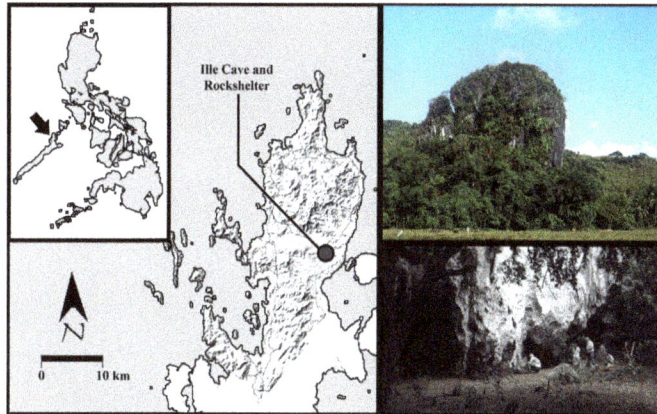

Figure 2. The location of the Ille Cave and Rockshelter site in the Philippine map (inset) and northern Palawan map (left). The site is located at the base of a karst tower (above right) and is composed of two major cave entrances (below right).

Source: Philippines map modified from http://www.palawanjoe.com/images/elnido_map2.jpg Ille tower on top right photo by author; Ille cave on bottom right photo by Victor Paz.

Baler Shell Remains in Philippine Sites

The Philippine archipelago has very rich archaeological evidence of baler shell exploitation and use; on current evidence, the richest in the Indo-Pacific region. Around thirty recorded sites within the archipelago have *Melo* remains, mostly located in the central and southern Philippines (Figure 3). The densest concentration of baler shells from archaeological sites is centred on the Palawan region, known for its rich diversity of shell artefact forms, and dubbed a 'major shellworking community of practice' (Szabó 2005). The notable concentrations of baler shell remains in Palawan are on Coron Island (3 sites) (Guthe n.d.; Solheim 1964, 2002), El Nido (12 sites) (Fox 1970, 1977; Paz 1998; Paz *et al.* 2008; Solheim 2004; Szabó 2005; UP-ASP 2005-2006; Vitales 2009a), and Quezon (5 sites) (Fox 1970; Kress 2000). Aside from Palawan, other sites with a presence of baler shells include the Bicol region of Luzon (Fox and Evangelista 1956, 1957), Bondoc Peninsula in Quezon Province, Luzon (UP-ASP unpublished data; Vitales 2009b), and the islands of Masbate (Solheim 1964, 2002), Samar (Guthe n.d.; Santiago and Barbosa 1977), Bohol (Roales 1985), Cebu (ACECI 2006; Nishimura 1992), and Saranggani Province in southern Mindanao (Dizon and Santiago 1996). Remains of baler shells found in Philippine sites generally range from the Neolithic Period around 4,000 years ago to as recent as 400 to 500 years ago (Vitales 2009a), although there are some baler shell fragments believed to date as early as c. 10,000 to 12,000 years ago at Ille Cave and Rockshelter in El Nido, Palawan (P. Piper pers. comm. 2006).

The species of baler shell identified from Philippine sites are given as *Melo aethiopica* (identified as *Cymbium aethiopicum* in Solheim's study, which is a junior synonym of *M. aethiopica*, for the baler shell artefacts from the Guthe collection (Solheim 1964, 2002)), *Melo amphora* (originally identified as *Melo diadema*, which is a junior synonym of *M. amphora* (Fox 1970, 1977; Kress 2000; Szabó 2005)), and *Melo broderipii* (ACECI 2006; Szabó 2005). Reassessment of these baler shell remains by Vitales (2009a) identified most of them as *Melo broderipii*.

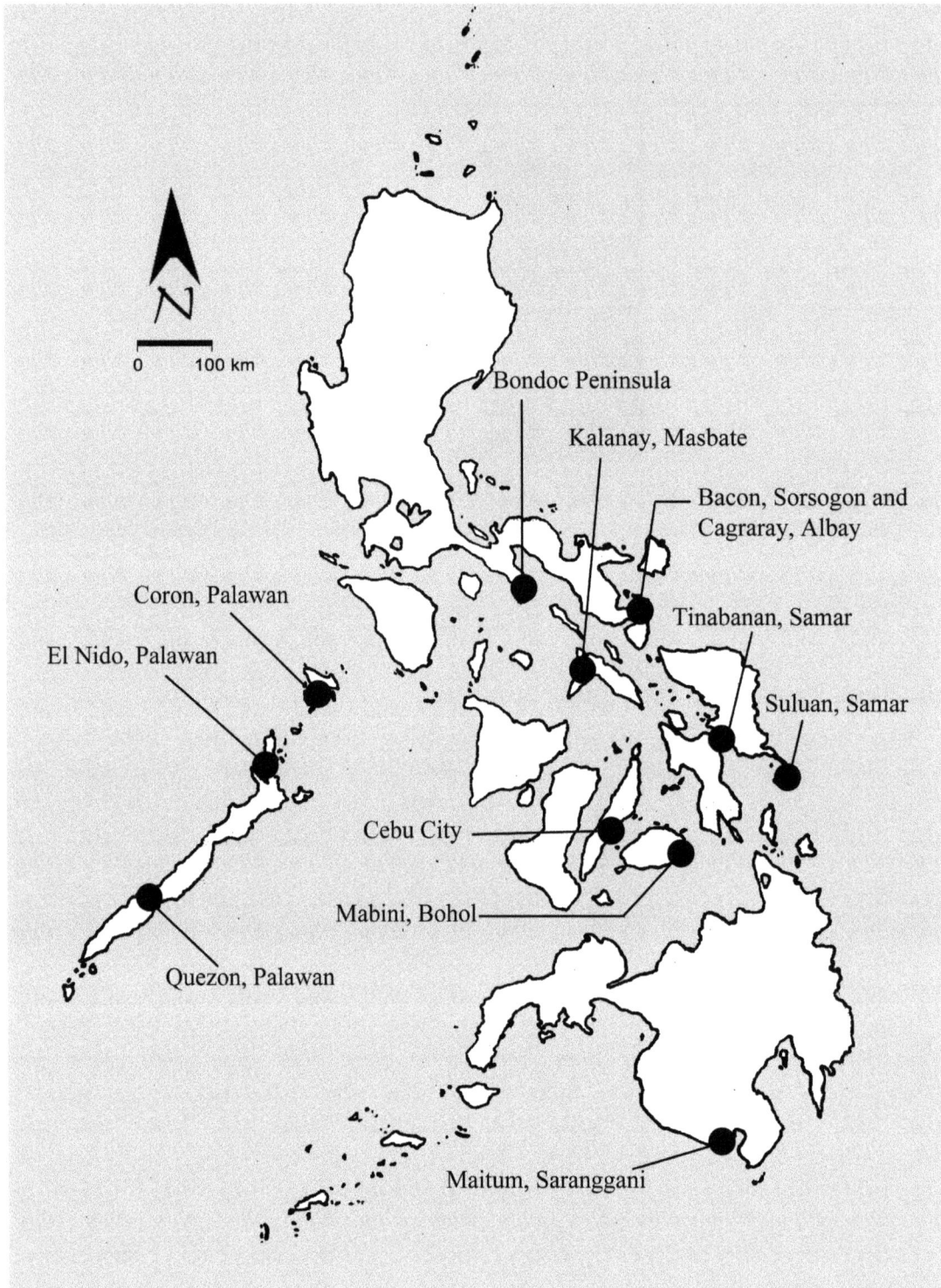

Figure 3. Map of the Philippines showing the sites with reported baler shell remains.

Source: Archaeological Studies Program (ASP), University of the Philippines.

Analytical Framework

The *Melo* shell assemblage in the Ille site is mostly composed of fragments, although there were baler shell remains found that are evidently whole artefacts, so these will be considered as well. Total identification (distinguishing between other molluscan fragments) and recovery of baler shell remains were done during the excavation. As for the fragments, each will be initially identified according to which part of the shell it corresponds to (Figure 4). The identification will be divided into six categories:

- *apical* - composed mainly of spire and shoulder
- *basal* - composed mainly of siphonal canal, sometimes with basal part of lip and exterior columellar folds
- *body whorl fragments* - composed mainly of the dorsal and/or ventral face
- *lip fragments*
- *apical and basal fragments* - spire and siphonal canal connected through lip or partial body whorl
- *columellar fragments* – composed primarily of the inner structure of the shell

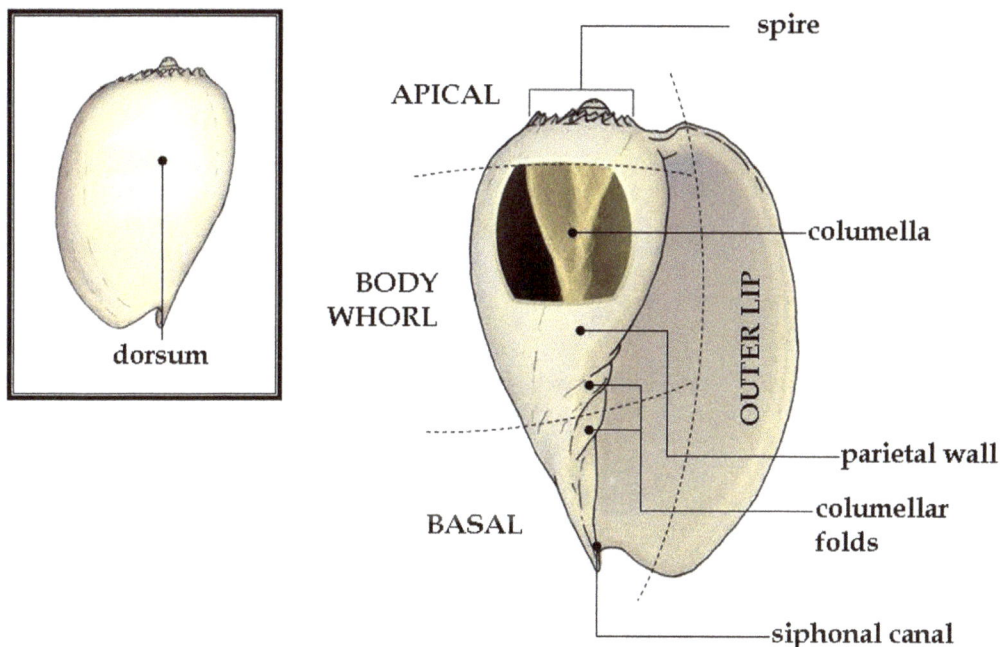

Figure 4. Six categories for identification of *Melo* shell.

Source: Timothy Vitales.

Individual fragments will be quantified as single specimens, although fragments that can be refitted will be counted as part of their aggregate specimen. Breakage patterns were also considered in the analysis using Szabo's (2005) method of distinguishing natural breakage, human-modified breakage related to subsistence, and human-modified breakage related to artefact production. The baler shell artefacts were analysed and classified according to their manner of working. Other variables were also considered, such as the surface condition of the shells and possible evidence of bioerosion, coral encrustation, and sponge borings, which would tell us whether the molluscs were collected fresh or post-mortem (Ibid.). Local knowledge from coastal communities that the author visited in the central Philippines regarding meat extraction from baler shells was also noted (although not systematically recorded) and served as a reference for identifying any subsistence-related shell remains.

Baler shell remains from other sites, particularly of the same period, were also analysed for comparative purposes. However, the baler shell remains found in later-period sites will be considered as well in order to understand the nature of its exploitation after the Neolithic and Metal Ages.

Results of the Analysis

Food discard or artefact fragments?

The question of whether there is evidence of purely subsistence-related baler shell remains can be addressed if we understand the processes of meat extraction of *Melo* spp. in the Philippines. Correspondence from the locals in Palawan, Cebu (central Philippines), and the Bicol region (eastern Philippines) reveals two methods of meat extraction. One involves hooking the meat and letting the shell naturally fall off onto to the ground. This is generally done when there is a desire to preserve the shell, which is sometimes used for decorative or commercial purposes. Another method of meat extraction for *Melo* spp. is by breaking through a large portion of the body whorl until the meat is accessible. With this method, the inner architecture of the shell usually remains intact, since breaking through the thin body whorl would be adequate for easily extracting the meat from the wide space inside the shell (Figure 5). It would seem unnecessary to break the thick columella in order to remove the meat. Based on local accounts, there is a possibility that similar meat extraction techniques were used in the past and, therefore, we should expect most parts of the shell, such as the body whorl, spire, columella, and basal portions, to be equally present in the site.

Figure 5. An example of a baler shell that was broken for meat extraction.

Source: Timothy Vitales.

The results of analysis of the *Melo* sp. fragments from Ille Cave (Figure 6) revealed that the shell parts recovered consist mainly of body whorl fragments (51%), as well as several fragments of spire and shoulder (12%), lip (10%), and basal portions, such as the siphonal canal (10%), with few apical-basal fragments (Figure 7). Only one columellar fragment, however, was recovered from the excavation. As for the body whorl fragments, it seems that only dorsal portions were found at the site. The ventral parts (characterised by the presence of a smooth parietal wall) were noticeably absent.

Baler Shell Remains from Ille Cave and Rockshelter

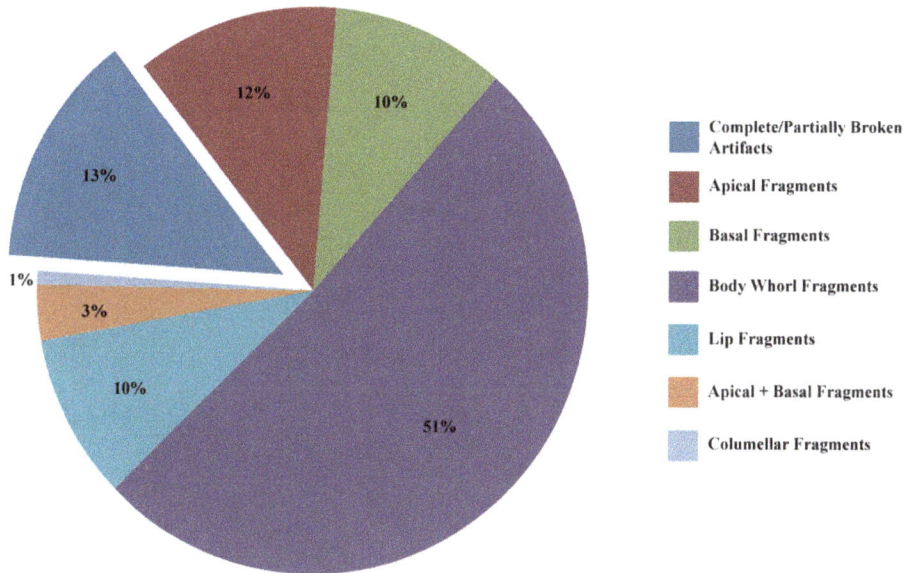

Figure 6. Percentages of identified baler shell artefacts and different fragments of baler shell remains found in Ille Cave and Rockshelter.

Source: Timothy Vitales.

Figure 7. Examples of different baler shell fragments found in Ille site. Some of the fragments belong to one piece and were restored. Scale in centimetres.

Source: Timothy Vitales.

The recognisable baler shell artefacts (complete and partially complete specimens), on the other hand, formed 13% of the total specimens. These artefacts resembled the 'scoop' forms similar to those described in previous literature on baler shell artefacts found in Palawan (see Alba 1998; Bautista 1988; Fox 1970; Szabó 2005). Three formal classes were observed in the artefact assemblage based on the type of working and the parts of the shells utilised (Figure 8) (Vitales 2009a):

- *Class 1* - The ventral portions of the shell are removed, including the siphonal canal and columella, leaving a deep concave form composed only of the spire and dorsal surface of the body whorl. The worked edges ('rim') are smoothed and cut, while the spines are often abraded.

- *Class 2* - Almost two-thirds of the shell is removed (including the spire and probably the lip), leaving a shallow concavity. Like Class 1 specimens, the worked edges are also cut, and the spines on the remaining shoulder are abraded.

- *Class 3* - Only the ventral face of the body whorl and columella are removed, leaving a deep concave form like that of Class 1 specimens, but including the rest of the lip and siphonal canal. The worked edges are irregular and show evidence of chipping, possibly through pressure flaking or indirect percussion. The spines on the spire and shoulder do not display signs of human modification, unlike Classes 1 and 2.

Analysis of the breakage patterns on most of the fragments revealed evidence of working as well, particularly in the body whorl, shoulder, and siphonal canal parts of the shell. Evidence of chipping, snapping, and cutting was found on the broken edges, which seems to be a departure from the natural fractural tendencies of the shell. Furthermore, apical fragments also showed a total removal of the thick columella connecting the interior of the spires—clearly evidence of working.

The particular fragments found at the Ille site, such as the spire, dorsal portions of the body whorl, and basal portions, seem to constitute the parts of baler shells utilised in manufacturing scoop forms as described above. This was further confirmed by the near absence of the columella and ventral portions of the body whorl. The identified parts from the shell fragments showing evidence of working also corresponded to the worked portions of the *Melo* shell artefacts. It can also be argued that the dorsal fragments, which showed the least evidence of deliberate working, could be parts of these shell scoops, since the dorsum is the main part utilised. From this evidence, we can therefore infer that the baler shell assemblage recovered from the Ille site were most likely artefact fragments rather than purely subsistence-related. In addition, it indicates that the reduction processes for the production of these artefacts were done outside the site.

Looking at other sites

To get a general view of the patterns of exploitation of *Melo* spp. in Philippines prehistory, it will be important as well to examine the *Melo* shell remains recovered from other Philippine sites. I focused particularly on the Neolithic and Metal Age sites since most of the baler shell remains were found in association with these periods and were contemporaneous with the Ille assemblage. However, I also considered studying the baler shell remains recovered from later-period sites (around 1500 to 500 years ago) to see any probable changes or continuity in these patterns after the Neolithic and Metal Ages.

The Palawan region has the densest concentration of baler shell remains, dating from the Neolithic to the Metal Age. Like Ille, all of these sites were cave or rockshelter sites that contained burial deposits. Only two Palawan sites, however, contained significant amounts of subsistence-related deposits: Duyong Cave and Sa'gung Rockshelter from Quezon, southern Palawan. Neolithic midden deposits from Sa'gung Rockshelter have already been analysed by Kress (2000) and, so far, only one baler shell was identified in the molluscan assemblage. Initial examination identified the baler shell as worked for artefact purposes. The process of reduction was similar to those found in the Ille assemblage (removal of columella and ventral face). The Duyong shell midden analysis, on the other hand, has been included in Fox's (1970) monograph of the Tabon caves. The shells were mostly coastal marine, brackish, and freshwater species (see also Kress 2000) and no *Melo* spp. were identified from the assemblage, dated around 7000 years ago. There were, however, *Melo* shell remains on the upper levels of the excavation, not associated with the midden deposits. All of the baler shell specimens from Duyong were worked and were similar to the baler shell scoop forms from Ille. One specimen, in fact, still had an intact basal portion of the columella, similar to the columellar fragment recovered from Ille. It is likely, therefore, that this fragment is part of the artefact as well. The rest of the baler shell remains from other Palawan burial cave sites were worked and manufactured into scoop forms, with the exception of one unmodified sub-adult baler shell found in Tadyaw Cave in Quezon, southern Palawan.

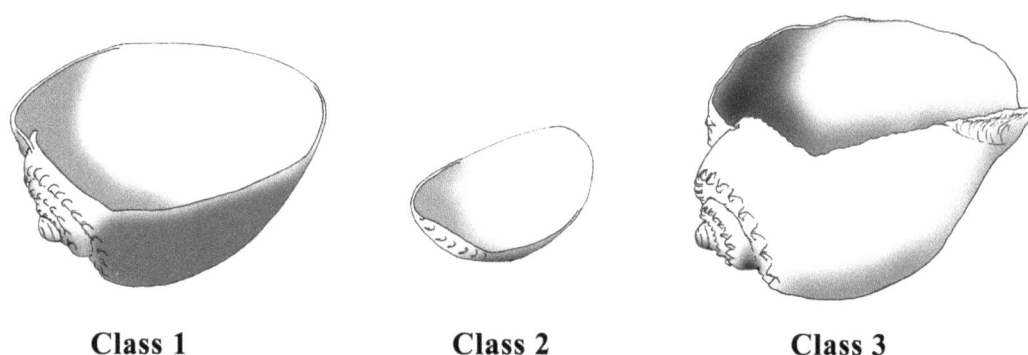

Class 1   **Class 2**   **Class 3**

Figure 8. The three class forms of baler shell 'scoops' generally found in Philippine archaeological sites.

Source: Timothy Vitales.

Aside from Palawan, other Neolithic and Metal Age sites containing baler shells were mostly burial cave sites; however, one site in the Bondoc Peninsula in southeastern Luzon was identified as an open midden and jar burial site (Paz *et al.* 2008). The baler shell remains recovered from the sites in the Bicol region (Fox and Evangelista 1956, 1957), Bondoc Peninsula (see Vitales 2009b), Bohol Island (Roales 1985), Saranggani Province (Dizon and Santiago 1996), and Samar (Guthe n.d.) were mostly worked and manufactured into scoop forms similar to the Palawan specimens. Maitum site in Saranggani Province, southern Philippines, on the other hand, seemed to have both worked and unworked shells, based on the initial examination of the zooarchaeological materials recovered from the site (Dizon and Santiago 1996). A seemingly unworked young *Melo* shell was recovered from a pot, while a *Melo* shell scoop, recovered from the surface in association with the Metal Age artefacts and burial jars. Another 'unworked' baler shell was recovered from an excavation of a cave site in Kalanay, Masbate, by Solheim (1964, 2002) and was associated with Metal Age deposits, including human remains.

Fewer baler shell remains were found in later-period sites. Only two later-period sites were known to have baler shell remains: Suluan Island in Samar, and Cebu City, both in the central Philippines. The baler shell found in a burial cave site in Suluan Island was a scoop artefact (Santiago and Barbosa 1977) similar to the scoop forms typically found in Neolithic and Metal

Age sites in Palawan and other areas. However, the time-depth of the associated materials (deliberately modified skulls) placed the site between c. 10th century CE to c. 17th century CE. Cebu City, on the other hand, yielded baler shell remains at sites dating from the 16th to 18th centuries (ACECI 2006; Nishimura 1992). The earlier excavation of these sites (Nishimura 1992) mentioned the presence of *Melo* spp. in the midden deposits and no indication of shell working from this taxa. The recent excavation (ACECI 2006), however, has only one unworked *Melo broderipii*, also found in possible subsistence-related deposits.

Evidence from the shell material

Previous studies on molluscan exploitation in Philippine prehistory indicate subsistence and diet as primary reasons for its collection, with utilisation of the shell as a raw material for artefact manufacture being a secondary consideration (Alba 1998). Szabo's (2005) technological studies on worked shells in the Philippines, on the other hand, revealed the contrary. Evidence of certain worked shells, such as *Conus* spp., from post-mortem collections of molluscs were observed, indicating that they were collected mainly for artefact production and not primarily as a food source. Subsequently, physical examinations were also done on *Melo* shell remains to see if there was evidence of post-mortem collecting similar to the other worked shells analysed by Szabó.

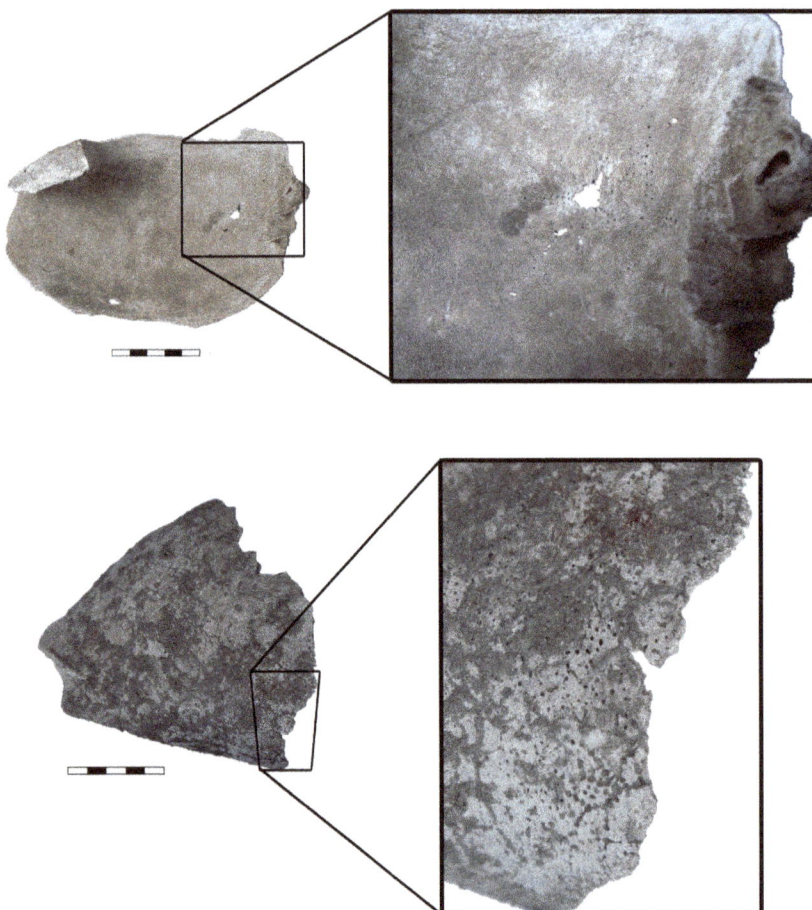

Figure 9. Baler shell scoop fragments from Batu Puti Cave in Quezon, Palawan (above) and from Ille Cave and Rockshelter (below) with evidence of animal borings. Scale in centimetres.

Source: Timothy Vitales.

Virtually all of the worked *Melo* shells in Ille were most likely collected fresh; some, in fact, had retained their porcelaneous interior surface. However, there were two baler shell remains at the site that showed signs of post-mortem collecting. Animal borings, such as those made by clionid sponges, were seen on the interior surface of these remains, an indication that the baler shells were long dead before collection, manufacture, and deposit at the site (Figure 9). Baler shell remains from sites other than Ille were also examined, revealing at least three baler shells with evidence of post-mortem collection. Two of these were baler shell artefacts from Batu Puti Cave in Quezon, southern Palawan; one contained clionid borings on the interior surface, while the other was evidently water-worn prior to its manufacture and usage. The third specimen was an unworked baler shell from the later-period site in Cebu City. Evidence of calcareous encrustations and possible animal borings were found on the interior surface of the lip, clearly indicating the inhabitancy of a post-mortem deposit.

Based on the physical analysis of the baler shell remains, it seems that most of the *Melo* sp. molluscs were collected fresh and their meat most likely eaten. However, their collection as a food source was certainly not the end in itself. During the Neolithic to the Metal Ages, most of these shells were apparently manufactured into artefacts, which seemed to be the primary purpose for their acquisition. Evidence of post-mortem collections of some of the shells further supports this inference.

Understanding the Significance of Baler Shells in Philippine Prehistory

The abundance of baler shells from Neolithic and Metal Age sites in the central and southern Philippines, particularly in Palawan, clearly demonstrates the frequent and continuous exploitation of these gastropods in this region over the past 3000 years. The high occurrence of worked baler shells, along with evidence of post-mortem collecting, indicates that they were not primarily collected for subsistence purposes but, rather, for shell-working and utilisation. This evidence seems to signify the shell's cultural importance in the past.

The mortuary role of baler shells

The ubiquity of baler shell remains in burial cave sites from the Neolithic and the Metal Ages suggests that their occurrences somehow played an important role in mortuary practices during that particular period. The most conspicuous, perhaps, would be the Neolithic burial in the Ille site, wherein two baler shell (*Melo broderipii*) scoops were found on top of human remains: one on the chest area and the other on the pelvis (UP-ASP 2005-2006). In other sites in Palawan (Fox 1970), the Bicol region (Fox and Evangelista 1956, 1957), and the Maitum site in Saranggani Province (Dizon and Santiago 1996), baler shell artefacts were found associated with other funerary items, such as burial jars. Even the unworked baler shells found in Tadyaw Cave in southern Palawan (Vitales 2009a), Kalanay site (Solheim 1964), and Maitum site (Dizon and Santiago 1996) were found in mortuary contexts. The presence of red pigments or colourants applied on several *Melo* artefacts from Ille and other Palawan sites were also observed, suggesting, again, the mortuary role of the shells. The colour red has a deep ritual significance in Philippine societies, both in the past and in the present (Fox 1970; Peralta 2000). Such pigments were mostly associated with mortuary practices in the past, usually found on human remains and other artefacts from burial sites (Fox 1970, 1977; Peralta 2000; Thiel 1986-87).

The ritual role of baler shells

Aside from their mortuary role, baler shells in the Philippines seem to have played some active part, as well, in particular ritual practices in the past, and this was observed in the Ille assemblage. While most of the breakage patterns found in the baler shell remains of Ille indicated working related to artefact production, there was also evidence of deliberate modification that seemed to be unrelated to artefact production. This type of breakage was first observed on some complete and partially complete artefacts, wherein the dorsal parts were punctured, most likely by a direct percussion technique, creating a perforation (Figure 10). Some dorsal fragments analysed also showed such patterns through evidence of semicircular notches, representing a total deviation from the natural fractural tendencies of these shells. Such practice of breaking or perforating the shell artefact closely resembled the ritual or ceremonial killing practice observed in other past and present cultures (Grinsell 1961; Leach 1976; Parker Pearson 1993), wherein they primarily apply this form of breaking to pottery. These breakage patterns on baler shell artefacts were also found in the neighbouring sites of Ille; furthermore, it seems this practice is confined to the northern Palawan region.

Figure 10. Baler shell scoops found within northern Palawan (including Ille site) with evidence of deliberate breakage. Scale in centimetres.

Source: Timothy Vitales.

This practice involving *Melo* shells has yet to be understood, and, therefore, further studies are needed to address such enquiries. On the other hand, it must be remembered that their inclusion in mortuary assemblages indicates a conscious or deliberate selection of these artefacts for burial purposes, which clearly reflects a particular cultural belief associated with this practice (Parker Pearson 1993). The possible practice of ceremonial killing involving baler shell scoops also indicates the special role of these materials in rituals and highlights their significance in society.

Looking at the Bigger Picture: The Significance of Baler Shells as Raw Materials in the Indo-Pacific

It is highly evident from the archaeological record that baler shells (*Melo* spp.) were among the molluscs selectively exploited during the Neolithic and Metal Ages in the Philippines. The results of the analyses from the baler shell assemblages at Ille and other Philippine sites clearly showed that most of these shells were actively selected primarily for artefact production (particularly in scoop forms), as evidenced by shell-working, as well as the post-mortem collection of some worked shells. Their inclusion in burial deposits also signified their particular role in mortuary and ritual practices in the past.

Figure 11. A baler shell 'gong' collected from a Pala'wan elder in southern Palawan.

Source: Timothy Vitales.

The significance of baler shells as raw materials in prehistory, however, is not confined to the Philippine archipelago. The selection of baler shells beyond subsistence purposes was apparently widespread in the Indo-Pacific. The 32,000-year-old baler shells (*Melo amphora*) found in northwest Australia are believed to have been utilised as value goods rather than food items (Brumm and Moore 2005; O'Connor and Chappel 2003; O'Connor and Veth 2000). This was also observed in other early sites in Australia (Bowdler 1999; O'Connor 1996, 1999; O'Connor and Veth 2000; Przywolnik 2003; Veth 1999). In a Hoabinhian site in Sumatra, baler shells (*Melo melo*) found in midden deposits were clearly worked, as evidenced by the perforated ventral faces of the shells' body whorls (see van Heekeren 1972). The baler shell remains in the Niah Caves Complex in Sarawak (Szabó *et al.* 2008) and in Vietnam (Szabó unpublished data) were modified into disc beads. Such examples of the shell's importance have also been observed ethnographically (see Introduction), attesting to the persistence of the conscious selection of baler shells for raw materials through to the ethnographic present.

In the Philippines, evidence for the exploitation of baler shells as raw materials seemed to have waned in the later periods, as shown in the archaeological record, but it has not disappeared entirely. Evidence of the post-mortem deposition of unworked *Melo broderipii* in the 17th to

18th century site in Cebu City opened a window to the possibility of such exploitation around this period. As a matter of fact, baler shells were still utilised for several purposes during the ethnographic present. In southern Palawan, baler shells were sometimes used for ritual purposes as gongs by the Pala'wan group (Vitales 2009a) (Figure 11). Baler shells were also used as heirloom boat balers in Sulu, southern Philippines (R. Santiago pers. comm. 2007) and as cocoa crushers in the Visayan Islands (National Museum of the Philippines unpublished data).

Baler shell exploitation in the Indo-Pacific, especially in the Philippines, clearly indicates the special role of these shells in several cultures. Their significance, however, still needs to be explored to further understand the underlying conscious reasons for their acquisition and utilisation. It must be remembered that selection of particular shell taxa was not random. Through the practices of shell collecting, working, and utilisation, as inferred in the archaeological evidence, we might also understand how these shells were being perceived as food items, raw material, or even symbolic goods, and how such cultural knowledge is continuously being maintained, transformed, and transmitted through time.

References

Akerman, K. 1973. Aboriginal Baler Shell Objects in Western Australia. *Mankind* 9(2):124-125.

Akerman, K. 1975. Baler Shell Implements from North West Australia. *Mankind* 10(1):16-19.

Alba, E.D. 1998. Modified Bones and Shells from Philippine Archaeological Sites. *National Museum Papers* 8(1):45-80.

Archaeological, Cultural, and Environmental Consultancy, Inc (ACECI). 2006. *Cebu Colonial Period Revisited: The Rescue Archaeology of Plaza Independencia*. Unpublished report.

Bautista, A.P. 1988. The Exploitation of Animals in the Neolithic of the Philippines. *Archaeozoologia* 2(1-2):349-366.

Bowdler, S. 1999. Research at Shark Bay, WA, and the Nature of Coastal Adaptations in Australia. In J. Hall and I. McNiven (eds), *Australian Coastal Archaeology*, pp. 79-84. Canberra: The Australian National University.

Brumm, A. and M.W. Moore. 2005. Symbolic Revolutions and the Australian Archaeological Record. *Cambridge Archaeological Journal* 15(2):157–175.

Chen, C.-L. 1969. *Material Culture of the Formosan Aborigines*. Republic of China: The Taiwan Museum.

Dizon, E.Z. and R.A. Santiago. 1996. *Faces from Maitum: The archaeological excavation of Ayub Cave*. Manila: National Museum of the Philippines.

Faylona, M.G.P.G. 2003. A Preliminary Study on Shells from Ille Rock Shelter. *Hukay* 5:31-49.

Fox, R.B. 1970. *The Tabon Caves: Archaeological explorations and excavations on Palawan Island, Philippines*. Manila: National Museum of the Philippines.

Fox, R.B. 1977. Leta-Leta Cave: The science and art of cave archaeology. In A.R. Roces (ed.) *Filipino Heritage: The Making of a Nation, vol. 1*, pp. 228-234. Manila: Lahing Pilipino Publishing Inc.

Fox, R.B., and A. Evangelista. 1956. *The Bato Caves, Sorsogon Province, Philippines: A preliminary report of a jar burial - stone tool assemblage*. Unpublished report. Manila: National Museum of the Philippines.

Fox, R.B. and A. Evangelista. 1957. *The Cave Archaeology of Cagraray Island, Albay Province, Philippines: A preliminary report of explorations and excavations*. Unpublished report. Manila: National Museum of the Philippines.

Grinsell, L.V. 1961. The Breaking of Objects as a Funerary Rite. *Folklore* 72(3):475-491.

Guthe, C.E. n.d. *The University of Michigan Philippine Expedition: Field Catalog 1922-1925*. Ann Arbor: University of Michigan.

Hughes, I. 1977. *New Guinea Stone Age Trade*. Canberra: The Australian National University. *Terra Australis* 3.

Irwin, G. 1985. *The Emergence of Mailu*. Canberra: The Australian National University. *Terra Australis* 10.

Kress, J.H. 2000. The Malacoarchaeology of Palawan Island. *Journal of East Asian Archaeology* 2(1-2):285-328.

Leach, E. 1976. *Culture and Communication: The logic by which symbols are connected*. Cambridge: Cambridge University Press.

Lewis, H., V. Paz, M. Lara, H. Barton, P. Piper, J. Ochoa, T. Vitales, A. J. Carlos, L. Neri, V. Hernandez, J. Stevenson, E.C. Robles, A. Ragragio, R. Padilla, W. Solheim, and W. Ronquillo. 2008. Terminal Pleistocene to Mid Holocene Occupation and an Early Cremation Burial at Ille Cave, Palawan, Philippines. *Antiquity* 82(316):318-335.

Lewis, H., V.J. Paz, J.H. Kress, M.G. Lara, J.G.L. Medrana, A.J. Carlos, P. Piper, V. Hernandez, H. Barton, E. Robles, T.J. Vitales, A. Ragragio, W.G. Solheim, and W. Ronquillo. 2006. *Early Occupation at Ille Cave, New Ibajay, El Nido, Palawan, Philippines: Report on the 2005 excavation season*. Report submitted to the British Academy, NERC/Orads, and the National Museum of the Philippines.

McCarthy, F.D. 1967. *Australian Aboriginal Stone Implements*. Sydney: The Australian Museum.

McCarthy, F.D., and F.M. Setzler. 1960. The Archaeology of Arnhem Island. *Records of the American-Australian Scientific Expedition to Arnhem Land* 2:215-295.

Morse, K. 1993. New Radiocarbon Dates from North West Cape, Western Australia: A Preliminary Report. In M.A. Smith, M. Spriggs, and B. Fankhauser (eds), *Sahul in Review*, pp. 155-163. Canberra: The Australian National University.

Mulvaney, J. and J. Kamminga. 1999. *Prehistory of Australia*. Washington: Smithsonian Institution Press.

Nishimura, M. 1992. *The Role of Long Distance Trade in the Development of Complex Societies*. Unpublished doctoral dissertation. University of Michigan.

O'Connor, S. 1996. Where are the Middens? - An overview of the archaeological evidence for shellfish exploitation along the Northwestern Australian coastline. *Indo-Pacific Prehistory Association Bulletin* 15:165-180.

O'Connor, S. 1999. *30,000 Years of Aboriginal Occupation: Kimberly, North-west Australia*. Canberra: The Australian National University.

O'Connor, S. and J. Chappell. 2003. Colonisation and Coastal Subsistence in Australia and Papua New Guinea: Different timing, different modes. In C. Sand (ed), *Pacific Archaeology: Assessments and Prospects. Proceedings of the International Conference for the 50th Anniversary of the First Lapita Excavation (July 1952), Koné-Nouméa 2002*, pp. 15–32. Nouméa: Le Cahiers de l'Archéologie en Nouvelle-Calédonie 15.

O'Connor, S. and P. Veth. 2000. The World's First Mariners: Savannah dwellers in an island continent. In S. O'Connor and P. Veth (eds), *East of Wallace's Line: Studies of past and present maritime cultures of the Indo-Pacific region, vol. 16,Modern Quaternary Research in Southeast Asia*, pp. 99-137. Rotterdam: A.A. Balkema.

Paz, V.J. 1998. *Archaeological Survey of El Nido, Palawan: with ethnographic notes May 3 to 14, 1998.* Unpublished fieldnotes. Quezon City: Archaeological Studies Program, University of the Philippines.

Paz, V., W. Ronquillo, H. Lewis, P. Piper, J. Carlos, E. Robles, V. Hernandez, T. Vitales, J. Ochoa, T. Reyes, and H. Xhauflair. 2008. *Palawan Island Palaeohistoric Research Project: Report on the 2008 Dewil Valley field season.* Report submitted to the University of the Philippines-Archaeological Studies Program and the National Museum of the Philippines.

Paz, V., A. Ragragio, E. Robles, and M. Oxenham. 2008. *The Catanauan Archaeological and Heritage Project: Report on the excavation of Napa site, Locality 1 and 2, Catanauan, Bondoc Peninsula, Quezon Province.* Report submitted to the University of the Philippines-Archaeological Studies Program and the National Museum of the Philippines.

Parker Pearson, M. 1993. The Powerful Dead: Archaeological relationships between the living and the dead. *Cambridge Archaeological Journal* 3:203-229.

Peralta, J.T. 2000. *The Tinge of Red: Prehistory of art in the Philippines.* Manila: National Commission for Culture and the Arts.

Przywolnik, K. 2003. Shell Artefacts from Northern Cape Range Peninsula, Northwest Western Australia. *Australian Archaeology* 56:12-21.

Roales, T.M. 1985. *Pupog Burial Rockshelter: Preliminary Report.* National Museum of the Philippines.

Santiago, R.A., and A. Barbosa. 1977. Archaeological Exploration in Suluan Island, Samar. *Leyte-Samar Studies* 11(2):52-56.

Schall, A. 1985. *Aboriginal Use of Shell on Cape York Peninsula.* Brisbane: Archaeology Branch, Department of Community Services. *Cultural Resource Management Monograph* 6.

Shnukal, A. 2004. The Post-Contact Created Environment in the Torres Strait Central Islands. *Memoirs of the Queensland Museum, Cultural Heritage Series* 3(1):317-346.

Solheim, W.G. II. 1964. *The Archaeology of Central Philippines: A Study chiefly of the Iron Age and its relationships.* Manila: National Institute of Science and Technology.

Solheim, W.G. II. 2004. *Excavations of Ille Rock Shelter, Palawan, Philippines (Preliminary Report).* National Museum of the Philippines.

Springsteen, F.J. and F.M. Leobrera. 1986. *Shells of the Philippines.* Manila: Carfel Seashell Museum.

Szabó, K. 2005. *Technique and Practice: Shell-working in the Western Pacific and Island Southeast Asia.* Unpublished doctoral dissertation. The Australian National University.

Szabó, K. 2008. Shell as a Raw Material: Mechanical properties and working techniques in the tropical Indo-West Pacific. *Archaeofauna* 17:125-138.

Szabó, K., P.J. Piper, and G. Barker. 2008. Sailing Between Worlds: The Symbolism of death in northwest Borneo. In G. Clark, F. Leach, and S. O'Connor (eds), *Islands of Inquiry: Colonisation, seafaring and the archaeology of maritime landscapes,* pp. 149-170. Canberra: The Australian National University. *Terra Australis* 29.

Thiel, B. 1986-87. Excavations at Arku Cave, Northeast Luzon, Philippines. *Asian Perspectives* 27(2):229-264.

Thomson, D.F. 1934. The Dugong Hunters of Cape York. *The Journal of the Royal Anthropological Institute of Great Britain and Ireland* 64:237-263.

Tindale, N.B. 1977. Further Report on the Kaiadilt People of Bentinck Island, Gulf of Carpentaria Queensland. In J. Allen, J. Golson, and R. Jones (eds), *Sunda and Sahul: Prehistoric Studies in*

Southeast Asia, Melanesia and Australia, pp. 247-274. London: Academic Press.

University of the Philippines–Archaeological Studies Program (UP-ASP). 2005-2006. *Report on the Archaeological Investigation of Dewil Valley, New Ibajay, El Nido, Palawan.* Unpublished report. Quezon City: University of the Philippines

van Heekeren, H.R. 1972. *The Stone Age of Indonesia* (revised edition). The Hague: Martinus Nijhoff.

Vanderwal, R. 2004. Early Historical Sources for the Top Western Islands in the Western Torres Strait Exchange Network. *Memoirs of the Queensland Museum, Cultural Heritage Series* 3(1):257-270.

Vermeij, G.J. 1993. *A Natural History of Shells.* New Jersey: Princeton University Press.

Veth, P., M. Spriggs, S. O'Connor, and A.D. Saleh. 2005. Wangil Midden: A late prehistoric site, with remarks on ethnographic pottery making. In S. O'Connor, M. Spriggs, and P. Veth (eds), *The Archaeology of the Aru Islands, Eastern Indonesia,* pp. 95-124. Canberra: The Australian National University. *Terra Australis* 22.

Vitales, T. 2009a. Form, Function, and Meaning: An Approach in Understanding *Melo* Shell Artefacts in Philippine Sites. Unpublished master's thesis. University of the Philippines.

Vitales, T. 2009b. *Melo Shells in Philippine Archaeology.* Paper presented during the Wilhelm G. Solheim II Foundation meeting on March 14, 2009 in Ortigas Center, Pasig City.

Weaver, C.S. and J.E. duPont. 1970. *Living Volutes: A monograph of the recent Volutidae of the world.*

7

The History and Culture of Dolphinfish (*Coryphaena hippurus*) Exploitation in Japan, East Asia, and the Pacific

Hashimura Osamu, Tokyo Gakugei University, Faculty of Education, Japan

Introduction

What is the history behind human exploitation of dolphinfish (*Coryphaena hippurus*), and why were they so sought after by groups in the Pacific over such long periods of time (Figure 1)? The purpose of this paper is to examine the relationships between humans and dolphinfish, a highly migratory species that requires trolling technologies in order to catch.

Figure 1. Dolphin fish (*Coryphaena hippurus*).

Source: Photo by the author.

Research Background

The Japanese Archipelago is situated along the northwestern Pacific Rim, at the juncture where numerous species of migratory fish pass through nearby waters. In total, there are 350 species of endemic fish and two types of migratory fish. These include: 1) fish found in the warm Kuroshio Current, such as tuna, bonito, yellowtail, Spanish mackerel, sword fish, dolphinfish, and flying fish; and 2) fish found in the cold Oyashio Current, such as saury, herring, and salmon. In general, the warm water surface fish arrive from the south, while the colder water fish arrive from the north.

Dolphinfish (Coryphaenidae) consist of two subspecies in Japan: *Coryphaena hippurus* and *C. equiselis*. They originate in the Pacific, are found widely in tropical and sub-tropical seas, and reach approximately 0.5m to 2m in length. Dolphinfish migrate in groups from May to December and move northward (*agari shiira*) in waters around Japan during the summer season, moving south (*modori shiira*) again after late summer.

Dolphinfish are an extremely valuable resource for small-scale fisheries and are popular among recreational fishers in Japan. Both species are often exploited by taking advantage of behaviour aggregates under floating devices (Scientia Marina 1999), behaviour also found in other fish species, especially in their juvenile stage. However, dolphinfish have less value economically than tuna, bonito, and herring in Japan and, as such, are not as frequently caught. Their value, however, is different depending on locality. Consumers in Japan, for example, especially in urban areas, tend to prefer tuna, bonito, and sea bream over other species, though dolphinfish catches in Japan have been increasing in recent years.

Because dolphinfish are known to have been an important resource in Japan and East Asia, as well as in the Pacific Islands and South America prehistorically, and given the paucity of information known about their species, I review and discuss two major aspects of research: 1) the regional distribution of the *tsuke* method, one of the known FADs (Fish Aggregative Devices), and the cultural and historical use of dolphinfish in Japan; and 2) the relationship between dolphinfish and human societies in various regions from a view of comparative cultural and historical perspective.

Figure 2. Bamboo rafts (*tsukegi*).

Source: Photo by the author.

Tsuke Fishing and Dolphinfish Exploitation in Modern Japan

Description of fishing methods

In modern Japan, the capturing of dolphinfish is either done through net fishing with bamboo rafts (*tsukegi*) or angling/luring (Figure 2). The Japanese "*shiira-zuke*" (*shiira*=dolphinfish, *zuke*=*tsuke*=float) fishing method mainly targets dolphinfish using a method that takes advantage of migratory fish behaviour, such as when skipjack (*Katsuwonus pelamis*) and yellowfin tuna (*Thunnus albacares*) congregate under floating objects like driftwood and floating seaweed. Fishermen set out bamboo rafts, called *tsukegi* ("floating wood" in Japanese), on the surface of the sea, and fish are then caught using a purse seine net. This type of fishing is considered a form of a fish aggregation device (FAD) (Kakuma 2000, 2002:39-59), which restricts the potential fishing grounds to relatively shallow waters over the continental shelf and areas devoid of strong currents.

In the Kochi District in Western Japan (Figure 3), for example, these rafts are situated 30-40 miles offshore in waters that normally do not exceed 1000 metres in depth. During the fishing season (June-November), more than 2000 *tsukegi* may be set over these areas. To avoid excessive competition for space, the setting line of respective *tsukegi* is decided by lottery every year. In principle, a vessel will only operate along their assigned line, unless there is agreed cooperation with other vessels.

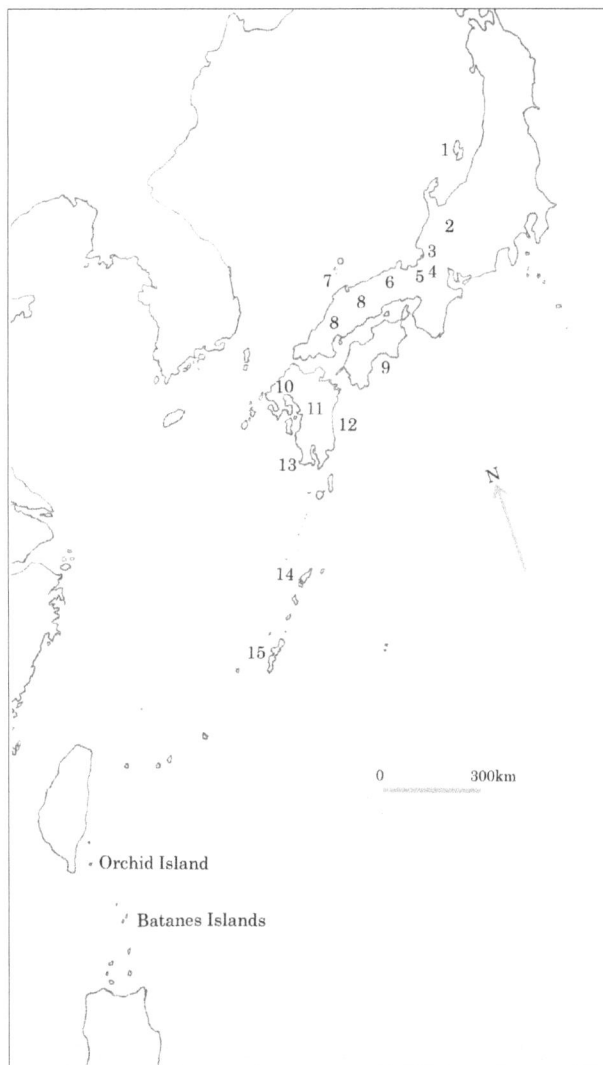

Figure 3. Major fishing grounds for Tsukegi fishing in Japan and Taiwan.

Source: Map by the author.

Major fishing grounds for this type of fishing technique are widely distributed along the western coast facing the Sea of Japan (see Table 1 and Figure 3). The only exceptions are the districts of Kochi and Miyazaki, which face the Pacific coast. Although the *shiira-zuke* has traditionally been a fishing method that targets dolphinfish, in recent years the major catch by this method has been amberjack (*Seriola lalandi*) (Sakamoto and Kojima 1999:375-385).

Table 1. Regional distribution of dolphinfish consumption and festival use in Japan.

No.*	Place Name	Host	Subject
1	Niigata, Sado island	Fishing village	Festival in Aikawa
2	Gihu, Hida	City	Seafood. salting fish
3	Fukui, Mikata Tsunekami	Fishing village	New year festival
4	Shiga, Takashima Kutusuki	Farm village	New year festival
			Harvest festival in autumn
5	Kyoto	City	Harvest festival in autumn
6	Totutori	Fishing village	New year festival
7	Shimane, Oki	Fishing village	Sushi seafood
8	Okayama. Hiroshima	Mountain village	New year festival
			The festival of the Dead in summer
			Harvest festival in autumn
9	Kochi	Fishing village	First fishing festival of a year
10	Ngasaki. Saga	Fishing village. City	New year festival, called "Shargi" (happy tree).
			"Okunchi" festival.
			Harvest festival in autumn
11	Kumamoto	Mountain village. City	New year festival
			The festival of the Dead in summer
			Harvest festival in autumn
12	Miyazaki	Fishing village	Promote the development of regional resources
13	Kagoshima	Fishing Village	Summer festival in 19thC
			First fishing festival of a year
14	Kagoshima. Amami Island	Fishing village	New year festival
			Harvest festival in autumn
15	Okinawa. Main island	Fishing village	The year's first fishing display by fishermen. "ishinougan"

* Numbers above correspond to Figure 3 above.

Source: Table by the author.

Trolling and longline fishing have also been popular along the eastern coast facing the Pacific. For trolling, one- to five-metric-ton vessels use cut riggers to tow two main surface lines and several subsurface lines, each employing one to three hooks and artificial bait. These typically operate between June and August, about five to 30 miles from shore. The longline fishery uses larger three- to 10-metric-ton vessels, which deploy 10-16km of multi-hook, subsurface (9-12m depth) longlines. These vessels usually operate between five and 30 miles from shore between May and July (Sakamoto and Kojima 1999:375-385).

Figure 4. The cutting ceremony in Kutsuki, Takashima City, Shiga Prefecture.

Source: Photo taken by the author.

Figure 5. Narezushi in Ginama Village, Okinawa.

Source: Photo taken by the author.

Human consumption patterns of dolphinfish in Japan

Daily use as food

Currently, dolphinfish are used primarily in fresh sashimi in areas where they are actively caught. However, because the flesh spoils relatively quickly, the fish is often sold as fillets in many urban supermarkets. They are typically deep-fried, served a la meuniére, or boiled slowly in a soy broth. There are many areas, such as Ibusuki, Kagoshima Prefecture, where dolphinfish and flying fish are minced as raw materials for Satsuma-age or Kamaboko. Once sold as a fillet or minced, however, consumers no longer know exactly what fish they are consuming. In the mountain regions, migratory fish are widely used. It is known that whales, dolphins, and sharks are delivered to and eaten in the mountain regions of northeast Japan to Kyushu.

Traditional ritual use

In terms of traditional uses, there are many rituals related to dolphinfish exploitation in Japan. For example, the ritual cutting of dolphinfish, using chopsticks and knives during the New Year's celebration, is widely preserved in the districts of Kinki (e.g., Shiga, Kyoto), Hokuriku (Fukui), the mountainous areas of Chugoku (Tottori, Shimane, Hiroshima), Kyushu districts (Miyazaki, Kumamoto, Nagasaki, Kagoshima), and in the Ryukyu Islands of Amami and Okinawa (see Table 1 and Figure 3 above). In Aso, Kutsuki, Takashima City, and Shiga Prefecture, a dolphinfish is offered to a community god first before the cutting ceremony is conducted, using a knife and chopsticks on New Year's Day (Figure 4). For example, dolphinfish or shark meat are usually recognised as a special fish for New Year's events among mountain villages in the Chugoku District of western Japan. Along the Gonokawa River in Shimane Prefecture, the dolphinfish is called *mansaku* and is usually eaten on the west side of the river, while the shark, called *wani*, is eaten on the east side. In Chizu town in Tottori Prefecture, the dolphinfish is commonly eaten as narezushi (fermented fish with rice) during New Year's.

People have also used the dolphinfish as one of the special foods for various rituals relating to life ceremonies, autumn harvest festivals, and other annual events. In these cases, narezushi is usually consumed. In Ginama Village in Okinawa, September 1 in the lunar calendar is regarded as the beginning of the fishing season and so-called "Ishinou-gan". During these times, a prayer for inviting dolphinfish is accompanied by serving the boiled fish to participants (Figure 5).

The reasons why the dolphinfish appears in traditional rituals in Japan might be related to the ease with which its meat can be preserved using salt, and to its size, which seems to represent good luck and fortune. However, the introduction and expansion of the use of electric refrigeration after World War II drastically reduced such customs, while dramatically increasing the importance of raw fish (tuna and other fishes) for sashimi and sushi. This eventually led to the decline of traditional food culture surrounding fish consumption.

Historical Transition of the Dolphinfish Exploitation in Japan

Before Tokugawa Period (before AD 1603)

In Japan, there have traditionally been two types of fisheries: one subsistence-based and the other revolving around commercial or industrial use. As noted in the archaeological record, fishing for subsistence has been a prominent feature throughout Japan's prehistory since the Jomon Period (ca. 13,000 to 2500 BP) and perhaps even earlier, during the Palaeolithic. Presently, the earliest traces of dolphinfish exploitation date back to the early Jomon Period around 11,000 BP. At the Torihama shell midden site in Fukui Prefecture, which dates back to 11,180 ± 180 BP, dolphinfish bones were excavated together with yellowtail, black sea bream, porcupine fish, skipjack tuna, shark, forktail, bullhead, sea bass, and Japanese Spanish mackerel (Research group of Torihama Kaizuka 1987). At the San-nai Maruyama site in Aomori Prefecture, dolphinfish bones were also excavated from layers corresponding to the mid-late Jomon Period between 6,000 and 5,000 BP (Fukuda 2006:1-16). There are also traces of dolphinfish exploitation at the Nishinoshou site, which is estimated to be the production site for salt-making earthenware during the 5th century in Wakayama Prefecture (the Educational Board of Wakayama Prefecture 1997). Much later, dolphinfish bones were unearthed at the ruins of Nakijin Castle on Okinawa (Ryukyu Islands), dating back to the 13th century (Okinawa Prefecture, Nakijin Village Educational Committee 2009:179-238).

The Tokugawa Period (AD 1603-1862)

Today, dolphinfish are generally treated as low-grade fish in Japan. However, historical documents from the late Muromachi Era to the Tokugawa Period and Meiji Era (the 15th to 19th centuries), indicate that dolphinfish were treated as higher-grade fish than various tuna species (including skipjack). The ease with which the fish could be salted or smoked might be one reason why this particular fish species was deemed more important, considering the fact that the electric refrigerator had not yet been invented.

During the Tokugawa (or Edo) Period, rapid technological advancements in commercial fisheries led to changes in the kinds of species that were harvested and how they were procured. In the Wakasa region (Fukui Prefecture) around the 16th century, for example, dolphinfish were treated as more expensive than Tai (red snapper/Pagrus major) (Hashimura 2003:199-223). At this time, local fishermen caught them by using floating FADs such as *tsukegi*, which were made of bamboo. It was during the Meiji and Taisho Periods that seine pursing began.

Among the Goto Islands in Nagasaki Prefecture (Kyusyu District), local fishermen also captured dolphinfish, one of the primary species caught, along with whale and tuna, from the 17th to the 19th centuries (Hashimura 2009a:30-85). The main method for capturing dolphinfish was netting. For example, during the end of the 18th century in Kisyuku Village on Fukue Island, dolphinfish and tuna were usually caught by using a fixed net. Tuna were then pickled in sake, while some were exported from Goto to Osaka and other parts of Kyushu. Salted dolphinfish were also distributed to northern Kyushu as food during the festival of Okunchi.

Despite the prolific existence of fixed-net tuna fishing, as well as whaling, the question remains as to why dolphinfish have been continually caught. In part, I believe that it may be due to their role in long-term sustainable fishing practices throughout the Japanese archipelago. The targeting of species such as dolphinfish, while often small in terms of catch size, nevertheless provided a stable and relatively easy way to capture a reliable food source. On the other hand, fishing for larger migratory fish, such as tuna and whales, was sometimes very dangerous and presented a higher risk of coming back empty-handed.

The Meiji and Taisho Periods (AD 1850-1920)

In the Kyushu and Chugoku regions, the treatment of dolphinfish varied between mountain villages and fishing villages, and even towns and urban areas in the same region (Hashimura 2003:199-223). Historical documents at this time also refer to large quantities of dolphinfish being harvested in Shimane and Nagasaki Prefectures (Hashimura 2005:273-291) as well as in Okinawa.

With regard to fishing methods and technology, the seine FAD known as *tsukegi* began sometime between the Meiji and Taisho Periods among Kochi, Miyazaki, Kumamoto, Nagasaki, Shimane and Ishikawa Prefectures. As such, it is clear that the *tsukegi* method for capturing dolphinfish had expanded to the Pacific coast of Japan during this time.

The Showa and Heisei Periods (AD 1920 to present)

In the early Showa Period prior to World War II, the increased popularity of the refrigerator quickly diminished the importance of salting dolphinfish, which subsequently began to be perceived as a "trash fish". In terms of fishing technology and potential fishing grounds, during the post-war Showa Period up to the Heisei Period, people began to focus on areas farther from shore. This was made possible by the development of a large floating fish reef known as a *payao*. An FAD fishing method originally developed in the Philippines and Indonesian seas, the outcome was that fishing areas were extended to the coasts of the Ryukyu Islands from Meiji from the 1920s through to 1982. Although *payao* increased the offshore catch of tunas and dolphinfish, it also led to several problems. According to fishermen on Okinawa and Miyazaki, for example, while the migratory fish caught off the coast had increased with the establishment of *payao*, the number of migratory fish caught by net fishing in coastal areas has declined (Kakuma 2002:39-59).

Regional Differences in the Dolphinfish and Fish Food Distribution System

Distribution of name

Apart from archaeological and historical evidence, it is important to examine the linguistic evidence regarding the species to provide a more robust interpretation of dolphinfish exploitation over time. Here, I compare the dialectic distribution of the dolphinfish's name.

The dolphinfish was important in the East China Sea. In this area, names given to dolphinfish are generally positive in nature; for example: *hiiwo*, *fu-nyuiyu*, *hii*, *manbiki*, and *manriki*. *Fu-nyuiyu* is a local name for the dorado in Okinawa. *Fu* refers to wealth in the local Okinawan dialect, and *iyu* means "fish". *Hii* is the local name for the dorado on Amami Island. *Manbiki* is the local name for the dorado in the southern part of Kyushu and the southern part of Shikoku. *Hiiwo* is the local name for the dorado in western Kyushu.

In contrast, along coastal areas of the Sea of Japan, such as the Kanto region, it is hated. Consequently, negative terms are used; for example, *Siira* (empty rice husk), and *Shibitokurai* (fish that eats corpses). From an areal study of the dolphinfish names mentioned above, I next examine the differences in how dolphinfish are valued between the Japanese and East China Seas. As I suggest, altering perceptions of how dolphinfish are valued derives from a decline in catches at the level of local economies.

Dolphinfish exploitation in the China Sea

In Korea, dolphinfish are known as *manzegi* or *pusiri*. On Chin-do Island, salted dolphinfish used to be served on New Year's Day and Obon (mid-summer) festivals until as recently as 50 years ago. On Ranyu (Orchid) Island in Taiwan, a type of dolphinfish called *arayu* is the most valuable fish. People initially catch flying fish called *aribaban* as the bait for dolphinfish (Yamada 1967). In China, consumption of dolphinfish was common in the areas dominated by Westerners in Hong Kong, indicating a preference by certain groups for eating this particular fish. Along other coastal locations of China, dolphinfish fishing is not popular since the fishing grounds are remotely located, though today, when captured, they are typically ground up into meal.

Dolphinfish exploitation in Hawai'i

In Hawai'i, the dolphinfish is known as *mahimahi*, similar to other parts of Polynesia, and is popular among tourists today. Although dolphinfish has been exploited since prehistoric times, it was not considered a desirable fish to Native Hawaiians. It was only during the 1960s that *mahimahi* was recognised as the state fish (Takenaka 1984:1-20), after tourists became increasingly fond of the species for game fishing. Throughout the 1960s and 1970s, the import of frozen dolphinfish by several Asian countries—namely Taiwan, Japan, and Vietnam—began. In 1989, Costa Rica and Ecuador began exporting fresh dolphinfish to the U.S. and other locations, with Hawai'i becoming the centre for its distribution.

Dolphinfish use in Costa Rica

In Costa Rica, the consumption of terrestrial animals has been a central part of traditional subsistence, so the fishing industry has not been as popular (Hashimura 2007:269-300). Prior to the 1980s, commercial harvesting was limited to small-scale shark fishing by the Taiwanese, while near-shore fishing remained minimal. Domestic consumption of dolphinfish in Costa Rica was extremely limited, in part because it was not well-liked by locals (Hashimura 2007:269-300); however, the situation changed, beginning in the early 1980s, due to an expansion of the global distribution of marine products. As a result, common dolphinfish and striped marlin fishing were initiated by the opening of export markets to the U.S. The commercial value of dolphinfish increased due to heightened demand, and the U.S. later became the lead importer of Costa Rican dolphinfish. This pattern also led to greater consumption of dolphinfish by local American tourists after an appointment by the Natural World Heritage committee helped increase the demand (Chant 1992: 85-101).

The continued growth of the Costa Rican dolphinfish industry and high levels of tourism have generally led to greater demand. To cope with this situation, the government of Costa Rica (INCOPESSCA: Institute Costarricense de Pesca y Acuicultura) has introduced strict management rules for marine resources, including a total ban on fishing around the area of national parks; a seasonal restriction on fishing is also being considered.

Overall, I have compared how the recent relationships between humans and dolphinfish differ in Costa Rica and various parts of Asia. In the western Pacific, especially in Japan, dolphinfish are categorised as a minor fish, unlike tuna, bonito, or sea bream, which are classified as high-grade fishes. In contrast, dolphinfish in Costa Rica is treated as a high-grade fish, primarily given its value to U.S. markets.

In addition, the philosophies behind properly managing these types of marine resources are very different between Asia and Costa Rica. In Japan and Taiwan, more emphasis is placed on using a FAD (Fish Attractant Device) than in setting area restrictions or seasonal bans on fishing. On the other hand, in Costa Rica, the use of an FAD is forbidden, whereas the seasonal and zonal prohibition of fishing is widely practiced (Hashimura 2007:269-300).

Discussion and Conclusion

In this paper, I have briefly discussed the history of dolphinfishing across parts of the Pacific. It is important, however, to point out some newly clarified matters and future tasks.

As noted previously, the antiquity of dolphinfish exploitation in Japan may date back to as early as 11,000 years ago. This early emphasis on the harvesting of dolphinfish can also be compared to consumption patterns found on neighboring islands in the Asia-Pacific region. For example, archaeological studies on Guam (see the chapter by Amesbury in this volume), Taiwan (e.g., Lee 1997), and the Philippines reveal that dolphinfish were also exploited in prehistory, though not as early.

Additionally, this paper demonstrates that there are distinct temporal changes in how dolphinfish were utilised in Japan from the 16th century to the present. Although dolphinfish today in Japan are economically categorised as low-grade and are relatively inexpensive, it is clear that they have served some very important functions historically, often presented to local lords by the villagers, offered to the gods, and, in some cases, served at wedding ceremonies. Such customs are also practiced in the southern districts of Korea, Taiwan, and probably in certain areas of East Asia. It would also be interesting to compare these activities with those seen in the Mediterranean (Jeanne and Hiechmi 1999:469-472) in future studies.

The next question remains as to why dolphinfish were auspicious during the Edo Period until the first half of the 20th century. In my opinion, the reason why dolphinfish became a cheap and low-class fish is possibly related to the development of preservation technology through the introduction of refrigerators (Hashimura 2003:199-223), by which the widespread distribution of tuna and bonito fish became possible while dolphinfish became comparatively tainted.

However, dolphinfish is very popular as a light fish, similar to tilapia and codfish. With the increased scarcity of marine products in modern Japan, there is a re-valuation movement of minor fish resources, such as dolphinfish, which are not mass-harvested like tuna has been over the past couple of centuries. Subsequently, there is now a revitalisation movement of depopulated communities. Such movement should be socially expanded through an understanding of the history of dolphinfish and their place in culture (Hashimura 2010:190-214). Through the analysis of relationships between fish and humans, we can observe historical preferences in fish consumption across space and time, noting how and why specific variables have come into play to structure subsistence patterns.

References

Chant, S. 1992. Tourism in Latin America: Perspective from Mexico and Costa Rica. In D. Harrison (ed), *Tourism and the Less Developed Countries*, pp. 85-101. London: Belhaven Press.

Fukuda, T. 2006. The archaeological sites with shell remains in northern area of HONSHU Island, Japan. In Aomori Prefectural Museum (ed), *Proceedings of the Aomori Prefectural Museum* 31, pp. 1-16. Aomori: Prefectural Museum (in Japanese).

Hashimura, O. 2003. Regional Differences and History in the Use of Dolphinfish (Coryphaena hippurus Linne): The Case Study of Warm Current of Tsushima. *Senri Ethnological Reports* 46:199-223. (in Japanese).

Hashimura, O. 2005. Regional Differences of the fishery and the Use of Dolphinfish (Coryphaena hippurus Linne) in Japan Archipelago: The Case Study of Meiji era. *Kokugakuin University Archeology Museum Bulletin* 21: 273-291. (in Japanese).

Hashimura, O. 2007. Fishing, distribution, culture of dorado resource in countries of the Pacific rim especially of Hawaii, Costa Rica. In N. Kishigami (ed), *Indigenous Distribution and Management of Marine Resources*, pp. 269 -300. Suita: National Museum of Ethnology, Japan. (in Japanese).

Hashimura, O. 2009a. *Social history of marine tenure during the Tokugawa period in Japan*. Kyoto: Jinbunsyoin. (in Japanese).

Hashimura, O. 2009b. The folklore of migrate fishes in Okinawa, Amami Island. *Nampo-bunka* 36. (in Japanese).

Hashimura, O. 2010. The Ecological history of the use of Migratory fish resources in Japan Sea. In Kazunobu Ikeya (ed), *Wildlife-Human Relationships in Japan*, pp. 190-214. Tokyo: Sekaishisosha. (in Japanese).

Jeanne, Z. and M. Hiechmi. 1999. Small-scale Tunisian fishery for dolphinfish. *Scientia Marina* 63(3-4):469-472.

Kakuma, S. 2000. Current, catch and weight composition of yellow-fin tuna with FADs off Okinawa Island, Japan. In J.-Y. Le Gall, P. Cayré, and M. Taquet (eds.), Pêche thonière et dispoitifs de concentration de poisons, pp. 492-501. Plouzané: Ifremer.

Kakuma, S. 2002. The evolution and conflict of Payao fishery in Okinawa. In T. Akimichi and N. Kishigami (eds), *Conflict of maritime use*, pp. 39-59. Tokyo: Jinbunsyoin. (in Japanese).

Kraul, S. 1999. Seasonal abundance of the dolphinfish, *Coryphaena hippurus*. *Scientica Marina* 63(3-4):261-266.

Okinawa Prefecture Nakijin Village Educational Committee (ed). 2009. Archaeological Report of Nakijin Gusuku Excavation. Okinawa: Okinawa Prefecture Nakijin Village Educational Committee. (in Japanese).

Olson, R.J. and F. Galván-Magaña. 2002. Food habits and consumption rates of common dolphinfish in the eastern Pacific Ocean - *Coryphaena hippurus*. *Fishery Bulletin* 100(2):279-282.

Research group of Torihama Kaizuka (ed). 1987. *Torihama Kaizuka*. Fukui: Fukui Prefecture. (in Japanese).

Sakamoto, R. and S. Kojima. 1999. Review of dolphinfish biological and fishing data in Japanese waters *SCIENTIA MARINA* 63(3-4):375-385.

Takenaka, B. and L. Torricer. 1984. Trends in the Market for mahimahi and ono in Hawaii. *Southwest Fisheries Center Administrative Report* 84-9:1-20.

Wakayama Prefectural Archaeological Center 1997. *Annual report of Wakayama Prefectural Archaeological Center 1997*. Wakayama: Wakayama Prefectural Archaeological Center. (in Japanese).

Yamada, Y. 1967. Fishing Economy of the Itbayat, Batanes, Philippines with Special Reference to its Vocabulary. *Asian Studies* 5(1):137-219.

8

Oceanic Encounter with the Japanese: An Outrigger Canoe-Fishing Gear Complex in the Bonin Islands and Hachijo-Jima Island

Akira Goto, Nanzan University (Catholic University of Nanzan), Nagoya, Japan

Introduction

The sea that lies to the east of the Philippines and west of the Marianas is called the Philippine Sea (Figure 1). It is surrounded by the islands of the Japanese Archipelago and the Ryukyu Islands to the north. To the west, there are a series of islands comprising Taiwan, the Philippines, and Maluku of Indonesia. The southern edge includes New Guinea and the Melanesian islands. North of Melanesia, there lies a series of Micronesian islands – Palau, Yap, and the Marianas, the latter of which are connected to the Bonin Islands and the Izu Seven Islands in the Japanese archipelago. These areas have so far been studied as if belonging to different cultural regions: East Asia, Island Southeast Asia, Melanesia, and Micronesia.

In this paper, however, I will tentatively disregard this traditional division and propose the "Circum-Philippine Sea" as an alternative framework. I do not intend to argue that the Circum-Philippine Sea has been a coherent cultural unit, but instead, I would like to characterise this area as a maritime interactive sphere (Rainbird 2007). This means that if a certain cultural element originating from other areas (c.f. Spain, Hawai'i, etc.) is incorporated into the indigenous cultural system, that system, in turn, further develops as part of its interactive relationship with the Circum-Philippine Sea. The single-outrigger canoe design, brought from outside—in this case, Hawai'i—to this area, was eventually combined with Japanese types of fishing gear and planking techniques. This cultural convergence resulted in a unique technological integration of the Hawaiian single-outrigger canoe and the Japanese fishing gear complex in the Bonin Islands and Hachijo-jima Island. I will subsequently demonstrate that these tiny islands have been a melting pot of human interaction in the Philippine Sea and the larger Pacific.

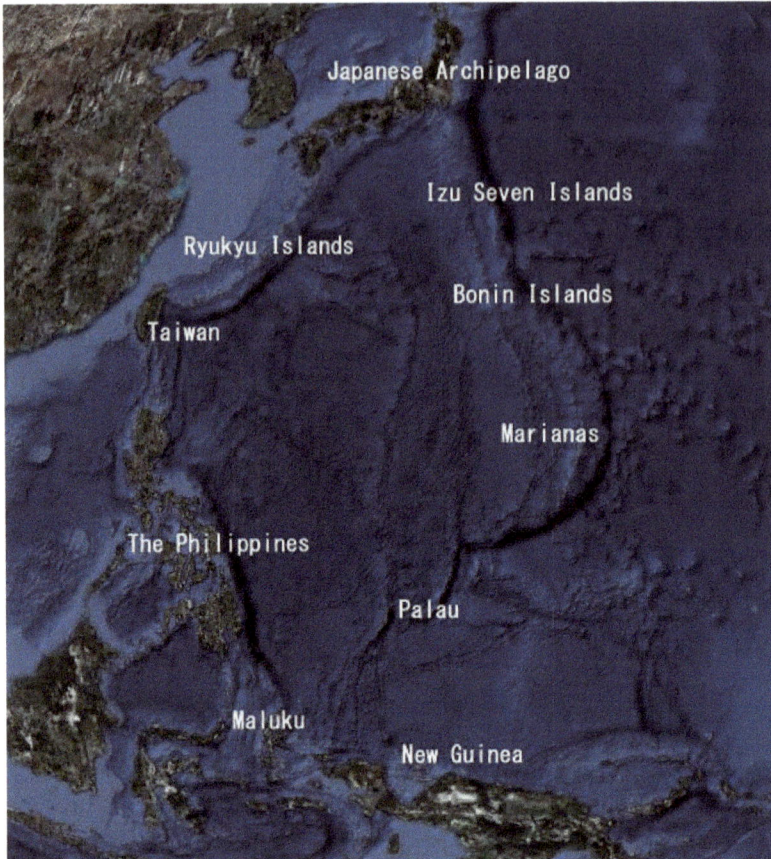

Figure 1. Map of the Circum-Philippine Sea.

Source: Map by author, based on a Google Earth map.

The Bonin Islands as a Centre of Maritime Interaction

Geography and prehistory

The Bonin or Ogasawara Islands (now part of the City of Tokyo) lie between the Izu Seven Islands to the north, and the Northern Marianas to the south. The Bonin Islands consist of 30 islands, about one third of which are inhabited. All of them are small, with a total landmass of 104 square kilometres. The Bonin Islands are geographically remote from all other major landmasses in the Circum-Philippine Sea: 1000km from Tokyo, 1000km from Guam, and 1500km from the Ryukyu Islands.

Although they appear to be isolated, these tiny islands have been characterised by a frequent flow of peoples from varying origins. In prehistory, the Bonin Islands seem to have been inhabited by people from the Marianas. A discovery of polished stones adzes with oval bodies and concave edges is indicative of wood working, such as canoe making. Most archaeologists agree that these adzes have an affinity with those of the Latte Period in the Marianas (around the first millennium BC). They are not similar to those of the Jomon or Yayoi axes of mainland Japan, which is separated from the Bonin Islands by the strong Kuroshiwo Current. Similar adzes, however, have been found on Hachijo-jima Island, south of the Kuroshiwo Current. Recent archaeological surveying by the Tokyo Metropolitan Historic Preservation Office has also uncovered shell artefacts and reddish plain pottery, the stylistic features and temper analyses of which reveal that they are indicative of the Austronesian tradition (Oda 1990; Oda *et al.* 1992).

Abandonment and re-habitation

The Bonin Islands were abandoned around the first millennium A.D. The name "Bonin" is considered to have come from the Chinese words, "*bu*" (=no) and "*nin*"(=people). Explorers' records suggest that castaways, beachcombers, and whalers had started to settle the islands after the 19th century (Ohkuma 1985).

In 1830, during the reign of Hawai'i's King Kamehameha III (Kuykendall 1938), pioneers from Hawai'i (Sandwich Islands) emigrated to the Bonin Islands. They consisted of five Westerners (American, British and Danish), 20 Native Hawaiians, and possibly people from other Pacific Islands. They brought with them crops and domesticated animals, along with Hawaiian style houses, clothes and tools.

In 1836, an American ambassador who visited the islands wrote, "I embarked with a friend in a small canoe, paddled by two Sandwich Islanders, and crossing the bay, ran through a natural tunnel, or rocky cave…" (Ruschenberger 2005:446). It has also been written that, "a canoe loaded with melons and pumpkins, floated on its surface; and a Sandwich Islander, asleep in the shade of a rock hard by, declared it to lead to some habitation or cultivated ground" (Ibid.).

In 1861, the Tokugawa Government, surprised by the presence of Westerners on the islands, delegated officials to explore the islands and declare their possession. Soon after (1868), Japan came into the Modern Era following the Civil War. The new government named the islands "Ogasawara", after a legendary *samurai*, Ogasawara Sadayori, who is said to have found these islands at the end of the 16th century. In 1876, the Japanese possession of the islands was internationally recognised.

After modernisation, the number of Japanese immigrants increased in the islands, where they mixed with the existing inhabitants of Caucasian and Hawaiian origin. During WWII, the Bonin Islands became the most important strategic location of the Japanese Army in defending the capital city; consequently, many military facilities were constructed.

After World War II, the Bonin Islands were occupied by American troops, and only the descendents of Caucasian origin were allowed to remain in the islands. The inhabitants of Japanese origin were forced to go back to Japan. Only after the return of the islands to Japan in 1968 did Japanese start to resettle the islands.

As a result, the Bonin Islands developed a complex history. For instance, the Bonin Islands dialect, formed by a "pidgin-Creole" process since 1830, has a complicated feature: the language consists of several dialects of English (c.f., Hawaiian English, standard American English, etc.) fused with several dialects of Japanese, Hawaiian, and even Micronesian (Long 2002).

Outrigger Canoes

The tradition of Hawaiian canoes

The Hawaiian Islands are part of Polynesia, and the canoes used there have a Polynesian heritage. There were two types of canoes in Hawai'i: the single-outrigger and the double-hulled canoe. Both types could be propelled either by paddling or sailing. Hawaiian canoes were further divided into many types according to function, structure and hull shape (Hiroa 1975:255; Holmes 1981:70).

Both the bow and stern of Hawaiian canoe hulls were pointed and curved upward. Although the inside of the hull was supported by transverse frames, they seem to be degenerate or vestigial. If Hawaiian canoes were rigged, the sail was shaped like a "crab-claw" or reverse triangular shape. This basic feature is most similar to that of the Tahitian half-claw sail (Bowden 1952; Horridge

1986; Lewis 1994:62-64). Both of them probably developed from the Oceanic spritsail used in the Marquesas and by the New Zealand Māori; they are different from the Oceanic lateen sails of Micronesia, Tonga, Sāmoa, and Fiji.

Concerning outriggers, single outriggers were mainly used throughout Oceania, including the Hawaiian Islands, so there were many varieties of boom and float assemblies. Hawaiian canoes consisted of two curved booms directly lashed to the float on the port side; no connective or peg was used. The paddle had a board and short blade that was either cordate, ovate, obovate, or elliptical (Hornell 1936:442).

Since Hawaiian canoes have changed rapidly since first Western contact in the late 18th century, there is not enough detailed information on canoe features from the time when the first emigrants from the Hawaiian Kingdom came to the Bonin Islands. The most detailed drawing is given by the 1804 Russian expedition (Barratt 1987:A-14).

Rev. William Ellis, whose record is one of the most valuable on Hawaiian life at that time, wrote:

> The canoes of the Sandwich Islands appear eminently calculated for swiftness, being long, narrow, generally light, and drawing but little water. A canoe is always made out of a single tree; some of them are upwards of 70 feet long, 1 or 2 feet wide, and sometimes more than 3 feet deep, though they are seldom in length more than 50 feet. The body of the canoe is generally covered with a black paint, made by the natives with various earthly and vegetable materials, in which the bark, oil, and burnt nuts of the *kukui* tree form the principal ingredients. On the upper edge of the canoe is sewed, in a remarkably neat manner, a small strip of hard white wood, from 6 to 8 inches in width, according to the size and length of the canoe. (Ellis 1826: 315).

Although Hawaiian canoes often were drawn in the late 18th century, photos of canoes came after the 1880s (Holmes 1986:79-80). Thus, there is little visual information of Hawaiian canoes from around 1830. In the drawing recorded by the Russian, Langsdorff, curved booms are directly connected to the float, whose head was shaped like a "lizard". By 1839, when Admiral Paris visited Hawai'i, the old type had disappeared and been replaced by:

> ...a [European] spritsail laced to a boom as well as the mast. This latter, which is stepped in the bottom, is secured to the outrigger boom and stayed on each side by two shrouds, and also by a stay attached at the bow. All these spars are of ordinary wood, bamboo appearing to be very rare in these islands. (Paris 1941: 141; cited by Hornell 1936: 25).

In a picture taken around 1885, the rectangular sail was supported by a fixed mast, boom and sprit. The bow and stern were curved upward like the indigenous type, and a paddle with an elliptical blade was shown. Although this picture was taken after the first emigrants from Hawai'i arrived at the Bonin Islands, this canoe was most similar to the one drawn in 1861 by the Tokugawa Government discussed below.

Canoe drawing in the Bunkyu Period (1861)

The emigrants from Hawai'i introduced single outrigger canoes to the islands. They have been called "*kano*" until today (Figure 2). The oldest Japanese record of the presence of canoes on the Bonin Islands came from the end of the Tokugawa (Edo) Period.

Figure 8.3 illustrates the picture drawn by the officials delegated by the Tokugawa Government in the Bunkyu Period, 1861. The structure of the canoe was Hawaiian, but the sail already had a Western influence: it did not have a typical Hawaiian crab-claw shape but rather a rectangular sail with a split. The bailer drawn under the canoe had an inner handle, that is, a typical Oceanic bailer. The shape of the paddle blade was similar to that of the Hawaiian paddle. Hence, the original Bonin Islands canoe was a copy of the Hawaiian canoe already influenced by Western design.

As cited above, Rev. Ellis wrote that the canoe hull was painted black. The upper part of the canoe hull in the above picture was also blackish, although hull bottom and float were white, indicating its possible succession from the Hawaiian tradition.

Figure 2. The Bonin Island Canoe with Sail, Visitor Center, Chichi-jma Island.

Source: Photo by the author, 2008.

Figure 3. The Canoe Drawing in 1861 Expedition.

Source: Tokyo Metropolitan Archives. Photo by the author, 2008.

Canoes of the Bonin Islands seen in Hornell's volume

Canoes in the Bonin Islands were mentioned in Hornell's *Canoes of Oceania, Vol . 1*, following the section regarding Hawai'i:

> The hull of the canoe is a double-ended dugout. The ends are almost identical, curved, sharp, and capped above by short and pointed triangular end pieces sharply curved upward; Weatherly qualities are given by a short, slight arched deck at each end, butting against the after side of the small end piece. These canoes run to 30 feet in length…

> The outrigger consists of two similarly shaped booms curved downward in their distal part to their insertion into the float at the distance outboard of about 8 feet. The pointed end of each is forced into a hole made in the ridged midline of the float and is further secured by a collar lashing to a peg inserted on the inner aspect of the float.

> The proximal ends of the booms lie athwart the dugout hull and rest upon the gunwales. Crossing the hull a short distance immediately below each boom is a convexly bowed wooden thwart bar or boom brace; its ends pass through the sides and show on the outside a couple of inches below the gunwale. To this the inboard part of the boom is secured by two collar lashings. A method of attachment of the same type is found in the South Celebes and in a varietal form is generally throughout Indonesia. (Hornell 1936:26).

Concerning the nature of the boom attachment, Hornell wrote, "The boom lashings, though essentially Indonesian in method…must yet be considered a simplification of the Hawaiian U-shaped spreader" (Hornell 1936:28). As for the float, Hornell wrote:

> …[the] float is two-fifths of the length of the hull. The ends pointed and the upper surface is ridged longitudinally; the sides and bottom are rounded as in the dugout hull. A curious feature is its compound construction; it consists of a basal part hollowed out in canoe fashion, and an upper part made of long board broadly triangular in transverse section, fitting over the hollowed under part like the ridged cover of sarcophagus. (Hornell 1936:26).

The overall shape of the float resembled that of a canoe hull, and I have heard that the Bonin Islanders call the float a "small canoe".

Introduced in 1830, Bonin Islands canoes have since acquired modifications: "The half-sprit rig employed is a rough adaptation of ordinary European sprit sail, the rig which the peripheral Polynesians have found it most easy to adopt when abandoning the old Polynesian type of triangular sail which was tied to the mast" (Hornell 1936:28-29).

Concerning the paddles, Hornell wrote, "The paddles used are essentially of the Japanese sculling type, long-shafted and cross-handled, with the blade elongated and narrowed" (Hornell 1936:29). The last point is not adequate, since both the Oceanic type of paddle with oval blade (*maru-gai*, or round paddle) and the Japanese sculling type with rectangular blade (*hira-gai*, or flat paddle) have been used. As discussed later, only the Japanese sculling type came to be used on the Hachijo-jima Island.

Further Discussions

An interesting characteristic is the masks that were recorded as being painted on canoe bows as a kind of charm (Figure 4). These masks were certainly not Japanese or Hawaiian; rather, they appear to be of a Melanesian style. The proportions of the head with the face and the large tusk are reminiscent of the Malanggan type of masks from New Ireland in the Bismarck Archipelago (Helfrich 1973:Plates 9a-10b). Since further information is not available, we simply do not know why Melanesian-style masks were used in the Bonin Islands in association with Hawaiian canoes; nevertheless, it certainly indicates a complex interaction between the Bonin Islands and other islands of the Circum-Philippine Sea.

Another interesting item is a canoe paddle on which a human face was painted (see Figure 3, above). Although Oceanic canoe paddles were often decorated, this kind of concrete expression of the human face was not widely used. I would argue that the most similar example comes from Bougainville, Papua New Guinea. If these Melanesian-style elements actually existed together with Hawaiian-type canoes, it indicates another route of cultural transfer in the Circum-Philippine Sea. It does not necessarily mean that indigenous Melanesians themselves arrived by some means in the Bonin Islands. I rather suspect that Westerners either introduced these cultural elements, or brought indigenous Melanesians with these elements to the Bonin Islands.

With these further modifications, single outrigger canoes of Hawaiian origin have been used mainly for fishing and transportation until today. In particular, they are used for catching turtles and spearing Spanish mackerel. The harpoons used are of Tokyo Bay and Izu Seven Island types. Eyeglasses of wood used for dive fishing are of the Okinawan type. Modification is also seen in hull building. Originally a hull was dug out from *Hernandia sonora*, but later, hulls came to be made by combining planks of Japanese cedar trees and using a Japanese-type boat nail.

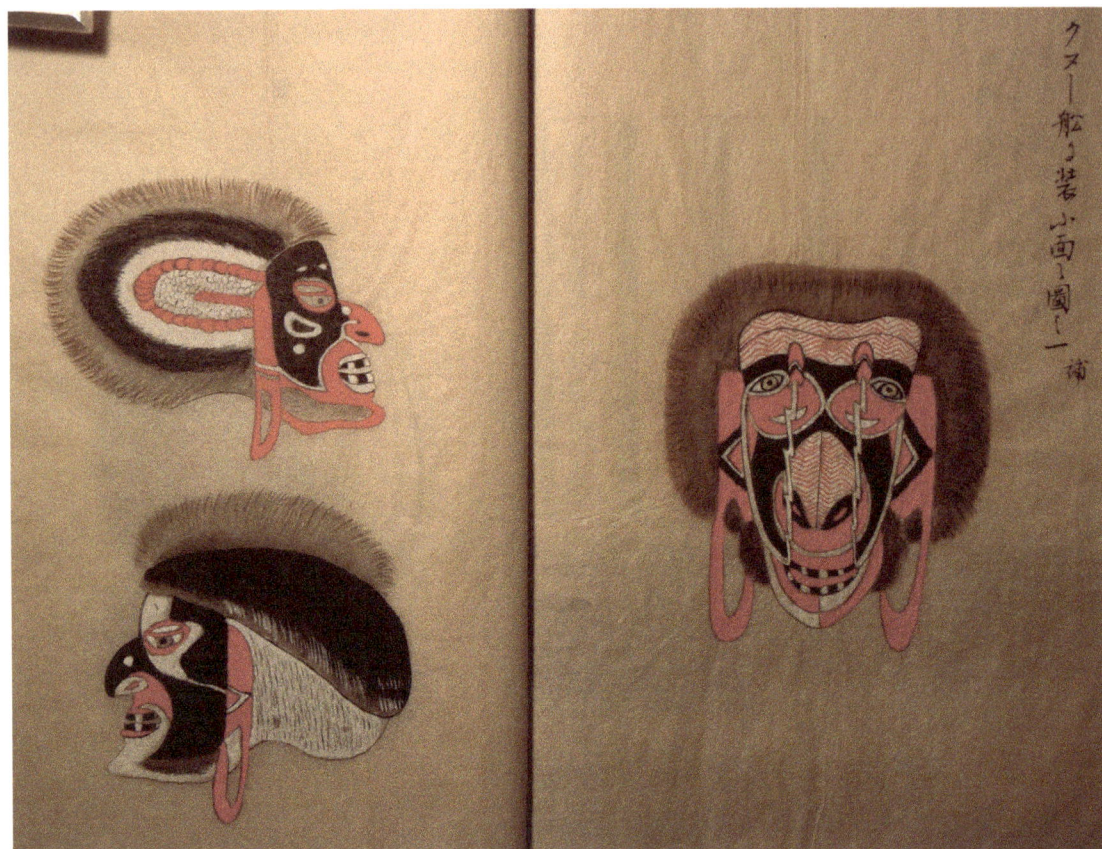

Figure 4. The Mask Drawing in 1861 Expedition.

Source: Tokyo Metropolitan Archives. Photo by the author, 2008.

After the Japanese were forced back to Japan following WWII, canoe builders continued making Bonin Islands type canoes in the Tokyo area. One canoe builder, Mr. A., who was born on Haha-jima Island and was living in Ichikawa, near Tokyo, at that time, made several canoes (Figure 5). These were the most recent wooden canoes recorded, constructed using cedar trunks for the keel parts (Figure 6); the basic shape of the dugout keel, however, still retained the tradition of the original canoes. These canoes were ordered by the American inhabitants during the American occupation period. Curved outrigger booms that were originally made of one kind of wood eventually came to be made, combining straight athwart parts and curved parts directly attached to the float. They were sent to the Bonin Islands by American navy ships and distributed to the inhabitants. There were islanders of Japanese origin who had obtained some of them for fishing and transportation after returning to the islands.

The fiberglass canoes used today were molded from one of the wooden canoes introduced at that time. Now, the canoes are propelled by outboard engine and the sail is seldomly used. However, fiberglass canoes still retain a projection on the stern board that is a remnant of the attachment for rigging a rope for sailing (Figure 7).

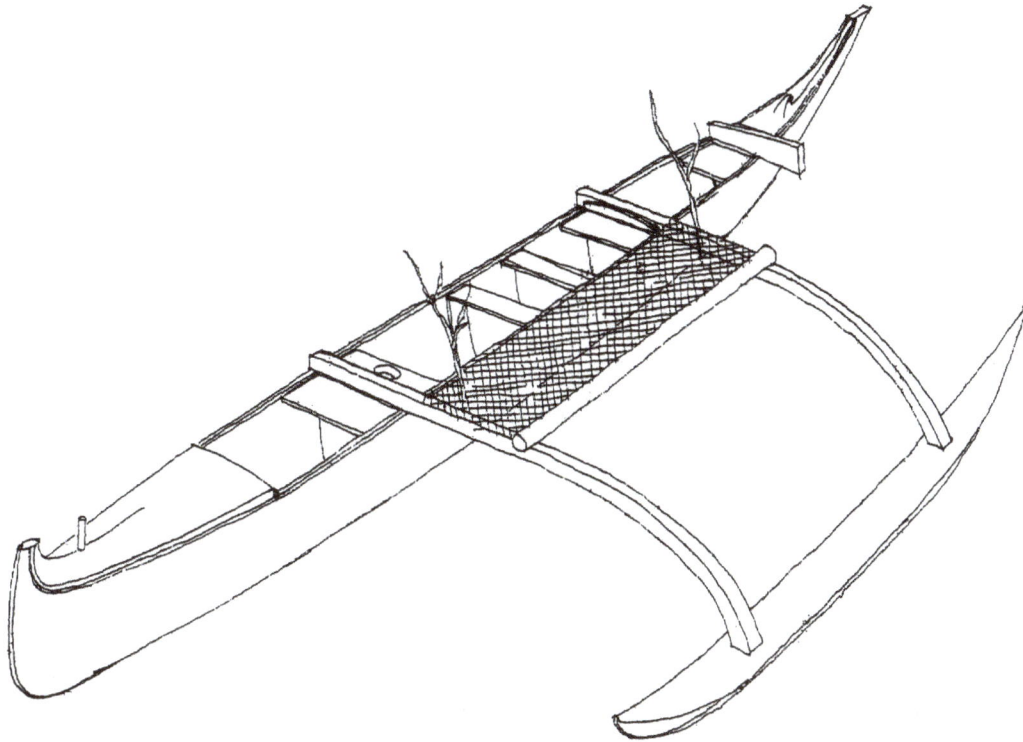

Figure 5. Sketch of the Canoe made around the 1950s: the hull length 7.3m, width 0.41m and depth 0.53m.

Source: Board of Education, Ogasawara Village.

Figure 6. Canoe Hulls at the Workshop of Canoe Builder, Mr. Asanuma.

Source: Photo taken around 1950 by Mr. Seitaro Asanuma (owner of the material).

Figure 7. Canoe of Glass-fiber used today, Chichi-jima Island. Notice the "hook" at the stern that is the remnant of the sailing canoe used in the past.

Source: Photo by author, 2008.

Thus, the canoes of the Bonin Islands were originally introduced from Hawai'i, already with some Western influences and possibly with a temporal influence from Melanesia, used with Japanese fishing and planking techniques until today. After the war, the tradition of "Bonin Islands Type Canoe" has been kept, not in the Bonin Islands, but in Tokyo. The canoe is very much a witness of multi-directional cultural interaction and transfer of technology encountered in the islands.

Hachijo-jima Island

Hachijo-jima Island is the southernmost island of the Izu Seven Islands. Before modernisation, the island had been used mainly as a penal colony. Fishing boats with a single outrigger have been in use until today. The hull is now made of fiberglass and shaped not as a canoe hull, but as a regular fishing boat; however, the hull is asymmetrical to facilitate the use of an outrigger on the port side.

Most of the islanders agree that these outrigger canoes came from the Bonin Islands. As I have already mentioned, after the war, the Bonin Islanders of Japanese origin were forced to return to Japan. There are some Bonin Islanders who came to live on Hachijo-jima Island, as well as some Hachijo-jima Islanders who went to the Bonin Islands as military workers before WWII and came back during the war. They were the ones who transmitted canoe building techniques. One canoe builder, Mr. S., born on Hachijo-jima Island, was sent to Chichi-jima Island to build military facilities. He then learned canoe building there. After coming back to Hachijo-jima Island, he started experimenting with canoe building following the advice of the immigrants from the Bonin Islands.

Although it seems reasonable that the introduction of the canoe to Hachijo-jima Island was during or after WWII, I found one picture taken before the war in which a canoe was used on Hachijo-jima Island (Figure 8). The overall shape of the canoe was identical to that of Bonin Islands canoes, so the experimental use of outrigger canoes by local fishermen dates back to before the war. The difference between the canoes of the Bonin Islands and Hachijo-jima Island is that the canoes of the Bonin Islands were propelled by paddle (like an Oceanic canoe), but those of Hachijo-jima Island were propelled by a Japanese-style oar or "*ro*" (Figure 9).

Figure 8. Canoe in the Hachijo-jima Island, before the War. Note that the man sitting in the middle is using Japanese type oar or "*ro*". situated at outrigger boom. Photo taken at the Hachijo-jima Historical Museum.

Source: Photo by the author.

Figure 9. Canoe Manipulated by the Japanese Style Oar. Note that the standing fisherman is using Japanese type oar: this is the special body technique for using "*ro*".

Source: From *Living in the Kroshiwo Current: Izu Islands*, 1981:248. Tokyo Tosho Village.

Unlike the Bonin Islands type, canoes of Hachijo-jima Island were later modified with considerable influence from fishing-boat building in Japan. A canoe builder, Mr. Y., said that he was the first builder to use plastic hulls with an outrigger device. Gradually, since then, the shape of the hull has changed and become more similar to a regular fishing boat; they still retain uniqueness, however; that is, an asymmetrical shape to accommodate an outrigger to one side (Figure 10).

Figure 10. Canoe Fishing Boat at the Hachijo-jima Island, today.

Source: Photo by the author, 2008.

The Bonin Islands and Hachijo-jima Island: A Melting Pot in the Circum-Philippine Sea

In addition to canoes, other artefacts used in the islands also show maritime interaction. For example, the water jar used on the Bonin Islands is of typical Ryukyu Island-type pots for containing alcohol. Historic records show that immigrants came from Ryukyu Island to the Bonin Islands as sugarcane laborers. There were also specialised fishermen (including divers) from Okinawa.

Nanyo Odori, or the "South Sea Dance", is also evidence of the interaction between Japan, Micronesia, and the Bonin Islands. The dance was introduced from Micronesia to the Bonin Islands before WWII. After WWI, Japan came to govern the previous German colonies of Micronesia while Japanese troops settled in the major Micronesian islands. Carolinians witnessed the marching of the Japanese army and incorporated soldiers' marching behaviour into their traditional dance. The dance was thus formed, mixing traditional Micronesian dance with Japanese soldiers' athletic motion (Konishi 2006). Then the dance was introduced to the Bonin Islands by a Bonin Islander who had returned from Micronesia, and it became an "indigenous" dance there as well. The dance is now qualified as a form of intangible cultural property of the City of Tokyo.

Hachijo-jima Island is also an important location in the discussion of maritime interaction in the Philippine Sea. There is a legend of Gramdam *Tana*. The legend has it that there lived an old lady, called *Tana*. One day, she predicted the coming of a big tsunami. She was saved by clinging to a boat, while all the other people were drowned in the wave. She was pregnant, and later she begat a boy. Since there were no other people who survived, she mated with her son, and they had children. They are the ancestors of the present islanders.

This legend clearly contains motifs of original myths that are often found in the Austronesian and Austro-Asiatic traditions (Walk 1949; cf. Goto 1999, 2010). This example, together with those from the Bonin Islands, indicates that these islands south of Tokyo have been a melting pot of maritime interaction in the Circum-Philippine Sea.

In conclusion, the Circum-Philippine Sea, including Japan, Taiwan, the Philippines, Indonesia, and other Oceanic islands, is a rich field that has not been explored enough yet. We should explore these interesting aspects of culture history in this area. The technological integration seen in the canoe-fishing gear complex of the Bonin Islands was not a mere result of "diffusion", but it is rather explained by the "dynamics of self-interested technical agents, the artifice of technical acts" (Dobres 1999:126). As Pfeffenberger (1999:159) notes, the canoe builders must have built canoes by:

> …drawing from conventional modes of social, economic, and legal relationships, including partnership, kinship, auctions, speculative investment, markets, and contracts; but it weaves them together into a unique and distinctive totality – an artifice resulting in a socio-technical phenomenon that actors themselves recognize to be distinctive.

References

Barrat, G. 1987. *The Russian Discovery of Hawai'i*. Honolulu: Editions Limited.

Bowden, R.L. 1952. Eastern sail affinities. *American Neptune* 12:81-117, 185-211.

Dobres, M.-A. 1999. Technology's links and chaînes: the processual unfolding of technique and technician. In M. Dobres and C.R. Hoffman (eds), *Dynamics of Technology: Practice, Politics, and World Views*, pp. 124-146. Washington D.C.: Smithsonian Institution Press.

Goto, A. 1999. *Talking Fishes: South Islands Myths of Eels and Snakes*. Tokyo: Shogakukan. (in Japanese).

Goto, A. 2010. Mythicization of tsunami in the Ryukyu Islands: a process of seascape formation in island societies. In P. Wallin and H. Martisson-Wallin (eds), *Selected Papers from the VII International Conference on Easter Island and the Pacific: Migration, Identity, and Cultural Heritage*, pp. 465–471. Visby: Gotland University.

Helfrich, K. 1973. *Malanggan •1: Bildwerke von Neuirland*. Berlin: Museum für Völkerkunde.

Hiroa, T.R. 1975. *Arts and Crafts of Hawaii, Section IV 6: Canoe*. Honolulu: Bishop Museum Press. *Bishop Museum Special Publications* 45.

Holmes, T. 1981. *The Hawaiian Canoe*. Hanalei: Editions Limited.

Hornell, J. 1936. *Canoe of Oceania, Vol I: The Canoes of Polynesia, Fiji, and Micronesia*. Honolulu: Bishop Museum Press. *Bishop Museum Special Publications* 27.

Horridge, A. 1986. The evolution of Pacific canoe rigs. *Journal of Pacific History* 21:83-99.

Konishi, J. 2006. *A Comparative Study of the Performing Arts Being Spread by Cultural Exchange between Micronesians, Ogasawarans and Okinawans Focusing on its Reception and Changing Aspects*. Report for the Grand-In-Aid Scientific Research (B), JSPS. Tokyo: Japan Society for Proceeding of Science.

Kuykendall, R.S. 1938. *The Hawaiian Kingdom, 1778-1854: Foundation and Transformation*. Honolulu: The University of Hawaii Press.

Lessa, W.A. 1961. *Tales from Ulithi Atoll: A Comparative Study in Oceania Folklore*. Berkeley: University of California Press. *Folklore Studies* 13.

Long, D. (ed). 2002. *An Invitation to Bonin Islands Studies*. Kagoshima: Nanpo Shisha. (in Japanese).

Oda, S. 1990. A review of archaeological research in the Izu and Ogasawara Islands. *Man and Culture in Oceania* 6:53-79.

Oda, S, I. Hayakaya, M. Okazaki and S. Kobayashi (eds). 1992. *Collection of Archaeological Materials from the Ogasawara Island*. Tokyo: Board of Education of Metropolitan area. (in Japanese).

Ohkuma, R. 1985. *The Records of Foreign Ship Arrivals to the Bonin Islands*. Tokyo: Kondo Publisher. (in Japanese).

Pfaffenberger, B. 1999. Worlds in the making: technological activities and the construction of intersubjective meaning. In M. Dobres and C.R. Hoffman (eds), *Dynamics of Technology: Practice, Politics, and World Views*, pp. 147-164. Washington D.C.: Smithsonian Institution Press.

Rainbird, P. 2004. *The Archaeology of Micronesia*. Cambridge: Cambridge University Press.

Rainbird, P. 2007. *The Archaeology of Islands*. Cambridge: Cambridge University Press.

Ruschenberger, W.S.W. 2005. *A Voyage round the World, including an Embassy to Muscat and Siam, in 1835, 1836, and 1837*. Philadelphia: Elibron Classics.

Walk, L. 1949. Das Flut-Geschwisterpaar als Ur- undn Stammelterpaar der Menschheit. *Mitteilungen der Anthropologischen Gesellschaft in Wien* 78/79:60-115.

9

The Technique and Ecology Surrounding Moray Fishing: A Case Study of Moray Trap Fishing on Mactan Island, Philippines

Takashi Tsuji, National Museum of Ethnology (Minpaku), Japan

Introduction

The Republic of the Philippines is made up of over 7,100 islands and archipelagos of all sizes. The Visayas region of islands is centrally located south of Luzon and north of Mindanao, and is surrounded on the east and west by the Panay and Negros islands, and the Samar and Leyte islands, respectively. The residents of the Visayas region fish masterfully, applying fishing methods and tools that are suitable to this inland sea ecology (Balogo 1996; Calderon-Hayhow et al. 1994; Green et al. 2004; Rau 1979; Schoppe et al. 1998; Tawa 1981, 2006; Tsuji 2007a; Yano 1994; Yano and Kobayashi 1994; Zayas 1994, 2004).

The research findings reported in this paper focus on one of the fishing tools and fishing methods utilised in the Visayas inland sea area, the bamboo fishing trap, which is used primarily to trap moray eels.

Fish traps are widely used in various locations across the globe including the target region of this study. Inhabitants of Mactan Island, Cebu, use bamboo traps extensively. Trap fishing of morays at shallow depths is the primary method used in this region, especially by the offshore fishing businesses off the coast of Cebu (Green et al. 2004).

Previous research on fish traps and moray trap fishing activities in the Philippines is limited. As for the traps themselves, Balogo (1996) cited the Gimbaleños trap as an example of a bamboo made trap used as a fishing tool. However, Balogo only provided a name for the trap and a brief description. Calderon-Hayhow et al. (1994) and Umali (1950) published illustrations of fishing tools and fishing methods from the eastern region of Negros and the whole of the Philippines, but again, only included brief descriptions. Cadeliña et al. (1986) studied traps used on Siquijor Island from an archeological material-culture perspective, but document the collected information without offering any analytical discussion. From this body of research, we can determine the variety of traps in each region and their distribution, but we cannot know the technology used to create the traps, usage techniques, the environment in which they were utilised, or their structural and functional attributes from a fishing ecology perspective. In contrast, Rau (1979) studied the methods of small fishing businesses in the areas surrounding Cebu from an ecological perspective, reporting the names of the fishing methods, the structure of the tools, the targeted fish and fishing seasons, the environment in which the traps are used, and the productivity of these fishing methods. Rau's research is therefore valuable as a baseline reference point.

A rough understanding of moray fishing can be gleaned from the preceding studies and newspaper articles (Garcia 2003), but to date, ethnographic research focusing on moray fishing in the Philippines has not been conducted. Given this backdrop, in 2005, the author conducted a preliminary ecological anthropological study of moray trap fishing on Mactan Island, Cebu. This study describes the actual construction of the moray trap and an analysis of the time periods during which the trap is used in relation to tide and weather conditions at the trapping locations (Tsuji 2007b). Due to scheduling constraints, the author was only able to do an on-board study once, making it impossible to conduct a sufficient weight study necessary for productivity discussions. In order to compensate for this deficiency, another study was conducted in 2008. This report documents the information from that study, intermingling data from 2005 as needed.

The primary objectives of this report are 1) to disclose the true condition of moray fishing in Cordova on Mactan Island in Cebu, Philippines, and 2) to document and discuss the technique and ecology of moray trap fishing including a) the structure of the trap, b) the times and usage of the trapping grounds, and c) the effectiveness of the trap. An additional goal of this document is to clarify how the moray trap fishing technique reflects the ecological environment of the region.

The supplemental study for this report was carried out from 29 June through 25 August 2005, while the on-board study was conducted on 31 July. A second study was conducted from 28 May through 31 May 2008. The primary research methods were individual tracing[1] using participant observation and a Global Positioning System receiver, and weight studies using a spring scale and interviews. Written surveys were incorporated as well.

Overview of the Investigated Site

Mactan Island is located on the east side of Cebu Island, in Cebu Province (Figure 1). There is an international airport and a Mactan Export Processing Zone (MEPZ) along with many beach resorts. Mactan Island has a relatively dry climate, receiving a mean rainfall value of approximately 100mm of precipitation monthly from February through May. There is a marked rainy season from June to January. The average precipitation rate and temperature per year is 1,547.1mm and 28.1°C, respectively (Cebu Pagasa Complex 2005).

This study was conducted in Sitio Kawayanan, the Kawayanan borough, within the Barangay Poblacion District in the centre of the Municipality of Cordova on the southeast side of Mactan Island. Cordova is located approximately 22km from Cebu City, and in 2007, it had a population of 45,713. The residents use Cebuano as their common language and 95% are Christian (Roman Catholic) by faith. The service industry and manufacturing companies employ a majority of the workforce while approximately 20% of the households have a family member working at the MEPZ. Thirteen percent of households are in the fishing business (Ator 2007;

---

1   The Individual Tracing Method is used primarily as a means of capturing the activities and allotment of time in everyday living in the fields of ecological anthropology and human ecology. An individual surveyor constantly moves about with the target individual being surveyed. The advantage of this method is that the researcher observes the surveyed subject's activities in detail. That data from multiple surveys cannot be collected has been pointed out as a disadvantage to this method (Suda 1994). The author would like to acknowledge that the data from the individual tracing method used in this report (on-board survey) is a record of only two moray trap fishermen. This report discusses in detail an aspect of the state of moray trap fishing in Cordova on Mactan Island. However, providing a comprehensive picture of this issue is beyond the scope of this study, and is a topic for future research.

Municipality of Cordova 2004; San Carlos Publications et al. 2004). Approximately 300 people living in 53 households reside in the Kawayanan borough and have easy access to the ocean and public markets. Fourteen households acquire their primary income from the MEPZ, twelve of whom have a member working as a driver for a *trisikad* (a bicycle with a sidecar used for public transportation). There are eleven households in the fishing business, three of which are currently engaged in harvesting moray eels with fish-traps (*mamakasi*). Besides this method of fishing, people also engage in practices aimed at gill netting (*manukut*) of mottled spinefoot *danggit*; shellfish diving (*manaon*); trap fishing (*maneming*) for *kasag* (swimming crab) or *ibis* (cardinal fish family); night-fishing for *tama* (*Octopus oliveri*) and general gleaning (*manginhas*), as well as catching peanut worms *salpo* (*Sipunculus robustus*) and wedge sea hares *dunsol* (*Dolabella auricularia*) (Tsuji 2007a).

Figure 1. The location of the field survey.

Source: Drawn by the author, based on a Google Map.

Figure 2. The Moray Festival.

Source: Photo by the author.

Thirty-four percent of all households in Cordova are in the fishing business and 43% have a member who is employed full-time in fish harvesting (Municipality of Cordova 2004). These statistics demonstrate the presence of an intimate link between the people of Cordova and their marine environment. The *Dinagat Festival* (Sea Festival), which was held in Cordova every August from 1999 through 2004, arose from this close relationship and provided a means of promoting tourism. In 2005, leveraging their primary local marine resource with the aim not only of promoting tourism, but also supplementing the fishing household livelihood and income, the festival was changed to the *Bakasi Festival* (Moray Festival). It is now a focus of economic stimulus for the region (Figure 2).

Figure 3. Live Morays at the market.

Source: Photo by the author.

Moray and Moray Traps

Moray (bakasi)

The target of moray trap fishing is a moray eel called *bakasi*. This is a relatively small size species of moray eel (unidentified) of about 10-25cm. Mixed into the catch are also snowflake moray (*Echidna nebulo*) *halawig*, and *ubod* (not confirmed), but they are considered ancillary prey taxa.

The hardiness of these morays allows the fishermen to hold them in a container for up to four days before taking them to market. This enables fisherman to harvest a sufficient number before taking them to be sold. Morays are sold on the open market in Cordova, but middlemen transport live morays by truck to locations such as Cebu's largest market, Carbon Market, and presumably onto Mabolo in Cebu City as well as Tabunok, which is located 9km west of the city centre (Garcia 2003).

Fishermen sell the morays to middlemen for 50 to 70 pesos per caltex. About 15 living morays are placed in a sack and lined up for sale at the market (Figure 3). One sack is sold for about 20 pesos. They are sold with the smaller snowflake moray mixed in together. Some morays are processed, dried, and sold at the market. Some people say that the moray eels are harvested and sold live because they are fresher that way, but morays are also considered an aphrodisiac, so it can be inferred that there is a significant marketing advantage to delivering the conduit to improved virility while it is still alive. These smaller morays are rich in gelatinous fatty tissue and are mainly prepared in soups (*tinola),* or fried together with black beans and spices (*linarang*) or grilled over open coals (Sollano 2005). The larger morays are not preferred for consumption because their flesh is tougher and they contain many bones.

Moray traps (bantak)

The moray trap (*bantak*) (Figure 4) discussed in this study is woven with bamboo (*kawayan*). The height of the basket trap is approximately 23cm; it is 32cm around at its widest point, and 16.5cm at the thinnest point of its body, and weighs about 100g. Given its name, it is believed that in the Kawayanan borough (Sitio Kawayanan), there used to be many bamboo groves, but they are hard to find today. Baskets are made from either bamboo that is found nearby or purchased.

Figure 4. Moray traps (*bantak*).

Source: Photo by the author.

I was unable to confirm the exact type of bamboo, but a green bamboo about 2m in length and 40cm in circumference can be purchased for 45 pesos (1 peso was approximately 0.02 USD at the time in 2008). The bamboo is sliced into thin strips with a knife or hatchet. Eleven strips (approx. 40cm long, 7mm–1cm wide, 1mm thick, with both ends sharpened to a point and one end used as a fold-back) are used for the vertical frame. Six strips (1.5m long, 3.5-5mm wide, and 1mm thick) are used for the horizontal frame and together, they form a jar-like shaped weave leaving no openings. On the bottom of the jar portion, strips are left folded back to prevent a moray from exiting. The opening of the jar is where the moray enters the trap and where the bait is inserted. In order to reinforce yet preserve suppleness, 2mm wide polypropylene bands are woven into both portions of the trap.

It is said that in the past, bamboo strips were used to reinforce the traps, but after the year 2000, polypropylene bands began to be used. It is reported that rattan had been used as reinforcement on Siquijor Island in the 1980s (Cadeliña et al. 1986). A stopper for the trap is made by cutting out a portion of used rubber beach slippers (whose strap may be broken) and inserted into the mouth of the trap. Until around 1990, wood was used for the stopper, while fishing nets or rags were used on eastern Negros Island (Calderon-Hayhow et al. 1994). Somewhat centrally located between the body and the mouth of the trap are loops made of polypropylene bands. The trap is secured at the fishing ground by pinching these loops with a forked bamboo stick to keep the trap from being washed away by the waves. In Cordova, these forked bamboo sticks are used to secure the trap (Rau 1979), but it is reported that on Siquijor Island, rocks are tied to the trap to secure it to fishing spots (Cadeliña et al. 1986).

It is a man's job to weave bamboo traps. An aged pair of brothers who are veterans of weaving these bamboo traps live in the Kawayanan borough. The elder brother weaves traps for morays (*bantak*) while the younger brother weaves square traps (*teming*). *Kasag* (swimming crab) or *ibis* (cardinal fish family) are caught for bait of *maneming*-fishing. These brothers also engage in fishing activities using these types of traps. They learned the art of making these traps from their father and have been weaving them since they were young. They can weave 1 trap in about 40 minutes. A *bantak* sells for about 20 pesos and a *teming* for about 25 pesos. They weave and sell the traps once an order is placed. In general, a moray trap will last about 5 months.

In addition to bamboo traps, *buhi-an* containers are also woven to hold live morays. *Buhi* means (life) in the Cebuano language and with the suffix "*-an*" means a container to allow them to remain living. Besides strapping this container to the cross arm of the boat along its side to keep morays alive while harvesting, it is also used as the holding tank until they are taken to market. The size of this woven *buhi-an* differs according to the size of the boat or the need, but the largest ones are as long as 155cm long and 94cm in circumference at their widest point. Both ends are reinforced with bamboo tubes in order to maintain their strength. The body of the *buhi-an* is woven with bamboo in a similar fashion to the traps. Polypropylene bands are used in spots that easily fall apart. In the middle section of the *buhi-an*, there is an opening that is approximately 21cm long and 8cm wide using strips of wooden or rubber sandals, which is created for inserting and retrieving the moray eel. Worn out rubber sandals are used for the lid of this opening and are held down like a stopper with a piece of bamboo so that the morays cannot get out. These *buhi-an* are made to order and the larger *buhi-an* can be sold for 300 pesos.

The Technique and Ecology of Moray Trapping

Use of the trapping grounds

Moray eel trapping is conducted all around the Cordova coastal region, which is blessed with massive coral reefs, as well as around neighboring Gilutongan Island and other peripheral islands.

Trapping grounds are chosen in the intertidal flatlands that have a sandy bottom and are packed with *lusay* (probably a species similar to *Enhalus acoroides*) sea grass. The sea grass bed provides a hiding place for the organisms that are prey taxa for the moray eel. Morays are nocturnal and feed at shallow depths at night. Moray trap fishing is a method that takes advantage of these feeding behavioural traits.

Moray eel fishing is conducted during low tide, since during any low tide, irrespective of the season or time of day, the morays can be successfully caught. At this study site, fishing is usually conducted in the mornings, but Rau also reported that a time closer to sunset is sometimes preferred and that fishing is not good in November (Rau 1979). In the 2005 study, moray trapping was conducted even during the unstable rainy season as well as during thunderstorms, confirming that one can successfully harvest morays even under poor weather conditions. However, trapping was not conducted during strong winds (Tsuji 2007b).

Figure 5. Moray trap fishing.

Source: Photo by the author.

Boats that use a bamboo pole for propulsion are used for trapping in the shallow water if the trapping grounds are close to the shore, whereas a motorboat is used to go out to the surrounding islands that require longer travel time. Both types of vessels are double outrigger boats. Along with the traps, bamboo forks are loaded into the boat, which secure the traps to the trapping grounds. The basket *buhi-an* and bait are also assembled and loaded into the vessel. In this study, a de-shelled cockle (*litub*; *Anadara antiquata*) is used for bait.

During trapping, the boat is pulled with one hand while walking in the shoal water and securing the traps in the trapping grounds with the other hand (Figure 5). While the boat is primarily used for transportation, at this juncture it also plays the role of carrying the tools for trapping. In order to set a trap, a 1m long pole is created by splitting a 1 metre piece of bamboo. A slit is made into the pole's end into which the loop on the trap is fastened so that the trap will not be washed away by the waves, since the pole is then securely stuck into the sandy bottom. Additionally, due to the fact that during low tide these poles are exposed above the water, they serve as place markers for where the traps were set (Rau 1979; Tsuji 2007b). The traps are set at a few metre intervals apart, but with care so as not to lose sight of them.

At the locations where the traps are set, the bamboo poles protrude above the surface of the water in low tide. By simply walking along the line of poles, the traps can then be harvested. Other than designating the starting and ending points, extra poles can also be stuck in the sand to indicate a change in direction of the trap settings. If the traps cannot be easily relocated, the surrounding landscape may become the basis for finding them.

The traps that have been set are retrieved the next day at low tide and the harvested morays are transferred to *buhi-an*. Bait is inserted back into the trap and it is set again at a different location.

The characteristics of moray trapping ground usage described below are based on information gleaned from one fisherman's use of the trapping grounds captured with a GPS over the course of three days, beginning on 28 May and ending on 31 May 2008. This fisherman used a non-motorised boat for moray trapping. The GPS analysis showed that the trapping grounds are sought around the shoals of Cordova without moving long distances between trapping grounds (Figure 6).

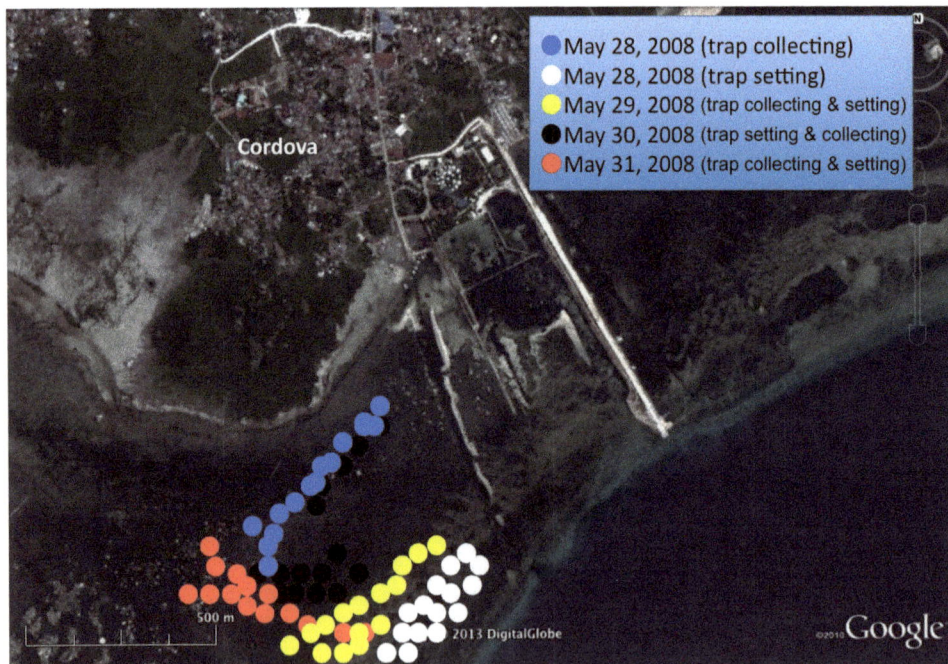

Figure 6. Moray trap setting and collection points.

Source: Drawn by the author, based on Google Map.

Several reasons can be given as to why trapping grounds are not sought over an expansive area. First, the tide dependency method requires that the trap setting and harvesting are done during low tide and completed before the tide rises too high. Thus, if trapping grounds are sought over an expansive area, the prepared traps cannot be harvested or set within the given timeframe. Furthermore, the stamina and economic condition of the individual fisherman may be contributing factors.

Date	Time Zone	Total time for operation
May 28, 2008		203 min.
May 29, 2008		170 min.
May 30, 2008		177 min.
May 31, 2008		183 min.

4:00   5:00   6:00   7:00   8:00   9:00

■ transportation time   ■ trap collecting   ■ trap setting   ■ boat maintenance
■ Creel transferring   ■ meal   ■ preparing the bait

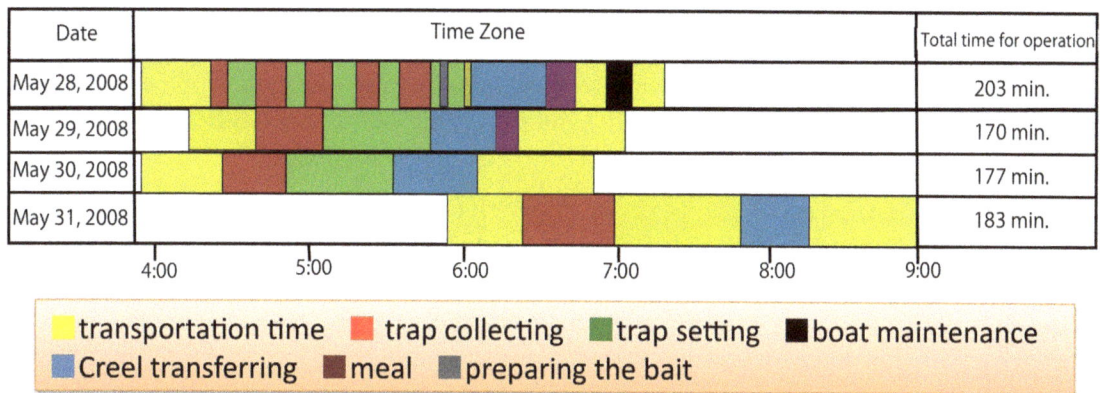

Figure 7. Time allocation for moray trap fishing.

Source: Chart by the author.

In this study, the targeted fisherman was 58 years old, and it is likely that to seek out trapping grounds over a wide area while operating speedily would take a toll on his stamina. If trapping grounds are sought nearby, the time and energy spent on moving is conserved. Furthermore, a rod or a scull is needed for non-motorised boats, which would require a great expenditure of time and energy.

Finally, the fact that trapping grounds are not sought over a wide area indicates that the moray supply is sufficiently rich to meet local demands. However, the shoals of the coastal regions also undergo other types of activities involving harvesting and collection of a variety of fish. Many of these fishing grounds overlap, potentially exposing these locations to population pressure. Thus, it is hard to say conclusively whether or not the location contains a plentiful supply of fish.

Time allocation

Moray trap fishing is a method that is strongly influenced by the tide. As a result of the fact that a boat is used during the fishing process, the trapping has to be initiated and completed during a time that is suitable for boat travel. Additionally, the harvesting and setting of traps must be conducted during low tide. The moray fish trapping times as well as the time allocation of the tasks involved are described in detail below, based on the results from the on-board study conducted using the individual tracing method.

According to Rau (1979) the time spent moray trap fishing is approximately 3 hours. As a result of the on-board study conducted from 28 through 31 May 2008, the work hours of a single fisherman using a non-motorised boat were 203 min., 170 min., 177 min., and 183 min., respectively, for each day, averaging 183.25 minutes (3 hours and 5 minutes) (Figure 7). These on-board study results roughly support the report by Rau (1979). As for the time of day the work was conducted, Rau (1979) stated that the evenings were more desirable, but the author found that in this study, moray eel trapping was conducted in the mornings. Fishing proceeded from just before 4:00 a.m. to around 9:00 a.m. During the 3 days in which this study spanned, 28 to 30 May, the fisherman went out to fish and returned between 6:40 a.m. and 7:20 a.m. On 31 May, the tide was high and the fisherman left to go fishing around 5:30 a.m. and returned around 9:00 a.m.

The workload was distributed to include: 1) transportation on land or sea, 2) setting the traps, 3) harvesting the traps, 4) transferring the morays to the *buhi-an*, 5) eating, 6) preparing the bait, and 7) maintenance of the boat. The aspect of the work that required the most time was transportation, requiring 36% (65.97 minutes) of the workload. Next was setting the traps, at

24% (43.98 minutes); harvesting the traps, at 19% (34.82 minutes); transferring the morays to the *buhi-an*, at 16% (29.32 minutes); eating, at 3% (5.5 minutes); and 1% (1.83 minutes) for both preparing the bait and boat maintenance. It is probably valid to say that 95% of moray trap fishing is taken up by transportation, setting and harvesting traps, and transferring the morays to the *buhi-an*.

Concerning the transferring of the harvested morays into the *buhi-an*, there are fishermen that wait until all of the traps have been collected to transfer them, and also those that transfer the moray into the *buhi-an* each time a trap is collected. Consequetly, it is possible that the time expenditure may vary greatly between individual fishermen. I would also like to point out that time expenditure for various tasks might also vary according to the number of traps that are set, the locations of the trapping grounds, and individual fishing techniques.

Above, I discussed the allocation of time required for the tasks involved in moray trap fishing when using a non-motorised boat. However, it is estimated that the work hours would be longer for a motorised boat, as the fisherman would cover trapping grounds over a broader area. Below, I present the time allocation of tasks in the case of two other individuals based on information obtained from the moray trap fishing study conducted on 31 July 2005, while recognising that this is a very limited sample.

The fisherman that offered to cooperate in the on-board study using a motorised boat was a 25-year-old moray trap fisherman, who set out to fish in the direction of Caohagan Island. The fisherman set out at 7:04 a.m. and returned at 2:44 p.m. Including the time to prepare the bait, the total time required for the operation was 489 minutes (8 hours, 9 min.). The time this fisherman spent on each task is broken down as follows: 1) land and sea transportation, 42% (205 min.); 2) time spent resting, 19% (92 min.); 3) harvesting the traps, 15% (72 min.); 4) setting the traps (including transferring the morays to the *buhi-an*), 10% (47 min.); 5) meal-time, 8% (39 min.); and 6) preparing the bait, 7% (34 min.). The transportation time required 205 minutes, but this was partially due to a thunderstorm on the return trip, causing visibility to be cut off by haze. The length of time spent resting was extended due to the fisherman visiting his family members on Caohagan Island before starting work.

Two hundred and five (205) minutes were required for transportation by the motorised boat operator in his trap fishing activities to and from his original destination, almost tripling the time used compared to the non-motorised boat operator's time of 65.97 minutes. There is almost no difference in the time expended for setting and harvesting the traps: 43.98 minutes versus 47 minutes. In harvesting of the traps (including the time required for transferring the morays into the *buhi-an*), the non-motorised boat operator expended 64.14 minutes and the motorised boat operator expended 72 minutes, showing an 8-minute difference.

However, the non-motorised boat operator averaged 96 traps set and harvested, whereas the latter set and harvested 120. Hypothetically, if the non-motorised boat operator had set 120 traps, the time expended setting them would be 55 minutes and 80 minute for harvesting them. It can be concluded that the motorised boat moray trap fisherman works more efficiently. The differences in theses results could reflect age differences, and the fact that by operating at a further distance with a motorised boat, one may have to be more conscious of the tide.

Moray trap fishing in nearby areas using a non-motorised boat can be conducted at a more relaxed pace. However, one is forced to compete with the other moray trap fishing businesses for both the supply and the fishing grounds, while continuing to operate under the disturbing conditions of the population pressure on the fishing grounds. On the other hand, with the motorised boat, it is possible to seek trapping grounds in areas where there is almost no moray trap fishing being conducted and a greater fish harvest can be anticipated. However, more financial expenditures and physical effort is required for the fuel to commute out to the trapping grounds, time for the commute, and for a faster operating pace, while remaining conscious of the shifting tide.

Above I have attempted to study and analyse the distribution of time allotted for each work task and the total work hours for moray trap fishing. I found that the work is being carried out at about the same tempo as Rau (1979) reported in 1970. Furthermore, I have found that moray trap fishing is being conducted with the use of motorised boats, leading to a significant increase in transportation time for moray fishing as well as a trend toward operating at an accelerated pace. From these facts, along with the changes in the shoreline environment and the moray boom, it can be implied that moray trap fishing is in a transitional period of change.

Productivity of moray traps

Generally speaking, fishing tools and fishing techniques have been refined throughout the years according to the behaviour of the fish, the environmental characteristics of the fishing grounds, and the choice of fish targeted for harvest. It is thought that the wisdom of the local fishing populace is reflected in the tools and the fishing techniques. For example, let us look at the three main types of traps that were used at the study sites. Pieces of fish are used as bait in the hemi-spherical *panggal* trap, which are attached to coral about 5m below the surface. With these traps, wrasse and mottled spinefoot are caught. The square trap called a *teming* is set in the coral shallows of sand or sea grass at about 1m below the surface and is used to catch non-palatable crabs of the box crab or spider crab families, *ibis* (cardinal fish family) or *kasag* (swimming crab) and other small fish. De-shelled cockle (*litub*; *Anadara antiquata*) are used as bait in the *bantak* trap, which are set in the same environment as the *teming,* to catch smaller morays. Each trap choice, the shape of the trap, the bait used, the environment in which it is set, and the targeted harvest is considered. Moreover, fishermen are engaged in the type of fishing that is suited to their needs and specialty skills.

The tools of the trade and techniques have been honed by trial and error over many years. The moray trap, *bantak*, has evolved into a jar or a Japanese *sake* bottle shape, used almost exclusively to catch *bakasi*.

Below, I discuss the productivity of the moray trap with reference to harvest data from moray trap fishing gleaned during the study period. During the 2008 study, 384 traps were used over a period of 4 days and 907 morays were caught. The combined weight of the morays is 18,295g (Table 1), resulting in an average harvest per day of approximately 4.57kg, or 226 moray caught with 96 traps. A range of one to eight morays were captured in 1 trap (an average of 2.4 morays).

Table 1. Moray Trap Fishing Yield Volume.

Date	No. of traps ( ) ... No. catch	No. of Moray	Weight (g)	Income (Pesos)
May 28, 2008	96 (23)	184	3,565	300
May 29, 2008	95 (17)	237	4,860	480
May 30, 2008	87 (11)	253	5,195	500
May 31, 2008	106 (25)	233	4,675	?
Total	384 (76)	907	18,295	1,280
Average	96 (19)	226.75	4,573.75	426.67

Source: Table by the author.

Out of the 384 traps, there were 77 traps in which no moray eels were caught. Consequently, 80% of the traps were productive. In the 2005 study, 115 out of 120 traps (95.8%) yielded at least one moray with a range of 1 to 5 morays captured in a single trap. These numbers reflect the raw data from only 2 fishermen over a period of five days. Without taking into consideration the fisherman's skill level, the difference in the conditions and environment of the fishing grounds, and the seasonal difference, a meaningful discussion on the productivity may not be entirely accurate.

Although interpretation of this information is an issue to be taken up in future studies, it is noteworthy to discuss particular episodes, which may show that the fisherman's ecological knowledge or skill level based on their experience might hold the key to the productivity of the yield. First, during the 2005 study, an area was discovered in which no morays were found in a consecutive number of traps. Again, during the 2008 study when a fisherman, who had just recently become a moray trap fisherman, set a homemade, ill-shaped trap, instead of *bakasi* morays, the trap yielded snowflake morays, which have almost no market value. These episodes could be mere coincidences, but are noteworthy because they could lead to an understanding of moray trap fishing in terms of the fisherman's ecological knowledge and technical skills based on experience.

Next, the productivity of moray trap fishing from the standpoint of profitability is considered. During the 2008 study, the sales volume of the morays was recorded for 3 of the 4-days surveyed. Sales volumes of 300 pesos, 480 pesos, and 500 pesos, respectively, for each day were recorded, averaging 426 pesos per day of work. During the 2005 study, data on sales volume and moray yields was obtained by means of a paper survey administered to moray fishermen over a 21-day period. The results demonstrate that morays were harvested 17 out of 20 days for an average of 6.4 caltex (the smallest was 3 caltex with the greatest being 10 caltex). The average sales volume was 320 pesos (150 pesos for the lowest volume and 500 pesos for the highest volume). On average, the time spent working was 3 hours (using a non-motorised boat). Considering that at the time of the 2008 study, the legal minimum wage for 1 day in the region of the study site was 185 to 200 pesos, moray fishing is a rather profitable occupation.

In the future, there will likely be a demand for comparative studies including the individual differences between fishermen, differences in socio-economic conditions, and income and labour effectiveness ratios in relationship to other methods of fishing, as well as yield volumes by season, which may affect the fishing business profitability. However, at present, the future of fishing operations in Cordova looks bright due to the area's rich resource of marine morays, a regional demand for morays, and support from local events such as the Moray Festival.

Summary and Conclusion

I have discussed and analysed the techniques and ecological aspects of moray trap fishing primarily based on the results from an on-board survey of moray trap fishing. The on-board survey was based solely on observations and the recorded activities of two individual fishermen and thus cannot be said to elucidate the comprehensive state of moray fishing in this field survey site. However, one can say that a rough sketch of the characteristics and issues has been adequately highlighted.

First, the moray trap fishing business targets morays for their harvest, but given the structure of the trap, it is clear that the actual targets are smaller morays (*bakasi*). More specifically, the trap is designed so that smaller moray eels can enter. The moray trap is tightly woven without any spaces in between, suggesting that this is done intentionally so that a long thin small moray may be able to escape. However, the purpose of tightly weaving the trap may be to reproduce more closely the preferred environment of the moray by creating a dark location within the trap. This supports the idea that the moray trap-making technology stems from an awareness of moray ecology and a grasp of design technology that prevents the catch from escaping.

Second, in terms of selecting the trapping grounds, it appears that moray trap fishermen choose them randomly. During the study, it was confirmed that morays enter most of the traps. However, small stretches of trapping grounds where morays did not enter the traps, as well as trapping grounds where other types of morays other than the targeted type entered the traps were also found. It is conceivable that a strong contributing factor to the fisherman's technique of selecting and using trapping grounds is a reflection of his experience and ecological knowledge of the moray routes and behavioural characteristics. However, at this time we do not have sufficient data to explain these factors. These are topics for consideration in future studies.

As for the allocation of time spent on various tasks for moray trap fishing, operations are greatly affected by the tide, requiring the fisherman to fish with a constant eye on the tide. Additionally, the number of traps used is determined by the fisherman's physical endurance in relation to his ability to complete an operation within the timeframe of a tide-change as well as the fisherman's socio-economic condition. Under such restrictive conditions, a fisherman must utilise his labour capacity, skill, experience, and knowledge of the ecology to set traps within the appropriate location and timeframe when it is probable that a moray will enter the trap.

Future studies that work towards unraveling the fishermen's experience-based techniques and ecological knowledge should focus on documenting more details about fishermen's usage strategies for their trapping grounds and their allotment of time spent on various tasks.

Today, moray trap fishing is in flux. While continuing to maintain the static aspects described above, it is being carried out under dynamic environmental conditions. The moray trapping grounds are being exposed to danger from land development, dynamite fishing, and population growth, as well as overlapping operational activities from other fishing businesses. They have experienced hardship from incidences where the trapped morays or the morays in the fisherman's *buhi-an* have been stolen. The results from this field survey, and based on information about the yield ratios from neighbouring regions, the trapping grounds at the survey site were productive. However, keeping in mind that each individual fisherman's situation varies, a large problem remains in the possibility that the results from this study only disclose specific fishing activities conducted under favourable conditions by particular fishermen who happen to fish wisely.

Neighbouring regions are using motorised fishing boats to fish in areas further offshore. This may be due to the fact that the moray resources are not at satisfactory levels, or perhaps fishermen are seeking safe and more productive trapping grounds. In a simple comparison of the incomes from the moray fishermen who used motorised and non-motorised boats in this study, it was found that the fisherman using a non-motorised boat in close vicinity earned a higher income.

However, it is possible that there is a significant difference in these fishermen's knowledge of fishing ground ecology and usage skills, given that the more productive fisherman's age is more than double that of the less productive fisherman. Perhaps trapping grounds at further distances offer a more stable yield even with poorer fishing skills and knowledge. In terms of allocation of time allotted to operation tasks, the difference between the two fishermen was almost double. It should also be pointed out that the expense of gasoline and the additional labour effort required to complete operations while being further limited by the tide change should be factored into the price of seeking distant trapping grounds with motorised boats.

While facing such contemporary challenges head-on, fishermen have high hopes and expectations for future moray fishing and the continued supply of moray at this site. Praising the rich marine supply of moray, the government started the Moray Festival and its promotional policies are producing events that spotlight the importance of this resource.

However, to date, explicit management of the supply of morays has never been conducted. Instead, the residents have a blind sense of expectation of the continuation of their rich moray marine resource. The marine moray supply has been maintained thus far because the moray trap fishing business is controlled not only by the tides, but also by physical and socio-economic constraints such as the fishermen's limited economic resources available to procure a boat and moray traps. In the future, studies need to focus on how the local moray promotional policies affect future tourism and the economy. Other important issues include how the moray trap fishing operations will evolve as a result of the increase in moray demand and heightened expectations, and how these factors will affect the livelihood of the fisherman, the marine supply, the value of morays, and the ecological environment.

References

Ator, L.A. 2007. *Municipality of Cordova, Cebu Brief Profile*. Unpublished manuscript. Cebu: Municipality of Cordova.

Balogo, O.G. 1996. Bamboocraft: The Guimbaleños Fishing Traps and Gears. In *Center for West Visayan Studies. Proceedings of the 6th Conference on West Visayan History and Culture*, pp. 16-22. Iloilo City: University of the Philippines-Visayas.

Cadeliña, R.V., J.V. Perez, and R.V. Mascuñana. 1986. *Artifacts from the Visayan Communities: A Study of Extinct and Extant Culture*. Dumaguete: Silliman University.

Calderon-Hayhow, et al. 1994. Appendix: Fishing Material Culture of Fishermen in Barrio Ajong, Sibulan, Negros Oriental. In I. Ushijima and C.N. Zayas (eds), *Fishers of the Visayas: Visayas Maritime Anthropological Studies I: 1991-1993*, pp. 393-464. Quezon City: CSSP Publications.

Cebu Pagasa Complex. 2005. *Cebu PAGASA Complex Climatological Normalstremes (1973-2004) 32 year Period*. Unpublished maunscript.

Coast and Geodetic Survey Department. 2005. *Tide and Current Tables: Philippines 2005*. Makati City: Coast and Geodetic Survey Department.

Garcia, J.R. 2003. Epektib Gyud. *The Freeman* 13 July.

Green, S.J., J.O. Flores, J.Q. Dizon-Corrales, R.T. Martinez, D.R. Nuñal, N.B. Armada and A.T. White. 2004. *The Fisheries of Central Visayas, Philippines: Status and Trends*. Coastal Resource Management Project of the Department of Environment and Natural Resources and the Bureau of Fisheries and Aquatic Resources of the Department of Agriculture. Cebu City: Department of Agriculture.

Hutchins, M., D.A. Thoney, P.V. Loiselle, and N. Schlager (eds). 2003. *Grzimek's Animal Life Encyclopedia* (2nd Edition). Farmington Hills: Gale Group.

Luchavez, J.A. and B.T. Abrenica. 1997. Fisheries Profile of Bais Bay, Negros Oriental. *Silliman Journal* 37(3-4):93-171.

Municipality of Cordova. 2004. *Comprehensive Municipal Profile: Including Plans, Programs, and Accomplishments*. Cebu: Municipality of Cordova.

Rau, N. 1979. Small-Scale Fishing Methods Used around Cebu City, Philippines. *The Philippine Scientist* 16:1-27.

San Carlos Publications and Office of Population Studies of San Carlos. 2004. *Cebu: A Demographic and Socioeconomic Profile Based on the 2000 Census*. Cebu: San Carlos Publications and Office of Population Studies of San Carlos.

Schoppe, S., J. Gatus, P.P. Milan and R. Seronay. 1998. Gleaning Activities on the Islands of Apid, Digyo and Mahaba, Inopacan, Leyte, Philippines. *The Philippines Scientist* 35:130-140.

Sollano, J.P. 2005. Cordova Town to Launch "Bakasi" Fest Aug. 14. *The Freeman* 21 July.

Suda, K. 1994. Methods and Problems in Time Allocation Studies. *Journal of Anthropological Science* 102:13-22.

Szanton, D. 1971. *Estancia in Transition*. Quezon City: Ateneo de Manila University Press.

Tawa, M. 1981. The Fishing Business in Sapian, Panay Island, Capiz: The Fishing Tools and Fishing Methods of Coastal Fishing in Sapian, the Northern Region of Panay Island. In the compilation of the Hiroshima Shudo University compilation of Philippine Study Projects (eds), *A Comparative Study of Japan and Philippines Inland Sea Regions Focusing on Hiroshima Prefecture and Panay Island*, pp. 52-63. Hiroshima: Hiroshima Shudo University Research Institute. (in Japanese).

Tawa, M. 2006. *People who Fish in Southeast Asia*. Tokyo: Nakanishi Publishing. (in Japanese).

Tsuji, T. 2007a. Coastal Gleaning and Resource Utilization of *Sipunculus robustus* and *Dolabella auricularia* in Mactan Island, Philippines. *Tropical Ecology Letters* 68:6-12. (in Japanese).

Tsuji, T. 2007b. A Note about Moray Fishing Activity in Mactan Island, Cebu, Philippines. *Humanities and Sciences* 22:141-151. (in Japanese).

Umali, A.F. 1950. *Guide to the Classification of Fishing Gear in the Philippines*. Washington: United States Government Printing Office.

Yano, T. 1994. The Characteristics of Fisherfolk Culture in Panay: From the Viewpoint of Fishing Ground Exploitation. In I. Ushijima and C.N. Zayas (eds.), *Fishers of the Visayas: Visayas Maritime Anthropological StudiesI: 1991-1993*, pp. 3-51. Quezon City: CSSP Publications.

Yano, T. and T. Kobayashi. 1994. Continuity and Change to the Manughudhod. In I. Ushijima and C.N. Zayas (eds), *Fishers of the Visayas: Visayas Maritime Anthropological StudiesI: 1991-1993*, pp. 163- 177. Quezon City: CSSP Publications.

Zayas, C.N. 1994. Pangayaw and Tumandok in the Maritime World of the Visayan Islanders. In I. Ushijima and C.N. Zayas (eds), *Fishers of the Visayas: Visayas Maritime Anthropological Studies I: 1991-1993*, pp. 75-131. Quezon City: CSSP Publications.

Zayas, C.N. 2004. Atob and Bato: Two Sides of Philippine Lithic Heritage. *Pilipinas* 43:55-70.

10

Marine Resource Use in Transition: Modern Fishing in Tonga, Western Polynesia

Kazuhiro Suda, Faculty of Humanities, Hokkai-Gakuen University

Introduction

Marine resources were very important as a protein source for the initial settlers of the islands of Oceania, where terrestrial animals were extremely scarce. The traditional subsistence of the area consisted of the horticulture of aroid tubers and bananas, arboriculture of breadfruit and coconut trees, and the intensive utilisation of marine resources. Islanders throughout Oceania were prominent horticulturists and fishermen. Anthropological and archaeological studies of fishing in Oceania have mainly focused on the classification and distribution of traditional fishing equipment, as well as the reconstruction of traditional fishing methods and resource use (Bellwood 1978; Lieber 1994; Oliver 1989; Reinman 1967). These studies elucidate the islanders' wealth of knowledge about the ecology of marine animals in order to efficiently exploit them.

After the intrusion of Europeans into this area, however, subsistence activities changed. Especially after the latter half of the 20th century, imported foods such as tinned fish and corned beef have become more important as protein sources. Furthermore, as globalisation of the economy permeates this area, commercial fishing is increasingly taking the place of subsistence fishing. In accordance with the changing socio-economic circumstances of this area, the role of marine resources has grown more varied. While marine resources are still important, the system of resource utilisation and the distribution of catches have drastically changed. The reciprocal exchange systems for fish catches have been disappearing. Instead, people in some islands often sell their catches to their communities. As commercial fishing has become more important, the problem of resource management has become more prevalent.

Taking these issues into account, I discuss the existing problem of contemporary marine resource use by focusing on the case of Ha'ano Island in the Kingdom of Tonga. On Ha'ano Island, subsistence fishing is still the main activity for acquiring animal protein, although outboard motorboats and modern fishing gear, such as nylon nets and lines, have been introduced. In order to elucidate the condition of the transformation of subsistence activities, I will describe the fishing activities in Ha'ano village based on direct observations and by measuring the weight of catches. Furthermore, I will discuss the variation in the choices of fishing activities amongst households in this paper.

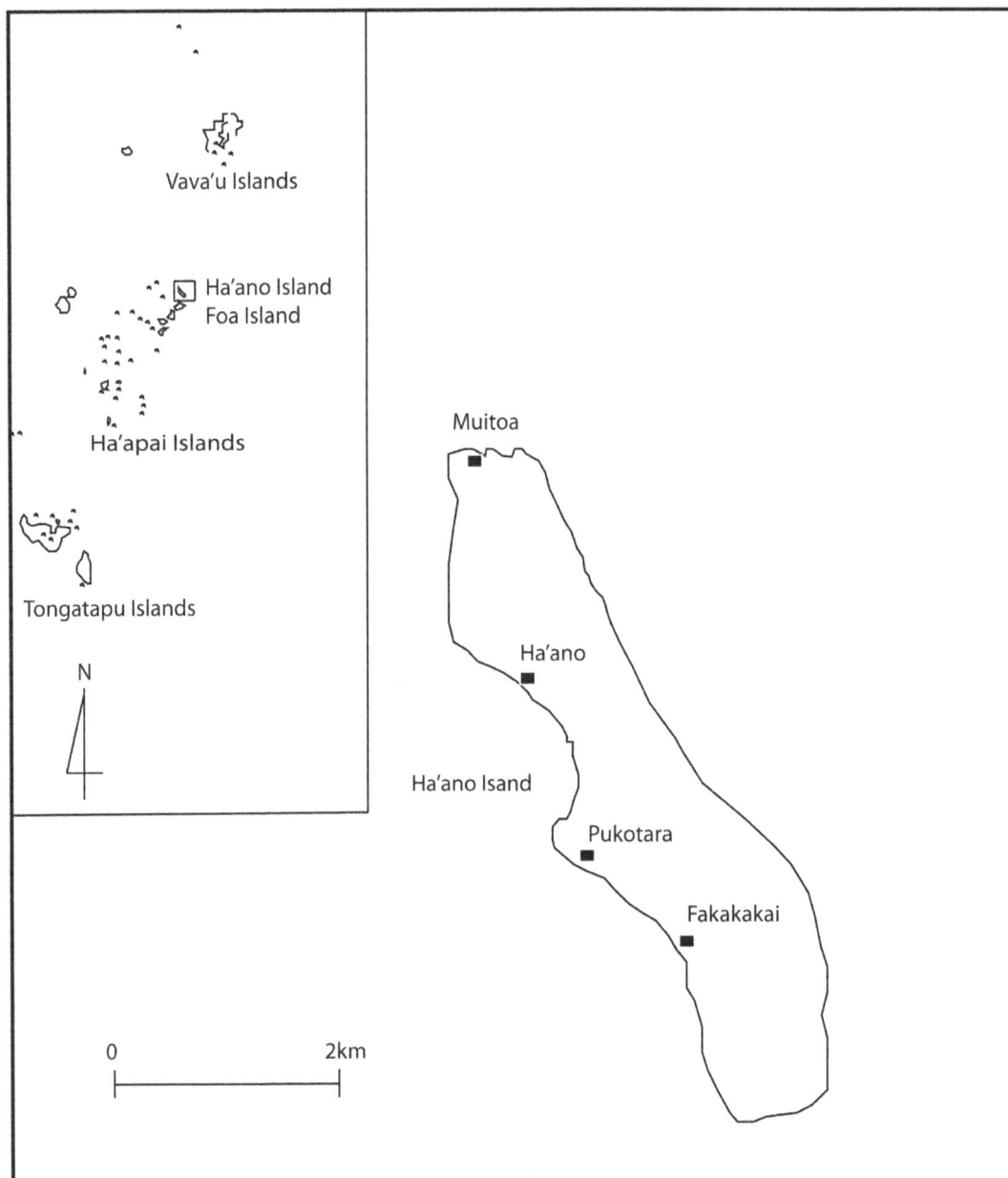

Figure 1. Ha'ano Island in Ha'apai Group of the Tongan Archipelago.

Source: Map by the author.

Ha'ano Village

Ha'ano Island is situated in the northern part of the Ha'apai Group of the Tongan Archipelago (Figure 1). The administrative capital village of the Ha'apai group is Pangai on Lifka Island, where administrative branches, business offices, middle and high schools, and the market are concentrated. It takes 45 minutes by outboard motorboat, as well as a half hour driving by truck-type buses to travel between Ha'ano Island and Pangai. There are four villages on Ha'ano Island: Muitoa, Ha'ano, Pukotara and Fakakakai, from north to south respectively. Although they have primary schools in Ha'ano and Fakakakai, they send their children to Pangai, Nuku'alofa (Tonga's capital), or New Zealand to receive secondary and higher education.

At the time of our fieldwork from 2001 to 2003, there was no wharf for big ships, no equipment for a water supply, and a small power generator to supply electricity was not installed until 2003. The only means of land transportation on the island was on foot, by bicycle, or in carriages. The insufficiency of infrastructure, furthermore, had confined the economic activities of the island: while some villagers ran the small shop (*falekoloa*) to sell necessities such as canned goods or soaps, for example, the range of items available was poor and items were sometimes out of stock altogether. Therefore, people often visited Pangai to buy daily living necessities, such as food and clothing.

The population of Ha‘ano Village has decreased from over 300 in the early 1970s to under 100 by the year 2000 as a result of emigration to Pangai and Nuku‘alofa, or to New Zealand and the United States in order to look for job opportunities (Evans 2001). The remittances from emigrant family members are the main source of income for villagers.

Our research was conducted during two visits, in October of 2001 (11 days) and in October of 2002 (19 days), in Ha‘ano Village. The population of Ha‘ano Village during our stay was 45 males and 43 females; the number of households was 22 during the research periods. Their subsistence activities consisted of the horticulture of taro (*Colocasia esculenta* and *Xanthosoma sagitifblium*) and banana (*Musa* sp.), arboriculture of breadfruit (*Artocarpus altilis*) and coconut (*Cocos nucifera*), fishing, and the raising of pigs and chickens. While the total arable land of the village was 92 acres (4.18 acres per household), only 34 acres (1.55 acre per household) were actually used by the villagers for subsistence food production at the time of our research. As each household planted a few breadfruit trees in their homestead, their fruits were consumed as staple foods between April and June, and between September and November. Although villagers raised livestock, such as pigs and chickens, they ate them only a few times a year, especially for communal eating ceremonies related to church activities. The main source of protein intake, therefore, came from marine resources.

While the above mentioned activities by men were for individual consumption, pandanus mats made by women provided a second important source of income to supplement the remittances from the emigrated family members. The mats were important exchange items in marriages and funerals, especially within the Tongan immigrant community in New Zealand.

Fishing Activities

The deep ocean around Ha‘ano Island is a good fishing ground for migratory fish, such as bonito, tuna and dolphinfish, while the shallows near shore provide a suitable environment for bottom fish, such as grouper and parrotfish, and for crustaceans, such as lobster and slipper lobster. As wind and waves are habitually high in the northeast area, fishing activities are mainly conducted in the southwest area; since there are no traditional divisions in the sea among the four villages, every fisherman could freely fish around the island.

Following the restrictive customary rules regarding the division of labour for fishing activities in Tonga, on the other hand, women's fishing activities are limited to gathering certain kinds of shellfish and small octopi from the shoals in front of the village. Unlike Muitoa, the nearest village, there was no shoal in Ha‘ano, and women seldom engaged in fishing. Only men engaged in the four fishing activities mentioned below. Out of twenty-two households, eleven engaged in line-fishing, four in diving and harpooning, four in encircling fish with gill nets, and two in the use of stationary nets (Table 1). Only three households engaged in more than one of these activities.

Table 1. Choice of fishing activities.

FISHING ACTIVITIES	LINE FISHING	DIVING	GILL NETTING	STATIONARY NETTING	TOTAL
No. of households	11	4	4	2	21

Source: Table by the author.

Eleven households engaged in line-fishing for tuna, bonito, dolphinfish, grouper, snapper, etc., with outboard motorboats (generally between 20 and 30 hp) costing about 3,000 pa'anga (over US$1,500) each (Figure 2). Usually, remittances from emigrated household members or their own earnings from overseas labour were spent for purchasing motorboats and fishing gear. Although the catches were mainly used for their own consumption or distributed to related households, if catches were extremely good, they were sometimes sold at the market in Pangai at three pa'anga per kg, irrespective of the fish species.

Figure 2. Line fishing.

Source: Photo by the author.

Four households engaged in diving and harpooning for lobster, parrot fish, etc (Figure 3). They did not need to used motorboats and did not invest in expensive fishing gear. Although this low-cost activity could bring good catches, villagers were reluctant to do it for fear of sharks. While the catches were also for a household's own consumption and distribution, they could sell lobster at 10 pa'anga per kg at the market in Pangai.

Only one household had an encircling gill net (Figure 4). When they used this fishing method, they asked other villagers to help. Usually three to four men worked together to encircle the net and chase the fish schools. The cost of the net was quite high (about 500 pa'anga), and, as of 2001, the catches were sold to other villagers on the beach. The stationary net was also a high-cost activity (over 1,000 pa'anga for an initial investment), which needed an iron fence and an impounding net (Figure 5). Two households jointly constructed one stationary net in 2001, after which their catches were also sold to the other villagers on the beach.

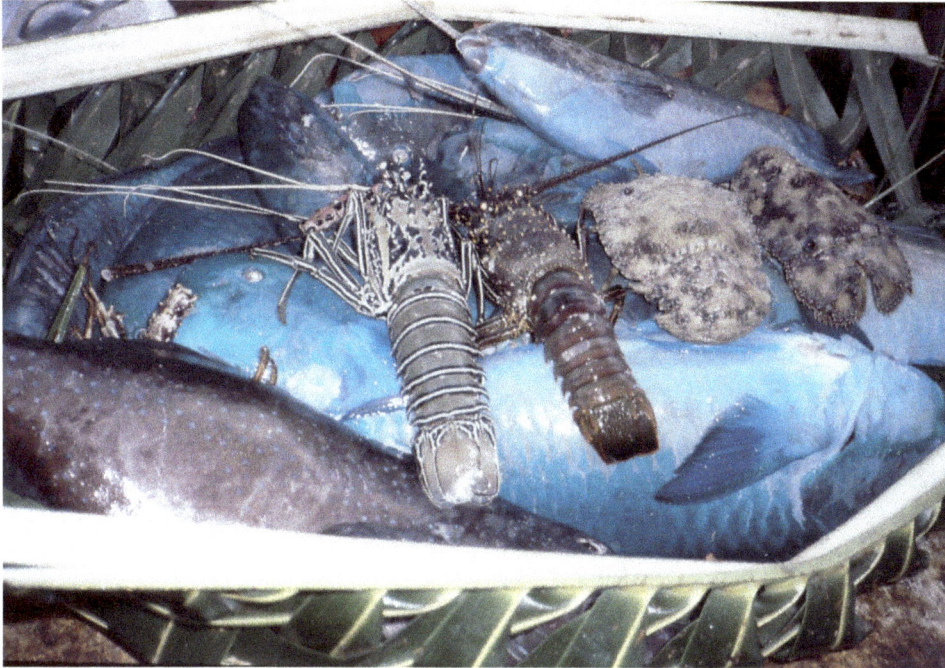

Figure 3. Catches of diving and harpooning.

Source: Photo by the author.

Figure 4. Encircling gill net.

Source: Photo by the author.

Figure 5. Stationary net.

Source: Photo by the author.

Choice and Productivity of Fishing Activities

Opportunities to earn money for purchasing fishing gear were very scarce in Ha'ano Village. Villagers usually depended on remittances from emigrated household members for their cash income (Evans 2001). This situation limited the choice of fishing activities. The most expensive investment was buying outboard motorboats, which numbered eight during our research period. Motorboats are important not only for fishing but also for transport to other islands (Figure 6), especially to Pangai to take children to school and purchase living necessities.

Figure 6. Transporting to other islands by motorboat.

Source: Photo by the author.

As shown in Table 2, average catches from the four fishing activities above were not so varied (from 14.36kg for daytime line-fishing to 21.65kg for an encircling gill net); however, the catch variation for line-fishing far surpassed the others. While eleven out of thirty-four line-fishing attempts were in vain, about 76% of the total catch during daytime (131.4kg) and 25% of nighttime catches (101.8kg) were acquired in one attempt. Although diving and harpooning was a steady activity from a cost-benefit standpoint, villagers could sell lobster at the market in Pangai, which was very difficult because they had to keep their catches fresh without a refrigerator. While the catches of encircling nets and stationary nets were not as good during our research period, villagers told us that they could catch hundreds of kilograms of fish when a large school migrated.

Table 2. Productivity of fishing activities.

FISHING ACTIVITIES	LINE FISHING	LINE FISHING	DIVING	NETTING	NETTING
	(day time)	(night time)	(harpoon)	gill net	stationary net
No. of sample	12	22	3	2	5
Main target	bonito, tuna, grouper	tuna, dolphin fish, snapper	lobster, parrot fish	yellow mackerel	yellow mackerel
Total catch (kg)	172.29	397.30	46.10	43.30	82.80
Max. catch (kg)	131.40	101.80	26.00	29.30	40.00
Min. catch (kg)	0.00	0.00	7.70	14.00	3.00
Aver. Catch (kg)	14.36	18.06	15.37	21.65	16.56

Source: Table by the author.

Marine Resource Use in Transition

The number of fishing activities was extremely scarce in comparison to those reported by Vaea and Straatmans (1954), who identified over 40 kinds of fishing activities in Tonga during the first half of the 20th century, and compared to Kirch and Dye (1979), who recorded 37 kinds of fishing activities in the northernmost island of Tonga, Niuatoputapu, in 1976.

The decrease in the variety of fishing activities might be caused by modernisation. The villagers were fond of new activities with modernised fishing gear, which improved fishing efficiency and allowed intensive resource use. As a result, fishermen were prone to concentrate on a few of the most productive activities.

The most popular fishing activity in Haʻano Village was line-fishing with a motorised boat, which requires a considerable amount of money to buy fuel. Furthermore, as catches were mainly used for household consumption or distribution, villagers rarely got cash from this activity; however, from their viewpoint, food acquisition activities were not for earning cash, but for subsistence, which was a fundamental activity for survival. Earning money from selling fish was simply a by-product of catch sizes that exceeded their expectations.

Remittances from emigrated family members, however, made it possible (Evans 1999). While farmers on Tongapapu, Tonga's main island, have often sold their harvests to earn cash at the various markets in the islands (Stevens 1999), there were few or no opportunities for the villagers on Haʻano Island to earn cash.

However, this situation is changing. As mentioned above, two households began to sell the catches from their encircling nets and stationary nets within the village in 2001. Both households' husbands were emigrants who had returned from New Zealand. They sold their catches, not in Pangai, but on the beach just after fishing. Although other villagers initially felt odd about this commercial—rather than reciprocal—exchange, they gradually accepted it. Subsequently, when these households engaged in these two fishing activities, they found other villagers would come to the beach to buy fish. Although these two households owned outboard motorboats, they seldom went line-fishing, instead choosing the activities that would earn them a steady income.

It was difficult for the villagers to obtain fish on a daily basis, to some extent because the catches of the major fishing activity—namely, line-fishing—in Ha'ano Village fluctuated. As a result, catches using encircling nets and stationary nets were much in demand.

Circulation of money within the village might cause changes in the socio-economic system. On Mangaia Island, where the sale and brokerage of fish was undeveloped, selling fish assisted the flow of money from those who had enough to spare to those who needed it (Takekawa 1997). In Ha'ano Village, however, it may cause the transformation from a reciprocal economy to one of commercialisation, in which those who have more capital may get more money by investing in modernised fishing gear and a sufficient number of motorboats.

The impacts of commercialisation in Ha'ano Village, however, have been limited in comparison to Southeast Asian regions. For example, in Visaya, Philippines (Torikai 1990) and Saba, Malaysia (Ono 2007), subsistence fishing had shifted to commercial fishing due to the adoption of modernised fishing gear. Along with population growth, the demand for sizeable catches has increased in these regions. As some wealthy fishermen have invested more capital, disparities in income have tended to increase, and the structures of fishing economies have changed drastically. In Ha'ano, however, the changes in the fishing economy have been limited thus far because of a population decrease and isolation from larger consumer markets. The cash circulating within the village is still primarily from the remittances of emigrated family members and, as such, is quite limited. It might be an early sign of the changes caused by economic globalisation. As long as the circulation of the catches is locally restricted, the possibilities of marine resource decline might not be so high.

Conclusion

While marine resources are still important to the islanders of Oceania even in the face of economical globalisation, the role of those resources has changed. The system of resource utilisation and distribution of catches has shifted from one of reciprocity to one of Western commercialisation.

As discussed above, the Ha'ano villagers rarely sold their catches in the market of Pangai. One of the major reasons for this was that they did not have electric freezers in their village. Because of this, local marine resources and money primarily circulated within the village. The influence of economic globalisation has been very limited in Ha'ano Village thus far. Under these conditions, therefore, they hardly overused marine resources simply because demand for those resources is localised and small.

However, with the financial aid of New Zealand, the Tongan government began to offer nighttime electric power to Ha'ano Village in 2003. As electric power would be in ample supply in the near future, the opportunity for using freezers to sell their catches at the market in Pangai would increase. As a result, they might utilise marine resources more intensively in order to earn money to meet their needs and spend on the necessities of modernised life. This, in turn, might result in the circulation of resources and money beyond the village or island and lead to the overuse of their marine resources. We should, therefore, pay attention to the dynamic between intra- and inter-resource management.

References

Bellwood, P. 1978. *The Polynesians: Prehistory of an Island People*. London: Thomes and Hudson.

Evans, M. 1999. Is Tonga's MIRAB economy sustainable? A view from the village and a view without it. *Pacific Studies* 22:137-166.

Evans, M. 2001. *Persistence of the gift*. Ontario: Wilfrid Laurier University Press.

Lieber, M.D. 1994. *More than a Living: Fishing and Social Order on a Polynesian Atoll*. Boulder: Westview Press.

Kirch, P.V. and T.S. Dye. 1979. Ethno-archaeology and the development of Polynesian fishing strategies. *Journal of the Polynesian Society* 88:53-76.

Oliver, D.L. 1989. *Oceania: The Native Cultures of Australia and the Pacific Islands*. Honolulu: University of Hawaii Press.

Ono, R. 2007. "Tradition" and "Modernity" in Fishing among the Sama, Eastern Coast of Borneo, Malaysia. *Bulletin of the National Museum of Ethnology* 31(4):497-579. (in Japanese).

Reinman, F.M. 1967. Fishing: An aspect of Oceanic Economy – An Archaeological Approach. *Fieldiana Anthropology* 56:95-208.

Stevens, C.J. 1999. Taking over what belongs to God: The historical ecology of Tonga since European contact. *Pacific Studies* 22:189-219.

Takekawa, D. 1997. Fishing activity as a minor subsistence in Mangaia, Cook Islands: Between subsistence activity and monetary economy. *Bulletin for the 50th Anniversary of Kita-Kyusyu University*: 341-359. (in Japanese).

Torikai, Y. 1990. Economic Structure of Fishing Villages in the Philippines. *Southeast Asian Studies* 27(4):406-26. (in Japanese).

Vaea, H. and W. Straatmans. 1954. Preliminary report on a fisheries survey in Tonga. *Journal of the Polynesian Society* 63:199-215.

11

Territoriality in a Philippine Fishing Village: Implications for Coastal Resource Management

Shio Segi, Department of Resource Management and Geography, Melbourne School of Land and Environment, The University of Melbourne

Introduction

The study of local territorial arrangements has been an important approach to common property resource management including that of fisheries and coastal marine resources among scholars and practitioners over the last few decades (Pollnac and Johnson 2005:34). These scholars have been critical of the fact that modern 'top-down' style management based on economic models can be inappropriate in many parts of the world (Ostrom 1990). That common property resources in the sea be under an open-access regime is an assumption on which these centralised systems are often based and they can be both enormously costly as well as ineffective, and in the case of archipelagic nations the matter can be even more difficult (Ruddle 1996:334-335).

The management of resources in tropical waters is a daunting task as one needs to address the diverse variety of marine species captured by the diverse gear types of often diverse cultural groups in highly complex ecological systems (e.g., Johannes 1998). Further, as Ruddle and Hickey (2008) point out, an underlying and continuing colonialism and cultural imperialism, often embodied in donor-assisted resource management projects, intensify the challenge. Self-sustaining site-specific resource management practices embedded in a local cultural and socio-economic context can thus have a significant role in the modern effective management of marine resources (Ruddle 2007:7).

Based on their rich local ecological knowledge, resource users have been practicing their pre-existing local management systems in nearshore waters in many parts of Oceania, East Asia, Southeast Asia, and the South Asia region, and a customary marine tenure system is commonly in place in some areas (e.g., Peterson and Rigsby 1998; South et al. 1994). According to Johannes and Ruddle (1993:23), customary marine tenure is "a practice which involves the observation of exclusive fishing rights…[that] apply to specific areas, and may include rights to particular species, or to use of a particular gear type."

In other parts of Southeast Asia at present, the concept of customary marine tenure is, however, neither common nor evenly distributed (Ruddle 1994:1-4). In the areas where a customary marine tenure system and traditional institutions continue to be present, such as in island-nations in Oceania, the recognition of the application of these management practices is being sought (e.g., Hviding 1998; Ruddle 1998a). In places where 'a strong traditional base' (Pomeroy 1995:145) for revitalising the pre-existing local management institution is absent, however, it seems that scholarly interest has been largely concentrated on establishing new regulatory regimes for community-based resource management. The Philippines provides a good example of this case. From archival records, Lopez (1985:196) noted that in the early Spanish colonial period in 17th century, some coastal Tagalog settlements in Luzon reserved some portion of the sea and river for their exclusive use. These areas were subjected to payment of a usage fee when used by non-constituents of the settlement. In some cases, according to him, these fishing grounds were bartered in the same manner as other commodities. Presumably, the concept of customary marine tenure with exclusive rights to usage once existed in at least some regions of Philippine communities, but, with a few exceptions (e.g., in Batanes Islands, see Mangahas 1994) these practices have long vanished over the more than 300 years of the colonial period (Ibid.:196). Under the open-access and centralised regime which was established during this period, resource depletion is taking place due to increasing fishing effort and technological advancement over the last century (e.g., Spoehr 1980).

Responding to decades of constant failure of such intrusive management strategies, the participation of local resource users in a decentralised manner became widely acknowledged as the key to more effective conservation of resources (Agrawal and Gibson 1999:631-633). In the case of the Philippines, the national government has shifted its approach to more localised control over resources since the 1990s.

In the course of the devolution, territorial restriction was used for controlling access to the resources under a co-management regime between the government and the resource users. Under the current legal framework (most importantly, the Fisheries Code of 1998 and the Local Government Code of 1991), municipal governments have major authority in the management of marine resources within their newly delineated jurisdictional waters. Meanwhile, local fishers are required to register to gain the right to exploit the resources. Upholding the tradition from the time of American occupation (Lopez 1985:196), the municipal governments have the authority to grant registered fishers the privilege of erecting fish corrals; oyster, mussel, and other aquatic beds; and milkfish fry areas in designated places within the municipal waters. At a more collaborative level, the creation of a marine protected area (MPA), managed by locally institutionalised organisations, has been one of the most common management tools in a growing number of coastal resource management projects (Pollnac et al. 2001:684). As a whole, recent resource management is characterised by the control of access to the resources by defining the eligible users and demarcating the accessible and non-accessible areas.

In many cases, but not all, the local marine resource management system is considered to be valuable in resource conservation as it involves autonomous control over access to the resources (McGoodwin and Dyer 1994:1). Even though there is on-going debate over how much local management contributes to actual resource conservation, locally appropriate management is "a vital aspect of the social and cultural constitutions of the complex resource system" (King 1997:424).

Despite the trend towards a strong focus on the creation and implementation of co-management of resources in the Philippines, there has been little attention to these non-traditional and informal practices for controlling the access to resources (Mangahas 1994:55). Regulating the access to resources through territorial control helps conservation, and a good understanding of the human dimension in this practice is essential (Christie 2004). The examination of locally practised territoriality should provide a valuable basis for the development of alternative approaches. Taking two case studies in a small fishing village in the Central Visayan region, this paper will focus on local claims of territoriality over fishing areas. It will examine how they are operated, rationalised, and related to the formal fisheries and coastal resource management framework.

The first case study represents the local territorial system practised by small-scale fishers to define the location of bottom-set gill nets in coastal waters. Fishers claim their exclusive right of use of certain netting spots where the operation is governed by a set of rules. The second case study deals with the small-scale fishers' territorial claim over distant waters where they compete fiercely with illegal commercial ring-netters. Unlike the first case, their claim is more discursive and unstructured, but there is a strong sense of territoriality based on the differentiation of social groups. While the first case involves a practical solution for avoiding risk and smoothing the fishing among local fishers, the second case involves the fishers' compelling case against exploitative outsiders and is motivated by perceived resource degradation.

This paper examines qualitative data that were collected through multiple semi-structured and unstructured interviews with small-scale fishers, non-fishing villagers, ring-netters, and government officers in the course of 14 months fieldwork (February 2006 to April 2007). Data were also collected through participatory observation of village life and a total of 15 fishing trips with ring-netter crews.

Case Studies

Research setting

The municipality of Boljoon is located on the southeast coast of Cebu Island facing Bohol (Cebu) Strait, approximately 100km south of Cebu City (Figure 1). Small in population and a considerable distance from commercial centres in the region (such as Cebu City and Dumaguete City), the town has no substantial commercial industry other than small-scale and primarily subsistence farming and small-scale fishing. Nevertheless, fishing is economically and nutritionally important, and compared to neighbouring towns, a larger percentage of the of the population of Boljoon engages in fishing (CRMP 2004).

Barangay[1] Granada is a well known fishing centre in the municipality. Among 180 households along the coast, 68 regularly engage in fishing, and for most, it is their main source of household income. From these households, at least 101 small-scale fishers use more than 20 types of fishing methods, which differ according to target species and fish habitat. Situated in an area of two relatively healthy coral reefs, some fishers use gill nets to target reef species in the coastal waters adjacent to the village. A larger number of fishers use hook-and-line methods, mainly targeting small pelagic species in off-shore waters close to Bohol Island, across the strait.

Case study I: Allocation of netting spots

In the approximately 400-metre stretch of coastal waters and directly facing the most densely populated part of the village of Granada, small-scale fishers using bottom-set gill nets have established a territorial (*teritoryo*) system[2] and operational rules. The area has a coral reef at each end. The area of sandy substrate between the reefs is the preferred fishing zone for net fishing

1   The *Barangay* is the smallest administrative unit in the Philippine system and it is similar to the notion of a village.

2   Though the exact origin of this is unknown, the fishers thought it had developed after the late 1980s, when the number of bottom-set gill nets in the coastal water gradually increased. Similar development of territorial systems for beach seining was observed in southern Palawan (Veloro 1992).

because of its high productivity, low risk of gear damage and easy access to the fishers' residences. Three types of bottom-set gill nets used in this area are locally called *pamo*, *pangmalangsi*, and *pangsolid* for overnight set (*pana-an*), mainly targeting reef-associated species such as fusilier (*Caesio* sp.), herring (*Spratelloides* sp.), and emperor (*Gnathodentex* sp., *Lethrinus* sp.). In general, local fishers from both Granada and adjacent *barangays* use this area for various methods, but it is only Granada fishers who use the above-mentioned nets.

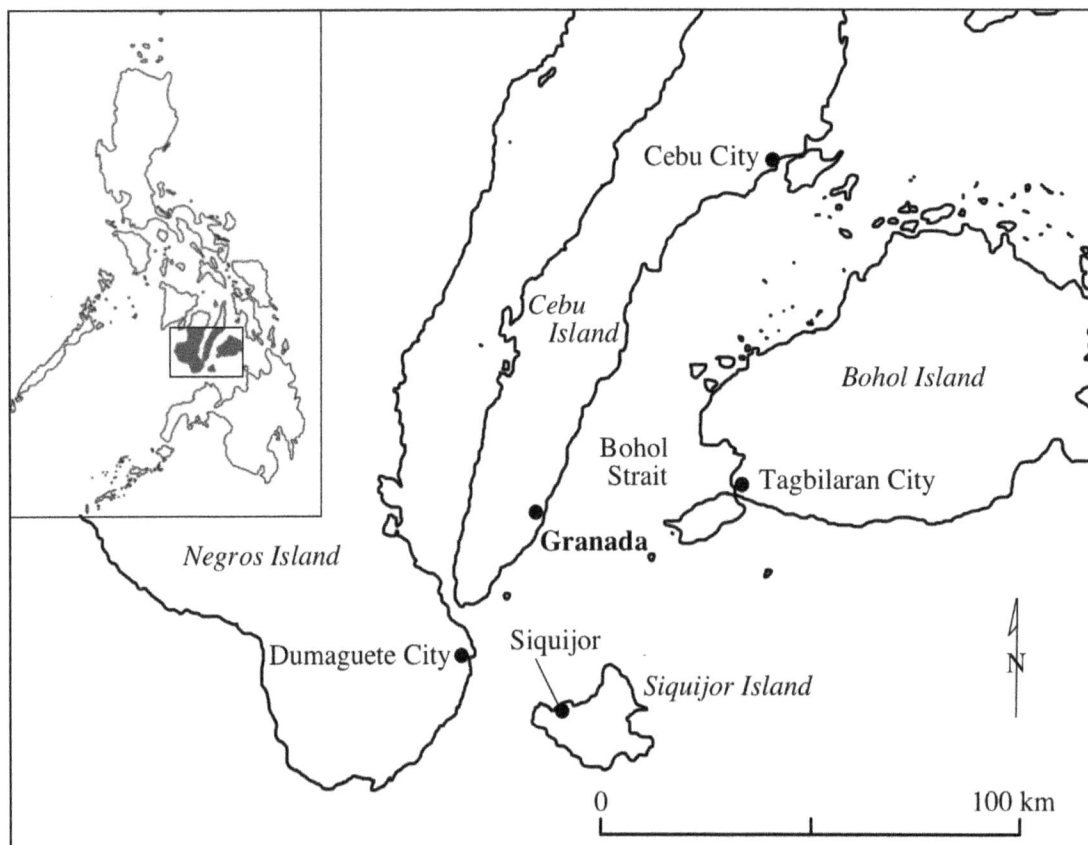

Figure 1. Map of the research area in Central Visayas.

Source: Map by Shio Segi.

These coastal waters are divided into 25 territories as a 'netting location' (*taktak-an*) shared by 18 Granada fishers, some of whom have multiple territories (Figure 2). In each territory, a right-holder has an exclusive right to place the net at roughly right angles to the shoreline. He sets it in late-afternoon and hauls it in early on the following morning. An individual's territory is usually located near his house or the land he owns and is the same as the beaching location of his boats. Although some spots are more scattered, owing to their perceived lower productivity, others, perceived as either more productive or easily accessible, are clustered tightly at intervals of about 5 metres. Nets are not set in coral reefs or their immediate vicinity, since they would be easily entangled in the coral, thereby incurring damage which would be expensive to repair.

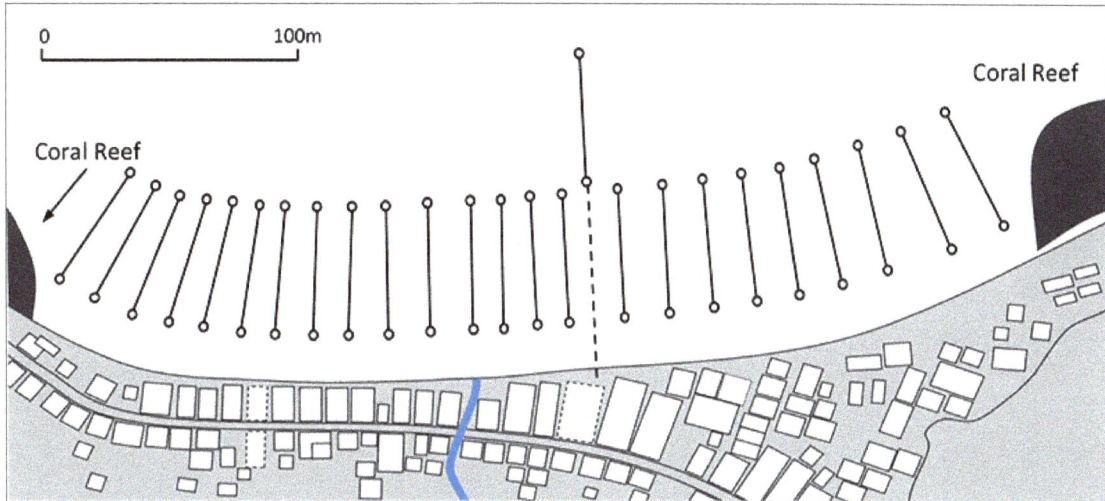

Figure 2. Territory for bottom-set gill net fishing in Granada.

Source: Shio Segi.

The rationale underlying these territorial claims is the fishers' long-standing and continuous use of the netting spots which are located close to their residences. Commonly, there is an implicit understanding among resource users that continuous use of the area for an extended period would generate a preceding use-right over others. Such a territorial claim based on the perception of long-standing use is not unusual in the Asia-Pacific region, including the Philippines (e.g., Cruz 1986; Veloro 1992), and often such claims are supported by formal as well as informal sets of rights and rules (Ruddle 1998b). In Quang Binh Province of Vietnam, for example, fishers hold several types of right which are structured according to a set of rules which define both socio-economic and operational aspects of fishing operation (Ibid.). Similar to this case, and in other parts of the Philippines (e.g., Russell and Alexander 2000:23), Granada fishers reinforce their territorial claim with a strong sense of 'household proximity right' which conceptually allows one to claim a prior use-right over the space close to one's residence or land. On the congested beachfront, this concept is used together with the first-comer rule when household proximity is a source of contestation for the preferential right holder.

This territoriality fulfils two main functions. The first is to secure an individual's netting location free from competition. Not only can the competition over the fishing spot easily lead to a souring of relations with others, but it is also an important concern for fishers to limit their fishing in order to keep it efficient (McCay 1978). When the fishing area is tightly limited and alternative fishing areas are not located within easy access, fishers face a situation in which they need to regulate others in their placing of nets. The fishing territory system thus both minimises the competition as well as setting the basis for operational arrangements in actual use.

As important as securing the fishing spot, the second purpose is to keep a certain distance between each net in order to avoid damage. Closely placed nets are vulnerable to entanglement (*gubot*) with other nets, particularly when current movements are less predictable. Also, when the nets are placed too close to each other, the catch may not be as good as it is when nets are better placed. In order to make sure each net is placed in the right way – that is, in the right fishing spot and at an appropriate distance from one another – fishers have made an operational rule to specify the time to place the nets collectively. Fishers who plan to put the net in that afternoon need to come out to the shore roughly before 5 p.m. so that they can place the net in collaboration with the other fishers. To put into operation each claimed territory, concurrent placement functions to reduce the risk of entanglement arising from uncertainty at each fishing trip. The placement of a net in relation to other fishers' nets needs to be adjusted to the movement of the current of the day, but most importantly, fishers find it important to place them together so that they know where others' nets are actually placed in relation to their own net.

The crucial difference to the above example from Vietnam, however, is the lack of a well-organised institution. While property rights and operational rules are rather clearly arranged, there is no clear decision-making structure, as no committee or organisation has ever been established. The *Barangay* council (the village legislative body) has no involvement in it either, as this informal arrangement is outside of the concern of formal political institutions. Nor does anyone seem to hold any special authority to administer the arrangement. Individual right-holders are equal constituents within the arrangement. Thus, detailed administrative rules over the rights and operations are certainly very vague. Because the territory has no legal legitimacy, no exclusive right-holder can claim against another fisher for infringement of his financial value. The territory can be lent, however, providing verbal permission has been obtained from the right-holder prior to fishing. Though no fee payment or other obligation is established for this, fishers who borrow a territory are morally expected to share the catch with the right-holder when it is sizable. While some fishers claim that territory also can be transferable to a successor, provided he owns a net, it seems there is no consensus among right-holders. Given that current right-holders are the first generation of this arrangement, the handing on of the rights has not yet been an issue.

Lack of organised institutions, however, does not mean that there is no form of an institution. Monitoring for whether fishers are following the arrangement is conducted mutually throughout fishers' day-to-day lives and particularly at the daily gathering in the late-afternoon before fishing. As for sanctioning the offenders, social criticism and compensation for the damage is likely if the wrongly placed net gets entangled with others. Though there was no case of breaching the rules by other fishers during the author's stay, one ring-net vessel, unaware of the net, damaged the net with its anchor and faced two full days of repairing the net for compensation. Social criticism resulting from deviating from the locally shared norms in general cultivates the grounds for further physical and verbal harassment (Russell and Alexander 2000:26). Although there is no organised institution governing the arrangement, right-holders are motivated to mutually respect each other's territory and rights. When the area is only used by fishers from the immediate village and pressure of new entrants to the territory is limited, loosely organised arrangements have been able to effectively and autonomously control access to the resources for at least a couple of decades.

Case study II: Fishing ground for small-scale fishers

Among lowland Filipinos, fishers generate their sense of territoriality in relation not only to the practicalities of fishing, but also to the security of minimal living standards based on status group. Russell and Alexander (2000) argue that small-scale fishers in Batangas Bay established the sense of territoriality for local fishers against foreign baby purse-seiners.[3] They argue that the local fishers institutionalised various forms of catch-sharing practice from the purse-seiners as a de facto 'tax' to access the resources in their territorial waters. As they point out, among local fishers this "relatively new strategy to keep other boats out of one's home bay" (Ibid.:23) is not unusual in the Philippines and a similar claim was made by small-scale fishers in Granada.

This type of claim is largely grounded in unequal power relations between the small-scale fishers and commercial fishers. Undoubtedly, it goes well beyond the realm of resource use at the village level. A fuller account of the underlying relationship requires a much wider understanding of the

---

3   Baby purse-seiners (locally called *pukotan*) are large double-outrigger motorised canoes crewed with 10-20 members. According to Philippine law, they are categorised as commercial fishing.

socio-political context. Also, as the case of Batangas Bay showed, such a catch-sharing practice constitutes an important way of smoothing out the relationship between local and foreign fishers at the site of this case study. Though these points are obviously important, full discussion of these issues is beyond the scope of this paper (for a full account on these issues, see Segi, forthcoming).

In Bohol Strait, the relatively calm sea and migratory movement of small pelagic species attracted a number of commercial ring-netters (*kobkob*) who visited the area annually from other parts of Central Visayas. Their major target species are bullet tuna (*Auxis rochei rochei*) from March until July and mackerel scad (*Decapterus macarellus*) from August until October. Fishing usually takes place around the southwest coast of the Province of Bohol and the adjacent Panglao and Balikasag islands. In this area, there is said to be a large number of Fish Aggregative Devices (FADs) called *payao*, installed mostly by the operators and associates of ring-net fishing in Bohol. Having their subordinating light boats illuminate the sea surface to aggregate the fish at the *payao*, ring-netters catch a large quantity of fish in one swoop. Employment of modern technology such as fish finders and sonar has contributed to the increase in excessively efficient operation. Fishing can be done up to three times a night and an overnight catch sometimes reaches over 4 metric tons. Though there are no data indicating the number of ring-netters operating in the area, the array of illumination at *payao*, almost forming a continuous line of light which can be seen from a distance, indicates the intense fishing effort in the area. Owing to their highly efficient fishing methods and the large number of boats in operation, everyone interviewed, both among resource users as well as those involved in resource management, agreed there had been significant resource depletion from over-exploitation.

Excessive use of the resources has affected the lives of small-scale fishers in Granada through resource competition over already depleted resources. These fishers employ a multiple hook-and-line (*palangre*) method to target the same species at the *payao* in the same area as ring-netters operate. In the perception of small-scale fishers, their catches drop significantly while ring-netters are in their prime season and it significantly affects their livelihood. Not only are they affected by the decreased catch, but they also suffer from a worsening fishing economy from price drops due to the consequent over-supply of fish to the local market by ring-netters. This situation has heightened their concern about the future prospects of the resources, as Granada fishers often commented that: 'fish will be exhausted (*mahurot na isda*)' because 'they will catch everything (*makuha nila tanan*)'. Because of the dual effect on quantity and price of the catch, Granada fishers have become extremely pessimistic regarding the future status of the resources and their vulnerable livelihood.

As a response, Granada fishers have been vocal about pushing out the ring-netters from the area by claiming that the area is for small-scale fishing. The rationale of their claim is at least partly based on the concept of delineated Municipal Waters. Under the Philippine Fisheries Code of 1998, the waters up to 15 kilometres off-shore are marked as 'municipal water' which the local government reserves for small-scale fishers, and usually no commercial fishing is allowed. Given that the narrow strait is less than 30 kilometres at its widest, all the ring-netters in this area are considered illegal fishers and only small-scale fishing is allowed.

Despite the fact that the law grants no more than the use right, small-scale fishers in Granada call the disputed fishing area 'our sea' (*dagat namo*) and claim the area is the territory for small-scale fishers. Continuous encroachment of ring-netters into the area is often described as 'stealing' the fish that small-scale fishers were supposed to catch. To support the territorial claim, Granada fishers often postulate two reasons. Firstly, Granada fishers explain that this area should be used only by locals (*taga diri*). With limited mobility in their fishing style, fishers claim that the resources are not abundant enough to share with non-locals who have access to their own waters.

This exclusivity based on the 'local-foreign' distinction is not only directed at the commercial fishers, but also at small-scale fishers who periodically visit the area from other places. Secondly, ring-netters are usually operated by capitalists and they have no trouble living a comfortable life and finding the means to make a living. By contrast, small-scale fishers live in poverty and are often unable to meet daily expenses and they are only able to gain a small livelihood. The gap in the reality of social class causes small-scale fishers to feel that ring-netters pose an unjustifiable threat to their humble livelihood. Thus, their claim to the territory of small-scale fishing is really a claim by the poor aimed at protecting their 'right to survive' against the rich who threaten the territory which provides their sole and irreplaceable livelihood.

Discussion

From two case studies, different types of territorial claims in both coastal and off-shore waters have been demonstrated to exist simultaneously in one small village. In this, it became clear that there are several rationales raised by fishers to justify their claim to the territory. As observed in many places, use of a location for an extended period of time is a powerful basis for the claim in the Philippine context. Obviously, the range of duration at the basis of their claim differs in each case. In regard to netting space, some referred to a period of two generations while others referred to about 10 years of use in their narratives. The important attribute is that they had been using the area with the stationary gear before anybody else and uncontested over the years. This generates some kind of a sense of 'title-by-occupancy' which gives moral support to their on-going exclusive use of the location.

Also, the sense of 'localness' is becoming an important trait as resource degradation continues. In Philippine fishing communities, a distinction in the social groups between 'local' and 'foreign' has been seen to influence their relationship to the resources (Russell and Alexander 2000; Zayas 1994). Again, there is no consistent definition of perceived 'localness' among fishers, as it may refer to the village-level or even the wider area over several municipalities, regardless of the jurisdictional borders. An important aspect, however, is that these fishers are heavily reliant on the area as the location of the daily earning of their livelihood and no alternative locations are easily accessible.

Finally, territorial claims are also made on the basis of the differentiation between social status groups. With less and limited means of production and vulnerability in their livelihood, poor fishers claim their local area must be used in order for them to survive, given their harsh living conditions.

As the central purpose of fisheries management is to place control over fishing, both cases suggest that the territorial claims are at least partially successful in restraining the fishing pressure. In the netting territory system, fishers acknowledge that the area is already fully occupied and there is no safe and productive spot for a new net to join in. As a result, this regulates the number of nets for overnight use because of the prospect of lower productivity and the higher risk of nets being damaged. Also, in the case of the territorial claims of small-scale fishers in off-shore waters, their claims led to stricter law enforcement. With active support of a conservation NGO, small-scale fishers along southeast Cebu managed to push local governments to introduce more systematic patrolling and fee collection activities, which discouraged ring-netters to intrude into municipal waters. Though there are no quantitative data to estimate the actual conservation effect, these examples show that the fishers' territorial claims have at least contributed to controlling access, which may slow down the depletion process of the resources.

Both cases show that fishers' territorial claims emerged out of necessity; however, this was not an inevitable result (Dyer and McGoodwin 1994:1). In coastal waters, increased risk of damaging expensive gear motivated fishers to creatively establish a self-restraining netting arrangement on their own initiative. Meanwhile, in off-shore waters, the impending threat of a degraded household fishing economy as a result of resource depletion and price fall triggered by ring-netters were the motives behind competing fishers' strong claim of territoriality. Although in both cases these fishers are aware that there is no legal basis for their claims, they choose to take active control over the fishing ground in order to protect their livelihood. While these issues are undoubtedly common to small-scale fishers in many societies, it is not the case that all fishers faced with this resource problem would make similar territorial arrangements. These territorial claims largely involve the cultural and socio-political dimensions of the locality in defining who they are and on what grounds they would have prior rights over others. These territorial claims are an active and practical response, based upon locally constructed legitimacy, to the risks and uncertainties in fishing and resource conditions.

In both cases, the articulation of the claim is aimed at keeping the fishers' livelihood economically viable as well as at the conservation of the resources, but only for their own use, not for solely environmental purposes. Similarities were also seen in a Tagalog fishing community (Russell and Alexander 2000:36) and elsewhere (e.g., Pollnac and Johnson 2005). Specifying the netting location does not only reduce the risk of entanglement, but also increases one's chance to catch more fish because of wider net-intervals and a smaller number of units. Similarly, reducing the number of exploitative commercial fishing vessels would likely return a greater catch to small-scale fishers. Thus, it is obvious that the impact on fishers' livelihood is the important determinant of the fishers' interaction with the resources and attempt to control them. This echoes and reinforces the argument that a perceived positive economic benefit on the part of small-scale fishers is the most significant indicator of success in coastal resource management projects, rather than resource conservation on its own.

Conclusion

Although its effect may be limited, the value of attempted local management can be considerable. King (1997:424) contends that the value of local management lies in "their social structural characteristics within which and by which resource appropriators…are able to, allowed to, or are willing to have a voice or play some role in determining the allocation and distribution of the [common property resources]." In this regard, these examples of local territoriality claims shed light on the ability and motivation of Philippine small-scale fishers to take an active and responsible role in controlling the resources for an even more autonomous, equitable, and socially inclusive management regime.

Because the sustainability of 'community-based' coastal resource management after the termination of a project is commonly an issue in the Philippines, meaningful participation of resource users who would like to generate the sense of 'ownership' in the project is a crucial issue (Pollnac and Pomeroy 2005:248-249). With the utilisation of territorial control in mind, these fishers' claims, which are deeply grounded in the cultural and socio-economic condition of the locality, may have important implications for the crafting of more effective coastal resource management strategies (Russell and Alexander 2000:37). Unfortunately, formally institutionalising this territoriality as marine tenure may not be a realistic option in the Philippines due to the unstable social structure and the lack of social institutions (Martin-Smith et al. 2004:184). Legal acknowledgement of the territorial claims and arrangements, however, coupled with supplementary formal resource management measures, may provide an increased moral investment on the part of locals in managing the resources, and this may help sustain such projects. Needless to say, substantial involvement of resource users in this formalisation process is essential (Palmer 1994:246). Resource managers should not overlook the often inconspicuous self-governing arrangements and territorial claims of resource users.

The above does not suggest, however, that territorial arrangement on its own is the solution for achieving more effective resource management. Indeed, as is evident in the case of fishers' claims over off-shore waters, one needs to note that the emergence of these territorial arrangements can be closely associated with the power struggle of resource users who are under threat of marginalisation and exploitation (Segi forthcoming). When unequal power relations penetrate the society and thus impinge on the use and management of resources, one needs to establish such territorial arrangements within the wider power relationships among stakeholders, not only at the local level but also within the vertical political structure from village to national level. In-depth research into local territoriality with multifaceted approaches to the social and political environment is thus necessary for designing meaningful and realistic forms of more socially sound management.

Acknowledgements

The research for this paper was undertaken with the support of The Australian National University. I am particularly grateful to Kenneth Ruddle, Nicolas Peterson, and anonymous reviewers for their insightful and constructive comments in the development of the manuscript. Also I would like to thank Madeleine Strong-Cincotta for assistance with editing. My sincere gratitude also goes to the people in Boljoon, especially small-scale fishers in Granada, ring-net crew members from Negros Oriental and Bohol, and the Coastal Conservation and Education Foundation, Inc. for their kind cooperation and engagement.

References

Agrawal, A. and C.C. Gibson. 1999. Enchantment and disenchantment: The role of community in natural resource conservation. *World Development* 27(4):629-649.

Christie, P. 2004. Marine Protected Areas as Biological Successes and Social Failures in Southeast Asia. *American Fisheries Society Symposium* 42:155-164.

Coastal Resource Management Project. 2004. Unpublished electronic database: Estimated number of municipal fishers and boats in the Municipality of Sibonga, Argao, Dalaguete, Alcoy, Boljoon, Oslob, and Santander.

Cruz, W.D. 1986. Overfishing and conflict in a traditional fishery: San Miguel Bay, Philippines, *Proceedings of the Conference on Common Property Resource Management*, pp.115-133. Washington D.C.: National Academy Press.

Dyer, C.L. and J.R. McGoodwin. 1994. Introduction. In C.L. Dyer and J.R. McGoodwin (eds), *Folk management in the world's fisheries: lessons for modern fisheries management*, pp. 1-15. Niwot: University Press of Colorado.

Hviding, E. 1998. Contextual flexibility: present status and future of customary marine tenure in Solomon Islands. *Ocean and Coastal Management* 40:253-269.

Johannes, R.E. 1998. The case for data-less marine resource management: examples from tropical nearshore finfisheries. *Trends in Ecology and Evolution* 13(6):243-246.

Johannes, R.E. and K. Ruddle. 1993. Human interactions in tropical coastal and marine areas: lessons from traditional resource use. In A. Price and S. Humphrey (eds), *Applications of the biosphere reserve concept to coastal marine areas*, pp. 21-27. Gland: International Union for the Conservation of Nature.

King, T.D. 1997. Folk management among Belizean lobster fishermen: Success and resilience or decline and depletion? *Human Organization* 56(4):418-426.

Lopez, M.G. 1985. Notes on Traditional Fisheries in the Philippines. In K. Ruddle, R.E. Johannes and UNESCO Regional Office for Science and Technology for Southeast Asia (eds), *The Traditional knowledge and management of coastal systems in Asia and the Pacific : papers presented at a UNESCO-ROSTSEA regional seminar held at the UNESCO Regional Office for Science and Technology for Southeast Asia, 5-9 December, 1983*, pp. 193-206. Jakarta: United Nations Educational Scientific and Cultural Organization Regional Office for Science and Technology for Southeast Asia.

Mangahas, M.F. 1994. *Traditional marine tenure and management in ASEAN.* In R.G. South, D. Goulet, S. Tuquri, and M. Church. (eds), *Traditional marine tenure and sustainable management of marine resources in Asia and the Pacific*, pp.48-58. Suva: International Ocean Institute-South Pacific.

Mangahas, M.F. 1994. *Indigenous coastal resource management: the case of Mataw fishing in Batanes.* U.P. Assessment Project on the State of the Nation; no.94/001, Quezon City: University of the Philippines Center for Integrative and Development Studies.

Martin-Smith, K.M., M.A. Samoilys, J.J. Meeuwig, and A.C.J. Vincent. 2004. Collaborative development of management options for an artisanal fishery for seahorses in the central Philippines. *Ocean and Coastal Management* 47:165-193.

McCay, B.J. 1978. Systems ecology, people ecology, and the anthropology of fishing communities. *Human Ecology* 6(4):397-422.

McGoodwin, J.R. and C.L. Dyer. 1994. *Folk management in the world's fisheries: lessons for modern fisheries management.* Niwot: University Press of Colorado.

Ostrom, E. 1990. *Governing the commonn: the evolution of institutions for collective action.* Cambridge: Cambridge University Press.

Palmer, C.T. 1994. Are folk management practices models for formal regulations? Evidence from the lobster fisheries of Newfoundland and Maine. In C.L. Dyer and J.R. McGoodwin (eds), *Folk management in the world's fisheries: lessons for modern fisheries management*, pp. 237-249. Niwot: University Press of Colorado.

Peterson, N. and B. Rigsby (eds). 1998. *Customary Marine Tenure in Australia.* Sydney: Oceania Publication, University of Sydney.

Pollnac, R.B., B.R. Crawford, and M.L.G. Gorospe. 2001. Discovering factors that influence the success of community-based marine protected areas in the Visayas, Philippines. *Ocean and Coastal Management* 44(11-12):683-710.

Pollnac, R.B., and J. Johnson. 2005. Folk management and conservation of marine resources: Towards a theoretical and methodological assessment. In N. Kishigami, J.M. Savelle and K.M. Hakubutsukan (eds), *Senri ethnological studies, no. 67: 33-50 Indigenous use and management of marine resources*, p. 455. Osaka: National Museum of Ethnology.

Pollnac, R.B. and R.S. Pomeroy. 2005. Factors influencing the sustainability of integrated coastal management projects in the Philippines and Indonesia. *Ocean and Coastal Management* 48(3-6):233-251.

Pomeroy, R.S. 1995. Community-based and co-management institutions for sustainable coastal fisheries management in Southeast Asia. *Ocean and Coastal Management* 27(3):143-162.

Ruddle, K. 1994. *A guide to the literature on traditional community-based fishery management in the Asia-Pacific tropics.* Rome: Food and Agriculture Organization of the United Nations.

Ruddle, K. 1996. Traditional management of reef fishing. In N.V.C. Polunin and C.M. Roberts (eds), *Reef fisheries*, pp. 315-335. London: Chapman and Hall.

Ruddle, K. 1998a. The context of policy design for existing community-based fisheries management systems in the Pacific Islands. *Ocean and Coastal Management* 40(2-3):105-126.

Ruddle, K. 1998b. Traditional community-based coastal marine fisheries management in Viet Nam. *Ocean and Coastal Management* 40(1):1-22.

Ruddle, K. 2007. Fishing rights: misconceptions, outright prejudice. *Samudra The Triannual Journal of the International Collective in Support of Fishworkers* Report No. 48:4-9.

Ruddle, K. and F.R. Hickey. 2008. Accounting for the mismanagement of tropical nearshore fisheries. *Environment, Development and Sustainability* 10:565-589.

Russell, D.S., and T.R. Alexander. 2000. Of Beggars and Thieves: Customary Sharing of the Catch and Informal Sanctions in a Philippine Fishery. In E.P. Durrenberger and T.D. King (eds), *State and community in fisheries management: power, policy, and practice*, pp. 19-40. Westport: Bergin and Garvey.

Segi, S. forthcoming. *Losing at sea, winning on land: a case study of Philippine small-scale and industrial fisher resource competition.* Society & Natural Resources.

Segi, S. 2011. *'Pinning Our Hope on the Seas': Conservation, Resource Depletion and Livelihood in a Philippine Fishing Village.* PhD Thesis, Canberra: The Australian National University.

South, R. G., Goulet, D., Tuquri, S., and Church, M. (eds). 1994. *Traditional marine tenure and sustainable management of marine resources in Asia and the Pacific*, Suva: International Ocean Institute-South Pacific.

Spoehr, A. 1980. *Protein from the sea: technological change in Philippine capture fisheries.* Pittsburgh: Department of Anthropology, University of Pittsburgh.

Veloro, C. 1992. Complementary adaptations, contrasting images. *Yakara* 19:76-110.

Zayas, C.N. 1994. Pangayaw and Tumandok in the Maritime World of the Visayan Islanders. In I. Ushijima and C.N. Zayas (eds), *Fishers of the Visayas,* pp. 75-131. Quezon City: CSSP Publications in co-operation with University of the Philippines Press.

www.ingramcontent.com/pod-product-compliance
Lightning Source LLC
Chambersburg PA
CBHW051309270326
41929CB00029B/3464